# MOVIES of the SEVENTIES

# MOVIES *of the* SEVENTIES

## EDITED BY ANN LLOYD
## CONSULTANT EDITOR
## DAVID ROBINSON

## ORBIS·LONDON

## Acknowledgments

Many of the illustrations come from stills issued to publicize films made or distributed by the following companies: ABC, Academy, Action/Citel/SSR/SFD, AIP, Albatross/ WDR/Trio, Apple, Arcola/Millfield, Argos, Artistes Associés, Avco Embassy, Aspen, A-Team, Australian Film Commission, BBC-TV, BBS, Benegal/Sahyadri, Boyd's Co/Virgin/ Matrixbest, Brandywine, British Lion, Brooksfilm, Canadian Film Development Corp, Cannon Films, William Castle, Chartoff-Winkler, Cinema Center, CIP, Columbia, Compton-Tekli, Concordia/ Champion/Rome-Paris Film/Georges de Beauregard, Coppola Co, Cupid Productions, Dino De Laurentiis, Directors Co, Dovemead, EMI, Enigma, Faces Distributing Corp, FC/PECF, Filmanthrope/FDL, Film House, Film Plan, Filmverlag der Autoren, Filmways, Margaret Fink, First Artists, Gaumont, Golden Harvest, Hammer, HandMade, Debra Hill, Hoyts Theatres, Italo-Judeo, Ladd Co, Joseph E. Levine, Lion's Gate, Lira Film, Long Road, Lorimar, Lucasfilm, Lux, MCA, Malpaso, Mara Film, Marceau/Cocinor/Mega, MGM, MKH, Mirisch/Phalanx/Jalem, Mosfilm, N.E. de Film, Neoplanta/Telepool, New South Wales Film Corp, NFFC, Omni-Zoetrope, Orion, Oshima Productions, Paramount, Pathé, PEA/Constantin/Gonzales, Persky-Bright/ Devon, Carlo Ponti, Praja Film, Raab-Litvanoff, RAI, Rank, Rapid/Terra Filmkunst, Raviraj, Renn/Burrell, Sandrews, Scimitar, Seven Arts, Shaw Brothers, Shibata Organisation, Sippy Films, Solar, South Australian Film Corp, Svensk Filmindustri, Swedish Film Institute, Tango Films, Titanus, 20th Century-Fox, Ultrafilm, United Artists, Universal, Vera Film, Vic Films, Vides, Warner Brothers, Wildwood, Won World, Woodfall, Zeno/Films du Losange, Zespoły Filmowe Unit X.

In addition we would like to thank Artificial Eye, Atmosphère, Australian Film Commission (London), Martyn Auty, Keith Bartlett, BBC, Bowerhouse Model Associates, Cactus Films, Ugo Casiraghi, Cinegate Ltd, Donald Cooper, Peter Cowie, Susan D'Arcy, Downton Advertising Ltd, Greg Edwards Archive, Phil Edwards, D. Elley, Joel Finler Collection, John Fleming, Ronald Grant Archive, K.G. Hall, Harris Films, David Hine, India House, Kobal Collection, Liberty Cinema, Mainline Pix, National Film Archive, National Film Theatre, David Robinson Collection, Scorsese Archive, Talisman Books, Paul Taylor, Adrian Turner, Bob Willoughby, Ken Wlaschin.

Although every effort is being made to trace the present copyright holders, we apologize in advance for any unintentional omission or neglect and will be pleased to insert the appropriate acknowledgment to companies or individuals in any subsequent edition of this publication.

## Abbreviations used in text

**add:** additional; **adv:** advertising; **anim:** animation; **art dir:** art direction; **ass:** assistant; **assoc:** associate; **chor:** choreography; **col:** colour process; **comm:** commentary; **cont:** continuity; **co-ord:** co-ordination; **cost:** costume; **dec:** decoration; **des:** design; **dial:** dialogue; **dial dir:** dialogue direction; **dir:** direction; **doc:** documentary; **ed:** film editing; **eng:** engineer; **ep:** episode; **exec:** executive; **loc:** location; **lyr:** lyrics; **man:** management; **mus:** music; **narr:** narration; **photo:** photography; **prod:** production; **prod co:** production company; **prod sup:** production supervision; **rec:** recording; **rel:** released; **r/t:** running time; **sc:** scenario/screenplay/script; **sd:** sound; **sp eff:** special effects; **sup:** supervision; **sync:** synchronization; **sys:** system. Standard abbreviations for countries are used. Most are self-evident but note: A = Austria; AUS = Australia; GER = Germany and West Germany after 1945; E.GER = East Germany.

**Editor**
Ann Lloyd
**Consultant Editors**
David Robinson, Richard Schickel
**Editorial Director**
Brian Innes

**Senior Editor**
Graham Fuller
**Senior Sub Editor**
Dan Millar
**Chief Sub Editor**
Maggie Lenox
**Sub Editors**
Lindsey Lowe, David Roper, Susan Leonard

**Research Consultant**
Arnold Desser
**Picture Researchers**
Dave Kent, Liz Heasman
**Research**
Paul Taylor, Sally Hibbin, Julian Petley

**Designers**
Ray Kirkpatrick, John Heritage, Wayne Léal

*Facing title-page:* far from his origins on the planet Krypton, Clark Kent's alter ego (Christopher Reeve) protects Metropolis in *Superman, The Movie* (1978)

# CONTENTS

# INTRODUCTION

The closer we are in time the harder it is to focus on history. Already our perspective on the Thirties or the Forties is fairly clear; but with the Seventies it is still sometimes hard to see the wood for the trees. In the long view of history, will Spielberg and Fassbinder still seem giants, or will other figures dominate and the landscape assume new contours?

The forces that shaped the Seventies are, however, already evident. One was the influence of politics. Political upheavals during the decade had strong effects upon the development or decline of national cinemas. New Third World cinemas had lately come into being, in Africa, Asia, Latin America and the Middle East. The cinema revived in Greece and Spain and as abruptly died in Iran and Brazil and Chile, as old dictatorships collapsed and new ones arrived. In East and West the start of the Seventies was deeply influenced by the events of 1968, the year which brought Eastern Europe the trauma of the Soviet invasion of Czechoslavakia, while the West experienced a widespread upsurge of radical and revolutionary consciousness comparable only to Europe's 1848. It was an era and spirit in which Underground and independent cinema flourished in many parts of the world, discovering an enthusiastic new audience, and in some cases succeeding in imparting new ideas and new personnel to mainstream production.

Hollywood was dominated during this period by a new generation – Francis Coppola, Steven Spielberg, George Lucas, Martin Scorsese, Brian De Palma, John Carpenter – talents which had not come through the traditional routes from within the industry, but were mostly the products of the university film schools. Such people brought to American commercial film-making a refreshing new and wider cultural experience, and an awareness of a new, young audience. The changed atmosphere in Hollywood provided easier acceptance for such wayward individualists as Woody Allen, Robert Altman, Mel Brooks.

The spirit of revolution and renewal largely passed Britain by: her time would come in the subsequent decade. History is unlikely to remember much from these years, except perhaps the musical egocentricities of Ken Russell, the lone radical voice of Ken Loach, and Bill Douglas's singular autobiographical trilogy.

Elsewhere, though, there were miracles. The Seventies saw the beginnings of the New Australian Cinema, with the pioneer work of Bruce Beresford, Peter Weir and Ken Hannam finding an international audience and market for films of resolutely indigenous character, determinedly independent of all outside influences.

The Seventies demonstrated more clearly than previous decades this characteristic of the cinema in producing sudden national resurgences and renascences. Usually a direct cause can be attributed. Sometimes it is the effect of an eruptive cultural or political mood that demands an outlet (compare the renascence of cinema in Greece after the fall of the Colonels or in Spain after the death of Franco). More often it is the availability of finance. Money – a measure of official subsidy for films – was a factor in the revival of both the Australian and the Swiss film in this decade. The German revival, the most characteristic phenomenon of the late Sixties and Seventies, was directly attributable to the availability of finance from official sources and the collaboration with television, which was a partner in many significant German productions of the period. (In the next decade, British films were to benefit in much the same way when Channel Four TV provided a continuity of production which the country's film industry had not known within memory). When opportunity offers, it seems, the artists will be found to grasp it. In Germany the Seventies produced a remarkable generation of film-makers, who, without the opportunity, would have probably found their medium in literature or the theatre – Fassbinder, Wenders, Schlöndorff, Herzog, Straub, Syberberg and a host of followers.

Paradoxically, in France and Italy, where the spirit of 1968 had been most forcefully experienced, few notable new film-makers emerged during the decade,

The director Stanley Kubrick films Adrienne Corri and Malcolm McDowell in a violent scene for his bleak futuristic fantasy *A Clockwork Orange* (1971), based on Anthony Burgess's novel

which continued to be dominated by the film-makers who had come to the fore in the Fifties and Sixties.

The most vital activity of these years was often to be found in the newly developing countries of the Third World. New directors like Ousmane Sembene of Senegal, Youssef Chahine and Shadi Abdelsalam of Egypt and Mohammed Lakhdar Hamina, who carried off the coveted Cannes Grand Prix in 1975 with an Algerian film, *Chronicle of the Years of Embers*, attracted international attention with films which were uncomprisingly indigenous to their own cultures. India was unique in having a commercial film industry which moved into a boom period such as had never been seen since Hollywood in the golden Twenties. Alongside the commercial production – and actually styled 'The Parallel Cinema' – there developed a movement of independent film-makers aiming to make films of social and artistic worth which would be, as one of them said, 'non-comprising without being non-commercial'. For a generation Satyajit Ray had been India's sole international film-maker. In the Seventies he was joined in the world film arena by such major talents as Shyam Benegal, Girish Karnad and Mrinal Sen.

The Czech trauma was a shock from which the Eastern Europe cinema was slow, for the most part, to recover. It was not until the late Seventies that Czech films were able to revive somewhat after the departure or inactivity of most of the major talents responsible for the films of the brief renascence in the Dubček era. New hardline policies affected other Eastern states. Yugoslavia could not return to the carefree years of Makavejev's *W.R. – Mysteries of the Organism*. The USSR and Eastern Germany struck doldrum periods. After 1968 Poland suffered from politico-cultural repressions and a wave of anti-Semitism which put several major film talents out of action.

The Hungarian cinema, alone of the Eastern Europeans, rode the storm and flowered in these years, with the maturing of a gifted new generation, stimulated by the international acceptance of Miklós Jancsó. Perhaps the Hungarian example, and particularly the Hungarian capacity for self-criticism, was useful encouragement to the reviving Polish cinema later in the decade as it braced itself – led by two major talents, Andrzej Wajda and Krzysztof Zanussi – to play a significant role in the political movements and brief euphoria of the Solidarity era.

In the East, in the West, and in the Third World, the cinema of the Seventies felt itself to be embattled. Not all the dust has cleared even yet, but the main outlines are emerging. In the contributions collected here, writers of varied backgrounds and viewpoints provide a fascinating insight into the developments of a turbulent decade.

DAVID ROBINSON

# STARTING OVER

A whole new generation of young film-makers, knowledgeable about film history, came to prominence in Hollywood in the Seventies, replacing the old guard they revered

The end of the Sixties can reasonably be seen as a watershed in the American cinema. Industrially, mounting costs and dwindling audiences, combined with the dismal box-office receipts of several blockbusters such as Paramount's *Darling Lili* and 20th Century-Fox's *Tora! Tora! Tora!* (both 1970), pushed more than one major studio to the brink of ceasing production. Artistically, the great veteran film-makers, the development of whose careers had largely coincided with the evolution of the cinema itself, were finally reaching the end of the road: Howard Hawks, for instance, made his last movie *Rio Lobo* in 1970, and the same year marked William Wyler's farewell with *The Liberation of L. B. Jones.*

In a climate of uncertainty, output – reduced to begin with – became to a large extent polarized. On the one hand, low-budget exploitation movies – associated in particular with Roger Corman's New World Pictures, founded in 1970 – flourished by attracting a predominantly teenage audience through a pre-tested supply of thrills and spills. On the other, a wider audience was courted by mega-dollar 'event' movies, often star-stuffed disaster epics such as *The Poseidon Adventure* (1972) and *The Towering Inferno* (1974).

However, the end of the Sixties witnessed the emergence of at least one distinctive medium-budget genre, the 'road' movie. The runaway box-office success of Dennis Hopper's *Easy Rider* (1969) set a trend that was to sustain some of the most interesting and ambitious of the American films which, in the early Seventies, sought to steer a middle course between 'event' and exploitation (though Hopper's film itself drew on the components of the disreputable bike movies of the Sixties). A whole range of films developed the motifs of the journey and the open road, whether they were clearly intended as symbolic of modern life, as in the case of Monte Hellman's *Two-Lane Blacktop*, or disguised as thrillers, like Richard Sarafian's *Vanishing Point* (both 1971). Sometimes, as in Jerry Schatzberg's *Scarecrow* (1973), their impetus was philosophical, whereas in other examples, such as Joseph Strick's *Janice* (1973), it was primarily sociological.

*Easy Rider* was the product of an adventurous new company, Raybert, founded by Bob Rafelson and Bert Schneider, who had been associated on the profitable television pop show *The Monkees*. When Raybert used the Monkees group in a feature film – *Head* (1968), directed by Rafelson and co-scripted with him by actor Jack Nicholson – the group was placed in a much more critical and abrasive

*Below: director Martin Scorsese (centre) had not yet grown his by-now familiar beard when he made* Mean Streets *(1973), starring Robert De Niro (left) as the irresponsible Johnny Boy and Harvey Keitel as the perpetually worried Charlie, two friends trapped by their environment in New York's Italian ghetto. Scorsese himself played a small role as the gunman who shoots Johnny Boy at the end of the film*

*Above: Lion (Al Pacino) and Max (Gene Hackman) go on the road in* Scarecrow, *in search of a meaning to their lives; Lion sets his hopes on the child he has never seen, while Max plans to start a car-wash business. Top: Michael Corleone (Al Pacino) seeks the paternal advice of* The Godfather (Marlon Brando) *as he takes over the family's criminal business. Top right: this tinted production shot from* Days of Heaven *vividly suggests the film's glowing depiction of the Texan wheat-belt*

context, a fact which testifies to the company's readiness to temper commercial considerations with a sense of relevance that was at least quasi-radical. After *Easy Rider*, Raybert was reorganized as BBS, named from the first initials of Bert Schneider, Bob Rafelson and Steve Blauner.

In his subsequent work for BBS, Rafelson established an unassailable place in the forefront of serious American cinema, first with *Five Easy Pieces* (1970) and then with *The King of Marvin Gardens* (1972), films that combined a European quality of elusiveness with a specifically American shrewdness of domestic observation, as well as providing memorable roles for Jack Nicholson, the Seventies actor *par excellence*. But *The King of Marvin Gardens* was, unfortunately, a commercial flop; and the same fate befell some other BBS movies, including Nicholson's directorial debut, *Drive, He Said* (1971), a rather puzzling account of relationships in a men's college, and Henry Jaglom's touching modern fairy-tale *A Safe Place* (1971). BBS's brave venture came to an end in 1973, although Schneider and Jaglom were to be reunited as executive producer and director of *Tracks* (1976), a spiky, hallucinatory film almost entirely set aboard a train, concerning the return home of a Vietnam war veteran.

Earlier, however, BBS had notched up a popular as well as critical triumph in Peter Bogdanovich's *The Last Picture Show* (1971). Austerely filmed in black and white, a fact that by this time could be exploited as a novelty, the movie elegiacally recounts the withering of a small Texas town in the early Fifties, and its nostalgic quality marks a sharp contrast with the contemporaneity of, say, *Five Easy Pieces*.

What is doubly significant about the film is that its nostalgia is also specifically cinematic: Bogdanovich makes stylistic references to the work of John Ford and Orson Welles, and quotes directly from that of Howard Hawks, whose *Red River* (1948) is the closing attraction at the town's decaying movie theatre. (It is amusing to discover that in the source novel by co-scriptwriter Larry McMurtry, the film in question was far less prestigious – a minor Audie Murphy Western.) Bogdanovich temporarily became a hot ticket with the big studios, though his status declined when his movie buff's propensity for resurrecting Hollywood formulas and Hollywood history led to such resounding flops as *At Long Last Love* (1975) and *Nickelodeon* (1976).

Bogdanovich is himself a former critic and journalist, but his enthusiastic knowledge of film history puts him essentially at one with the slightly younger group of film-school graduates – Martin Scorsese, George Lucas, John Milius and François Ford Coppola among them – who, along with Steven Spielberg and Brian De Palma, were collectively termed the 'movie brats'. Some of them made, quite early in their careers, films of huge commercial success: Coppola's *The Godfather* (1972), Spielberg's *Jaws* (1975). But the other element that unites them more particularly is their indebtedness to the cinema's past, both in terms of using well-established genre material and of alluding directly or indirectly to old movies.

The explanation for this phenomenon is perhaps not hard to find. These men had as students been exposed systematically to the classic American cinema at the very time when it was finally becoming intellectually respectable – which was also, of course, the time when it was virtually ceasing to exist. Their work thus becomes a continuation – sometimes, as in *The Godfather*, on a grandiose scale – of the mainstream traditions otherwise largely dying out. It might be added that in their details these films sometimes seem less like an extension of that tradition than a reproduction of its past glories. In this light, it comes as no surprise that George Lucas should not only follow up on the success of his *American Graffiti* (1973) with an out-and-out genre movie, the space opera *Star Wars* (1977), but that he should include in *Star Wars* an overt homage to John Ford's famous Western *The Searchers* (1956), when Luke Sky-

walker returns to find his home burned down.

It has been a very different story for another director of the same film-school generation, Terrence Malick, who has not evinced the crowd-pleasing instincts, however sincere, of a Spielberg or Lucas. Malick's *Badlands* (1973), which retails a potentially melodramatic anecdote of a youthful Midwestern murderer on the rampage with a cool, almost abstract detachment, is in its way as original a film as those of Rafelson. But its uncompromising individuality cost it dear at the box-office, and it was not until 1978 that Malick directed a second film, the no less remarkable *Days of Heaven*, with its astonishing visual rendering of life on the land in Texas at the time of World War I.

The reworking of traditional genres was not confined to the 'movie brats'. Roman Polanski, a director who made his reputation in the Sixties, scored his biggest hit with *Chinatown* (1974). This is an elaborate revamping of the classic private-eye thriller, with the difference that by being set in the Thirties – the period when such writers as Dashiell Hammett first established the conventions of this type of story – it in effect becomes a costume movie.

## Old genres were revived in modern form by directors who remembered and loved Hollywood's rich past

There was certainly no shortage of nostalgic excursions into the cinematic past. Dick Richards, one of the more distinctive if less publicized of the decade's new directors, was responsible for a stylish remake of *Farewell, My Lovely* (1975), with Robert Mitchum wearing, a bit belatedly, the trenchcoat of Raymond Chandler's detective Philip Marlowe amid some briskly handled action and elegantly observed Forties decor. Richards, who subsequently ventured with less happy results into a Foreign Legion adventure, *March or Die* (1977), first made his mark with an extremely striking Western, *The Culpepper Cattle Co.* (1972).

This was probably the most accomplished of a group of revisionist Westerns to appear in the early Seventies, seeking to demystify the muddy realities of life on the frontier. An interesting, if less fully achieved, example of the same species was *Dirty Little Billy* (1972), a downbeat account of the early life of Billy the Kid. The director here making his first film was Stan Dragoti, who later played a different set of variations on another hallowed genre with the satirically humorous *Love at First Bite* (1979), an engaging spoof of Dracula movies.

The film-maker who has played the genre game to most consistently rewarding effect must, however, be John Milius. A flamboyantly colourful figure, a surf enthusiast and gun collector who forthrightly rejects fashionable liberal opinions, Milius first won notice by writing two notable studies in old-time individualism, Sydney Pollack's *Jeremiah Johnson* and John Huston's *The Life and Times of Judge Roy Bean* (both 1972). When Milius, besides writing, also took over the director's chair, the result was the quirkily brilliant *Dillinger* (1973), an account of the Depression-era bank-robber's career couched in terms of a latter-day folk-tale.

Its successor was *The Wind and the Lion* (1975). More ambitious but equally exciting, this film – dramatizing a curious incident of 1904 involving American gunboat diplomacy in Morocco – confirmed Milius' delight in tales of derring-do and in the odd byways of history, as well as his confident skill in staging action sequences. The casting of John Huston in a cameo role set an appropriate seal on the movie's lineage. When Milius moved from modernizing genre material to more openly personal concerns in the semi-autobiographical surfing story *Big Wednesday* (1978), the result was appreciably less appealing – an indication, perhaps, of the debt he owes to the traditional restraints of telling a story.

The other most notable promotion to direction from among the ranks of screenwriters was that of Paul Schrader, a former critic who wrote several scripts (eg. Scorsese's *Taxi Driver*, 1976) before making his directorial debut with *Blue Collar* (1978). This conspicuously well-crafted movie is on the surface a sharp thriller about trade-union corruption, and below the surface a gripping essay on alienation. Schrader's next film, *Hardcore* (1979), though often intriguing in its response to the Los Angeles underworld, is curiously lacking in narrative plausibility. But *American Gigolo* (1980) is a major achievement: again adopting the framework of a suspense story, the film combines a seductively fluid technique with a disquieting foray into the metaphysical realms of guilt and regeneration.

Another screenwriter who has contributed significantly to modern American cinema – though he has not turned to direction – is Robert Towne. After rising to modest prominence in the Sixties, he consolidated his position with two very different films. On the one hand, *Chinatown* is a consummate re-creation of an earlier model; on the other, *The Last Detail* (1973) is very much of its own time, and in fact its expletive-strewn dialogue represented something of a breakthrough in the permissible limits of naturalistic speech on the screen. This mordant tragi-comedy about two hard-bitten naval petty officers escorting a naive young sailor to military prison turned the 'road' format to pointedly distinctive use. It clinched the directorial reputation of former film editor Hal Ashby, who had earlier directed two off-beat comedies, *The Landlord*

*Top left: Harry Hannan (Roy Scheider) has a* Last Embrace *with the mysterious Ellie Fabian (Janet Margolin), who is suspected of multiple murder. Top: Jack (William Katt), Matt (Jan-Michael Vincent) and Leroy (Gary Busey) are Californian surfing friends in* Big Wednesday. *Above: Peter Sellers, in one of his last roles, as Chance – the illiterate gardener who gains an undeserved national reputation for wisdom in* Being There

(1970) and *Harold and Maude* (1971).

Ashby went on to make *Shampoo* (1975), an attractive satirical comedy, changed pace with *Bound for Glory* (1976), a large-scale biopic about folksinger Woody Guthrie, and subsequently returned to the mood of *Shampoo* with an impressively witty and inventive political satire, *Being There* (1979), in which Peter Sellers gave a memorable comedy performance as a near-imbecile who becomes a Presidential candidate.

It is somewhat surprising that of the many directors of television movies recently to graduate to the cinema few have stamped much of a personality on their big-screen work. A partial exception is Gilbert Cates, who showed himself a fluent director of actors in two rather old-fashioned and literary movies, *I Never Sang for My Father* (1970) and *Summer Wishes, Winter Dreams* (1973). But his later *The Last Married Couple in America* (1980) is a merely tiresome sex comedy.

Apart from television, the most potentially fertile breeding ground for new directors has been in 'exploitation'. Easily the most important figure to have emerged from this area has been John Carpenter. His *Assault on Precinct 13* (1976) is a splendidly assured urban melodrama leavened by tongue-in-cheek humour. The horror movie *Halloween* (1978) is less appealing though no less well-crafted, but it proved a phenomenal box-office hit and spawned an endless series of inferior 'teen-jeopardy' chillers

by other hands.

Roger Corman, a key influence in encouraging new film-makers in the Sixties, has not on the whole produced a comparable range of talents from his intensive – and immensely profitable – engagement with New World Pictures in the Seventies. However, at least two directors to have come out of New World merit critical attention. Paul Bartel made in *Death Race 2000* (1975) a dynamic and witty comedy about a death-dealing transcontinental road race, which contrives to satirize the popular demand for violence at the same time as satisfying it. His follow-up, *Cannonball* (1976), is virtually a remake.

Jonathan Demme's *Crazy Mama* (1975), made for New World, is an energetic but uneven variation on the period gangster film. But his subsequent work elsewhere qualifies him as a director of real skill and versatility. *Citizens Band* (1977) is a spirited updating of Thirties-style populist comedy, whilst *Last Embrace* (1979) is a Hitchcock-like thriller of unflagging style and assurance. Demme's more recent *Melvin and Howard* (1980) might plausibly be seen as a quintessential work of the new American cinema. Putting the 'road' movie formula to unpredictable and very likeable effect, it even manages – since the Howard of the title is the legendary Howard Hughes – to invoke a reference to Hollywood's vanished past as well as pointing encouragingly into the future.          TIM PULLEINE

*Below: shades of the prison-house begin to close around Julian Kay (Richard Gere) as he is framed for the murder of a female client. Below right: Bob Rafelson, director of* The Postman Always Rings Twice *(1981), examines a video playback of the scene just shot with Jessica Lange and Jack Nicholson, who play a passionate couple conspiring to kill the lady's husband. Bottom: Henry Jaglom (centre) directs* Sitting Ducks *(1980), which stars Zack Norman (left) and Michael Emil as a couple of inexperienced but ambitious thieves, on the run from New York to Miami and blissfully unaware that their lives are in deadly danger*

He's the highest paid lover in Beverly Hills. He leaves women feeling more alive than they've ever felt before.

Except one.

*American Gigolo* x

Paramount Pictures Presents  A Freddie Fields Production  A Film by Paul Schrader  Richard Gere in "American Gigolo" Lauren Hutton
Executive Producer Freddie Fields  Produced by Jerry Bruckheimer  Music Composed by Giorgio Moroder  Written and Directed by Paul Schrader

# Coppola Now

Above: Francis Ford Coppola – doing 'a Hitchcock' – as the director of a TV crew filming GIs in action in Apocalypse Now

'Francis Coppola likes to think of himself as a film-maker,' says Roger Corman. Coppola is a big boy now but his career is as diverse and sprawling as his films. In his search for creative autonomy – which began in the early Sixties when he was an employee on the Corman production line – he has woven a wide-angle saga of financial and technological overkill, setting himself up as a Hollywood godfather and producing several masterpieces along the way

Francis Ford Coppola's story to date has been an occasionally spectacular drama about making films – as opposed to directing them. His carefully nurtured public image is that of the artist struggling to change and control the means and conditions of production through which his work is realized. The parodoxes involved go beyond the usual, simple 'artist versus industry' opposition, climaxing perhaps in the grotesque notion of a weeping Coppola thanking his Zoetrope studio employees for agreeing to continue working on the musical *One From the Heart* (1981) without being paid.

## The hustler

Coppola's aspirations to mogul status are hinted at when he describes how, as a child (he was born in Detroit, Michigan, in 1939), he made 'a little money' from showing the home movies his parents made. He would cut up the films and construct narratives with himself as the hero, but was more interested in 'the exhibition end' and in technical matters. He was to become one of the new wave of young American film-makers in Hollywood in the Seventies and his career developed in archetypal 'movie brat' style. After obtaining a degree in theatre arts he moved on to the UCLA (University of California at Los Angeles) film school in 1960. Then he made some 'nudie' movies, won the Samuel Goldwyn Award for a screenplay (*Pilma, Pilma* – never filmed), and was picked up by producer-director Roger Corman. Work on several of Corman's pictures led to Coppola's first feature, *Dementia 13* (1963), shot in Ireland and using the cast and crew that had been assembled for Corman's *The Young Racers* (1963). Corman agreed to put up half the budget ($20,000) on the basis of Coppola describing a scene involving a lady, a lake, a drowned child and an axe murder. He then supposedly developed the storyline in three-and-a-half days to contain these elements. Certainly individual images and scenes in the film are stronger than the actual plot. Perhaps most significant is Coppola's account of 'big disagreements' with Corman over the editing. This led to Coppola's quitting.

Next followed a spell as a writer with the Seven Arts company, a job obtained largely as a result of the Goldwyn award. Coppola's script for *Reflections in a Golden Eye* (1967) was not used, but his name appears on *This Property Is Condemned* (1966) – 'it was all very depressing' – and on *Paris Brûle-t-il?* (1966, *Is Paris Burning?*), of which he says, 'I could write a book about the troubles we had'. In 1964 he worked on *Patton*; it wasn't filmed until 1970 but, according to Coppola, 'the best scenes in the film, like the opening, are word-for-word from my script'. Coppola regards *You're a Big Boy Now* (1966), his next directorial credit after *Dementia 13*, as 'a con job' worked by himself and the producer Phil Feldman on Seven Arts. He wrote the script on Seven Arts time, but used his ownership of the book rights to get the director job. The film itself was very much a Sixties piece – a zany, Dick Lester-influenced fantasy about a young man trying to cope with

13

women. Again, more interesting is Coppola's hustling attitude to the financing company:

'The way we worked was the way I work now, which is, I don't ask anybody if I can make a movie, I present them with the fact that I am going to make a movie, and if they're wise they'll get in on it.'

Already Coppola was setting his creative flair against the restrictive pressures of the film industry (the management and unions): 'You would never believe the thinking of some of those guys.'

His relationship with Warner Brothers-Seven Arts (the two companies had merged in 1967) was not improved during the making of *Finian's Rainbow* (1967), which was offered to Coppola while he was scripting *The Rain People* (1969). He wanted to film the musical (involving a dancing Irishman, a crock of gold, leprechauns, plus a very mild race issue that inspired Coppola to call the film 'a hot potato') on location, a desire almost totally thwarted by the studio. Veteran dance director Hermes Pan quit the film, Warners blew it up to 70mm (cutting off Fred Astaire's feet in the process) but Coppola considered the final product as having 'humanity and joy', though it was 'not a personal film of mine'.

## Rain over America

Because Warners mistakenly believed that *Finian's Rainbow* would be a hit, they were prepared to back Coppola's next venture, the very 'personal' *The Rain People*. The film's narrative core – a pregnant woman (Shirley Knight) journeys across America and defines her maternal feelings through an encounter with a brain-damaged football player (Bruce Dern) – allowed Coppola a literal escape from the pressures of Hollywood as industry. He packed his tiny crew into a few vehicles and set off, armed with specially purchased light-weight equipment and prepared to improvise and edit *en route*. As an attempt at an early feminist movie, *The Rain People* was somewhat compromised by Coppola's fantasies about women:

'There's a kind of feminine, magical quality, dating back to the Virgin Mary or something I picked up in Catechism classes, that fascinates me.'

His paranoia about unions, arising this time from problems over the size of the crew, was meanwhile growing hand-in-hand with his image of himself as the isolated artist:

'They're [the unions] at my door every day . . . they feel I'm a sort of rat I guess. . . . How can I take a crew like that for a picture that's a personal statement. . . . Nobody wants to make it but me.'

All in all, Coppola's move in 1969 – along with George Lucas for whom he would later produce *American Graffiti* (1973) – to his own San Francisco studio, American Zoetrope, seems in retrospect an inevitable next step. The idea of independently producing low-budget features by young directors, exploiting technological developments and escaping not only the unions (more powerful in Los Angeles) but also what Coppola called 'the management breed . . . packages and deals' seemed fine. But Coppola's hustling streak backfired and Warner Brothers, whom he had persuaded to back Zoetrope, so intensely disliked its first feature, Lucas' *THX 1138* (1970), that they instantly withdrew their support. As a result, Zoetrope simply collapsed.

## Day of the Godfather

At this point, the strands and oppositions within the Coppola story come together in the double-faced form of *The Godfather* (1972) and *The Conversation* (1974). He was seemingly chosen by Paramount to direct the former as much for his Italian blood as for any particular directorial aptitude for the task. But he was clear about the effects of its extraordinary commercial success: '*The Godfather* made me very rich . . . Part of me really wants to take some control and own a piece of that film business.' Paramount offered as much when it set up the Directors Company to fund 'small' features directed by Coppola, Peter Bogdanovich and William Friedkin in conditions of relative autonomy. When the project folded, mainly because of the directors' commitments to other companies, Coppola had produced only one film for it. *The Conversation* is a combination of European 'art movie' and Hollywood thriller, and centres on a great performance by Gene Hackman as a paranoiac, alienated surveillance expert who becomes involved in a murder plot. The film was a critical success, but the formula whereby the commercial blockbuster – in this case *The Godfather* – subsidizes the 'personal project' is an unrealistically simplistic one. In this light *The Godfather, Part II* (1974) seems to occupy a gap – a film made by Coppola while he chose which path to take.

Despite statements since *The Godfather* like 'I don't want to make big commercial pictures', and his professed desire to make 'modest films about contemporary human situations', Coppola has plunged headlong into becoming the

*Above: a cop (Robert Duvall) attempts to rape Natalie (Shirley Knight) in* The Rain People. *Top: Petula Clark and Tommy Steele in the happier* Finian's Rainbow. *Top right: Mafia revenge – Woltz (John Marley) loses by a short head in* The Godfather. *Right: Harry Caul (Gene Hackman), all wired-up in* The Conversation. *Below right:* The Black Stallion *(1979), one of Coppola's 'by-productions'*

last tycoon. In 1974 he purchased a theatre, a radio station and San Francisco's *City* magazine (from which he fired the entire staff). He also bought new production premises and a large share in a distribution company. Most important of all, Coppola resurrected *Apocalypse Now*, a project started by John Milius in 1969 which was originally intended for George Lucas. Shooting began in the Philippines in March 1976 with a budget of $12 million. This would eventually soar to $31.5 million. When the film finally appeared in 1979, critical responses to its vision of Vietnam as a psychedelic nightmare – filtered through Conrad's *Heart of Darkness*, Michael Herr's *Dispatches*, a *film noir*-style voice-over and the music of the Doors – were in a sense superfluous. More significant was the fact that Coppola had mortgaged his home to complete it and almost ruined his marriage, that a typhoon had wrecked the shooting, that it was entered as a 'work in progress' at Cannes, and that there were various different endings, and so on. Coppola himself played his part, informing the world that '*Apocalypse Now* is not a movie. It is not *about* Vietnam, it is Vietnam'. So much for 'modest films'.

## After the Apocalypse

Since *Apocalypse Now*, showmanship has turned into total brinkmanship. The list of Coppola's activities is bewildering. It ranges from the distribution of Godard's *Sauve Qui Peut (La Vie)* (1980, *Slow Motion*) and the financing of a new Godard feature, to the roadshow presentation of Abel Gance's *Napoléon* (1927); the financing of Wim Wenders' *Hammett* (1982) – suspended after 10 weeks' shooting; the rebirth of Zoetrope with the purchase of Hollywood General Studios; the hiring of Michael Powell as director in residence and Gene Kelly as house choreographer; a massive investment in new video technology. But the thin ice on which all this was happily skating became apparent when, after the problems with *Hammett* emerged, investors began to withdraw money from Coppola's own *One From the Heart* – and so he wept for his unpaid workers. Once again it was up to Paramount to dry his tears with a million-dollar investment to keep him afloat, at least temporarily.

That this was the same man who never hesitated to criticize the attitudes of film-workers' unions is not only ironic, but also suggestive as regards the real importance of his career. The interest of his directorial efforts is overshadowed by his status as the embodiment of the new Hollywood who, through his relationships with the industry, gradually evolved into a caricature of the old. Possibly he has only been trying to live up to his claim that 'the most powerful man on earth is a film director. When he makes a picture, he is a god'. Certainly, an earlier statement that his most admired director was Howard Hughes now makes a great deal of sense.

STEVE JENKINS

### Filmography
**1960** Ayamonn the Terrible (short). **'62** The Magic Voyage of Sinbad (co-sc. only on re-ed. and dubbed version of USSR film: Sadko, 1952) (GB: Song of India); Tower of London (dial. dir. only). **'63** Battle Beyond the Sun (co-sc; +add. dir. under pseudonym on re-ed. and dubbed version of USSR film: Nebo Zobyot, 1959); The Young Racers (sd. only); The Terror (co-dir, uncredited; +assoc. prod); Dementia 13 (+co-sc) (USA-EIRE) (GB: The Haunted and the Hunted). **'66** This Property Is Condemned (co-sc. only); Paris Brûle-t-il? (co-sc. only) (FR) (USA/GB: Is Paris Burning?); You're a Big Boy Now (+sc). **'67** Finian's Rainbow. **'68** The Wild Racers (2nd unit dir. only). **'69** The Rain People (+sc). **'70** Patton (co-sc. only) (GB: Patton: Lust for Glory); THX 1138 (exec. prod. only). **'72** The People (orig. TV) (exec. prod. only); The Godfather (+co-sc). **'73** American Graffiti (co-prod. only). **'74** The Great Gatsby (sc. only); The Conversation (+co-prod; +sc); The Godfather, Part II (+prod; +co-sc). **'77** The Godfather (re-ed. version of The Godfather and The Godfather, Part II for TV with add. footage). **'79** Apocalypse Now (+prod; +co-sc; +co-mus; +act); The Black Stallion (exec. prod. only). **'81** The Escape Artist (exec. prod. only); One From the Heart (+co-sc). **'82** Hammett (exec. prod. only). **'83** The Outsiders (+exec. prod); Rumble Fish (+exec. prod; +co-sc); The Black Stallion Returns (exec. prod. only). **'84** The Cotton Club (+co-sc).
*1960–62: Coppola directed a number of 'nudie' shorts, including* The Peeper *and* Tonight for Sure *(intercut and re-released as:* The Wide Open Spaces*);* Come On Out*;* The Playgirls and the Bellboy/The Belt Girls and the Playboy.

As *Apocalypse Now* approaches its climax, Captain Willard listens to Colonel Kurtz recalling an incident from his Special Forces days, when the Vietcong came and hacked off the arms of children who had been inoculated against polio:

'There they were in a pile, a pile of little arms, and I remember I . . . I . . . I cried . . . and then I realized like I was *shot*, like I was shot with a diamond, a diamond bullet right through my forehead, and I thought, my God, the genius of that, the genius, the will to do that – perfect, genuine, complete, crystal, pure!'

It is this revelation that has led Kurtz and his cadre of Montagnard tribesmen to go on the rampage in Cambodia, mass-murdering and mutilating the enemy 'without judgment' in order, he claims, to shorten the war.

Earlier in his journey Willard has witnessed the devastation of a coastal village by the American Ninth Air Cavalry. Kilgore, the officer who orders the air strike, squats on the beach with the jungle

1

2

3

5

*Production shots showing: Phillips, top left; Willard, top right; 'Chef', bottom left; 'Clean', bottom right; and Lance, inset.*

In Vietnam, Captain Benjamin Willard is instructed by his superiors to locate and 'terminate . . . with extreme prejudice' Colonel Walter E. Kurtz, who is waging his own ferocious war against the

Vietcong with an army of Montagnard tribesmen who worship him as a god. Willard begins his journey on a patrol boat crewed by Chief Phillips, 'Chef', Lance and 'Clean' (1).

They are escorted to the Nung River by the helicopters of the Ninth Air Cavalry under Colonel Kilgore (2), who orders an attack on a Vietcong beach-head (3).

As the boat proceeds upriver,

6

7

behind him engulfed in a cliff of flame. 'I love the smell of napalm in the morning,' he informs Willard. 'It smells like . . . victory.'

And so, at first glance, Francis Coppola seems to be showing, in Kurtz, the insane, neo-fascist barbarism of the Vietnam War and, in Kilgore, the ironically respectable side of the same coin. It is tempting to see Kurtz, who has reverted to the Dark Ages and created a primordial holocaust in the jungle, as resembling in spirit the Khmer Rouge; and to see the destructive apparent 'victory' of Kilgore, a latter-day Hollywood Custer in a black stetson with 'DEATH FROM ABOVE' daubed across his chopper, as summing up the ruinous achievement of American military intervention in Indo-China. This may be true as regards Kilgore; but the Kurtz half of *Apocalypse Now* has its roots in a deeper and more ancient legend.

Willard's odyssey is based on that of the narrator, Marlow, in Joseph Conrad's Edwardian novel *Heart of Darkness*, in which there is a character named Kurtz – not a soldier but a white trader in Africa who has resorted to head-hunting to keep the natives in check. 'The horror! The horror!' – Kurtz's dying words in both Conrad's book and Coppola's film, and an existential acceptance of the consuming evil present in the human soul – was the phrase used by T. S. Eliot as an epigraph to the original manuscript of his poem *The Waste Land*, a despairing indictment of post-war western values, published in 1922. Eliot's poem also drew on such anthropological works as Jessie L. Weston's *From Ritual to Romance* and Sir James Frazer's *The Golden Bough*, raising the spectre of the impotent 'fisher king' of Arthurian mythology who must be ritually sacrificed by a younger, stronger man before his barren lands can be replenished. In the twentieth-century waste land of Vietnam, Kurtz, a fated lord, and Willard, aspirant and assassin, fit neatly into this literary framework. Col-onel Kurtz even possesses copies of the Weston and Frazer books and reads from Eliot's poem *The Hollow Men*, invoking the overwhelming shadow of darkness to be found between 'the conception and the creation' of human civilization.

That still leaves Kilgore and the war. Coppola has stated that his intention was to create 'a film experience that would give its audience a sense of the horror, the madness, the sensuousness and the moral dilemma of the Vietnam War'. The film succeeds most powerfully in the area of sensuousness. For better or worse, *Apocalypse Now* displays the warped, foul beauty of war, its rank voluptuousness and epic chaos.

Perhaps Coppola's masterstroke was his collaboration with Michael Herr, whose voice-over commentary for the incredulous Willard (spoken by Martin Sheen) reveals, like Herr's book *Dispatches*, that Vietnam was more like a crazy, obscene movie than like a war. But Coppola also spent $31.5 million, much of it in creating the staggering set-pieces that comprise the film's main episodes: these include the *Playboy* show in the glittering warehouse-arena; the battle for the psychedelically lit Do Lung Bridge, fought on LSD and Jimi Hendrix cassettes; and, most astonishing of all, the helicopter attack on the beach-head. In this awesome sequence an armada of hideously lit choppers glides silently through the breaking dawn, and then swarms down at a sickening pace on the unsuspecting village, spewing rockets and fire as Wagner's 'The Ride of the Valkyries' belches from the stereo speakers in Kilgore's cockpit.

*Apocalypse Now* is a film to despair at. It is a film about going beyond the limits, and its prevailing message is its title, or, as Jim Morrison, the lead singer of the Doors, intones over the first hallucinatory images of choppers ghosting into view on the edge of the blazing jungle: 'This is the end . . .'

GRAHAM FULLER

supplies are collected from the base at Hau Phat, where *Playboy* Playmates entertain sex-starved troops (4). The boat passes the embattled Do Lung bridge (5), entering Cambodia. 'Clean' and Phillips are killed in surprise attacks from the river banks.

The Montagnards await Willard (6). Corpses festoon the approach to Kurtz's compound. Willard (7) is taken to Kurtz (8), who explains

the necessity of his brutal methods before imprisoning him. A crazy American photo-journalist expounds Kurtz's cause to Willard, who is later presented with Chef's severed head.

Accepting the inevitable, however, Kurtz allows Willard (9) to kill him, carrying out a ritual decapitation. Refusing the chance to become the new god, Willard begins the return journey.

**Directed by Francis Coppola, 1979**
**Prod co:** Omni Zoetrope. **prod:** Francis Coppola. **co-prod:** Fred Roos, Gray Frederickson, Tom Sternberg. **assoc prod:** Mona Skager. **sc:** John Milius, Francis Coppola, from the novel *Heart of Darkness* by Joseph Conrad. **comm:** Michael Herr. **titles:** Wayne Fitzgerald. **photo** (Technicolor, Technovision): Vittorio Storaro. **sup ed:** Richard Marks. **ed:** Walter Murch, Gerald B. Greenberg, Lisa Fruchtman. **prod des:** Dean Tavoularis. **art dir:** Angelo Graham. **sp eff:** Joseph Lombardi, A. D. Flowers. **mus prod:** David Rubinson. **mus:** Carmine Coppola, Francis Coppola; Richard Wagner's *Die Walküre* by The Vienna Philharmonic Orchestra; Patrick Gleeson (master synthesist), Richard Beggs, Bernard L. Krause, Don Preston, Shirley Walker, Nyle Steiner, Randy Hansen, Mickey Hart, Airto Moreira, Michael Hinton. **songs:** 'The End' by The Doors, 'Satisfaction' by The Rolling Stones, 'Love Me, and Let Me Love You', 'Let the Good Times Roll' and 'Suzie Q' by Flash Cadillac; excerpts from 'Mnong Gar Music from Vietnam'. **sd:** Walter Murch. **sd ed:** Richard Cirincione. **stunt co-ordinator:** Terry Leonard. **aerial co-ordinators:** Dick White, David Jones. **marine co-ordinators:** Pete Cooper, Dennis Murphy, Shane Edwards. **ass dir:** Jerry Ziesmer, Larry J. Franco, Tony Brandt. **prod man:** Leon Chooluck, Barrie Osborne. **r/t:** 141 minutes in 70mm version (153 minutes in 35mm version with end title sequence).
**Cast:** Marlon Brando (*Col. Walter E. Kurtz*), Robert Duvall (*Lt.-Col. Bill Kilgore*), Martin Sheen (*Capt. Benjamin L. Willard*), Frederic Forrest (*'Chef' Hicks*), Albert Hall (*Chief Phillips*), Sam Bottoms (*Lance B. Johnson*), Larry Fishburne (*'Clean'*), Dennis Hopper (*photo-journalist*), G. D. Spradlin (*Gen. Corman*), Harrison Ford (*Col. Lucas*), Jerry Ziesmer (*civilian*), Scott Glenn (*Capt. Richard Colby*), Bo Byers (*first MP sergeant*), James Keane (*Kilgore's gunner*), Kerry Rossall (*Mike from San Diego*), Ron McQueen (*injured soldier*), Tom Mason (*supply sergeant*), Cynthia Wood (*Playmate of the Year*), Colleen Camp and Linda Carpenter (*Playmates*), Jack Thibeau (*soldier in trench*), Glenn Walken (*Lt. Carlsen*), George Cantero (*soldier with suitcase*), Damien Leake (*machine-gunner*), Herb Rice (*Roach*), William Upton (*aircraft spotter*), Larry Carney (*second MP sergeant*), Marc Coppola (*radio announcer*), Daniel Kiewit (*major from New Jersey*), Father Elias (*Catholic priest*), Bill Graham (*agent*), Hattie James (*voice of Clean's mother*), Jerry Ross (*Johnny from Malibu*), Dick White (*helicopter pilot*), Francis Coppola (*director of TV crew*), Ifugao people of Banaue, Philippine Islands (*Montagnard tribesmen*).

# MEAN

1

# STREETS

### Directed by Martin Scorsese, 1973

**Prod co:** Taplin-Perry-Scorsese for Warner Brothers. **exec prod:** E. Lee Perry. **prod:** Jonathan T. Taplin. **sc:** Martin Scorsese, Mardik Martin, from a story by Martin Scorsese. **photo** (Technicolor): Kent Wakeford. **add photo:** Norman Gerard. **visual consultant:** David Nichols. **sp eff:** Bill Bales. **ed:** Sid Levin. **songs:** 'Jumping Jack Flash', 'Tell Me' by The Rolling Stones, 'I Love You So' by The Chantells, 'Addio Sogni Di Gloria', 'Conta per' Me', 'Monasterio Di Santa Chiara' by Giuseppe De Stefano, 'Marruzella', 'Scapricciatiello' by Renato Carosone, 'Please Mr Postman' by The Marvelettes, 'Hideaway', 'I Looked Away' by Eric Clapton, 'Desiree' by The Chants, 'Rubber Bisquit' by The Chips, 'Pledging My Love' by Johnny Ace, 'Ritino Sabroso' by Ray Baretta, 'You' by The Aquatones, 'Ship of Love' by The Nutmegs, 'Florence' by The Paragons, 'Malafemmina' by Jimmy Roselli, 'Those Oldies But Goodies' by Little Caesar and the Romans, 'I Met Him on a Sunday' by The Shirelles, 'Be My Baby' by The Ronettes, 'Mickey's Monkey' by The Miracles. **sd:** Glen Glenn. **sd rec:** Don Johnson, John K. Williamson, Bud Grenzbach, Walter Goss. **stunts co-ordinator:** Bill Katching. **animal trainer:** George Toth. **prod man:** Paul Rapp. **ass dir:** Russell Vreeland, Ron Satloff. **r/t:** 110 minutes.
**Cast:** Harvey Keitel (*Charlie*), Robert De Niro (*Johnny Boy*), David Proval (*Tony*), Amy Robinson (*Teresa*), Richard Romanus (*Michael*), Cesare Danova (*Giovanni*), Victor Argo (*Mario*), Robert Carradine (*assassin*), Jeannie Bell (*Diane*), D'Mitch Davis (*cop*), David Carradine (*drunk*), George Memmoli (*Joey*), Murray Mosten (*Oscar*), Ken Sinclair (*Sammy*), Harry Northup (*soldier*), Lois Walden (*Jewish girl*), Lenny Scarletta (*Jimmy*), Robert Wilder (*Benton*), Martin Scorsese (*car gunman*), Dino Seragusa (*old man*), Peter Fain (*George*), Julie Andelman (*girl at party*), Jaime Alba, Ken Konstantin (*young boys*), Nicki 'Ack' Aqualino (*man on docks*), B. Mitchell Reed (*disc jockey*), Catherine Scorsese (*neighbour on staircase*).

The opening credits of *Mean Streets* – a haphazard sequence of hand-held home-movie shots backed by the punchy music of the Ronettes singing 'Be My Baby' – end on a shot of Charlie, the small-time gangster, shaking hands with the parish priest. Both men are smiling at the camera. Over this image the final title reads 'directed by Martin Scorsese'. It is a shot that encapsulates the two career choices Scorsese reckons were offered to him by his upbringing in New York's Little Italy district.

He had already failed to stay the course in a Catholic seminary, and his slight stature and asthmatic condition did not mark him out as a future Lucky Luciano, though the hit-man fantasy is fulfilled briefly at the end of *Mean Streets* when the director himself plays the killer hired to exact revenge on Johnny Boy. For the rest of the movie, however, the feeling that Scorsese is living *through* the character of Charlie is inescapable, and the persona had already been sketched in by Harvey Keitel in Scorsese's earlier movie *Who's That Knocking at My Door?* (1968).

The key to the critical and commercial success of *Mean Streets* lies in the circumstances of its financing and in Scorsese's own background: the common denominator is rock music. Determined to make the film he had been planning in his head for years and resisting the temptation to film another Roger Corman quickie after *Boxcar Bertha* (1972), Scorsese found a backer in Jonathan Taplin, who managed bookings and tours for Bob Dylan and The Band.

From the start Scorsese had conceived the film in terms of its picture track and its music track simultaneously. His own experience as an editor on several rock-concert movies in the early Seventies testified to his professional knowledge of the music business. But above all it was Scorsese's memory of Sixties rock'n'roll with its revolutionary power to influence people's lives and behaviour that made *Mean Streets* such an exciting proposition for Taplin and Warner Brothers.

In the film, music is always of equal importance to the other elements of *mise-en-scène* – lighting, positioning of actors, movement of camera, and so on. The fight in Joey's pool-room, for example, lasts exactly the length of the Marvelettes' number 'Please Mr Postman' and the action – filmed in a combination of threatening close-ups, giddy overhead shots and rapid, hand-held takes pursuing the brawlers around the room – is cut neatly to the rhythm of the song. For once, the epithet 'operatic' is entirely appropriate, especially given Scorsese's use of Italian popular classics and the cultural importance of opera within the Italian immigrant society depicted in the film.

But *Mean Streets* also distances Scorsese from his background; ironically, the film was shot not in the New York streets where it is set but in Los Angeles. More importantly, it reveals the gap between Scorsese the film-maker and those adolescent options of priest or gangster. It is a distance that is measured in the film by quotations from other movies. When Michael and Charlie go to a cinema on the proceeds of a con-trick, the film they see is John Ford's *The Searchers* (1956) and Scorsese shows a clip with John Wayne in a brawl. But when Charlie and Johnny Boy go on the run from Michael, the cinema they shelter in is showing a horror movie with Vincent Price about to be consumed in the flames of hell.

Earlier, when Charlie and Teresa make love in a hotel room, Scorsese quotes quite consciously from the director Jean-Luc Godard – Harvey Keitel and Amy Robinson replay the Jean-Paul Belmondo and Jean Seberg roles from *A Bout de Souffle* (1960, *Breathless*). The director even ventures a jump-cut, more as an acknowledgment of Godard's influence than as a device within the narrative.

All the examples of cine-literacy (referring, within one film, to a whole context of cinematic influences, both European and American) are characteristic of the 'movie brat' generation of film-makers. In *Mean Streets* they are brilliantly combined with superb ensemble, improvisatory acting from Keitel, De Niro and Romanus, to produce a work that is, if anything, even more exciting on a formal level than in its gripping, breathless narrative.

MARTYN AUTY

2

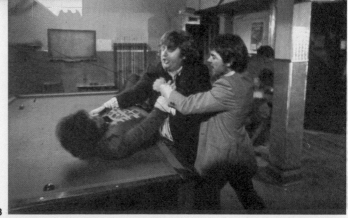

3

4

5

Home-movie footage introduces the principal characters – Charlie, Johnny Boy and Michael – in their neighbourhood of Little Italy, New York. Charlie (1), a practising but spiritually anguished Catholic, works as a collector for his mafioso uncle, Giovanni. Michael, a small-time crook, has loaned money to the irresponsible Johnny Boy who cannot hold down a job long enough to make regular repayments to him.

Charlie stands surety for Johnny Boy, but in the back-room of Tony's club (2) he berates him for his irresponsible attitude.

Later, Charlie, Johnny Boy, Tony and another associate, Jimmy, call at Joey's pool-room to make a collection. A fight breaks out over an insult (3) but just as all is settled between the two sides, Johnny Boy throws a final punch and is bundled out.

Meanwhile, Charlie is dating

Johnny Boy's cousin Teresa (4), despite a warning from uncle Giovanni not to associate with the family at all (5).

When Johnny Boy shows up over an hour late at Teresa's, Charlie attacks him (6) and then drags him off to Tony's, where they have a crucial meeting with Michael. At Tony's, Michael demands his repayment from Johnny Boy, who offers him ten dollars, insults him and then pulls

a gun on him (7). Michael walks out in a rage.

Charlie hustles Johnny Boy out of the club, knowing that Michael will come looking for revenge. As Charlie, Johnny Boy and Teresa are driving out of town, Michael's car pulls alongside and a hired gunman fires several shots, hitting Johnny Boy in the neck (8) and wounding the other two. Charlie staggers from the crashed car and slumps to his knees (9).

6

7

8

9

# Scorsese, Scorsese

Peter Hayden's 1978 documentary about Martin Scorsese is appropriately entitled *Movies Are My Life*, for no other director of the new American cinema has quite so completely managed to merge the concerns of his personal life with older film genres which helped to form his consciousness of life and cinema. An Italian-American of the third generation, Scorsese was born in 1942 in Flushing, New York, but his parents moved to Little Italy in 1950, so that it was in the Italian, Catholic milieu of Manhattan that he grew up. His asthma prevented the more strenuous pastimes; as partial recompense his father took him to the movies at least twice a week, which inspired him to draw his own story-boards for imaginary films. He now says that when thinking back over his childhood, he often confuses events that really happened with events from Alice Faye vehicles or the films of John Ford and Samuel Fuller.

At 14 he decided he wanted to be a priest, but rock'n'roll, movies on 42nd Street and his gang pals on Lower East Side, New York, interested him more than the Church and took more of his time than his studies. Instead, in 1963, he enrolled in the English Department of New York University where he found himself more interested in cinema courses and was encouraged in his interest by Professor Haig Manoogian, to whom *Raging Bull* (1980) is dedicated. Among his fellow students and friends were Brian De Palma (through whom he met Robert De Niro), cameraman Michael Wadleigh (who later directed *Woodstock*, 1970) and Mardik Martin, who worked on several scripts with Scorsese.

A growing awareness of the French *nouvelle vague* from screenings at the New York Film Festival helped him to see the possibility of making personal films under almost amateur circumstances. At any rate, it is clear from his second 16mm short made at NYU – *It's Not Just You, Murray* (1965) – what sort of cinema was to be Scorsese's major influence: that film ends with a production number ('Love Is a Gazelle') in the manner of Busby Berkeley, a perfect example of popular American movies of the Thirties and Forties. That same film also indicated other central concerns which were to be developed in later films: *It's Not Just You, Murray* is a semi-fictionalized portrait of his uncle, set in Little Italy.

## Dress rehearsals

In 1965 he attempted to make a 35mm feature – *Bring on the Dancing Girls* – a semi-autobiographical story. About a young man, raised in Little Italy as a Catholic, the film shows how a young girl brings confusion to his macho sense of 'angel or whore'. The $6000 Scorsese had borrowed for the film did not last

'People tell me that I am incapable of telling a story. I don't care. I have other things to say. And another way to say them.' For all his lack of concern with the commercialism of cinema, Martin Scorsese has nevertheless made pictures which have sold well. Starting out as a respected editor, he went on to exploit his Italian-American origins in the films he has directed. His success has certainly earned him a place in the vanguard of the new American cinema

long and he abandoned the project until 1967 when Haig Manoogian encouraged him to try it again, this time in an economically more realistic 16mm. The result was *I Call First* – released in 1968 under the title *Who's That Knocking at My Door?* – with Zina Bethune and Harvey Keitel. Seen now, the film has its own nervous intensity, a fine performance by Keitel, and striking black-and-white images, but seems something of a dress rehearsal for *Mean Streets* (1973) – itself already 'in the air' as a script.

After finishing *Who's That Knocking at My Door?* Scorsese made a 16mm short, *The Big Shave* (1967), which was a hit at the Experimental Film Festival in Knokke-le-Zoute,

Belgium. He stayed in Europe with cameraman Richard Coll and made publicity films for six months and co-wrote Pim de la Parra and Wim Verstappen's *Obsessions* (1969) in Holland. His reputation as an editor took him to Hollywood, and while editing and supervising post-production for François Reichenbach's *Medicine Ball Caravan* (1971), Scorsese met American International Pictures exploita-

*Above: between feature films, Martin Scorsese hopes to make a series of documentary profiles. He himself appears in* American Boy *(1978), the portrait of a friend. Below left:* Boxcar Bertha *– an outspoken, bloody drama about union activity*

tion producer Roger Corman who hired him to make an action film 'for the guys on 42nd Street'.

The producer expected something of a sequel to his own film *Bloody Mama* (1970). Instead, Scorsese's *Boxcar Bertha* (1972) is a strange meditation, with bursts of violence, on roving union organizers and other outcasts of the Depression. AIP was somewhat disconcerted and did not quite know what to do with the film, since Scorsese had doctored the screenplay to some extent. Nevertheless, *Boxcar Bertha* and its director had their supporters in the film industry and on the festival circuit, and they advised Scorsese to make a film to which he was more totally committed than this impersonal commercial exploitation work.

## Italy isn't here any more

That film was *Mean Streets*, made for $550,000, which became a hit at both the New York Film Festival and in the 'Directors' Fortnight' at Cannes. The film is a portrait of a generation of Italian-Americans in the ghetto of Little Italy, caught between the Mafia and the Church. Harvey Keitel again plays a variation of Scorsese himself, attempting to free himself of his Catholic background and yet to 'save' those around him, particularly his best friend and his friend's epileptic sister . . . with catastrophic

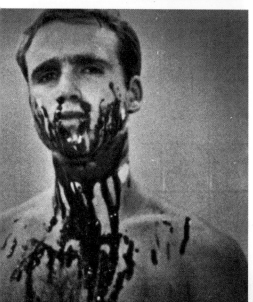

results. Part of the film's excitement comes from the use of rock music, not only to underscore period but to comment on emotional states and point to how popular culture helps determine character.

For all its personal concerns, *Mean Streets* is very much a genre film, in a tradition that dates back at least as far as *Angels With Dirty Faces* (1938). Looked at from one angle, however, Scorsese has never made anything but genre films . . . but always with a difference. His next feature, *Alice Doesn't Live Here Any More* (1974) – the story of a widow's search for happiness on a trip across America in which she vacillates between the dream of a career and 'true love' – was in every way a woman's picture in the tradition of Sirk or Capra. It is probably the director's least personal film – Ellen Burstyn, who won an Oscar for her performance, had as much or more to say about the script as Scorsese or writer Robert Getchell. But Scorsese's own concerns are certainly not absent: the beginning in which an extract from an Alice Faye film is used to show how popular movies formed consciousness of identity, for example, or the unbalanced 'angel or whore' violence of the character played by Harvey Keitel, who is at one and the same time generous and loving with Alice, yet brutal to his own wife. *Alice*

*Left: Ellen Burstyn stars in* Alice Doesn't Live Here Anymore, *a 'road' movie about a young widow and her son drifting in search of love and money. Bottom left: just after he graduated, Scorsese made the black comedy* The Big Shave *– a prize-winning short in which a minor accident turns into an arterial tragedy. Below: Jodie Foster as Iris and Robert De Niro as the* Taxi Driver

*Doesn't Live Here Any More* showed that at least some of the problems found in Little Italy are also a part of Anglo-Saxon Protestant culture.

## Street life

In 1976 New York City became not only the setting but a major character in *Taxi Driver*, the film which won the Golden Palm at Cannes and secured Scorsese's reputation as the most talented director of the new American cinema. While the script is by Paul Schrader, there are definite connections between *Taxi Driver* and *Mean Streets*. Here, however, the would-be 'saviour' becomes an exterminating angel, a killer praised and honoured for slaughtering a pimp. Ironically, though, it is praise for a paranoid murderer who could easily strike again. The film is a trip through hell with the 'real' city dissolving into an hallucination of odd colours and visual distortions – a hell from which there is no redemption.

Those who praise Scorsese for his 'realism' are missing the point, unless it is his emotional realism they have in mind. There is little difference finally between the way he uses the actual streets of New York in *Taxi Driver* and the purposely artificial sets of the city he uses in *New York, New York* (1977). What he had in mind was:

'A movie called *New York, New York* shot entirely in Los Angeles, which goes back to the old films I used to see as a kid, which reflected part of New York, but that was a fantasy of New York up on the screen. So, in the picture I tried to fuse whatever was a fantasy – the movies I grew up with as a kid – with the reality I experienced myself.'

In *New York, New York* Scorsese wants to take the viewer through the changes in the American consciousness from the open-ended,

high-energy optimism following hard on the tail of World War II to the repressed disillusion of the Fifties. While he glories in the artificiality of the form – something akin to *The Glenn Miller Story* (1953) – he attempts to make the human relationships realistic, in part to determine whether those old forms can contain emotional realism without bursting open. He is only relatively successful, at least in the version of the film that was released – the original four-and-a-half hours were edited down to just over two. There is now an imbalance in the structure which loses sight of the character played by Robert De Niro in the second half, so that the emotional drive of the film is weakened.

## The last round

*The Last Waltz* (1978), a documentary about the last performance by The Band, is a genre film – the 'concert' film with interviews. Aside from the fact that it was shot and edited with musical grace and energy, the film is easily the best of its type because it has a moving thesis which grows from the material rather than being imposed on it. Its theme is one that is shared in part by *New York, New York* – the portrait of the end of a musical and cultural era which, for all its excitement, is finally autumnal in tone.

*Raging Bull* is in the boxing-biography genre of the *Somebody Up There Likes Me* (1956) variety, but with a difference. Set more or less in the Italian milieu and again with something of the sexual angel-whore problem, of the love-hate relationship with the Anglo-Saxon blonde which is also in *Taxi Driver*, the film describes in one scene how Jake La Motta (the hero) is driven to a violent frenzy when he fears that his idealized, teenage wife might have been sleeping with his brother. But Scorsese has developed other favourite themes in new ways: redemption, love, friendship between men, the unconsidered act. Scorsese refuses to think of *Raging Bull* as a boxing film:

'I don't like boxing. What interested me was what was going on in the heads of the characters. Jake, on a certain fundamental level, is perhaps an animal, but he's closer to a human life less complicated. He doesn't know what he is doing, he can't verbalize his acts. There's the mystic side of the film, why I made it. Everything in the film remains strange.'

DAVID OVERBEY

*Above: the Forties' musical drama* New York, New York *follows the romance of singer Francine Evans (Liza Minnelli) and musician Jimmy Doyle (Robert De Niro)*

*Below: De Niro in* Raging Bull. *Bottom: Dr John, Neil Diamond, Joni Mitchell, Neil Young, Rick Danko, Van Morrison, Bob Dylan, Robbie Robertson in* The Last Waltz

### Filmography
**1964** What's a Nice Girl Like You Doing in a Place Like This? (short) (+sc). **'65** It's Not Just You, Murray (short) (+co-sc; +act). **'67** The Big Shave (short) (+sc). **'68** Who's That Knocking at My Door? (+sc). **'69** Obsessions (co-sc. only) (HOLL-GER). **'70** Woodstock (doc) (ass. dir; +sup. ed); Street Scenes (doc) (prod. sup; +add. dir. only). **'71** Medicine Ball Caravan (doc) (assoc. prod; +sup. ed. only (USA-FR) (GB: We Have Come for Your Daughters); Minnie and Moskowitz (ass. ed. only). **'72** Elvis on Tour (doc) (montage sup. only); Unholy Rollers (sup. ed. only); Boxcar Bertha (+act). **'73** Mean Streets (+co-sc; +act). **'74** Italianamerican (doc. short) (+co-sc; + appearance as himself); Alice Doesn't Live Here Anymore. **'76** Taxi Driver (+act); Cannonball (actor only) (GB: Carquake). **'77** New York, New York. **'78** The Last Waltz (doc) (+appearance as himself); Roger Corman; Hollywood's Wild Angel (doc. short) (appearance as himself only); American Boy (doc) (+appearance as himself); Movies Are My Life (doc) (appearance as himself only). **'80** Raging Bull (+act); Il Pap'occhio (actor only) (IT). **'83** The King of Comedy (+act).

# The trouble with Harry...

. . . is that he tends to get into things over his head, into professional situations that viciously rebound on his private life. Harry Caul that is, or Harry Moseby, or indeed any of the middle-aged, menopausal males superbly portrayed on the American screen by Gene Hackman – one of the most relevant of modern superstars

For most moviegoers the first conscious encounter with Gene Hackman came with his portrayal of Buck Barrow, Clyde's elder brother in *Bonnie and Clyde* (1967), though he had previously played small roles in such films as *Lilith* (1964) and *Hawaii* (1966). But however impressive his performance as Buck Barrow was, it would have taken an act of clairvoyance to predict that Hackman would become a major box-office star of the Seventies, ranking as high as third in world popularity in 1972.

In appearance Hackman has always seemed middle-aged and his looks might best be described as 'everyday'. His face was never going to make his fortune in a business peopled by Newmans, Redfords and McQueens . . . or was it? Perhaps because Hollywood heroes of the Sixties were traditionally cast from the blue-eyed, blond-haired mould, a bulkier figure and more mature face like Hackman's would stand out from the crowd. Even so, under the old Hollywood star system, this ex-marine – 6ft. 2in. and weighing over 200lbs – would have found himself restricted to 'character' parts rather than top-lining roles such as 'Popeye' Doyle in William Friedkin's *The French Connection* (1971), the part that made him a star.

Because he arrived in Hollywood at the moment when the old studio system was breaking up, Hackman could see that casting was becoming more fluid, that 'types' mattered less than talent, and that a man who was heading for middle age – he was 37 when he appeared in *Bonnie and Clyde* – was not necessarily condemned to playing character parts.

## Just an ordinary guy

At the outset his 'ordinary man' image enabled him to keep comfortably in work over the four years that separated *Bonnie and Clyde* from *The*

*French Connection*. Later Francis Ford Coppola was to say of his casting of Hackman in *The Conversation* (1974):

'Hackman was ideal for this role because of his utterly everyday appearance, the most important feature of the character.'

Hackman himself calls the films of this pre-stardom phase 'forgettable' but the period contains two performances of distinction by him – the ski-team trainer in Michael Ritchie's

*Above: Hackman as a man whose impending marriage to his girl (Elizabeth Hubbard) is threatened by his cantankerous widowed dad in* I Never Sang for My Father. *Top left: as Harry Moseby up to his neck trying to rescue a runaway girl (Melanie Griffith) who has just discovered the corpse of her lover in* Night Moves. *Top right: as a boorish Southern husband in* Lilith, *an asylum drama with Warren Beatty and Jessica Walter*

23

*Above: Hackman in his Oscar-winning role of 'Popeye' Doyle, grimly intent on getting his man in* The French Connection. *Right: as a priest saving souls from sea disaster in* The Poseidon Adventure, *with Pamela Sue Martin*

*Downhill Racer* (1969) and the middle-aged son who has to look after an elderly father (Melvyn Douglas) in *I Never Sang for My Father* (1970).

Eugene Hackman's own relations with his father were disrupted in his mid-teens when his parents were divorced; his mother brought him up in Danville, Illinois. The biographical detail at this point is almost identical to that supplied by the scriptwriter Alan Sharp for the character of Harry Moseby in Arthur Penn's *Night Moves* (1975), for many Hackman's finest screen performance. In 1946 Hackman lied about his age (which was 16) and got into the Marines. It was an experience that would serve him well physically in the business of being a star of action pictures like *The French Connection* and *French Connection II* (1975). After being discharged he took odd jobs and small parts in theatre and TV until he gradually carved himself a niche in Hollywood.

## Hackman's method

On his approach to acting Hackman is quite candid. He told an interviewer in *Films in Review*:

'There's something of me in all the roles I play. It's finding this little something of you in the character and developing it. That's the art of acting.'

It may not be a profound definition perhaps, but it is a clear-headed and conscientious attitude to the business of creating a character as distinct from the mystification often indulged by actors talking of their craft. Hackman admits that he will think constantly about a new role for days but he does not 'become' the character. 'I live with him', he avers.

In the early Fifties when he was playing in summer stock and still ten years away from Hollywood, he used to watch Marlon Brando. In an interview in *Film Comment* he said:

'Really, I think I began in this profession because of Brando. I saw in Brando a kind of kinship, not because of his appearance, but because of something in his performance which made me think "I can do that". I'm sure that's why he has so many followers. People

see in Brando a kind of strength which can at the same time be an everyday approach to life.'

By 1978 Hackman had his name just beneath Brando's on the billing for *Superman, The Movie*.

To trace the run up to Hackman's 'arrival' with *The French Connection* is to discover a subtle alternating of sympathetic roles – for example, Buck Barrow and the stranded astronaut in *Marooned* (1969) – with downright unpleasant parts such as the gangleader in *Riot* (1968) and the corrupt cop in *Cisco Pike* (1971). Thus by the time he was cast in *The French Connection* his screen image, insofar as it existed in the mind of the moviegoer, was a decidedly ambiguous one. No-one could be sure whether 'Popeye' Doyle was a good guy or a bad guy. And that was the strength of his characterization.

Required to play a tough and streetwise cop on the trail of narcotics smugglers, Hackman served 'an apprenticeship' in Harlem with Eddie Egan, the real-life detective on whose exploits the source novel was based. 'It was scary as hell', Hackman told *Time* magazine. In the movie Hackman borrowed tricks from Egan such as shoving a suspect into a telephone booth to subdue him. He also did most of the hair-raising driving in *The French Connection* and constantly refused to have a double for action scenes. Asked what he thought of 'Popeye' Doyle's morality, Hackman made clear his broadly liberal politics:

'Most cops like the idea of a movie showing something of the reality they know, with a hero who is a very right-wing conservative – shit, let's be honest, Doyle is a fascist.'

Though the actor may choose to distance himself from the role, the sense of isolation that allowed Doyle to say 'Never trust a nigger. Never trust anyone' became a key feature of the Hackman screen persona. It was a stance that would alienate that persona further and consolidate the image of a loner that *The Conversation* and *Night Moves* would exploit to such advantage in the Hackman roles of Harry Caul and Harry Moseby respectively.

In the interim, however, there were three

films that variously extended the public's awareness of Hackman as a major star. *The Poseidon Adventure* (1972) saw him as a somewhat unorthodox priest attempting to save people caught in the submerged ship but who insisted on helping 'winners not quitters'. In *Scarecrow* (1973) he played the egotistical tramp who dreams of running his own carwash. In *Zandy's Bride* (1974), opposite Liv Ullmann, he was a brutal, self-centred husband.

## Private hell

*The Conversation* involves the lacing together of sounds and images from a conversation overheard by a professional eavesdropper who has picked up on a murder. The tables are turned in the course of the film and it is the 'bugger's' – Harry Caul's – privacy that is suddenly invaded, rendering him finally more paranoid than everyone else. The appearance of this movie at the time of Watergate was crucial to

*Below left: 'Popeye' Doyle still pursuing a heroin czar in* French Connection II – *he is drugged and nearly drowned for his pains. Below: Hackman and Ned Beatty as the villains of* Superman, The Movie

*Above left: in* Zandy's Bride *Hackman is a Californian farmer who maltreats the wife (Liv Ullmann) he buys from a newspaper ad. Above right: 'Harry Caul' discusses* The Conversation *with Francis Ford Coppola*

*Young Frankenstein* (1974) – he was a blind old man who welcomes the monster into his pathetic home only to spill boiling soup inadvertently into the creature's lap. *Bite the Bullet* (1975) saw him as a disillusioned cowboy entering an endurance horserace with his rival (James Coburn). *French Connection II*, directed by John Frankenheimer, had Hackman back as 'Popeye' Doyle, put through even more physical exertions as he raced a motorboat along the Marseilles waterfront and simulated 'cold turkey' in an underworld cell. For a change of image Hackman accepted the role of Major Foster, an American in the French Foreign Legion, in *March or Die* (1977). He remained in uniform for a small role – earning himself a small fortune – in Joseph E. Levine's colossal *A Bridge Too Far* (1977).

Hackman's admirers have since been divided over his portrayal of the arch-criminal Lex Luthor in *Superman, The Movie* and *Superman II* (1980). It seems clear, however, that his much-undervalued comic timing is well appreciated by Richard Lester, director of the latter, who allowed the star to play his role more tongue-in-cheek than in the first film – bringing an essentially cardboard villain to life. Now in his fifties, Gene Hackman has no publicly declared ambitions, apparently no plans to become a director or to enter politics (having been deeply disillusioned over the deaths of both Kennedys), but if he is offered parts as challenging and potentially subversive as Caul and Moseby, there may well be more 'trouble' with Harry.              MARTYN AUTY

its success but the casting of the 44-year-old Hackman is also an essential factor. In his face and through his obsessive but outwardly normal behaviour, Hackman suggests the anxiety of the menopausal male who 'gets in over his head' and is bugged by his own technology. His portrayal of Harry Caul stands as a personification of the fear and loneliness at the heart of all the American conspirators in the mid-Seventies – not just Nixon's men but the CIA men and the big businessmen whose 'dirty tricks' were coming into the open.

To follow such a consummately low-key performance with that of the middle-aged private-eye in *Night Moves* was for Hackman a question of merging one 'Harry' into the next. In *Night Moves* Harry Moseby is hired to find the daughter of a movie mogul's widow. All around him things are collapsing, including his marriage, or becoming distorted – the missing-person job becomes a murder and larceny case – but Moseby appears to be

muddling through until he realizes that he is in over his head and that there is no way out of the twists and turns of the plot. Hackman's characterization is built on a series of shifts from tenderness to blind anger, clear-sightedness to confusion, suggesting that Moseby's ambivalence would have been well suited to the uncertain world of Forties *film noir*. Indeed, what is genuinely disturbing about *Night Moves* lies in the tension between its *film noir* structure and the 'where-do-we-go-now?' ambience of post-Watergate America. The essential unease of this fine thriller is attributable in no small measure to Hackman's depiction of a man desperately trying to make sense of a world where marriages break up, presidents get shot and detectives do find trouble if they go looking for it.

## Mainline connections

Around the time of *Night Moves* Hackman contributed a brilliant cameo to Mel Brooks'

**Filmography**
1961 Mad Dog Coll. '64 Lilith. '66 Hawaii. '67 A Covenant With Death; First to Fight; Banning; Bonnie and Clyde. '68 The Split; Riot. '69 The Gypsy Moths; Downhill Racer; Marooned. '70 I Never Sang for My Father. '71 Doctors' Wives; Confrontation (short); The Hunting Party; The French Connection; Cisco Pike. '72 Prime Cut; The Poseidon Adventure. '73 Scarecrow. '74 The Conversation; Zandy's Bride; Young Frankenstein. '75 Night Moves; Bite the Bullet; French Connection II; Lucky Lady. '77 The Domino Principle (GB: The Domino Killings); A Look at Liv (doc) (appearance as himself only); A Bridge Too Far; March or Die. '78 Superman, The Movie; Formula 1, Febbre della Velocità/Speed Fever (doc) (appearance as himself only) (IT). '80 Superman II. '81 All Night Long. '83 Eureka (GB-USA); Under Fire.

# Both sides of

# John Cassavetes

One of the most paradoxical and controversial of all the American independents, John Cassavetes has always placed actors and acting at the centre of his film-making conceptions. An actor himself, he has used his craft as a means of financing his own productions – which are themselves celebrations of acting. 'Directing really is a full-time hobby with me,' he confessed in an interview in the late Sixties. 'I consider myself an amateur film-maker and a professional actor.'

Born on December 9th, 1929 in New York City, the son of a Greek immigrant who made and then lost a fortune in business, Cassavetes attended Colgate College as an English major. It was there that his interest in acting was sparked, and he enrolled in the American Academy of Dramatic Arts shortly after graduation.

### Delinquent turns director
Following a stage debut in a stock company and a bit part in a Hollywood feature, *Fourteen Hours* (1951), Cassavetes gradually acquired his reputation as a young actor by appearing in television dramas, where he specialized in

**The lean, hungry delinquents that actor John Cassavetes played in his youth and the intense villains of his middle age have made him a familiar face in American films. And as lucrative Hollywood assignments they have all helped finance his other career as an independent film-maker – one whose maverick methods were a shining example for kindred spirits working outside 'the system' in the early years of the Sixties**

juvenile delinquent parts. By the mid-Fifties, he was re-creating one of these roles in a film about a family being held captive by hoodlums, *The Night Holds Terror* (1955). Juicy parts followed in *Crime in the Streets* and *Edge of the City* (both 1956).

Probably the most popular of Cassavetes' television appearances was as the star of the detective series *Johnny Staccato* (1959–60). He used his own earnings from that programme to support his experimental feature, *Shadows* (1960), which grew out of an acting workshop that he taught. Shot in 16mm on a minuscule

budget, and improvised by a talented cast of unknowns out of sketchy material provided by Cassavetes, the film had an unusual genesis. The popular Manhattan radio personality Jean Shepherd visited the class one night, was mightily impressed by what he saw, and urged Cassavetes to appear on his late-night show, where listeners were asked to send in small donations so that a film could be made. The ploy worked, and the eventually released film created enough of a sensation to secure Cassavetes a Hollywood contract.

Undeniably flawed in many particulars,

Opposite page: John Cassavetes, actor, as the
devil's stand-in in Rosemary's Baby (left);
John Cassavetes, director, shooting the marital
drama A Woman Under the Influence
(right). Above left: Rupert Crosse, Hugh Hurd
and Lelia Goldoni in Shadows, an
unpatronizing look at race problems. Above: an
unhappy wife (Lynn Carlin) and her lover
(Seymour Cassel) in Faces. Left: Cassavetes
and Sidney Poitier in Edge of the City

*Shadows* had a sensitivity and power in relation to its subject – a closely-knit black family
of two brothers and a sister living in Manhattan – that came across as a revelation to
audiences. The film's tracing of racism and its
effects on an unsuccessful nightclub singer
(Hugh Hurd) and his younger siblings – a
juvenile delinquent (Ben Carruthers) and adolescent virgin (Lelia Goldoni) – is remarkable for
the fact that it remains observable almost
exclusively through the nuances of the performers; there is scarcely a reference to the
subject of race in the dialogue.

Cassavetes' directorial stint in Hollywood
proved unsatisfactory and frustrating for all
parties concerned, although it produced two
offbeat features. One was a mawkish yet
singularly haunting and memorable saga of
small-time jazz musicians, *Too Late Blues*
(1961), made for Paramount, with Bobby
Darin and Stella Stevens. The other – *A Child Is
Waiting* (1963) – starring Judy Garland and
Burt Lancaster, and set in an institution for
retarded children, was started for producer
Stanley Kramer who had Cassavetes replaced
after four months, apparently because of a

disagreement over the film's approach to its
subject. (According to Cassavetes, his own
thesis, in contrast to Kramer's, was that retarded children shouldn't be institutionalized.)
Also appearing in this film was the gifted Gena
Rowlands, Cassavetes' wife – a stage actress
who has since played the starring role in no
less than five of Cassavetes' seven subsequent
movies, all of them independently produced by
his own production company.

## About Faces

Five long years were to pass, however, before
Cassavetes' distinctively rough-hewn and
actor-centred cinema reappeared, dramatically and decisively, in the psycho-drama of
*Faces* (1968). By this time, his focus had shifted
to a more commercial subject – the American
suburban middle-class – which was further
explored in his next two features, *Husbands*
(1970) and *Minnie and Moskowitz* (1971).

Not that Cassavetes had remained idle in the
intervening five years. Apart from shooting
and editing the 16mm *Faces* piecemeal over
most of this period, he was doing some of his
best-known work as a Hollywood actor – still

usually playing heavies – in such films as *The
Dirty Dozen* (1967) and *Rosemary's Baby*
(1968), which were helping to finance his
independent project. (His role in the latter, as
an egotistical actor who sells his wife to the
devil for procreative purposes in exchange for a
good part, may have reflected some of his own
tenacity in getting *Faces* made.) Somewhat
earlier, he played in a version of *The Killers*
(1964) – directed by Don Siegel – in which he
was clearly out-ranked in villainy by one
Ronald Reagan, who was giving his last film
performance.

After editing *Faces* down from a six-hour
version to 129 minutes and blowing it up to
35mm, then devoting a lot of time and energy
to promotion, Cassavetes went on to enjoy a
substantial success with the film. A saga of
sexual frustration set in Southern California
which involved, among others, an estranged
suburban couple (Lynn Carlin and John
Marley), a call girl (Rowlands) and a gigolo
(Seymour Cassel, a Cassavetes regular), the
film obviously hit a raw nerve. Spectators
identified closely with the nervous laughter,
embarrassment and anguished responses to
loneliness of the characters, and the Cassavetes manner – which less sympathetic
viewers could describe as giving actors enough
space and rope with which to hang themselves
– was firmly established.

*Husbands*, Cassavetes' first independent feature in colour and 35mm, is also his only
attempt to date to write, direct *and* play a
leading part in one of his films (and the film
was produced by his production company). He
joined forces with two actor friends, Ben
Gazzara and Peter Falk, to depict a trio of
drinking companions out on an extended spree
to mourn the recent death of a friend. In the
ensuing jaunt that takes the men all the way
from suburban New York to London and back
again, Cassavetes pushed the compulsively
macho, carousing side of his style about as far
as it could go.

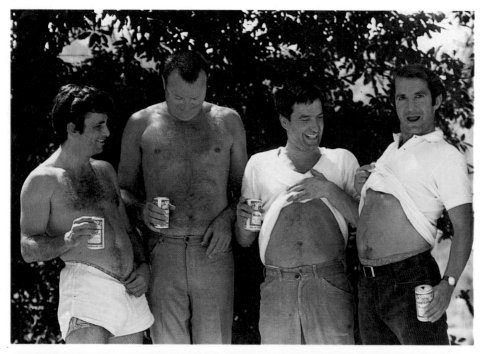

*Left: Charles Bronson, Cassavetes, Telly Savalas, Donald Sutherland – a third of* The Dirty Dozen. *Below left: nightclub entertainer Mr Sophistication (Meade Roberts) and assistants in* The Killing of a Chinese Bookie. *Below: Cassavetes, Ben Gazzara and Gena Rowlands rehearse for* Opening Night. *Below right: production shot from* Gloria, *with Rowlands, in the title role, and John Adames*

Around the beginning of the Seventies, Cassavetes was preparing one of his most remarkable acting roles in a film written and directed by Elaine May. This was the nightmarish and infernal *Mikey and Nicky* – a paranoid parable of betrayal between gangster friends, set in Philadelphia during a single night, and a film that, due to diverse complications, wasn't completed or released until roughly six years later in 1976.

Cassavetes' next film, *Minnie and Moskowitz*,

*Above, far left: beerguts on display in* Husbands – *they belong to Peter Falk, an unidentified colleague, Cassavetes and Ben Gazzara. Above: Seymour Cassel and his daughter, Cassavetes' wife Gena Rowlands and their daughter, Katharine Cassavetes (John's mother), Lady Rowlands (Gena's mother) – stars of* Minnie and Moskowitz. *Above right: with Sophia Loren in* Brass Target *(1978)*

was a more relaxed and conventional romantic comedy about a parking-lot attendant (Seymour Cassel) and museum curator (Rowlands). Following this, he returned to whipped-up psycho-drama with a vengeance in *A Woman Under the Influence* (1974), another big commercial success. Charting the nervous breakdown of a working-class wife and mother (Rowlands, married to Falk) over two and a half hours, the film resumes the almost 'pointillist' manner of *Faces* in which fleeting

behavioural tics are liberally applied by the actors on a broad canvas as if they were tiny dabs of paint.

## All in the family

In the same film, one can see Cassavetes' impulse to enlist friends and family reaching some sort of apogee: members of the Cassavetes, Rowlands and Cassel families – including parents and children – are all present in the cast. And it seems worth noting that familial groupings, both real and enacted, are at the centre of Cassavetes' three subsequent features – *The Killing of a Chinese Bookie* (1976), *Opening Night* (1977) and *Gloria* (1980).

'I Can't Give You Anything But Love' – the sentimental anthem that resounds so significantly throughout the closing moments of *The Killing of a Chinese Bookie* – might not be too inappropriate an expression of what Cassavetes' warm, loose and intuitive cinema is all

about. It implies a radical commitment to people and their outsized emotions that goes beyond the usual dictates of thought and logic, and a position that necessarily accepts more than it can understand.

Even while Cassavetes continues to play unsympathetic parts in the films of others, as in Brian De Palma's *The Fury* (1978), his own productions reveal nothing but unconditional empathy for the varied plights of a soft-hearted nightclub owner (Gazzara in *The Killing of a Chinese Bookie*), an ageing actress (Rowlands in *Opening Night*) and a tough broad with little taste for kids (Rowlands again, in *Gloria*). As we find him coming full circle from his juvenile delinquent acting parts in the Fifties to the violent gangster melodramas of *The Killing of a Chinese Bookie* and *Gloria*, what has grown in the process is a sense of character – rich, vibrant and full of life.

JONATHAN ROSENBAUM

### Filmography
1951 Fourteen Hours (extra only). '53 Taxi (actor only). '55 The Night Holds Terror (actor only). '56 Crime in the Streets (actor only); Edge of the City (actor only) (GB: A Man Is Ten Feet Tall). '57 Affair in Havana (actor only). '58 Saddle the Wind (actor only); Virgin Island (actor only) (GB). '60 Shadows (dir; +prod;+act). '61 Too Late Blues (dir;+prod;+co-sc). '62 The Webster Boy (actor only) (GB). '63 A Child Is Waiting (dir. only). '64 The Killers (actor only). '67 The Devil's Angels (actor only); The Dirty Dozen (actor only). '68 Rosemary's Baby (actor only); Faces (dir;+sc); Roma come Chicago (actor only) (IT) (GB/USA: Bandits in Rome). '69 Gli Intoccabili (actor only) (IT) (GB/USA: Machine Gun McCain); If It's Tuesday, This Must Be Belgium (guest appearance only). '70 Husbands (dir;+sc;+act). '71 Minnie and Moskowitz (dir;+sc;+act). '74 A Woman Under the Influence (dir;+sc). '75 Capone (actor only). '76 The Killing of a Chinese Bookie (dir;+sc); Two-Minute Warning (actor only); Mikey and Nicky (actor only). '77 Opening Night (dir;+sc;+act). '78 The Fury (actor only); Brass Target (actor only). '80 Gloria (dir;+sc). '81 Incubus (actor only) (CAN); Whose Life Is It Anyway? (actor only). '82 Tempest (actor only). '84 Love Streams (dir; +co-sc; +act).

# THE LAST PICTURE SHOW

On its first appearance in 1971, *The Last Picture Show* had a potent effect on audiences everywhere. This evocative depiction of small-town life, recalled with such affection and loving detail, seemed like the kind of film that American cinema had well-nigh stopped producing for twenty years or more.

Reduced to a mere synopsis, the incidents depicted could easily appear no more than a slice of life from some Texan Peyton Place. But in Peter Bogdanovich's hands they unerringly convey the lost dreams, foolish aspirations and rivalries – the whole texture of life in a community in decline with not much of a remembered past and scant hope for a future. Chekhovian is the word which, without hyperbole, springs to mind.

All the film's adolescent sexual encounters bring their attendant disappointments and pain, but there is the wry implication that, with the passing years, nostalgia may well turn the pain into a treasured memory, so blur its edges that it can even be recalled with comfortable ruefulness as the one great chance that was missed. Thus it is that Sam the Lion, in the only long speech in the film, waxes lyrical to Sonny, as he fishes, about an idyllic moment from his youth when he and a girl

went swimming in the nude. The object of these reminiscences is by now a cynical fading beauty, alienated from her husband, capable of caustically advising her own daughter to do something about losing her virginity. She, too, clings to this long-ago attachment as her big moment: 'I guess if it wasn't for Sam, I'd just, about have missed it, whatever it is,' she muses. The young folk, meanwhile, are amassing similar double-edged experiences to be nurtured and mellowed in memory's chest.

Bogdanovich's approach to his characters' shallow lives is never sentimental and often slyly humorous. Sitting in the tacky cinema, watching Minnelli's *Father of the Bride* (1950), Charlene removes her chewing-gum to kiss Sonny absently, fatuously absorbed in the never-never-land problems of Spencer Tracy coping with Elizabeth Taylor's coy pre-nuptial tantrums; later, in the last film to be shown before the cinema's closure (Hawks' *Red River*, 1948), John Wayne's herds making their impressive progress across the great prairies are a far cry indeed from the forlorn tumbleweed encroaching on this dying township where the only cattle seen are crowded in the back of a truck. The film clips

make their point as opiates, unquestioned grist to the fantasy mill which, with the demise of the old cinema, will now be supplied with coarser fodder by the new monster, television.

Already, in his first feature, *Targets* (1967), Bogdanovich had revealed an exceptional capacity for directing his actors and here he consolidates it. In the meticulously observed cramped interiors and grey exteriors (the whole film was shot in Archer City in north Texas) everyone finds his unobtrusive, unstarry place, superbly served by Robert Surtees' expressive black-and-white camerawork. For here is a film not so much shot in black and white but conceived in shades of those colours, best able to capture the period and the elegiac mood.

It seems perfectly natural that Ruth Popper should reward a spontaneous gesture of kindness from Sonny by inviting him into her kitchen for a drink; equally natural that the same neglected, middle-aged wife should entreat him to stay with her a little longer. A flutter of unrest clouds his face for a moment until the adolescent, himself in a state of emotional unrest, finds himself responding sympathetically to an older frustration he dimly apprehends. Their subsequent affair seems perfectly plotted and Ruth's transition from drabness to radiance and thence to shrill virulence when Jacy lures Sonny away from her is most movingly achieved by Cloris Leachman. All the relationships bear the same stamp of truth.

Bogdanovich's film is, in the Chekhovian sense, a comedy of empty lives where the characters occasionally go to ludicrous lengths to assert the fact that their existence is notable and their actions of importance. Jacy's bid for acceptance by the rich set is made by stripping naked on a diving board; she incites her mother's lover to rape her, and her elopement with Sonny, she hopes, will make her the talk of the town and provide her with a colourful *entrée* to her first year in college.

*The Last Picture Show* has about it that kind of purity of expression that only the very greatest directors – Donskoi, Ford, Mizoguchi, Satyajit Ray – are able to sustain consistently throughout their careers. Most achieve it only once. It is one of those films whose characters linger in the memory, and that is happily re-seen time and time again.
DEREK PROUSE

**Directed by Peter Bogdanovich, 1971**
**Prod co:** A BBS Production/Last Picture Show Productions for Columbia. **exec prod:** Bert Schneider. **prod:** Stephen J. Friedman. **assoc prod:** Harold Schneider. **sc:** Larry McMurtry, Peter Bogdanovich, based on the novel by Larry McMurtry. **photo:** Robert Surtees. **ed:** Donn Cambern. **prod des:** Polly Platt. **art dir:** Walter Scott Herndon. **mus:** 1951 recordings by Hank Williams, Bob Willis and His Texas Playboys, Eddy Arnold, Eddie Fisher, Phil Harris, Pee Wee King, Hank Snow, Tony Bennett, Lefty Frizzell, Frankie Laine, Johnnie Ray, Johnny Standley, Kay Starr, Hank Thompson, Webb Price, Jo Stafford. **sd:** Tom Overton. **ass dir:** Robert Rubin, William Morrison. **prod man:** Don Guest. **r/t:** 118 minutes. Premier, New York Film Festival 1971. **Cast:** Timothy Bottoms (*Sonny Crawford*), Jeff Bridges (*Duane Jackson*), Cybill Shepherd (*Jacy Farrow*), Ben Johnson (*Sam the Lion*), Cloris Leachman (*Ruth Popper*), Ellen Burstyn (*Lois Farrow*), Eileen Brennan (*Genevieve*), Clu Gulager (*Abilene*), Sam Bottoms (*Billy*), Sharon Taggart (*Charlene Duggs*), Randy Quaid (*Lester Marlow*), Joe Heathcock (*sheriff*), Bill Thurman (*Coach Popper*), Barc Doyle (*Joe Bob Blanton*), Jessie Lee Fulton (*Miss Mosey*), Gary Brockette (*Bobby Sheen*), Helena Humann (*Jimmie Sue*), Loyd Catlett (*Leroy*), Robert Glenn (*Gene Farrow*), John Hillerman (*teacher*), Janice O'Malley (*Mrs Clarg*), Floyd Mahaney (*Oklahoma patrolman*), Kimberley Hyde (*Annie-Annie Martin*), Noble Willingham (*Chester*), Marjory Jay (*Winnie Snips*), Joye Hash (*Mrs Jackson*), Pamela Keller (*Jackie Lee French*), Gordon Hurst (*Monroe*), Mike Hosford (*Johnny*), Faye Jordan (*nurse*), Charlie Seybert (*Andy Fanner*), Grover Lewis (*Mr Crawford*), Rebecca Ulrick (*Marlene*), Merrill Shepherd (*Agnes*), Buddy Wood (*Bud*), Kenny Wood (*Ken*), Leon Brown (*cowboy in café*), Bobby McGriff (*truck driver*), Jack Mueller (*oil pumper*), Robert Arnold (*Brother Blanton*), Frank Marshall (*Tommy Logan*), Otis Elmore (*first mechanic*), Charles Salmon (*roughneck driver*), George Gaulden (*cowboy*), Will Morris Hannis (*gas station man*), and the Leon Miller Band.

1951. In Anarene, a small, dust-laden, one-horse town in Texas (1), there are few distractions for the local youth apart from their sexual exploits and the weekly picture show. Sonny Crawford – having broken with his bovine, steady girlfriend Charlene, and though envious of his friend Duane (2), who seems to have found favour with the local belle Jacy – drifts into a liaison with Ruth (3), the neglected wife of the football coach.

Jacy has higher aspirations than Duane and leaves him at the local Christmas dance to attend a much smarter, nude swimming party where she attracts the attention of Bobby Sheen, a rich,

2

3

5

6

8

9

young playboy. To vent his frustration Duane, with Sonny, plays a cruel joke on Billy, a retarded boy, and is severely chastized by Sam the Lion (4), the cinema owner and Billy's protector. But Sam relents and on a fishing trip with Sonny reminisces (5) about how he once went swimming, naked, with a girl. Returning from a trip to Mexico with Duane, Sonny learns that Sam has suddenly died.

Sam's old flame was Lois Farrow, Jacy's mother, who now advises her daughter to lose her virginity (6). Jacy consents to go with Duane to a motel (7), mainly because Bobby Sheen has curtly told her he has no time for

virgins. It is an unsatisfactory session and Duane leaves town to enlist for Korea. Jacy learns of Bobby's imminent marriage and, out of pique, lures Sonny (8) away from Ruth. Duane returns and in the ensuing fight (9) Sonny's eye is badly hurt. Jacy is delighted to be the focal point of this row and coerces Sonny into eloping with her, making sure that her parents will find out in time and send her off to college.

Duane, due to leave for Korea, spends his last night in town with Sonny at the cinema's final show before it closes. Sonny sees Billy struck dead by a passing lorry and wretchedly returns to Ruth for consolation (10).

10

# Uphill racer
## Robert Redford

**TV star, sex-symbol, superstar. In just twenty years Robert Redford has achieved star status by successfully combining all three attributes, but at the peak of his profession he seems to be forging himself a new career, this time in the field of direction**

With his blond hair, blue eyes and clean-cut all-American appearance, Robert Redford seems to be perfectly cast as a star in the grand Hollywood tradition of the male romantic lead. Nevertheless, Redford's emotional entanglements have usually been subsidiary to the main plot of his films: with the exceptions of Barbra Streisand and Jane Fonda he has rarely played opposite actresses of equal calibre. Indeed, some would argue that his only screen love affair has been with Paul Newman.

The films that work best are those in which there is a quiet questioning of the stereotyped American male, and which thereby gently subvert Redford's own pretty-boy image. He has attacked the notion of the attractive athletic winner – *Downhill Racer* (1969), *Little Fauss and Big Halsy* (1970), *The Electric Horseman* (1979) – commented on the heroic legends of the Hollywood West – *Butch Cassidy and the Sundance Kid*, *Tell Them Willie Boy Is Here* (both 1969), *Jeremiah Johnson* (1972) – and played the naive American caught up in somebody else's politics – *The Candidate* (1972), *The Way We Were* (1973), *Three Days of the Condor* (1975), *All the President's Men* (1976).

### The cream on its way to the top
Redford's early life was not that of the well-to-do middle-class American that his appearance would seem to suggest. Born in 1937, the son of a milkman, Redford grew up in Santa Monica, California, in the shadow of the 'dream factory' itself. But he despised the movies, often shouting at the screen on visits to the cinema with his friends. Despite rebelling against the discipline of school, he won a baseball scholarship to the University of Colorado, but soon dropped out, believing there was more to life than sport. After hitch-hiking around various European capitals, painting, and 'loitering' in bars and cafés, he returned to America to study art at New York's Pratt Institute, and eventually found himself at the American Academy of Dramatic Arts. He had several minor roles on Broadway before the breakthrough came – the lead part in Neil Simon's domestic farce *Barefoot in the Park*. The play, directed by Mike Nichols, had rave reviews and Redford earned recognition for his comic ability. With a growing reputation on television, it was not surprising that he was soon much sought after by Hollywood.

### Skimming the heights
However, his first film, *War Hunt* (1962), was a second-rate, low-budget venture about a psychotic private in Korea. It was not a great success for either its producers or Redford, but during the filming he met and struck up a long working relationship with the then actor Sydney Pollack – who later directed several of Redford's films. Redford's career continued with *Inside Daisy Clover* (1965), the film version of Gavin Lambert's novel about the machinations of Hollywood. He then went on to make a total flop, *Situation Hopeless, But Not Serious* (1965); turned in a highly praised performance as Bubber Reeves, the escaped convict whose presence brings out the mercenary tendencies of his home-town folk in *The Chase* (1966); starred with Natalie Wood in a Tennessee Williams' small-town melodrama, *This Property Is Condemned* (1966); and was sued by Paramount for walking out on the Western *Blue* (1968) (a wise decision on his part since the completed film, starring Terence Stamp, was not a success).

In 1967 he returned to Hollywood to fulfil an obligation to film *Barefoot in the Park*. Echoing his stage success, Redford's role as Paul Bratter, the straitlaced lawyer whose new wife (Jane Fonda) complains about his lack of spontaneity – he cannot even walk barefoot in the park – swept him to fame. Although Redford disliked Bratter's image he found a niche for himself as the fall-guy to his more active partner and he and Fonda made an

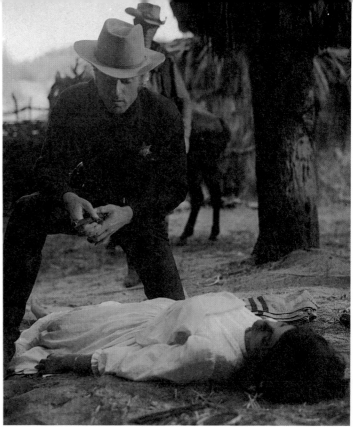

Opposite page: Redford with Gene Hackman, skiing champion and coach in Downhill Racer (left), and with Natalie Wood and the director Sydney Pollack filming This Property is Condemned (right). Left: Michael J. Pollard and Redford as Little Fauss and Big Halsy

Above left: Redford as Paul Bratter who drunkenly loses his inhibitions in Barefoot in the Park. Above: Sheriff Cooper finds his quarry's fiancée (Katharine Ross) dead in Tell Them Willie Boy Is Here. Below: Jeremiah Johnson with Bear Claw (Will Geer)

effervescent duo.

Redford was subsequently offered several major roles which he turned down – including the diffident Benjamin in *The Graduate* (1967). It was well worth the wait for 1969 was Redford's year – he had a critical success with *Tell Them Willie Boy Is Here*, made his long-cherished project *Downhill Racer*, and after Marlon Brando, Steve McQueen and Warren Beatty had all dropped out of the running he was offered what will probably remain his most memorable role, that of the Sundance Kid in *Butch Cassidy and the Sundance Kid*. The attractive vitality of the relationship between the two heroes, and their tongue-in-cheek humour, made the film a smash hit. Redford may not say much in the film, but his laconic, fast-shooting Sundance Kid complemented Newman's thoughtful Butch. The male camaraderie and slick repartee encouraged the quick growth of buddy-buddy movies and four years later Newman and Redford were reunited on

Far left: the partners in crime (Paul Newman and Redford) act out their charade in front of the victim (Robert Shaw) in The Sting. Left: a man with a past to hide – Redford as The Great Gatsby. Below left: as Bob Woodward in All the President's Men.

the screen in *The Sting* (1973). Once again under the direction of George Roy Hill, it is a witty story concerning a successful confidence trick on a racketeer. It was another hit.

## How the West was

*Butch Cassidy and the Sundance Kid* made Redford a valuable property and enabled him to pick and choose his parts. Having deserted Hollywood for the mountains of Utah and a commitment to ecological preservation, many of his films comment on the values he left behind, with a recurrent theme being the false heroics of the Western. *Tell Them Willie Boy Is Here*, with Abraham Polonsky making a return to direction after years on the blacklist, tackles the treatment of the American Indians. Redford was originally offered the part of Willie Boy – the Paiute Indian who kills a chief while claiming his bride and finds himself hunted as a renegade – but, feeling that Indian roles should be played by Indians, he opted for the role of Sheriff Cope who learns to respect the Indian traditions. *Jeremiah Johnson*, a legendary story of a lone trapper who braves the elements to live his own life in the mountains, is another film that challenges Hollywood's heroic notions. Redford's Johnson is neither braver nor wiser than others: he is simply more determined to live free from interference. In a totally different setting, the wealthy Twenties as depicted by Scott Fitzgerald in *The Great Gatsby* (1974), Redford portrays another loner who rejects 'modern' society's materialism. However, the film failed because it was one of the few Redford films that indulged itself as a love story.

Redford has expressed his dislike of the born competitor who smiles as he clocks up the wins and the girls:

'What about the athlete who is a creep? We do tend to tolerate creeps if they win. They can behave any way so just forget that swell guy whom everyone loves and who came second.'

With 20,000 feet of unofficial footage from the Grenoble Winter Olympics, and after a two-year struggle, Redford was finally able to embody these views in *Downhill Racer* – a couple of seasons in the life of David Chappellet, a skier who is only admired so long as he keeps winning. That Redford's looks made it difficult to believe Chappellet is such a jerk

### Filmography
**1962** War Hunt. **'65** Situation Hopeless, But Not Serious; Inside Daisy Clover. **'66** The Chase; This Property Is Condemned. **'67** Barefoot in the Park. **'69** Butch Cassidy and the Sundance Kid; Tell Them Willie Boy Is Here; Downhill Racer. **'70** The Making of Butch Cassidy and the Sundance Kid; Little Fauss and Big Halsy. **'72** The Hot Rock (GB: How to Steal a Diamond in Four Uneasy Lessons); Jeremiah Johnson; The Candidate (+ co-exec. prod). **'73** The Way We Were; The Sting. **'74** The Great Gatsby; Broken Treaty at Battle Mountain (doc) (narr. only). **'75** The Great Waldo Pepper; Three Days of the Condor. **'76** All the President's Men (+ co-exec. prod). **'77** A Bridge Too Far. **'79** The Electric Horseman. **'80** Brubaker; Ordinary People (dir. only). **'84** The Natural.

emphasizes the very point the film is trying to make. *Little Fauss and Big Halsy* develops the same theme, this time on the motorcycle racetrack. The misguided admiration that Fauss (Michael J. Pollard) holds for his more confident fellow competitor Halsy (Redford) leads only to disillusionment. However, the most revealing image of the American athletic winner is in *The Electric Horseman*; the drunken, ex-rodeo champion rides out of town on the prize horse he has rescued from the breakfast-cereal company he publicizes. All that can be seen of him against the night is his illuminated outline – a visual indication of the hollowness of that kind of success.

## A man for the people

Several of Redford's films have examined the manipulations and threats of modern politics: in *The Way We Were*, the McCarthy witchhunt is the cause of the break-up of a young Hollywood couple's marriage when the wife Katie (Barbra Streisand) becomes involved in the campaign against the blacklist; *The Candidate* looks at competition in the electoral fight as a certain-to-loose well-intentioned contender (Redford) becomes seduced by the political arena; *Three Days of the Condor* is a spy thriller about a desk-worker for the CIA who, on returning to his office, finds all his colleagues shot dead, possibly by his own side; *Brubaker* (1980) investigates the clash of interests between a prison governor bent on reform and the corrupt local businessmen and politicians.

But undoubtedly Redford's major intervention into political film is *All the President's Men*. He had negotiated a film deal with Woodward and Bernstein even before the book of the Watergate cover-up investigation had been written. He then spent a long time researching the journalistic background by talking to the reporters and staff of the *Washington Post*. The resulting film – with Dustin Hoffman and Redford as the two intrepid reporters – is a strong indictment of power politics and the distortions which ensue.

## Bridging the gap

Despite being one of Hollywood's highest-paid stars – he commanded a fee of $2 million for 20 days work on *A Bridge Too Far* (1977) – he declined to appear in his directorial debut, *Ordinary People* (1980). It is a highly emotional and perceptive study of family tensions based upon the guilt that the son Conrad (Tim Hutton) feels over his brother's drowning. When talking about his brother's death Conrad is unable to express his feelings and wonders what John Boy – of the popular television series *The Waltons* – would have said, an astute observation of the powerful effect America's 'heroes' have on ordinary lives. But at the end of the film, when the mother (Mary Tyler Moore) has gone away leaving husband (Donald Sutherland) and son contented together, it is interesting to note that Redford still seems to be perpetuating the male-orientated world of *Butch Cassidy and the Sundance Kid*.

SALLY HIBBIN

*Left: Redford played a small role in* A Bridge Too Far, *the story of the Allied defeat at Arnhem. Above right: an ex-rodeo rider decides to leave the bright lights behind in* The Electric Horseman. *Right: Redford discusses a scene from* Ordinary People *with Donald Sutherland*

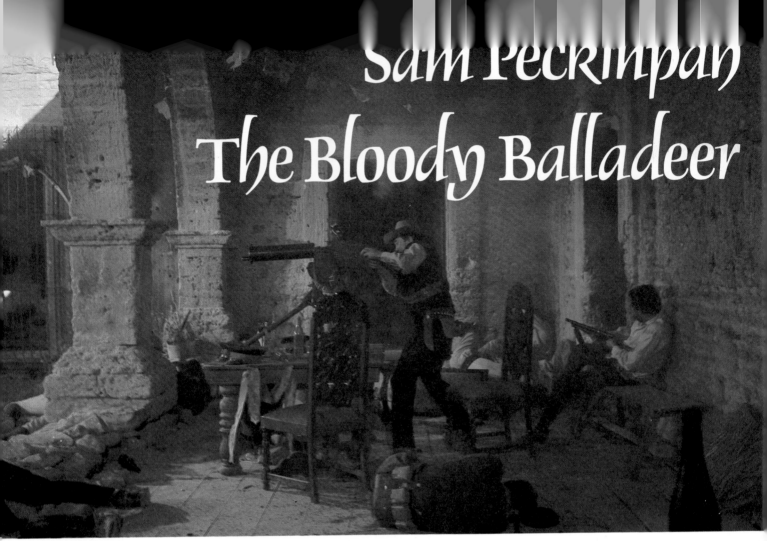

# Sam Peckinpah
# The Bloody Balladeer

**Who could possibly forget the ritualized bloodbath at the end of *The Wild Bunch*, or the rape and resultant savagery in *Straw Dogs* – and all in the name of entertainment? But maybe for Peckinpah's heroes violence and death are the only truly glorious ways to fulfilment**

It would be neither hyperbole nor cliché to say that Sam Peckinpah burst onto the Hollywood scene in the Sixties with two films that outraged the expectations first of his producers (*Major Dundee*, 1965) and then of the world at large (*The Wild Bunch*, 1969). This, of course, was not the beginning of Peckinpah. *Major Dundee* was his third film and he had worked in television since 1955; nor, despite its apocalyptic tendency, was *The Wild Bunch* to remain for long the ultimate in screen violence. But the controversies that the two films sparked off have remained central to the director's image – to a distorting degree – ever since. He is a man of violence, whether falling out with the producers who have failed or betrayed him, or dwelling in loving slow-motion on the moments of death and mutilation in his films.

What seems most remarkable about the fuss Peckinpah caused was that it should have happened in the Western, which had been Hollywood's staple since time immemorial and was, in the Sixties, a particularly quiescent form. It was so quiescent, in fact, that various film-makers – spearheaded by Sergio Leone with the Dollar films – were not only knocking on the gates of the genre from outside Holly-

wood, but threatening to transport it wholesale to Italy or Spain. The Hollywood Western, in other words, was ripe for overhaul; and Peckinpah, a man of the industry and a genuine Westerner, was admirably qualified to launch a revolution from within. If he had not been there at the time, Hollywood might have had

to import him – as, in a way, by recalling Clint Eastwood from his spell with Leone, it finally did incorporate the 'spaghetti' Western.

## The end of the Western world
The Europeans, of course, approached the genre from outside, and treated its conventions with an absurdist exaggeration. They produced a mannerist Western, one of extreme but ritualized violence in which the traditional idealism was replaced by cynicism, self-seeking

*Above: Ben Johnson and Warren Oates as two of* The Wild Bunch, *living and dying the only way they know how. Below: Peckinpah directs the gentler* Junior Bonner, *a rodeo story*

and materialism. They gave the genre a dose of economic realism, even if their plots of vengeful oneupmanship were more Jacobean than Marxist in impact. Though his Westerns often match the 'spaghetti' Westerns in stylization and exaggeration, Peckinpah is moving in another direction. He does not 'play' at the Western as, say, Leone did. Indeed, 'It's not a game' is a line of dialogue that recurs in his films about the values and beliefs, the way of life that his characters represent. For Peckinpah also, the old Western codes and traditions are on the way out, but their passing occasions painful spasms rather than a cynical shrug.

What his films share with the Italian Westerns is a novel (for a while) amount of grubby detail – the stubbly chins, the muddy streets and the dubious motives of heroes and villains alike. But from his own first-hand acquaintance with the West, Peckinpah – born in 1925 to a pioneer family in Madera, California (with a grandfather who gave his name to a mountain in the region) – gained not just an interest in portraying the West 'like it was'. His father was a Superior Court Judge, and apparently he also had uncles on the bench. Dinner-table discussions about law and justice had a strong biblical flavour, Peckinpah remembers, and he put an aphorism of his father's, 'I want to enter my own house justified', into the hero's mouth in one of his earliest films, *Ride the High Country* (1962, known in Britain as *Guns in the Afternoon*).

Concepts of honour and personal morality, then, are crucial to Peckinpah, despite the supposed amorality of the 'new' Westerns. The true violence of his films is not in the balletic displays of slow-motion slaughter but in a kind of internal shock – the displacement of characters who cannot or will not compromise or change, even to survive. Peckinpah's slow-motion orgies, it is often objected, are both unrealistic and indulgent, which is, in a sense, true yet not a criticism. What these agonized

action montages commemorate is the characters' heroic annihilation, and also the director's own wilful, obdurate and unrealistic attachment to the loner, the misfit, the outmoded and the outsider.

## Heading for the last round-up

Violence, however, is no more important to Peckinpah's view of the West than another element that has hardly been noticed at all – his lyricism. 'Elegiac' might be a fair if general description of all his Westerns, ringing down the last sunset on a landscape that is not exactly the West as it really was – more a promise of freedom whose passing Peckinpah bitterly regrets. His heroes seem headed for the end of their trail before the films even begin, but there is often a surprising dignity, warmth and even comedy to their passing. Peckinpah's stories are as likely to take the form of a ballad as they are a dirge.

His first film, *The Deadly Companions* (1961), is a little-seen revenge Western that he himself considers to be a failure. But his second, *Ride the High Country*, was a revelation – tough but serene, rumbustiously atmospheric but

*Top right: a Rebel officer (Richard Harris) skirmishes with an Apache in* Major Dundee. *Right: in* Straw Dogs *a sluttish wife (Susan George) teases yokels into rape. Below: Jason Robards Jr as the drunk – no example for muchachos – in* The Ballad of Cable Hogue

The knock at the door meant the birth of a man and the death of seven others.

ABC PICTURES CORP presents

**DUSTIN HOFFMAN**

in SAM PECKINPAH'S

"STRAW DOGS" x

A DANIEL MELNICK Production

Starring SUSAN GEORGE as Amy

Music by JERRY FIELDING Screenplay by DAVID ZELAG GOODMAN and SAM PECKINPAH Produced by DANIEL MELNICK Directed by SAM PECKINPAH

meditative. Old Western stars, Joel McCrea and Randolph Scott, were persuaded to play two over-the-hill gunslingers who take jobs as payroll guards, which leads them to a final reckoning with themselves and each other. Peckinpah picked up this mood again with *The Ballad of Cable Hogue* (1970), in which the hero (Jason Robards Jr) also has to lose himself before he can be found. In this case, the film's lyricism is boosted not only by some interspersed songs but a charming dream dimension: Cable (as one of the songs declares) found water where it wasn't, a home where he shouldn't have, and a nemesis where Peckinpah always expects it (the twentieth century, in the shape of an automobile). Two films later, *Junior Bonner* (1972), about a coming-home crisis in the life of a middle-aged rodeo star (Steve McQueen), evoked a gentle, almost loving, pessimism about failed dreams and closing frontiers.

## Down Mexico way

*Major Dundee* and *The Wild Bunch*, however, remain the two colossi that dominate Peckinpah's career, as much because of their epic dimensions as because of the controversies that surround them. Peckinpah won the first battle over *Major Dundee* – to shoot it on location in Mexico – but subsequently lost the war when it was cut against his wishes. Even in its maimed state, the film survives as one of his finest. Towards the end of the American Civil War, the Union officer Dundee (Charlton Heston) leads a raggle-taggle command of black troops, Confederate prisoners and assorted rejects and misfits south of the border in pursuit of a band of marauding Apache. The mission, and the film, is barely contained anarchy, as the leader's frustrated ambition and his unit's festering hostilities constantly threaten to self-destruct. But a precarious nationhood prevails, and Dundee's outfit makes a costly but triumphant return across the bloody Rio Grande. This is Peckinpah's first foray into Mexico, the first twinge of his alienation from America – and the last time that coming home will seem a positive option.

Following his disagreements over *Major Dundee*, Peckinpah ran straight into producer trouble on his next project, *The Cincinnati Kid* (1965), from which he was fired (the film was

completed by Norman Jewison). During the following three years, unable to find work as a film director, he wrote scripts and worked in television, directing a highly praised adaptation of Katherine Anne Porter's story *Noon Wine* (1966). *The Wild Bunch* was his comeback, a more virulent, savagely pessimistic version of the odyssey undertaken in *Major Dundee*. Here a gang of outlaws, pursued by scavenging bounty hunters, seek refuge in Mexico, a land as innocent and primitive as themselves. There is a languorous idyll in a friendly village, a little arms-dealing with peasant guerrillas on one side and rapacious federal soldiers on the other, and then the underlying anarchy tears loose in a bloody riot of we'll-all-go-to-hell-together-when-we-go. In one exchange, the Bunch's leader (William Holden) declares, 'We're getting old. We've got to think beyond our guns. I'd like to make one good score and back off.' To which his lieutenant (Ernest Borgnine) replies, 'Back off to what?'

The climactic blood-letting of *The Wild Bunch*

*Above: the price paid by German soldiers hoping to win the* Cross of Iron. *Below: one of many violent scenes in* Bring Me the Head of Alfredo Garcia, *with Warren Oates*

may not be cathartic in the usual sense – purging the desire for bloodshed – but it is a kind of merciful release from the no-exit hopelessness in that dialogue. There is no release at all in the film Peckinpah made in 1973, *Pat Garrett and Billy the Kid*, perhaps as the final comment on the predicament of the ancient Westerner. All options north of the Rio Grande are now in the hands of big business, and the sheriff (James Coburn) and the outlaw (Kris Kristofferson), old friends and inevitable enemies, circle each other in the twilight. Mexico shimmers somewhere across the horizon, promising freedom but also threatening anonymity, a life-in-death in limbo.

That last dilemma sums up the tensions of Peckinpah's non-Western subjects, which have a way of looking like almost-Westerns. In both *Straw Dogs* (1971) and *Bring Me the Head of Alfredo Garcia* (1974), the heroes have left America, but the drama – and the resulting violence – still gathers darkly around the problem of their making themselves 'at home'. In the first, a mathematics professor (Dustin Hoffman) determines to defend to the death the house he has rented in the Cornish countryside; at the end, he drives off into the night, at peace with himself but no longer sure where to find home. The second discovers Warren Oates as a bar piano-player suffering the hell of exile in Mexico, a fallen state out of which he tries to climb – at one point, literally, from the depths of his own grave – his ticket home being the price on a dead man's head.

## Señor Peckinpah

Both these films have elements in common with Peckinpah's Westerns, but they relate to them mostly as reverse propositions – what if one abandoned the West, moved beyond the borders of America? The result is a flight into some imaginary, interior realm, in which the horrors of exile are courted and the imagery, appropriately, is more Gothic than Western. Only in a relatively light and inconsequential work, *The Getaway* (1972), can Peckinpah contemplate with equanimity a happy ending which has hero (Steve McQueen) and heroine (Ali McGraw) disappearing into Mexico. Interestingly, after spending many years in exile himself – including a sojourn in Europe and his assumption of Mexican citizenship – Peckinpah tried to make a move in the opposite direction in the early Eighties with an uncompleted Western, *The Texans*.                RICHARD COMBS

**Filmography**
**1954** Riot in Cell Block 11 (dial. dir). **'55** Seven Angry Men (dial. dir); The Annapolis Story (dial. dir; + act) (GB: The Blue and the Gold); Wichita (dial. dir; + act). **'56** Invasion of the Body Snatchers (act; + stunts only). **'61** The Deadly Companions. **'62** Ride the High Country (GB: Guns in the Afternoon). **'65** Major Dundee ( + co-sc); The Glory Guys (sc. only). **'68** Villa Rides! (co-sc. only). **'69** The Wild Bunch ( + co-sc). **'70** The Ballad of Cable Hogue ( + prod). **'71** Straw Dogs ( + co-sc) (GB). **'72** Junior Bonner; The Getaway. **'73** Pat Garrett and Billy the Kid. **'74** Bring Me the Head of Alfredo Garcia ( + co-sc) (USA-MEX). **'75** The Killer Elite. **'77** Cross of Iron (GB-GER). **'78** Convoy; China 9, Liberty 37/Amore, Piombo e Furore (actor only) (IT). **'82** Jinxed! (2nd unit dir). **'83** The Osterman Weekend.
*Around 1953 Peckinpah directed 3 experimental shorts, titles unknown; 1954–57 no complete listings for work as dialogue director/actor.*

# Westward Ho!

# British directors find fame and finance in Hollywood

Ever since Alfred Hitchcock first went to America in the Thirties – where he found the money necessary to continue making his sophisticated thrillers – crossing the Atlantic has become the British public's measure for assessing the success of its film-makers. Five decades later the options for the British film-maker were essentially still those of Hitchcock's early days: make low-budget British films; secure American finance and stars for 'mid-Atlantic' movies; or, for more expensive projects, actually go to work in America.

Despite television's massive rise in popularity a dynamic 'New Wave' of film-making came to the fore in Britain in the late Fifties. The work of John Schlesinger, Karel Reisz, Lindsay Anderson and Tony Richardson heralded a new film culture of socially critical realism reflecting post-war political concerns in the country. These directors produced cheap films set in cities like Liverpool and Nottingham, and used home-grown actors. However, when a director like Richardson – who had made his name with such working-class films as *A Taste of Honey* (1961) and *The Loneliness of the Long-Distance Runner* (1962) –

wanted to branch out into the lavish costume-drama *Tom Jones* (1963), no British company was prepared to take the financial risk. Richardson had to look to America for backing: United Artists stepped in and the film was a popular and commercial success. At once the floodgates were re-opened for American-backed British films.

## The crest of a New Wave

Then came the Swinging Sixties. With British music dominating the world's pop charts and British talent flowering in a burgeoning film industry, American money poured in. By the late Sixties an estimated 90 per cent of British films were made with American capital. In the ensuing recession the Americans withdrew, leaving behind a disastrously under-financed industry. Many directors were forced to leave Britain for America in order to continue working, and of the 'New Wave' directors only Lindsay Anderson remained – which perhaps explains why *Britannia Hospital* (1982) was his first film for seven years.

Some directors, such as Michael Winner, entered the mainstream commercial cinema in

*Above: John Irvin's* The Dogs of War, *based on Frederick Forsyth's novel about European mercenaries in Africa*

America. Winner had made his name with British films steeped in Sixties culture – *The Jokers* and *I'll Never Forget What's-'is-Name* (both 1967) – but in America turned his hand to more typically American 'action pictures' such as the Charles Bronson vigilante films *Death Wish* (1974) and *Death Wish II* (1982). Other British directors also showed that they could make films firmly in the tradition of American cinema, as witness Peter Yates' *Bullitt* (1968) and John Boorman's *Deliverance* (1972), but still retained their ability to make 'non-action' films: for example Yates' tale of pre-college youth in *Breaking Away* (1979) and Boorman's science-fiction story *Zardoz* (1974). Tony Richardson attempted a comedy based on Evelyn Waugh's novel *The Loved One* (1965), but was unable to transfer to the screen Waugh's biting satirical observation of the way in which Americans react to death.

John Schlesinger and Karel Reisz have both kept one foot on either side of the Atlantic.

39

*Above: Michael Winner and* Won Ton Ton, the Dog That Saved Hollywood *(1975). Above right: when the children are away adults will play – Alan Parker showing the wrist-action needed for* Bugsy Malone. *Right: the youngsters gain the upper hand at their elders' expense in* Fame. *Below right: Ridley Scott with* The Duellists – *Keith Carradine and Harvey Keitel*

Reisz returned to England after completing two moderately successful American movies – *The Gambler* (1974) with James Caan and *Who'll Stop the Rain?* (1978) with Nick Nolte and Tuesday Weld – to make *The French Lieutenant's Woman* (1981) from the novel by John Fowles. To star in this very English story he used the American actress Meryl Streep. The decision produced much controversy, but also a fine performance from Streep who portrayed both heroines – contemporary and Victorian – with immense feeling. Schlesinger successfully used his 'foreigner' status to view from the outside the weaknesses of American society with both *Midnight Cowboy* (1969) and *Day of the Locust* (1975). In 1979, he returned to Britain to make *Yanks*, an American film about GIs stationed in Lancashire during World War II. The story compares the life-styles and values of the two countries, but when his American backers insisted that he tone down the Britishness of the script it lost a lot of its bite. Back in America he completed *Honky Tonk Freeway* (1981), a social satire on a small town's attempts to attract the tourist trade. This film was heavily criticized in the United States for the anti-American attitudes of its British director.

### Crying all the way to the bank

In the early Eighties inflation and the escalating costs of film production – coupled with the ever-decreasing number of cinemas – meant that only low-budget features stood a chance of recouping their cost from the British market alone. The prolific producer David Puttnam argued that what British films needed, in order for the industry to survive, was international appeal. In practice this meant that Puttnam's successful 'mid-Atlantic' movies *Midnight Express* (1978) and *Agatha* (1979) helped to give a new lease of life to the ailing British film industry – alongside more specifically British movies like *The Long Good Friday, Gregory's Girl* (both 1980) and *Chariots of Fire* (1981) – but it also meant that yet more British directors reached the limitations of home finance and went to the States to make the kind of films they wanted. At one point in 1980 there were so many British directors in America that Britain's *Daily Express* newspaper noted:

'These days when the Hollywood director shouts ''action'' he is likely to be bellowing through his megaphone . . . in broad Cockney.'

Examples included Adrian Lyne working on *Foxes* (1979), Ken Russell on *Altered States*, John

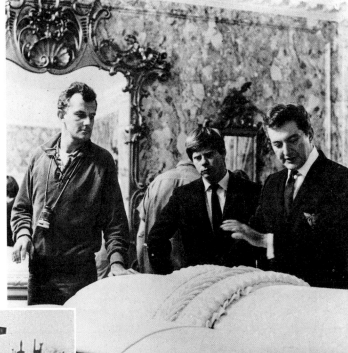

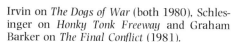

*Left: Dustin Hoffman on Harrogate station, returned to its former glory for Michael Apted's* Agatha. *Above left: Apted, Tommy Lee Jones and Sissy Spacek consider a problem during the shooting of* Coal Miner's Daughter. *Above: a casket fit to be seen dead in – Tony Richardson and stars Robert Morse and Liberace consult while filming* The Loved One

After *Stardust* Apted had numerous offers from America but he preferred to try and make a successful career for himself in England. As he commented at the time:

'I'm really one of those starry-eyed idiots who believe my roots are here and that there's still useful work to be done in this country.'

But Apted's idealism was much tested, for it was not until 1979 that he managed to raise the money for another commercial movie. *Agatha*, a Puttnam production, starred Vanessa Redgrave and Dustin Hoffman and centred on the mystery surrounding the disappearance of the detective-novelist Agatha Christie in the Twenties. The film provided Apted with the international kudos he needed in order to go to America on his own terms. His *Coal Miner's Daughter* (1980), with Sissy Spacek playing the part of the renowned country singer Loretta Lynn, is an inside look at the American Country-and-western scene, and it is perhaps ironic that this fine portrayal of American rural life should come from an Englishman. Having finally made it to America, Apted seems to have opted for a prolonged stay.

## Advertising his talents

Alan Parker established his reputation with over five hundred TV commercials made by his own company before completing a 50-minute love story, *The Evacuees*, in 1975 for the BBC. To find the finance for his first feature

Irvin on *The Dogs of War* (both 1980), Schlesinger on *Honky Tonk Freeway* and Graham Barker on *The Final Conflict* (1981).

Three of the directors who have had the most success in Hollywood – Michael Apted, Alan Parker and Ridley Scott – all began in British television and were given a helping hand with their careers by Puttnam. Apted entered television by way of a Granada Television Company training scheme and quickly became a researcher for the current-affairs programme *World in Action*. He graduated to direction with episodes of the retrospective programme *All Our Yesterdays* and the soap-opera *Coronation Street*, and followed these with numerous plays. His first sortie into the film world was with the anti-war *The Triple Echo* (1972), starring Glenda Jackson and Oliver Reed, but it was *Stardust* (1974), produced by Puttnam, that gave him his first commercial success. The sequel to *That'll Be the Day* (1973), the story of an aspiring rock star, *Stardust* traces the career of the same musician (David Essex) who has finally 'made it big' and suffers the consequences.

*Bugsy Malone* (1976), he hawked the script around production companies for over a year, but finally raised the $1 million he needed. Starring Jodie Foster, *Bugsy Malone* is a musical gangster story entirely acted by children. It was co-produced by Puttnam and Parker's long-standing associate Alan Marshall, as was Parker's next project *Midnight Express*, the controversial story of an American youth who is serving a long sentence in a Turkish jail on charges of drug-smuggling. Parker wanted to remain in England but recognized that only America could supply the level of finance he needed. *Midnight Express*, a relatively expensive British film, cost $2.8 million; his next film, the 'American' *Fame* (1980), was budgeted at $8 million.

However, money was not the only factor involved in Parker's transatlantic migration. He has, as he admits, spent his entire life watching American movies, and was probably influenced by the tensions of a polyglot society so often touched on by Hollywood. *Fame* was an ideal project. It is based on the story of seven children at the High School of Performing Arts in New York, and is a typical American story of class and race integration:

'What specifically appealed to me about *Fame* was that it was set in New York . . . The idea of a dozen different races each having their own crack at the American dream intrigued me.'

Parker is now equally happy on either side of the Atlantic, completing the American *Shoot the Moon* (1981) with Diane Keaton, filming *Pink Floyd – The Wall* (1982) in Britain and planning to film the novels of Tom Sharpe for the American Ladd Company.

Ridley Scott graduated from London's Royal College of Art before working as a photographer in New York. On his return to London he became an art director for BBC television, and followed Apted's footsteps on a training

programme that led him to direct episodes of such series as *Z-Cars* and *The Informer*. Like Parker, Scott went into commercials and among his three thousand or so creations are some of the most innovative on British television. His first film was *The Duellists* (1977), funded by Paramount, the British National Film Finance Corporation and private sources. Keith Carradine and Harvey Keitel play two members of Napoleon's Hussars who become obsessed with duelling. Paramount insisted on the American actors against Scott's wishes but he was not dissatisfied with the result, agreeing that their inclusion gave the film the kick it needed. *Alien* (1979), a science-fiction 'horror', was an American film financed by 20th Century-Fox, although shot at Shepperton studios in England. Its success ensured Scott's continuation in Hollywood.

With Franc Roddam (*Quadrophenia*, 1979) and Tony Garnett (*Prostitute*, 1980) working in America it seems that transatlantic travel thrives. Most of these directors would rather work in their home country, a point emphasized by Colin Welland, the scenarist on *Chariots of Fire*, who said:

'We've got the best actors, directors and writers in the world . . . All we need now is to persuade the entrepreneurs . . . to put a bit of money into our films and we'll really have something to brag about.'     SALLY HIBBIN

*Above: John Schlesinger's* Yanks *(1979) explored how the American army's arrival affected wartime Britain. It was made with American money but British know-how. Below: a scene from Ridley Scott's science-fiction movie* Alien

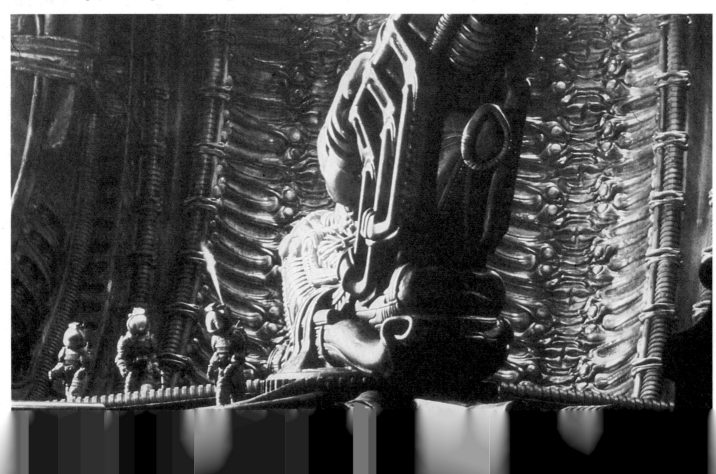

# Geoffrey Unsworth

## Shooting to the top

Geoffrey Unsworth – cinematographer supreme. When working with a camera he was both instinctive and inspired. Whatever effect was needed he would strive to supply it and the very fact that he was to work on a movie would lure top stars to appear in it. He was respected and admired by the entire film community, who universally mourned his death in 1978 – but his memorable photography remains a fitting epitaph

If directors are the superstar artists of the cinema, then cinematographers are the unsung heroes. Principal among their number was Geoffrey Unsworth. He was a quiet man beloved by all who knew him and admired and respected by those who did not. He gave directors courage because they knew he could do anything they wanted and actors felt safe with him because they knew they could trust him. When he died in 1978, while photographing Roman Polanski's *Tess* (1979) in Normandy, he left behind a legacy of fine films.

Geoffrey Unsworth regarded himself as the servant of the director, but that very self-effacement made him a star among cinematographers. The director John Boorman, who worked with Unsworth on *Zardoz* (1974), says:

'He helped the director maintain a coherent tone. Geoffrey did not bring a fixed style to his films as some cameramen do who have only one thing they can do, and do it from picture to picture. Geoffrey could do anything, give you precisely the photographic effect you required and, more important still, be utterly consistent once it was chosen.'

He was like an impressionist painter, preferring muted colours and atmosphere, but he never imposed a style on a film, believing that if the photography became noticeable it became too intrusive. And indeed, he never followed a formula or played safe. As John Boorman observes:

'Because he never fell back on formulae, each day's rushes were an agony for him. He risked, he extended himself, he reached out for excellence. And it was this that fed him, gave him his inexhaustible energy and passion for his craft. In a word, he was an artist.'

Geoffrey Unsworth was born in London in 1914. As a child his cinema-going was restricted to holidays, but he enjoyed seeing as many films as he could and realized this was a world of which he wanted to be a part.

He joined Gaumont British studios at Lime Grove, Shepherd's Bush, as a camera apprentice in 1932 with about fifty others. By the end of the first year just six remained. Not surprisingly, Unsworth was one of them. He began as a clapper boy and worked his way up through the ranks to become camera operator

for the likes of Victor Saville and Hitchcock.

Unsworth was in Africa working on the original *King Solomon's Mines* (1937) when he heard that Gaumont British had closed. On returning to England he joined MGM and worked as assistant cameraman on *A Yank at Oxford* (1938).

He was particularly fascinated by colour photography, which was in its infancy at this stage, and joined Technicolor where he mastered the new technique. He worked as camera operator with the legendary French lighting cameraman Georges Périnal, a man whose

*Below: Unsworth viewing the situation and (bottom) working on* A Bridge Too Far

colossus, though many were; he just enjoyed practising his skill. After a masterwork like *2001: A Space Odyssey* he made smaller scale films like *The Bliss of Mrs Blossom* (1968), *The Assassination Bureau* (1969) and *Baxter!* (1972). And he brought the same professionalism, caring and quiet authority to any production, irrespective of the size. In fact one of his favourite films was *Three Sisters* (1970), by no means a massive work, and the films he most liked were the period pictures to which he could add a mountain of mood – films such as *Becket*, *Cabaret*, *Murder on the Orient Express*, *The Abdication* and *Tess*.

## Flattering photography

Actresses adored him, not only because he brought a certain charm and courtliness to the hurly-burly world of film-making, but also because he believed every woman should look as beautiful as possible – 'He caressed them with light', comments John Boorman. Liza Minnelli was one of his biggest fans, asking for him on every film, and securing him for three – *Cabaret*, *Lucky Lady* (1975) and *A Matter of Time* (1976). The only thing he found difficult were scenes where the actress was required to look less than sensational. A scene like the

techniques he admired. At this time Technicolor not only supplied the film but the cameras and crew as well, and Unsworth worked as an operator with director Zoltan Korda on films like *The Drum* (1938), *The Four Feathers* (1939) and *The Thief of Bagdad* (1940). He later worked on Michael Powell's *The Life and Death of Colonel Blimp* (1943) and *A Matter of Life and Death* (1946).

In 1946 he joined the Rank Organization and, even before working with cinematographer Jack Cardiff on *Scott of the Antarctic* (1948), he became established as a director of photography in his own right. During the Fifties he worked with the Rank repertory of contract artists, which included Dirk Bogarde, on films such as *Penny Princess* (1952) and *Simba* (1955), and Peter Finch on movies like *Passage Home* (1955) and *A Town Like Alice* (1956). And his many lighting assignments included *Where No Vultures Fly* (1951), *A Night to Remember* (1958), *North West Frontier* (1959) and *The World of Suzie Wong* (1960).

### Wider angles

Unsworth stayed with Rank for 13 years but found himself on the open market when they turned away from major production. And, as

British film output declined during the years that followed, he moved with enormous success into big international pictures and gained a worldwide reputation for excellence. He became so sought-after that many producers wanted to cast him before they attempted to lure actors.

Over the last 15 years of his life Unsworth's camera operator was Peter MacDonald. He greatly admires Unsworth's work:

'Geoffrey was an intuitive cameraman, as he himself would readily admit, although no one would ever have believed him. He wasn't highly technical. He believed in his instincts and his gut feeling and very few cameramen had quite his daring in taking chances . . . . Geoffrey would never influence a director against doing a particular shot on the grounds of it being difficult. He would chew his viewing glass and walk away and maybe kick a box, but he would turn out the shot asked for.'

The Sixties and Seventies produced the films for which he will be most remembered – *Becket* (1964), *2001: A Space Odyssey* (1968), *Cromwell* (1970), *Cabaret* (1972), *Murder on the Orient Express*, *Zardoz*, *The Abdication* (all 1974), *A Bridge Too Far* (1977) and *Superman, The Movie* (1978). He did not insist that every film was a

*Above left: Sean Connery, Sid James, Patrick McGoohan and Stanley Baker in* Hell Drivers *(1957). Above: atmospheric lighting for the death of Becket (Richard Burton). Above right: Marlon Brando, John Hollis, Trevor Howard and Vass Anderson in* Superman, The Movie. *Right: Nastassia Kinski as Tess. Below: a stark interior from* 2001: A Space Odyssey

'morning-after' one in *Cabaret* where Minnelli, as Sally Bowles, had to look very ragged round the edges, was agony for Unsworth.

Minnelli wanted Unsworth to light *New York, New York* (1977), but he was already committed to *A Bridge Too Far*. Privately, he said that he believed *A Bridge Too Far* should be filmed in black and white, but producer Joseph E. Levine would never have agreed to allow his cast of superstars and his gigantic budget to be entrusted to a black-and-white end product. On location for the film in Holland, Unsworth found constant joy in the extraordinary light. 'It's the kind of light you find very prevalent in Dutch paintings. Everything is desaturated, you don't get harsh colours.' He thoroughly enjoyed working abroad and rest days often found him seeking out museums and art galleries, or wandering around the streets absorbing the atmosphere:

'I rather enjoy working abroad. If I can take my own crew with me then that is half the battle. You go just about anywhere and make films.'

He retained a profound love of the cinema:

'When I'm not working I sometimes see three or four films a day. Occasionally, of course, I'm aware of the craft, but generally I do get carried away with the story.'

There was also a dependability about him, an oasis of calm no catastrophe could shake. Others might have arguments or tantrums, but Unsworth quietly got on with the job, completely unperturbed. Says John Boorman:

'He always put me in mind of an old alchemist as he stooped over his exposure meter, peering at it with that bemused look. He transmuted our dross into golden light.'

## Filmography

**1938** The Drum (cam. op) (USA: Drums); A Yank at Oxford (ass. cam); Sixty Glorious Years (ass. cam) (USA: Queen of Destiny). **'39** The Four Feathers (cam. op). **'40** The Thief of Bagdad (ass. cam). **'42** The Great Mr Handel (cam. op); Teeth of Steel (short); Gardens of England (short); World Garden (short); Queen Victoria (compiled from: Victoria the Great, 1937; Sixty Glorious Years, 1938) (ass. cam). **'43** The Life and Death of Colonel Blimp (cam. op) (USA: Colonel Blimp); The People's Land (short); Power on the Land (short). **'44** Men of Science (short). **'45** Make Fruitful the Land (short). **'46** A Matter of Life and Death (cam. op) (USA: Stairway to Heaven); Meet the Navy; The Laughing Lady. **'47** Paris on the Seine (short); The Man Within (USA: The Smugglers); Jassy. **'48** Blanche Fury (ext. photo. only); Scott of the Antarctic (co-photo). **'49** The Blue Lagoon; Fools Rush In; The Spider and the Fly. **'50** Double Confession; Trio (ep only); The Clouded Yellow. **'51** Where No Vultures Fly (USA: Ivory Hunter). **'52** Penny Princess; Made in Heaven; The Planter's Wife (USA: Outpost in Malaya); The Story of Robin Hood and His Merrie Men. **'53** The Sword and the Rose; Turn the Key Softly. **'54** The Million Pound Note (USA: Man With a Million); The Purple Plain; The Seekers (USA: Land of Fury). **'55** Simba; Passage Home; Value for Money. **'56** A Town Like Alice; Jacqueline; Eric Winston's Stagecoach (short). **'57** Hell Drivers; Dangerous Exile. **'58** A Night to Remember; Bachelor of Hearts. **'59** North West Frontier (USA: Flame Over India); Whirlpool. **'60** The World of Suzie Wong. **'61** Don't Bother to Knock (USA: Why Bother to Knock); On the Double (USA). **'62** The Main Attraction; The 300 Spartans (USA); The Playboy of the Western World. **'63** An Evening with the Royal Ballet (co-photo); Tamahine. **'64** Becket. **'65** Genghis Khan (USA-GER-YUG); You Must Be Joking; Pop Gear (USA: Go Go Mania); Othello. **'66** Oh Dad, Poor Dad, Mamma's Hung You in the Closet and I'm Feeling So Sad (co-photo) (USA). **'67** Half a Sixpence. **'68** 2001: A Space Odyssey; The Bliss of Mrs Blossom. **'69** The Assassination Bureau; The Dance of Death; The Magic Christian. **'70** The Reckoning; Cromwell; Three Sisters; Goodbye Gemini; Say Hello to Yesterday. **'71** Unman, Wittering and Zigo. **'72** Cabaret (USA); Alice's Adventures in Wonderland; Baxter! **'73** Love and Pain and the Whole Damn Thing (USA); Don Quixote (AUS); Voices. **'74** Zardoz; The Internecine Project (GB-GER); Lenny (USA); The Abdication; Murder on the Orient Express. **'75** Return of the Pink Panther; Lucky Lady (USA); Royal Flash. **'76** A Matter of Time (USA-IT). **'77** A Bridge Too Far (USA); Exorcist II: The Heretic (USA). **'78** Superman, The Movie (USA). **'79** The First Great Train Robbery (USA: Great Train Robbery); Tess (co-photo) (FR-GB). **'80** Superman II (co-photo) (USA).

*No reliable listings exist for Unsworth's early work as focus puller and camera operator.*

## Lasting legacy

Unsworth worked on many films and won Oscars for two of them: *Cabaret* and *Tess* – a fact that was very important to him '. . . because they mean you have been favourably received by your fellow workers'. But the film for which he will be best remembered is *2001: A Space Odyssey*, possibly the most technically advanced and courageous movie venture of the Sixties. Everything that has followed in the same genre has been enormously influenced by this audacious and magnificent movie. And likewise all those who follow in the footsteps of Geoffrey Unsworth are bound to be influenced by his tremendous contribution to the cinema.

SUSAN D'ARCY

1

2

3

## The Aborigine and the girl 30,000 years apart ...together

WALKABOUT

Filmed in its entirety in the Australian wilderness

Just about the most different film you'll ever see

20th Century-Fox presents A MAX L. RAAB·SI LITVINOFF PRODUCTION WALKABOUT starring JENNY AGUTTER · LUCIEN JOHN · DAVID GUMPILIL executive producer MAX L. RAAB produced by SI LITVINOFF directed and photographed by NICOLAS ROEG screenplay by EDWARD BOND based on the novel by JAMES VANCE MARSHALL music by JOHN BARRY COLOR BY DE LUXE

*Walkabout* was to have been the first film directed by Nicolas Roeg, who had established himself by the mid-Sixties as one of Britain's leading cameramen for his work on such films as *The Caretaker* (1963), *Nothing But the Best, The Masque of the Red Death* (both 1964), *Fahrenheit 451* (1966) and *Far From the Madding Crowd* (1967). Roeg became fascinated by James Vance Marshall's novel, visited Australia to research settings and locations, and persuaded playwright Edward Bond to construct a screenplay. But the project then had to be shelved for lack of production support, and Roeg instead teamed up with Donald Cammell to make his joint directing debut with *Performance* (1970).

At first glance the two subjects could hardly look more different. *Performance*'s fetishistic study of a small-time London crook's metamorphosis in the claustrophobic home of a retired pop-star has little obvious connection with a trek through the Australian desert. But *Performance* too is about the fortuitous collision of opposites, their possible interaction and exchange, their final severance; and as it happens, the summary applies equally (with small variations) to Roeg's following films – *Don't Look Now* (1973), *The Man Who Fell to Earth* (1976) and *Bad Timing* (1980). It's all there in *Walkabout*, where the collision is both human (the white girl, the black Aborigine) and cultural (the city versus the outback); the interaction is a matter of both geographical and biological necessity (the girl is helpless in the aborigine's environment, as he would be in hers); and the severance is an inevitable consequence of two highly contrasted origins.

Roeg establishes the contrasts from the film's opening shots in which the bustling city is invaded by glimpses of desert, until, with a track from brick wall to open ground, he permits the wilderness to take over completely. At the end of *Walkabout* the pattern is reversed, with the invasion of the landscape by half-formed buildings, discarded equipment (the little boy actually sets an abandoned trolley in motion once more), and at last the city crowds themselves. As a result of Roeg's intercutting, city and desert appear symbiotic, each growing from the other; if the city-dwellers look disconcertingly like flowing sand, the wasteland, with its exotic wildlife, is also seen to have a teeming social structure, in which experience is the vital part of survival. Nature and civilization may be opposites, but they have the same roots, the same needs, and Roeg's examination of those needs reveals with each fresh illustration the special, even lethal, price that they demand.

The 'walkabout', explained in an opening title as an Aboriginal custom, is accordingly an education shared by the children of both cultures. For each, it provides the training for survival in a hostile environment. The Aborigine must learn how to find water, to kill lizards, to cook kangaroo meat. The girl, whom we first encounter in a classroom, must learn elocution, etiquette, and *haute cuisine*; education pursues her and her brother as they carry the radio on their journey, and ineffectual as its contribution may seem when there is no water, the measured tones of technology continue to echo across the outback long after the way home has become clear again and their brief benefactor has been left hanging from a tree. 'I can multiply 84 by 84', the six-year-old announces proudly to the smiling savage for

8

9

4

5

whom such skills are irrelevant; at the time, it seems incongruous, but it is the boy who lives and the Aborigine who dies.

*Walkabout* ends with the girl in her kitchen (as her mother was at the film's beginning). A voice speaks A. E. Housman's lines about 'the land of lost content . . . where I went and cannot come again' and we see a possibly remembered, possibly imagined bathing sequence with the girl, her brother and the Aborigine. Much enhanced by John Barry's soaring orchestration, this scene is a richly sentimental idyll, artificial enough to be subtly unconvincing. The viewer is invited, to recognize through it that while simplicity has many obvious attractions, and that nature specializes in simplicities, they are awesomely transient. The 'walkabout' provided the justification for the partnership and at the same time its limit; despite the many

erotic half-promises between boy and girl (and much of *Walkabout's* fascination comes from the delicacy with which it conveys their awareness of each other), they have no conceivable future together – which is why, having witnessed the gratuitous slaughter of wildlife by two white gunmen in a jeep, the Aborigine rises like a

skeleton from a landscape littered with bones to pay despairing homage to the female who has no further use for him. His time is past, even though Roeg's dislocated editing serves as a reminder that fragments of time, like bits and pieces of our upbringing, remain deeply embedded in the memories of us all.          PHILIP STRICK

---

**Directed by Nicolas Roeg, 1971**
**Prod co:** Max L. Raab – Si Litvinoff Films (Pty) Ltd (20th Century-Fox). **exec prod:** Max L. Raab. **prod:** Si Litvinoff. **assoc prod:** Anthony J. Hope. **sc:** Edward Bond, from the Novel by James Vance Marshall. **photo** (Eastman Colour): Nicolas Roeg. **sp photo:** Tony Richmond. **ed:** Anthony Gibbs, Alan Patillo. **prod des:** Brian Eatwell. **art dir:** Terry Gough. **mus:** John Barry. **add mus/songs:** 'Electronic Dance' by Billy Mitchell, 'Gasoline Alley' by Rod Stewart, 'Los Angeles' by Warren Marley, 'Hymnen' by Karl-Heinz Stockhausen. **sd rec:** Barry Brown. **sd re-rec:** Gerry Humphreys. **r/t:** 100 minutes. **Cast:** Jenny Agutter (*girl*), Lucien John· (*brother*), David Gulpilil (*Aborigine*), John Meillon (*father*), Peter Carver (*no-hoper*), John Illingsworth (*husband*), Barry Donnelly (*Australian scientist*), Noelene Brown (*German scientist*), Carlo Manchini (*Italian scientist*).

---

A teenage girl and her brother are taken for a drive in the Australian bush by their father. As she lays out the picnic, the father suddenly produces a pistol (1) and starts shooting; when the children take cover, he shoots himself. Reassuring her brother that it is nothing serious, the girl leads him away into the desert (2). By nightfall they are completely lost.

Next day they find an oasis – but soon the water is gone and their situation looks desperate (3). Unexpectedly an Aborigine youth appears out of the desert (4); he is on his 'walkabout' – the six-month period in the wilderness which, by tribal custom, will establish his manhood. He takes them under his protection and guides them through the vast wasteland (5).

At last they reach an abandoned homestead (6) which seems a natural place for them to stay. But the Aborigine then takes the boy (7) and shows him a nearby highway that could lead the way back to civilization. Disturbed that he and the girl may shortly have to part company, the Aborigine paints himself and begins a dance of courtship (8); the girl retreats from him in terror (9), fearing violence of some kind. He continues the ritual for hours, past the point of exhaustion, and in the morning they find him dead (10). Seemingly unconcerned, they take the road back to safety, only to be greeted with hostility at the first town they reach (11).

Years later, the girl receives her husband home from the office. As he chatters of minor triumphs in his business affairs, she recalls a time when three children swam together in the sunlit waters of a far-distant lake.

7

10

11

# ROBERT DE NIRO

# ODD MAN OUT

'You talking to me? Well, who the hell else are you talking to? You talking to me? Well I'm the only one here.' Travis Bickle, the rabid urban avenger played by Robert De Niro in *Taxi Driver*, affirms his solitariness in front of a mirror. As the Seventies wore on it seemed De Niro himself was the only one 'here' – the one actor immediately identifiable with lost souls on the streets of New York, fall-guys of the Vietnam fall-out, and other victims of the age. The brilliance he brings to such roles makes him the most authentic movie-hero of his generation

There is an agreeable symmetry to the fact that in *The Godfather, Part II* (1974) Robert De Niro played Vito Corleone, the young Sicilian who was to 'become' the old Mafia chief portrayed by Marlon Brando in *The Godfather* (1972). As Brando himself got older and his screen appearances rarer, it seemed for a long while that there was no-one to fill the void he was leaving: what other star was there possessed of such incredible sexual magnetism, who was at the same time a sensitive actor with a huge range, whose presence in even the most mediocre films lifted everything around him to a high level of intelligence and excitement?

Then in 1973 along came De Niro in *Bang the Drum Slowly* and, even more importantly, *Mean Streets*; it was not a 'new Brando' who had appeared, but an actor of the same class, and one who would obviously become, like Brando, a consummate *film* actor.

In 1973, however, De Niro – born on August 17, 1944 – was already 29 years old, and his career had begun much earlier:

*Top: Travis Bickle preparing for his one-man war on New York's vice-peddlers in Martin Scorsese's* Taxi Driver. *He gets a slug in the neck for his trouble but saves a child whore, kills a mafioso and becomes a hero. Back in his cab, though, he is still isolated in his madness; he remains, as Robert Philip Kolker says, 'his own passenger, threatening to take others for a ride.' Left: De Niro and Scorsese, a modern-day Wayne and Ford?*

*Left: De Niro as film producer Monroe Stahr, looking remarkably like Irving G. Thalberg, in* The Last Tycoon, *with Ingrid Boulting as Kathleen. Above left: as Vito Corleone, hustling, in* The Godfather, Part II. *Above: as Alfredo Berlinghieri in Bertolucci's 1900*

authenticity touched me, and I admire Walter Huston for his magic – remember *The Treasure of the Sierra Madre* (1948)? – and Jeanne Moreau because of something she emanates which always strikes me.'

In 1970 he played one of the gangster sons of Ma Barker (Shelley Winters) in Roger Corman's *Bloody Mama*, and the following year did three films – Ivan Passer's *Born to Win*, Noel Black's *Jennifer on My Mind*, James Goldstone's *The Gang That Couldn't Shoot Straight* – none of which won him fame and glory, but did get him noticed by other directors and producers.

'If I look back, I made a lot of films (independent or commercial, big and little) before I had any success, which was unforeseen. My luck was to be able to work and to learn; that's what an actor must never forget.'

His dying baseball player in John Hancock's *Bang the Drum Slowly* had audiences asking who he was and critics raving, and his Johnny Boy stole Martin Scorsese's *Mean Streets* (not an easy task when your co-star is the excellent Harvey Keitel), for which De Ni̶r̶o̶ ̶ ̶ the New York Film Critics Circle Award as Best Actor. The meeting with Martin Scorsese was particularly fortuitous:

'What matters to me is to work with a director who responds to me. That's been the case for a long time with Martin Scorsese. What's important in our work, which is very heavy and very s̶ ̶ ̶ ̶ ̶ ̶kind of complicity, solidarity, and a̶t̶ ̶ ̶ ̶ ̶ ̶m of fun – which prevents migraines.'

Scorsese refers to De Niro as 'Mr Perfection', and credits the actor as a major contributor to each of the films, from improvising new dialogue to rearranging troublesome scenes so that they work: 'Our collaboration is a *complete* collaboration. We work together in total trust.'

### The Italian job

From the almost crazy, self-destructive Johnny Boy, De Niro changed like a chameleon into Corleone, the Sicilian immigrant on his way to becoming the head of a Mafia family; the first role was all frenzy, the second a kind of elegant coolness. In Francis Ford Coppola's *The Godfather, Part II*, De Niro also worked extensively on his voice and intonation so that they

'I was born in Greenwich Village. I wanted to be an actor when I was 10, and then again when I was 16.' At 10, he attended New York's American Dramatic Workshop; at 16, he studied with Lee Strasberg and Stella Adler at the Actors' Studio.

'My parents were artists, and I thought they were Bohemian, and like all kids I wanted to rebel, so I decided to live a very conventional life. When it came time to make a real choice, however, I studied acting, which is what I always really wanted to do. My parents were very supportive; they were glad I hadn't become an insurance salesman.'

After working in semi-professional theatre outside New York City, he appeared Off-Broadway in a number of plays, including *One Night Stands of a Noisy Passenger* with Shelley Winters. In 1967, the director Brian De Palma, who had seen him on stage, hired De Niro to play a friend of the groom in *The Wedding Party*. They worked together again on the comedies *Greetings* (1968) and *Hi, Mom!* (1970). De Palma remembers:

'One day on *Greetings*, he came in to shoot a scene and I didn't recognize him. We had to put a label on him so that viewers would remember that it was the same character they had seen at the beginning. . . . He really lives his roles, and that changes him physically.'

### Living an illusion

People who know him have remarked that De Niro 'isn't here' during the making of a film, and he is well known for his 'isolation' between takes.

'I can't cheat when I act. I know that the cinema is only an illusion, but not for me. The qualities of an actor must be those which Faulkner said were those of a writer: experience, observation, imagination. The preparation of a role, the experience of making a film, are hard. When you are 10, you dream of beauty, of glory, and you aren't aware of the reality: study and work. If one is really in a film, the rest of the world disappears. No obligations, no telephone, no everyday details, no bothers. Then when it is finished and you return to reality you have to lose all the weight of the character, and go back to other disciplines. You have time for yourself, and that can be a source of new problems.'

Aside from the major influences of his teachers – Lee Strasberg, Luther James and Stella Adler (who he says was the first to give him 'a total sense of the theatre and of a character') – he says that the actors who 'marked' him include Montgomery Clift, James Dean, Marlon Brando, Kim Stanley, Geraldine Page – and also Spencer Tracy:

'I know, he was more conventional, but his

matched exactly those of Marlon Brando's Corleone in *The Godfather*. De Niro won the 1974 Best Supporting Actor Oscar for his performance. Entirely different again, he played the alienated, paranoid Travis Bickle, dedicated to purifying New York and 'saving' the virtue of an adolescent whore through slaughter in Scorsese's *Taxi Driver* (1976). The film won the Golden Palm at the Cannes Film Festival and De Niro became a solid international star.

De Niro has said that he constantly finds it necessary to change directors and kinds of roles 'in order to escape from that vicious circle in which we all find ourselves at any given moment.' A complete change came with *1900* (1976), made in Italy by Bernardo Bertolucci and an international cast of stars all acting in their own languages (later to be dubbed into Italian). De Niro played a sympathetic Italian landowner at the turn of the century trying to come to terms with the idea of revolution and maintain his relationship with his longtime peasant friend.

Although Elia Kazan's *The Last Tycoon* (1976) was made ineffective by its trowelled-on period decor and absolute fidelity to F. Scott Fitzgerald's unfinished Hollywood novel, De Niro came through unscathed. His elegant performance in a role modelled on Irving G. Thalberg suggested – more than did the leaden script – that the character was a part of the old Hollywood, that he knew about and loved film, and that he had been caught up in a love affair he knew was finally an illusion more hopeless than the films he was making.

More directly and authentically connected to the old Hollywood, Scorsese's *New York, New York* (1977), with its re-creation of the New York of movies (as opposed to the 'real' New York) and of the Big Band era, gave De Niro a chance to improvise whole sequences of dialogue, to demonstrate that he has a fine comic talent, and to walk the razor's edge between the comic and the emotionally touching. Jimmy Doyle was also De Niro's first fully romantic role and suggested that if he had been a less talented and ambitious actor he might have had a full career as a conventional matinée idol.

In *The Deer Hunter* (1978), De Niro played a metal-worker whose hellish experiences in Vietnam make it impossible for him to return to a normal life until he comes to terms with what has happened to himself and his friends. The actor has high praise for Michael Cimino, the film's director:

'I responded to him. From the time I met him, he was full of his project, of his subject, and I could see he was ready and felt the film had to be made. We were open to one another, ready to meet anywhere and anytime to work together to the end. As with John Hancock (to say nothing of Martin Scorsese) I felt there was something fresh and something good there.'

Although the film was politically and aesthetically controversial (some praised its view of America healing itself while others criticized its verbosity), De Niro's sensitive portrayal of a man learning to understand himself was universally acclaimed.

## Bring on the Bronx Bull

De Niro's work with Scorsese on *Raging Bull* (1980), the story of middleweight boxer Jake La Motta, again demonstrates the actor's incredible range and love of change. He played

La Motta as an inarticulate, instinctual animal. De Niro was fascinated by La Motta's 'destiny': 'He fought for everything and he lost everything.' The same passion for complete preparation that had made the actor learn the saxophone for *New York, New York*, here led him to take boxing lessons and gain 60lbs in four months for the scenes of La Motta in retirement. He also learned something about the inner character of the role:

'I don't like boxing. It's too primitive. But Jake is a more complex being than you think. Take his style: that way of uncovering his face to take blows and tire his opponents. In one way or another there has to be some feeling of guilt to deliberately look to get hit.'

De Niro's dedication earned him the Best Actor Oscar for 1981. It also persuaded him to reluctantly turn down another film with John Hancock, for he says he needed the eight months between *Raging Bull* and the next film with Scorsese in order to rid himself of Jake La Motta, and to get inside the next character.

In looking over the film career of Robert De Niro so far, it is clear that he is the outstanding talent and movie icon of his time. In 1977 *Newsweek* regarded him as:

'. . . the most exciting young American actor on the scene, the one with the greatest potential to combine superstardom with

*Top left: in the Vietnam movie* The Deer Hunter. *Top right: a guy, a suit and a sax – De Niro as Jimmy Doyle in* New York, New York. *Above: rest from the pressures of the ring for Jake La Motta (De Niro), his wife (Cathy Moriarty) and children in* Raging Bull

extraordinary creative ability . . . De Niro is the heir apparent to the post of American Cultural Symbol once occupied by Marlon Brando and the late James Dean. As Brando and Dean did . . . De Niro seems to embody the conflicting, questing energies of his generation.'

He is no teen idol but there is no doubt that in terms of Hollywood's image of post-Vietnam America and urban despair, Robert De Niro carries the burden more effectively than any other current star.      DAVID OVERBEY

**Filmography**
'67 The Wedding Party. '68 Greetings. '70 Hi, Mom!; Bloody Mama. '71 Born to Win; Jennifer on My Mind; The Gang That Couldn't Shoot Straight. '73 Bang the Drum Slowly; Mean Streets. '74 The Godfather, Part II. '76 Taxi Driver; 1900/Novecento (IT); The Last Tycoon. '77 New York, New York. '78 The Deer Hunter. '80 Raging Bull. '81 True Confessions. '83 The King of Comedy. '84 Once Upon a Time in America.

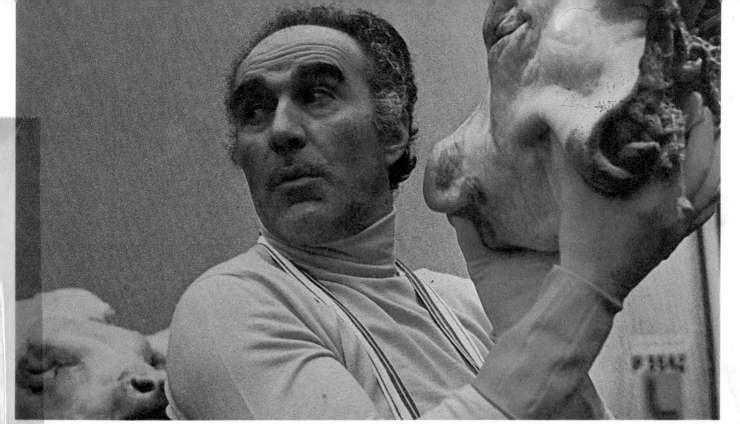

# Michel Piccoli
## Bourgeois or bizarre?

**For several decades a leading man and character actor on both stage and screen, Michel Piccoli lends all his roles – off-beat or conventional – a welcome degree of elegance and sardonic humour**

There is a certain irony, that Michel Piccoli would probably relish, in the fact that the films for which he is best known and most valued in England and America are those for which he was most reviled in France.

Born in Paris in 1925, Piccoli was on the stage for ten years before taking to the movies

*Above: gluttony comes to a head in Blow-Out. Below left: the film within a film, screenwriter (Piccoli), director (Fritz Lang), producer (Jack Palance) and assistant director (Jean-Luc Godard) as they appear in* Contempt

in the mid-Forties. In a working career spanning forty-odd years he has made something like three films a year. Yet, due to the vagaries of film distribution, the dozen or so that have been seen outside France are mostly those he made during the late Sixties and early Seventies.

This was, of course, the time of *les événements* of 1968, when everyone in Paris – even actors – nailed their colours to the mast. Piccoli's French audiences were surprised and then outraged at the sight of the man who had previously encapsulated all that they revered in suave, slightly foreign charm (he had played Don Juan in a long-running television serial) suddenly appearing in Luis Buñuel's surreal scourges of the bourgeoisie, financing and starring in the anarchic *Themroc* (1973), or eating himself to death in *La Grande Bouffe* (1973, *Blow-Out*).

### Contemplating contempt

In fact, the signs of his breaking out of the 'reasonable' mould had been there long before: witness his work for Jean-Luc Godard in *Le Mépris* (1963, *Contempt*) in which he plays a writer paid to do a re-hash of 'The Odyssey' for a megalomaniac producer. The only advice Godard gave him has since become famous: 'Your character is like a character from *Marienbad* who wants to play in *Rio Bravo*', and it is some measure of Piccoli's capabilities that not only does he embody that minimal direction perfectly, he also suggests an abrasiveness and hurt quite at odds with his recognized 'image' of that time.

Piccoli can certainly appear to be as withdrawn and insulated as the nameless participants in Resnais' *L'Année Dernière à Marienbad* (1961, *Last Year in Marienbad*), but it

clearly does not spring from any emotional indifference. As *Contempt* demonstrated, his awareness of the social pressures bearing down on him, the prostitution of his talents and his wife's contempt for him are almost too strong to allow his character any impassioned response. Yet it was Piccoli's urbanity that continued to appeal to his countrymen. *Les Choses de la Vie* (1970, *The Things of Life*) is a typical example of the middle-of-the-road commercial ventures in which Piccoli involved himself too often to enable his homeground audience to appreciate his more outlandish talents. *The Things of Life* gave him the role of another comfortable, suave womanizer, yet there are still moments that he made his own: a finicky taste in shirts – they had to be a certain shade of blue, a certain cut of collar – betrayed an appealing fastidiousness, a quality that film critic David Thomson pinned down with 'There is a marvellous note of the gloomy connoisseur in Piccoli'. It markedly resurfaces, albeit in different mood, in *Blow Out*

when he expands at length on the wonders of rubber gloves!

Indeed, *Blow Out* might be regarded as the pivot of his career, the moment when he finally alienated his French audience and appeared to the rest of the world as 'himself': scabrous but charming, immersed in – but subtly distanced from – the outrages of his surroundings. A man who could regard with perfect equanimity both the surreal fetishism of those rubber gloves and the proposition of eating himself to death.

## Having their cake and eating it

*Blow Out* is in many ways a mirror image of Buñuel's *El Angel Exterminador* (1962, *The Exterminating Angel*), where a party of house guests find themselves locked in a room without anything to eat. In *Blow Out* the director Marco Ferreri inverts Buñuel's world into a crueller version in which four men willingly withdraw from everyday life and commit group suicide in an orgy of gluttony. Whether continuing his ballet practice, flexing himself sedately at the wall bars or finally exploding on the verandah, Piccoli continues to convey the same slightly removed intellectuality that is perfectly suited to Ferreri's brand of Surrealism. By keeping his sceptical distance he also invites the audience to view the bizarre nature of ordinary objects or the cruelty of human appetites.

It is this quality that so enhances Ferreri's earlier *Dillinger è Morto* (1969, *Dillinger Is Dead*). Cinematically, the film achieves a tranquil perfection in terms of formal composition, but it is Piccoli's quiet concentration that makes it one of the most purely reflective films ever made. He roams the house, alone and silent; whether caressing the images that a projector throws on a wall, making a salad or dismantling an old revolver, he judges to perfection the distance between the spiritual needs of humans and the oppressive weight of the world of objects.

Similarly, the achievement of a man taking

*Below left: Renée (Jane Fonda) falls in love with the son of her husband (Piccoli) in* La Curée *(1966, The Game Is Over). Above: LeCoeur (Piccoli) presides over the ladies of* Le Moulin Bleu *in* Lady L *(1965)*

apart his life and striking out for freedom reaches a peak of anarchic enthusiasm in *Themroc*, a film financed by Piccoli and in which he unusually appears as a fully paid-up member of the working class. Throwing over his oppressive family and job, he reverts to a state of nature – knocking down the walls of his flat, sleeping with his sister and eating policemen. The cry of anger from this modern caveman revealed a rare side to Piccoli; a sheer physicality rarely glimpsed since.

## Semi-detached

Given his usual air of detachment, it is perhaps strange that he has not worked more with Claude Chabrol, the most sardonic observer of the French bourgeoisie. His role in *Les Noces Rouges* (1973, *Red Wedding*) personified the small-town urges of the petit bourgeois, but the best-remembered sequence – his seduction of Stéphane Audran in the local museum – has distinct overtones of Surrealism, especially the sly eroticism of his smoking a cigarette held between her toes.

It is the sort of touch that Buñuel has made his own and which certainly underlines Piccoli's presence in both *Le Charme Discret de la Bourgeoisie* (1972, *The Discreet Charm of the Bourgeoisie*) and *Le Fantôme de la Liberté* (1974, *The Phantom of Liberty*). Indeed, Buñuel's famous three-quarter-length shots seem ideally suited to capture Piccoli's talents: the imposing physical presence, broad chest, thick neck and leonine head can all be contained in the frame. The emotional intimacy of the close-up is rarely demanded, and the characters'

ironic detachment – itself held at a distance by the camera – underlines the bizarre aspects of any surrounding world. CHRIS PEACHMENT

*Below left: a wife (Rada Rassimov) imitates a doll in* Grandeur Nature *(1974, Life Size).*
*Above: the walls crumble in* Themroc

### Filmography
**1945** Sortilèges (GB: The Sorcerer). **'49** Le Point de Jour; Le Parfum de la Dame en Noir. **'50** Sans Laisser d'Adresse; Terreur en Oklahoma (short) (GB: Terror of Oklahoma). **'51** Chicago Digest (short). **'52** Torticola contre Frankensberg (short); Saint Tropez, Devoir de Vacances (short). **'54** Destinées *ep* Jeanne d'Arc (FT-IT) (USA: Daughters of Destiny; GB: Love, Soldiers and Women). **'55** Interdit de Séjour (GB: The Price of Love); French Cancan (FR-IT) (USA: Only the French Can); Tout Chante Autour de Moi; Les Mauvaises Rencontres; Ernst Thälmann, Führer seine Klasse (E.GER). **'56** Marie Antoinette (FR-IT) (GB: Shadow of the Guillotine); La Mort en ce Jardin (FR-MEX) (USA: Gina; GB: Evil Eden). **'57** Les Sorcières de Salem (FR-E.GER) (GB: The Witches of Salem); Nathalie (FR-IT (USA/GB: The Foxiest Girl in Paris). **'58** Rafles sur la Ville (GB: Trap for a Killer); Tabarin (FR-IT). **'59** La Bête a l'Affût. **'60** La Dragée Haute; Le Bal des Espions. **'61** Le Vergini di Roma (IT-FR-YUG) (USA/GB: Amazons of Rome); Le Rendez-vous de Nöel (short); Fumée, Histoire et Fantaisie (short); Le Rendez-vous (FT-IT); La Chevelure (short). **'62** Climats (GB: Climates of Love). **'63** Le Doulos; Le Jour et l'Heure (FR-IT) (USA: The Day and the Hour); Le Mépris (FR-IT) (USA/GB: Contempt). **'64** Le Journal d'un Femme de Chambre (FR-IT) (USA/GB: The Diary of a Chambermaid); Paparazzi (doc. short) (as himself). **'65** La Chance et l'Amour (FR-IT); De l'Amour (FR-IT) (GB: All About Loving); Le Coup de Grâce; Masquerade (GB); Marie Soleil; Lady L (FR-IT); Compartiment Tueurs (USA/GB: The Sleeping Car Murders); Café Tabac (short). **'66** La Guerre Est Finie (GB: The War Is Over); La Curée (FT-IT) (USA/GB: The Game Is Over); Les Ruses du Diable; Les Créatures (FR-SWED); Paris Brûle-t-il? (USA/GB: Is Paris Burning?); La Voleuse (FR-GER). **'67** Les Demoiselles de Rochefort (USA/GB: The Young Girls of Rochefort); Un Homme de Trop (FR-IT) (USA: Shock Troops); Belle de Jour (FR-IT); Mon Amour, Mon Amour (GB: My Love, My Love). **'68** Benjamin, ou les Mémoires d'un Puceau (GB: Benjamin, or the Diary of an Innocent Young Man); Diabolik (IT-FR) (USA/GB: Danger: Diabolik); La Chamade (FR-IT) (GB: Heartbeat); La Prisonnière (FR-IT) (GB: Woman in Chains). **'69** Dillinger è Morto (IT) (GB: Dillinger Is Dead); La Voie Lactée (FT-IT) (USA/GB: The Milky Way); Topaz (USA); L'Invitée (FR-IT). **'70** Les Choses de la Vie (USA/GB: The Things of Life); L'Invasion (FR-IT). **'71** Max et les Ferrailleurs; La Poudre d'Escampette (USA: Touch and Go); La Décade Prodigieuse (USA/GB: Ten Days' Wonder). **'72** Liza/La Cagna (FR-IT); L'Udienza (IT); Le Charme Discret de la Bourgeoisie (FR-SP-IT) (USA/GB: The Discreet Charm of the Bourgeoisie); L'Attentat (FR-IT-GER) (USA: The French Conspiracy; GB: Plot); César et Rosalie (narr. only) (FR/IT/GER) (USA/GB: César and Rosalie). **'73** La Femme en Bleu (FR-IT); Themroc; Les Noces Rouges (USA: Wedding in Blood; GB: Red Wedding); La Grande Bouffe (FR-IT) (USA/GB: Blow-Out); Le Far-West (BELG-FR). **'74** Touche pas à la Femme Blanche; Le Trio Infernal (FR-GER-IT) (GB: The Infernal Trio); Grandeur Nature (FR-SP-IT) (USA: Love Doll; GB: Life Size); Le Fantôme de la Liberté (USA/GB: The Phantom of Liberty); Vincent, François, Paul et les Autres (USA: Vincent, François, Paul and the Others). **'75** La Faille (FR-GER-IT); Léoner (FR-SP-IT); 7 Morts sur Ordonnance (FR-SP-GER). **'76** L'Ultima Donna (IT-FR) (USA/GB: The Last Woman); F. Comme Fairbanks; Mado (FR-GER-IT); Todo Modo (IT). **'77** René la Canne (FR-IT); Des Enfants Gâtés (USA: Spoiled Children); L'Imprécateur; La Part du Feu. **'78** L'Etat Sauvage; Strauberg ist da (GER); La Petite Fille en Velours Bleu; Le Sucre. **'79** Giallo Napoletano (IT); Le Divorcement; Le Mors aux Dents. **'80** Salto nel Vuoto (IT-FR); Der Preis für Uberleben (GER); Atlantic City USA (CAN-FR) (USA/GB: Atlantic City). **'81** La Fille Prodigue; Une Etrange Affaire; Espion, Lève-Toi. **'82** La Passante du Sans-Souci (FR-GER); Passion (FR-IT); Le Prix du Danger; Oltre la Porta (IT); Une Chambre en Ville; Que les Gros Salaires Lèvent le Doigt! **'83** Le Général de l'Armée Morte ( + prod; + co-sc) (FR-IT).

# Voyages of Discovery

# the films of Frederick Wiseman

**'I try to look at what is going on to discover what kind of power relationships exist and differences between ideology and the practice in terms of the way people are treated. The theme that unites the films is the relationship of people to authority'**

Frederick Wiseman makes films about institutions. He distributes them himself through his own company, Zipporah Films Inc., and the Zipporah publicity describes them in the dry, unemotional style of a legal textbook. He talks about them in the same pragmatic manner, stressing the number of weeks and months taken to make them, their shooting ratio, their editing structure and their length. It is no surprise to learn, from his own detailed *curriculum vitae*, that Wiseman, born in 1930, trained as a lawyer and spent three years as Lecturer-in-Law at Boston University.

Behind this prosaic façade, however, operates a dedicated and deceptively complex film-maker described by *The New Yorker* critic Pauline Kael as 'probably the most sophisticated intelligence to enter the documentary field in recent years'. Led into film-making through his concern with social problems and a deep and long-standing love of cinema, Wiseman received his first credit as a producer on *The Cool World* (1963), a fiction feature

about delinquent youth in Harlem directed by Shirley Clarke, whose *The Connection* (1961) had impressed him. In 1966, Wiseman co-founded the Organization for Social and

Technical Innovation (OSTI) with the aim of making constructive interventions in problematic social issues. Then, unhappy with the role of producer and scornful of the mystique of movie-making, he directed his first, and still his most controversial film, *Titicut Follies* (1967), a devastating study of the Bridgewater, Massachusetts, State Hospital for the Criminally Insane. Wiseman thus embarked on his almost obsessive cycle of documentaries about American institutions – social, military and

*Above: Frederick Wiseman. Left: a draftee contemplates life in the armed forces during an offduty moment in* Basic Training. *Bottom left: a shot from the same film shows the fledgling pride of the US Army. Right: young Christians in* Essene. *Below right: a youthful offender is frisked in* Juvenile Court. *Below, far right: one of the 'animal behaviour' experiments in* Primate

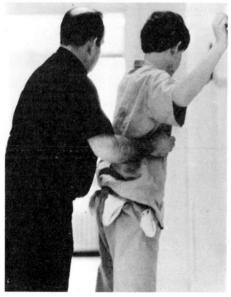

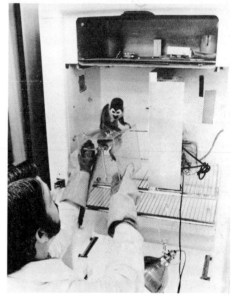

governmental – which comprises an unparalleled social history (or 'natural history' as he prefers to call it) of America in the Sixties and Seventies.

## Filming the facts of life

Wiseman's prime interest, in his own words, is 'in normal behaviour, what passes for normal behaviour', a dictum that echoes the assertion of John Grierson, one of the founding fathers of the documentary film, that 'the ordinary affairs of people's lives are more dramatic and more vital than all the false excitement you can muster'. But this is also the point at which Wiseman and the documentarists of the Thirties and Forties part company. Nowhere in Wiseman's films is there a hint of the lyricism, artiness or didacticism of the traditional documentary. His exclusive aim is to gather information, and to impart it, by the most faithful and unobtrusive means possible. His films are stripped bare of artifice, acting, false situations, narrative, dramatic structure and overt polemic. He uses no commentary, music or sound-effects to distract, influence or manipulate the viewer, and there is not even the visual seduction of colour, but rather a deliberate austerity induced by shooting in a grainy monochrome.

To be fair to Wiseman's predecessors, they too aspired occasionally to the ideal of capturing 'normal behaviour', but their efforts were hindered by bulky equipment, inadequate sound facilities and the need to create artificial light. Wiseman's good fortune is to be a beneficiary of the technical revolution of the Fifties, which liberated the film-maker and spawned *cinéma-vérité*, a film-style concerned only with trying to capture objective truth. That Wiseman has arguably come closer to achieving 'film truth' than any other documentarist is perhaps due as much to the development of portable, hand-held cameras, sensitive sound equipment and film that can be used in natural, even diminished light, as to his own practical skills.

## The search for normality

A doubt often raised by 'Wiseman watchers' is: to what extent can his subjects' behaviour really be 'normal' when they have a camera and crew staring at them and recording their every word and gesture? Wiseman's claim is that, particularly in the presence of a camera, non-actors ('ordinary' people) are more likely to behave in a manner in which they feel comfortable than to break their normal pattern and do something uncharacteristic. In any event, he believes that he can, from experience, detect 95 per cent of the exceptions, and those shots he automatically excludes from his films.

This is not to say that Wiseman is in any way deceived by notions of objectivity, despite his concern to mirror normality. He himself calls his films 'reality fictions': his own interpretation of his experiences, edited down and reconstructed in the cutting-room from perhaps fifty hours of film. Nor has Wiseman allowed himself to be fooled into believing that his films are weapons for change. They are, as he puts it, voyages of discovery painstakingly structured to present a balanced view of the situation he is investigating, in which the viewer is expected to become an active participant and to draw his or her own conclusions from what is on the screen. Condemnation of an institution may be implicit in the visual material, as in *Titicut Follies*, *High School* (1968) or *Basic Training* (1971), but it is not the result of intentional editorializing by the director.

There is evidence, nevertheless, that a Wiseman film can stimulate change, especially where it has aroused noisy controversy. *Titicut Follies*, for example, which exposes the appalling treatment of the prison inmates, became the subject of a legislative investigation (in which the judge condemned the film as 'a nightmare of ghoulish obscenities' as if Wiseman had invented the scenes he had filmed) and was banned by the Massachusetts State Supreme Court from being shown to anyone other than specialist professional groups. Yet soon afterwards, substantial reforms were made at the prison. There are similar indications that *High School*, a study of social indoctrination in a typical middle-class secondary school in Philadelphia, led to a rethinking of the school administrators' attitudes.

## Seeing every angle

A lesson learned by Wiseman at an early stage of his investigative odyssey was never to go in with preconceptions. He admits to having seen

his *Law and Order* (1969), which documents the routine activities of the Kansas City Police Department in Missouri and explores the complexity of the police role in American society, as 'a great chance to get the cops . . . to show what bastards they are'. His experience was entirely different, and for every scene of fascistic violence (such as that of a policeman trying to strangle a prostitute), there are numerous others showing the helplessness of the police in dealing constructively with domestic quarrels, lost children and drunkenness. Likewise in *Hospital* (1970), *Juvenile Court* (1973) and *Welfare* (1975), there is as much sympathy for the staffs of the institutions under scrutiny – trying to cope with the social ills of their community in the face of bureaucracy and faulty communication – as there is for their patients, charges and clients. *Basic Training* is a possible exception simply by dint of the self-condemnatory nature of what it reveals. It shows civilians being battered into soldiers by

the Army Basic Training Program – human beings trapped, brainwashed and destroyed by mindless disciplinary processes. There are echoes of this theme in *Primate* (1974), about the activities of an animal research centre concerned with primate behaviour (notably aggressive and sexual behaviour) which Derek Malcolm, film critic of *The Guardian*, neatly summarized as being 'essentially about one set of primates who have power, using it against another who haven't'. By contrast, *Essene* (1972), a moving and sympathetic look at life in a Benedictine monastery, has none of the latent outrage of Wiseman's other documentaries from this period.

As his work has progressed, Wiseman has seemed to take an increasingly dispassionate view of his chosen subject-matter, aligned with an obdurate persistence with repetitive and mundane detail. There are signs of this in *Meat* (1976) – a study of one of America's largest feed lots and packing plants – despite its

*Above left: a gruesome abattoir scene from* Meat. *Above: the aged await a sympathetic hearing in* Welfare. *Below left: Wiseman's artiest venture* – Model

unflinching abattoir scenes, and even more so in his trio of films about the activities of American military and governmental agencies abroad, *Canal Zone* (1977), *Sinai Field Mission* (1978) and *Manoeuvre* (1979). They are important and revealing, nevertheless, in their unmasking of individual behaviour and their questioning of American social values.

## Whither the truth-seeker?

Wiseman's *Model* (1980) was entertaining in its portrait of the fashion and advertising business and no less interrogatory than his previous work of the value Western society has placed on itself. With its 'showbiz' concern, it was a prelude to his first feature, *Seraphita's Diary* (1982), virtually a solo performance by a non-professional actress. Wiseman then made his first documentary in colour, *The Store* (1983), a study of the Neiman-Marcus department store in Dallas. He has not yet been put out of fashion by the more consciously polemical work of new young independent film-makers brave enough to take on the CIA and the FBI.

Whatever his next move may be, Wiseman can already rest on his laurels as one of the most intelligent, humane, creative and incisive chroniclers of contemporary American history. He is an innovative film-maker who has spared none of us in his efforts to show a twentieth-century Western society which has truly paved a road to hell with its good intentions.

CLYDE JEAVONS

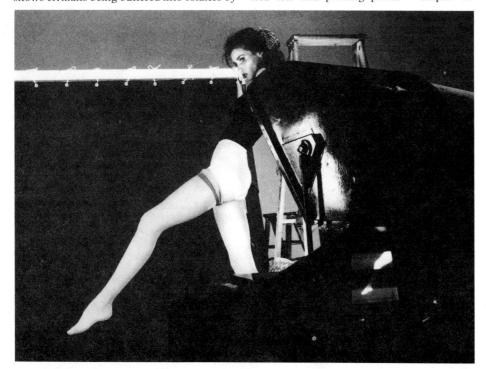

**Filmography**
1963 The Cool World (prod. only). *Director, producer and editor on following documentaries:* '67 Titicut Follies. '68 High School. '69 Law and Order. '70 Hospital. '71 Basic Training. '72 Essene. '73 Juvenile Court. '74 Primate. '75 Welfare. '76 Meat. '77 Canal Zone. '78 Sinai Field Mission. '79 Manoeuvre. '80 Model. '82 Seraphita's Diary (feature). '83 The Store.

# HIGH ANXIETY

**The New German Cinema has specialized in examining the German conscience and its intensely national concerns have brought international success**

The protagonist of Wim Wenders' *Im Lauf der Zeit* (1976, *Kings of the Road*) travels through Germany repairing the projection equipment in cinemas. Many are simply closed; the owner of one such place keeps her equipment in good repair but refuses to reopen until she no longer has to show pornography or book whatever the American-dominated distribution companies dictate. Another owner is full of nostalgia for the golden days of German cinema of the time of Fritz Lang. Yet another cinema seems to stay open on programmes of poorly-projected sex and violence.

This unhappy portrait of the state of German cinema was, and is, sadly accurate, if fortunately somewhat incomplete. At a time when the number of cinemas remaining open in West Germany has dropped to a little over 3000, as compared to more than 7000 in 1959, and the number of cinema tickets sold annually hovers around 100 million, as compared to 817 million in the peak year of 1956, the 'New German Cinema' has paradoxically become the most talked- and written-about, and the most highly praised, national cinema since the French *nouvelle vague*.

To see the New German Cinema in context, it is necessary to review briefly the developments since the end of World War II. The Allied Control Commission's policy, dominated by the Americans, was ideological and economic rather than cultural in motivation. Production was decentralized to Berlin, Munich, Hamburg and even Wiesbaden; small independent producers were forbidden by law to merge. This meant that there was a constant lack of finance for feature films. So German films could not compete internationally and the industry became oriented to films for the local market.

At the same time that the result of American policy was to discourage German film production, the Americans helped to rebuild the distribution and exhibition areas of the industry. Most of the distribution firms had, and have, major American investment; the sole major distributor not in American ownership, Constantin, went bankrupt in 1977. As no import control was permitted, American studios 'dumped' films that had already earned a profit in the USA and Great Britain on the German market at rates so low that no West German producer could compete. German films still account for only about a quarter of box-office returns in Germany.

During the Fifties, production consisted mostly of sex films, musicals, leaden comedies or historical romances, aimed at local audiences. Income from the export of German films was therefore always low. The federal and state governments tried to encourage film production with guaranteed bank credits, tax relief, subsidies and cash prizes. Most of these attempts were abandoned or sharply modified throughout the Fifties and Sixties as the results were seen to favour the distributors, the established producers who continued to churn out low-quality films and the makers of bland films which were politically acceptable.

Inspired in part by the *nouvelle vague* in France, 26 young film-makers who had been involved in short films – some of which had won prizes at international festivals – signed the Oberhausen Manifesto in 1962. Although vague and general in its proposals, it assumed the 'death' of the established industry and maintained that the hope of German cinema was in a new generation of directors 'who speak the international language of the cinema'. Through intense lobbying (led by Alexander Kluge, who is a lawyer as well as a film director), the Kuratorium Junger Deutscher Film (Board of Curators of the Young German Film) was established in 1965 to provide interest-free loans for first films. Between 1965 and 1968, DM 5 million was invested in a number of short films and 20 features, including Kluge's *Abschied von Gestern* (1966, *Yesterday Girl*) and Werner Herzog's *Lebenszeichen* (1968, *Signs of Life*), and the New German Cinema had begun.

This in turn brought about a counter-lobby by the established film producers and distributors who succeeded in 1967 in having the Film Development Act passed; this provided subsidies to producers based on the box-office performance of previous films. As the distributors then refused to handle the work of the directors involved in the New German Cinema, the Film Development Act's subsidies were not available to them – an undistributed film has no box-office performance. The effect was that a number of young directors 'went commercial' and established producers grabbed the easy subsidy money to make quickies – porn and comedies – which finally ruined the market.

Having previously ignored the all-important distribution area of the industry, several young directors (Wim Wenders, Werner Herzog, Rainer Werner Fassbinder and others) founded the Filmverlag der Autoren (Authors' Film Publishers) in 1971 for the distribution and international sales of their films. While the organization had some success, especially in getting films sold outside

*Top: Alexandra Kluge, the director's sister, as Anita G, the* Yesterday Girl *whose past as a Jewish refugee and a petty criminal catches up with her as she tries to adjust to life in West Germany. Above: Leni Peickert (Hannelore Hoger) dreams of improving the circus she inherited from her father in* Artistes at the Top of the Big Top: Disorientated; *but eventually she settles for a good job in television*

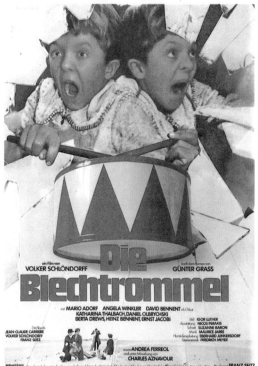

*Above:* Woyzeck *(Klaus Kinski) is a soldier much oppressed by poverty, humiliation and the infidelity of his common-law wife, whom he murders before accidentally drowning himself. Top: the German army on manoeuvres in* Germany in Autumn. *Top right: Heinz Schubert as Strongman Ferdinand, a security officer so obsessed with his work that he arrests his own boss and shoots a cabinet minister to emphasize the dangers of slack security. Right:* The Tin Drum *stars young David Bennent as a boy who decides to stop growing at the age of three in 1927, but, although tiny, later resists the Nazis with his shattering scream*

Germany, it never managed to deal with more than four hundred cinemas within West Germany and West Berlin. The Filmverlag continued to operate in much the same way after 1977, when 55 per cent was bought by the owner of the magazine *Der Spiegel*, Rudolf Augstein.

In addition to various small subsidies and cash prizes which still existed for serious directors, there was also television. If the introduction of the small screen in Germany in the Fifties helped to kill the box-office for cinema, it also provided the means by which many young directors made their films. Volker Schlöndorff has claimed that with television '70 per cent of the German cinema is subsidized'. Many directors, including Peter Lilienthal, Hans Jürgen Syberberg and Wolfgang Petersen, began in television and have continued to work directly for it. Werner Herzog produced most of his earlier films on a combination of small subsidies, prizes and television money. Fassbinder has also worked directly or indirectly for television; probably more Germans have seen his two successful television series. *Acht Stunden sind kein Tag* (1972–73, Eight Hours Are Not a Day) and *Berlin Alexanderplatz* (1980), than all of his cinema films together.

While television has allowed many directors to keep working and others to begin careers, the situation has not necessarily been ideal. Syberberg, for example, has commented that:

## Television launched many young German directors, but tended to curtail their creative freedom

'All the (political) parties are represented by television and they would never finance a film which really treated seriously, for example, atomic power or terrorism.'

Television did finance and show a number of films that touched such subjects obliquely, such as *Die verlorene Ehre der Katharina Blum* (1975, *The Lost Honour of Katharina Blum*), *Vera Romeyke ist nicht tragbar* (1976, *Vera Romeyke: Not Acceptable*), and *Messer im Kopf* (1978, *Knife in the Head*). But these remained studies of specific cases rather than general statements. The much tougher *Deutschland im Herbst* (1978, *Germany in Autumn*), a hard-hitting, episodic survey of the state of the nation, was made by a dozen directors; it was not only not financed by television, but contained a sequence parodying the problem of the political censorship

carried out by television. Other areas of subject-matter were also considered 'dangerous': Wolfgang Petersen's *Die Konsequenz* (1977, *The Consequence*), a fairly sympathetic treatment of a homosexual affair, was financed by television but then forbidden for screening, although it was later widely shown at festivals and became a commercial hit in France and Canada.

At times the difficulties of finding the money to make a film have been overwhelming for directors of the New German Cinema. Some, like Syberberg and Wenders, left to work in America. Some, like Reinhard Hauff and Schlöndorff, have managed to alternate between 'personal' and 'commercial' projects. Others, particularly Fassbinder, have become successful on the international market, so that producers know that budgets can be recouped abroad. The New German Cinema has continued to experience difficulty in distribution and in finding production funds, but has remained prominent among national cinemas, with about ten established directors and another two dozen or so minor but interesting directors actively working. Among those who established themselves solidly on the

international level were Alexander Kluge, Rainer Werner Fassbinder, Jean-Marie Straub, Werner Herzog, Reinhard Hauff, Volker Schlöndorff, Hans Jürgen Syberberg, Wim Wenders and, to a slightly lesser extent, Werner Schroeter and Daniel Schmid.

Alexander Kluge began with a strong admiration for the work of Jean-Luc Godard which was reflected in his shorts and his early features *Yesterday Girl* and *Die Artisten in der Zirkuskuppel: ratlos* (1968, *Artistes at the Top of the Big Top: Disorientated*). In *Gelegenheitsarbeit einer Sklavin* (1974, *Occasional Work of a Female Slave*), the story of· an ex-abortionist who becomes politically active, he continues to use Godardian devices, such as a fragmented narrative, printed quotations and deliberately shaky hand-held-camera images; but its very cool intellectual analysis of a woman's position in a male-dominated society marks it as clearly a Kluge film. Since then it has become apparent that Kluge's interests are indeed social and political. Even in *Der starke Ferdinand* (1976, *Strongman Ferdinand*), where he reveals both a sense of the comic and a sympathy for his unpleasant protagonist, the chief security officer of a factory, his final interest is in an

analysis of how a passion for 'security' develops into a fascist mentality. Kluge was later involved in straight political analysis in group-directed films, *Germany in Autumn* and *Der Kandidat* (1980, The Candidate), which concerned the ambitions of the right-wing Bavarian prime minister Franz-Josef Strauss for the Chancellorship.

Rainer Werner Fassbinder was also interested in social questions, such as terrorism and its relationship to the state in *Die dritte Generation* (1979, *The Third Generation*). But his theoretical viewpoint was often masked by melodrama, the analytical uses of which he learned from Douglas Sirk and Fritz Lang. Working very fast with, usually, the same team of technicians, he was the most prolific of the new German directors. He was the funniest and, in his way, the most courageous – his segment of *Germany in Autumn* was strongly personal and he allowed himself to be seen in a less than flattering way in recounting the story of his relationship with his male lover. As *Die Ehe der Maria Braun* (1979, *The Marriage of Maria Braun*) and *Lili Marleen* (1981) became box-office hits, he was accused of 'going commercial', although in the same period he made one of his most

*Top left:* The Marriage of Maria Braun *(Hanna Schygulla) is much interrupted by war and the imprisonment of her husband (Klaus Löwitsch) for a crime she accidentally committed; but she is ready to greet him when he returns from self-imposed exile in Canada. Top: Bach (Gustav Leonhardt) and musicians filmed and recorded on location in* Chronicle of Anna Magdalena Bach. *Above: Harry Baer as the last king of Bavaria in* Ludwig II – Requiem for a Virgin King; *the back-projected settings are economical as well as effective. Above left: Edith Clever plays a wife who asks her husband to leave their home so that she can find her own identity in* Die linkshändige Frau *(1977,* The Left-handed Woman), *the first film directed by Peter Handke*

59

personal and least popular films, *The Third Generation*. Until his death in 1982, he continued to do what he had always done: to make somewhat outrageous melodramas with a hard, serious (though also sometimes comic) core.

Jean-Marie Straub, who collaborates closely with his wife Danièle Huillet, must be mentioned for his early films, though he left Germany for Italy after the Sixties and no longer works regularly in the German language. *Nicht versöhnt* (1965, *Not Reconciled*) united memories of anti-Nazi resistance in the Thirties with the story of an architect's son who becomes a demolition expert in World War II and blows up his father's masterpiece. *Chronik der Anna Magdalena Bach* (1968, *Chronicle of Anna Magdalena Bach*) was a costume piece, structured around the imaginary journal of Bach's second wife and containing performances of a couple of dozen extracts from Bach's music. Straub's elliptical style makes few concessions to the viewer and his critical repute, especially in left-wing circles, is far in advance of his popular impact.

Werner Herzog is the mystic of the New German Cinema: his studies of people on the fringes of or outside society are part of his own personal vision of madness, isolation and a cataclysmic future. He has worked in the adventure genre with *Aguirre, der Zorn Gottes* (1973, *Aguirre, Wrath of God*), in original historical biography with *Jeder für sich und Gott gegen alle* (1975, *The Enigma of Kaspar Hauser*), in literary adaptation with *Woyzeck* (1979) and in his own private brand of visionary cinema with *Fata Morgana* (1971). Throughout this variety, Herzog's uniquely poetic style and his use of landscapes to

---

### The New German Cinema is much concerned with examining the past, both quite recent and more remote

---

reflect inner emotion have remained consistent.

Reinhard Hauff is one of the more varied of the New German directors in both style and subject-matter, having moved from the glowing antique colours of the historical tale about the hero-bandit *Mathias Kneissl* (1971), through a strong case-study of a prisoner, *Die Verrohung des Franz Blum* (1974, *The Brutalization of Franz Blum*), to the more personal *Der Hauptdarsteller* (1977, *The Main Actor*), in which he examines his own relationship with a youngster he had used as the main actor in an earlier film. *Knife in the Head* was a return to the case-study, concerning an amnesiac accused of being a terrorist.

*Above:* Geschichten aus dem Wiener Wald *(1979, Tales From the Vienna Woods) is a tragedy of small shopkeepers in pre-war Vienna, directed by Maximilian Schell; British playwright Christopher Hampton co-wrote the script. Below: Volker Schlöndorff's* Michael Kohlhaas – der Rebell *(1969, Michael Kohlhaas) is about one man's relentless quest for justice in 16th-century Germany, which leads to an uprising; the film was released in an English as well as a German version, and the controversial playwright Edward Bond worked on the adaptation from Heinrich von Kleist's novella*

Volker Schlöndorff, like Hauff, is a careful craftsman, without the personal style and vision of a Herzog or a Fassbinder. While he has made such purely commercial films as the bourgeois tale of adultery *Die Moral der Ruth Halbfass* (1972, The Morals of Ruth Halbfass), he is obviously intelligent and serious enough to be more at ease with subjects like the amateur criminals of *Der plötzliche Reichtum der armen Leute von Kombach* (1971, *The Sudden Fortune of the Poor People of Kombach*), in which he side-stepped every trap of romanticizing and sentimentalizing poverty-stricken farmers. His adaptation, with author Günter Grass, of *Die Blechtrommel* (1979, *The Tin Drum*) is strikingly intelligent and well-made.

Hans Jürgen Syberberg has moved with the times, beginning with fairly realistic motorcycle and sex dramas and moving on to his stylized trilogy about power and the German past: *Ludwig II – Requiem für einen jungfräulichen König* (1972, *Ludwig II – Requiem for a Virgin King*), *Karl May* (1974) and *Hitler* (1977, *Hitler – a Film From Germany*). Although he has said that his back-projected decors and his use of other non-realistic devices came originally from a lack of production funds, he kept the method when he saw that it worked far better than a realistic treatment of the subjects would have done. Later on, he moved to Hollywood to work on a project with Francis Ford Coppola.

Wim Wenders worked for Coppola on *Hammett* (1982) as well as releasing a semi-documentary, *Lightning Over Water* (1980), about his relationship with the dying American director Nicholas Ray. Wenders' features have usually concerned characters moving through time and space, learning about themselves, each other and the society around them. In *Alice in den Städten* (1974, *Alice in the Cities*), the characters were a young man and a little girl and the movement was from the United States to Germany. In his finest film, *Kings of the Road*, the characters are two adult men and the movement is through Germany, as the men come to terms with their pasts, both individual and collective, and with each other. While Fassbinder has been interested in the American 'presence' in German society since the war, Wenders has been the one who has tried to define it. In *Kings of the Road*, he has a character say: 'The Yanks have colonized our souls'. That, in relation to the portrait he gives of the German cinema, is as clear an indication as any of what indeed happened to the German cinema since the war, and why the New German Cinema is so important and significant not only in the national but also in the international context.

DAVID OVERBEY

# Nordic lights

By 1962, the decline in the Swedish film industry was at a drastic level, despite the international success of Bergman's productions. The following year, the government took the momentous step of founding the Swedish Film Institute; this was planned by Harry Schein, its first director, in recognition of the fact that, in a mixed economy like Sweden's, the native cinema could survive only with the help of subsidies. A punitive entertainments tax was replaced by a levy of 10 per cent on all box-office receipts. This sum, amounting initially to some £850,000 per annum, financed the Institute: 30 per cent was distributed to all Swedish productions in proportion to their earnings; 33.3 per cent was dispensed in the form of quality awards to Swedish films (valued by a jury of experts); and the balance was earmarked for the promotional, preservational and educational activities associated with more orthodox national film institutes. As a direct result, scores of films were made during the next decade. The prospect of an Institute award made producers willing to take risks.

The new directors who emerged, including Bo Widerberg, Jörn Donner and Vilgot Sjöman, were responsive to the influence of the French *nouvelle vague* and of American low-budget directors like John Cassavetes. Their first films had a raw, naturalistic texture; they dealt with social problems in modern Sweden, while Ingmar Bergman (as they

claimed) was immured in his private heaven and hell. Widerberg's talent was most discernible in *Kvarteret Korpen* (1964, *Raven's End*), which studies a young author's revolt against his depressing home background during the late Thirties. He achieved world-wide acclaim for *Elvira Madigan* (1967), *Ådalen '31* (1969) and a feature shot on location in the United States, *Joe Hill* (1971), about the life of the Swedish folksinger executed in dubious circumstances in Utah in ·1915. Widerberg's contribution consists of a lyrical style of film-making allied to an acute sense of social injustice.

In his time, Donner has served as writer, critic, producer and administrator as well as directing films – he was managing director of the Swedish Film Institute and then chairman of the Finnish Film Foundation. Of his own features, *Att Älska* (1964, *To Love*), a witty glance at contemporary sexual customs. *Anna* (1970), made in Finland, and *Män Kan inte Våldtas* (1978, *Men Can't Be Raped*) best demonstrate his dry, compressed and sardonic approach to life.

Vilgot Sjöman is the most incorrigibly rebellious of this group. He began in comparatively staid fashion with *Älskarinnan* (1962, *The Mistress*), but in 1967 he startled literally millions of people in Sweden and abroad with *Jag Är Nyfiken – Gul* (*I Am Curious – Yellow*), which interspersed an exuberant, lusty girl's search for personal liberty with a

*Above left: Ådalen '31 is based on a real-life incident in the small Swedish town of Ådalen in 1931; troops fired on an orderly march of strikers, killing five. Above: Anna Godenius as a rape victim in* Men Can't Be Raped; *she acquires a gun, but takes her revenge in sexually humiliating, rather than shooting, her assailant. Below: in* Som Natt och Dag, *Susanne (Agneta Ekmanner, right) has made an advantageous marriage which her sister Claire (Claire Wikholm) disrupts while Susanne's husband is away. Below left: Max Von Sydow and Liv Ullmann are two of* The Emigrants *who search for a new life in Minnesota*

Top: location filming of Hugo and Josephine, with Marie Öhman as the little girl Josephine and Beppe Wolgers as Gudmarsson, her father's gardener and the uncle of her friend Hugo. Above: Earth Is a Sinful Song is a Finnish film set in Lapland after World War II; it portrays a society much given to heavy drinking and guilt-ridden passions, and is based on a novel published when the author, Timo K. Mukka, was only 19

documentary inquiry into the shortcomings of Swedish democracy. The sex scenes were so overt that the film was banned in many states in the USA. Like Widerberg's, Sjöman's inventive fire waned somewhat during the Seventies. Only *En Handfull Kärlek* (1974, *A Handful of Love*), a period piece set against the general strike in Sweden in 1909, and *Linus* (1979), about a crime in a mysterious brothel, confirmed his talent.

Jan Troell, a brilliant cameraman as well as director, brought to film the eye of a painter and poet. He captured the sights and sounds of the Swedish landscape – and the people within it – in such masterpieces as *Här Har Du Ditt Liv* (1966, *Here Is Your Life*) and *Utvandrarna* (1971, *The Emigrants*). Troell earned a high reputation overseas for his picture of nineteenth-century Swedish workers making a new home in the United States, even being compared with John Ford. *Nybyggarna* (1972, *The New Land*) became its equally poignant and effective sequel. Troell's ventures into English-language film-making did not prove successful; but *Ingenjör Andrees Luftfjard* (1981, *The Flight of the Eagle*) marked a return to the epic genre he has enriched.

A second wave of film-makers followed swiftly during the later Sixties. Mai Zetterling came back to her native country to direct three scrupulously-made features from a feminist point of view, the most lasting of which will no doubt be *Älskande Par* (1964, *Loving Couples*),about some restless young society women during the period 1910–20. Jonas Cornell brought to the screen an ironic and detached vision of modern life in the comedy *Puss och Kram* (1967, *Hugs and Kisses*) and the social drama *Som Natt och Dag* (1969, *Like Night and Day*), both starring his wife, Agneta Ekmanner.

Kjell Grede made a splendid debut with *Hugo och Josefin* (1967, *Hugo and Josephine*), a children's film that appealed also to adults, and integrated the blithest and most touching of stories with the felicities of the summer landscape. Grede's subsequent films have grown more introspective, even mystical in tone, with *Harry Munter* (1969) the most rigorous and sensitive. By contrast, Jan Halldoff, starting in 1965, has kept his eye firmly on the everyday life and loves of young Swedes. His films are shot with authority, and often do well at the box-office, the most memorable being *Korridoren* (1968. The Corridor), about a young doctor. Johan Bergenstråhle is fierce in his social engagement, and has dealt with capitalist corruption in *Made in Sweden* (1969), the problems of immigration in *Jag Heter Stelios* (1972, *Foreigners*) and the forcible repatriation of political refugees after the war in *Baltutlämningen* (1970, *A Baltic Tragedy*).

In 1972, the statutes of the Film Reform of 1963 were amended so as to give more active encouragement to production, with grants being advanced ahead of shooting. This led to the emergence of yet a third wave of directors, although quality and talent remained scarce. Gunnel Lindblom, an actress in Ingmar Bergman's films, made her debut as a director with *Paradistorg* (1977, *Summer Paradise*), which, despite a schematic scenario, included some engaging conversations and a persuasive picture of the Swedish family under stress. Another woman director, Marianne Ahrne, announced her own idiosyncratic style of movie-making with *Långt Borta och Nära* (1976, Near and Far Away), about a love affair in a mental hospital involving a young man psychologically unable to speak and a social worker, while Mats Arehn quickly showed himself deft at handling both drama and comedy with *Maria* (1975), *Uppdraget* (1977, *The Assignment*) and *Mannen Som Blev Miljonär* (1980, To Be a Millionaire).

Stefan Jarl has made two remarkable and disturbing documentaries, *Dom Kallar Oss Mods* (1968, *They Call Us Misfits*) and *Ett Anständigt Liv* (1979, *A Respectable Life*), describing the punitive attitude to drug-use in a so-called free society. More entertaining, and a boon for jazz lovers, was *Sven Klangs Kvintett* (1976, *Sven Klang's Combo*), which evoked the Fifties through music and was made by a team including members of the radical October Group and intelligently directed by Stellan Olsson.

Denmark's establishment of the Danish Film Foundation, one year after its Swedish model, gave hope to new directors. Few Danish film-makers, however, have enjoyed more than intermittent success. Henning Carlsen, whose *Sult* (1966, *Hunger*) won the Best Actor Award at Cannes for Per Oscarsson, is the exception; he is unusually adroit at analysing the growth of relationships among people of disparate ages and backgrounds. Other directors of note include Jørgen Leth, whose films on cycle-racing are loved and admired in sporting circles; Henrik Stangerup, a novelist who made some sensitive features before leaving Denmark; and Morten Arnfred, with his humorous and perceptive studies of teenage development, *Mig og Charly* (1978, Me and Charly) and *Johnny Larsen* (1980).

Finland did not have a Film Foundation until 1969, and its inauguration by no means assured a renaissance. But four key figures (in addition to Jörn Donner) persisted with their personal films during the Seventies. Mikko Niskanen has worked for both television and the large screen, with *Kahdeksan Surmanluotia* (1972, Eight Deadly Shots) as his most trenchant accomplishment – an attack, like so many Finnish books and films, on the ravages of alcoholism and rural poverty. Rauni Mollberg is a painstaking artist who has brought the inhabitants of Lapland vigorously to life in three features, the best being *Maa on Syntinen Laulu* (1973, *Earth Is a Sinful Song*). Erkko Kivikoski has focused on social pressures and the interplay of domestic passions. The most significant Finnish *auteur*, Risto Jarva, had developed into a master of several kinds of film – comedy, science fiction, contemporary satire, social broadsheet – before being tragically killed in a road crash after the premiere of his finest film, *Jäniksen Vuosi* (1977, *The Year of the Hare*).

Two women directors should be noted. From Finland, Pirjo Honkasalo made, with Pekka Lehto, the striking epic *Tulipää* (1981, Firebrand); and from Norway, Anja Breien is best known for *Hustruer* (1975, *Wives*), a hilarious response to John Cassavetes' *Husbands* (1970), and for *Arven* (1979, The Legacy), dealing with guilt and rapacity in the archetypal Norwegian family. PETER COWIE

# WUNDERKIND

# Rainer Werner Fassbinder

If for each decade there is one country which shines in world cinema, for the Seventies it must have been West Germany. It is always difficult to say why this should be . . . what combination of social and economic forces with artistic tendencies . . . what totally unpredictable outbursts of individual talent. But even if one could suggest some tentative conclusions about the New German Cinema, it would be impossible to account for the appearance anywhere, at any time, of such an eccentric and many-faceted figure as the director Rainer Werner Fassbinder

Although in the eyes of posterity he may not prove to have been the most gifted of a generation which also includes Herzog, Wenders, Schlöndorff, Kluge and Straub, Rainer Werner Fassbinder undeniably made the biggest splash. It would have been difficult to guess at this from his obscure beginnings. When his first feature film *Liebe ist kälter als der Tod* (1969, *Love Is Colder Than Death*) was shown at the Berlin Film Festival in 1969, it left public and jurors alike nonplussed. Being a weird and pretentious combination of Maoist politics and static silences made it almost impossible to judge whether its maker actually had any talent which might possibly emerge once he had shed his two obsessive influences – Godard and Straub. But, it must also be admitted, the film had in full measure that ability to stick in the throat and irritate those who are normally peaceable to fury, and it was this which subsequently turned out to be one of Fassbinder's hallmarks.

Knowledgeable Germans said that this young man (23 at the time) had already done interesting work in the theatre as a writer, director, actor and general 'animator'. He was born in 1946 and was brought up largely by his mother after his parents' divorce. She had been a translator before becoming an actress, and she appeared as Lilo Pempeit in many of her son's films.

When he was 18 he entered a drama school where he met the first of his longtime associates, the actress Hanna Schygulla. In 1965 he made a ten-minute short – *Der Stadtstreicher* – the cast of which included another of his regular collaborators, Irm Hermann, and in 1967 he moved, with a group of friends, to a Munich fringe theatre called Action Theater, where he began directing productions and then writing his own texts. In 1968 the theatre was closed by the police, but Fassbinder and nine others (including Hanna Schygulla, Peer Raben, Kurt Raab and Irm Hermann) set up another group – Anti-Theater – also in Munich.

## Sharp shooter

Thus, by the time Fassbinder began making feature films, he had not only experience, but, crucial to his methods of working, a sort of stock company of actors round him who were used to his ways, able to take his lightning changes of direction in their stride, and work as complete collaborators in the evolution of new works, whether on stage, screen or – later on – television. It was through them that Fassbinder's legendary productivity was possible: where other, more conventionally minded film-makers would labour for months to set up, cast and shoot a film, he could, and frequently did, knock one off in a matter of days.

Hence the alarming statistic that once Fassbinder had embarked on a career in films, he made in the first two years (1969–70) no fewer than *ten* features. Most of them had a wild, improvisatory quality which Fassbinder never wholly shook off, and indeed, when he tried to, he seemed to be in danger of

*Top: favourite casting in his own films,*
*Fassbinder as Eugen in* Fear Eats the Soul.
*Far left: Katrin Schaake and Ron Randell in the*
*decadent melodrama* Whity. *Left: Wolfgang*
*Schenck as Baron von Instetten and Hanna*
*Schygulla as his young wife* Effi Briest

falling into the opposite trap of mandarin pretentiousness. The products of this period inclined towards Godard as the primary influence, both in their rough-and-ready shooting style and in their general commitment to a critique of bourgeois society.

A typical early Fassbinder film in these respects would be *Warum läuft Herr R. amok?* (1970, *Why Does Herr R. Run Amok?*), written and directed with Michael Fengler, in which an apparently happily married technical designer with a child, a lovely home and all the comforts of established middle-class life suddenly, for no stated reason, kills his wife, his son and a neighbour, then calmly goes to the office the next morning and there kills himself. What might have begun as a Marxist critique slips over into a refusal to comment that might be interpreted as Absurdist, anarchic or merely cool . . . according to taste.

## Transatlantic meditations

Fassbinder's own cinematic passions have embraced many other things besides recent political cinema. He had a passion for the Western and for overheated Hollywood melodrama, particularly when directed by Douglas Sirk. He had also been known to approve of Rossellini's brand of neo-realism. Thus it should have come as no surprise to find him, amidst his tributes to Godard, suddenly veering towards Samuel Fuller in *Der amerikanische Soldat* (1970, *The American Soldier*). In the more than usually bizarre *Whity* (1971) he is to be found pastiching a whole range of American Westerns and steamy tales of the Old South, with the mulatto hero darkly brooding on vengeance against the white master-race, represented here by a bunch of sadists and dribbling half-wits.

In 1971 Fassbinder began on the series of films which were to make him an important international figure. These were interspersed from 1972 with films and series intended wholly or partly for television, some of which – *Acht Stunden sind kein Tag* (1972–73, Eight Hours Don't Make a Day) and *Berlin Alexanderplatz* (1980) – are very extensive. The first of the theatrical movies was *Der Händler der vier Jahreszeiten* (1972, *The Merchant of Four*

*Seasons*), chronicling the economic rise and personal decline of a greengrocer in a sober style illuminated from time to time with flashes of bravura melodrama.

The second, *Die bitteren Tränen der Petra von Kant* (1972, *The Bitter Tears of Petra von Kant*), is a very literal but at the same time wholly cinematic transposition of a play by Fassbinder, who had continued throughout to work extensively in the theatre as well. It is the story of a spoilt fashion designer who has a brief lesbian affair, and in the course of a series of highly-charged meetings with her mother, her daughter, her best friend and most of the important people in her life, is finally deserted by them all and left alone.

The next to appear was *Angst essen Seele auf* (1974, *Fear Eats the Soul*) – an unexpectedly cheering view of a marriage between an elderly, widowed German char and a Moroccan immigrant worker younger than herself. For once, Fassbinder had told the subject in a minutely realistic manner which made it readily approachable by general audiences. With hindsight one may see that in the fourth, *Fontane Effi Briest* (1974, *Effi Briest*), a conspicuously well-upholstered adaptation of Theodor Fontane's famous turn-of-the-century novel about a dissatisfied wife and a fatal liaison, Fassbinder was already moving over, through a concern for surface polish and 'style', towards affectation and stuffiness.

## Gloss or floss?

Finally, however, in *Faustrecht der Freiheit* (1975, *Fox*), the relatively sensational – or at any rate unfamiliar – subject-matter (homosexuality) helped to obscure this tendency for the moment. Though married briefly to the actress Ingrid Caven, Fassbinder had never sought to disguise his own homosexuality, and, in his episode of *Deutschland im Herbst* (1978, *Germany in Autumn*), he offered a scarifying picture of his own home life with a lover who later killed himself. In *Fox* he plays a rough, homosexual fairground-worker who wins a lottery, is taken up by supposedly grand homosexuals and then eventually cast aside by his elegant businessman-lover once his money has run out. The picture the film presents of a

*Top left: in* The Bitter Tears of Petra von Kant *self-pitying heroine (Margit Carstensen) is deserted by her lesbian lover and in isolation sinks into a serious breakdown. Top: Fassbinder himself stars as Fox, the naive homosexual doomed to lose his lover after being exploited and humiliated. Above: 'I don't throw bombs, I make films,' claims Fassbinder on the poster for* The Third Generation (1979), *a six-part comparison of the origins and forerunners of the new strain of German terrorists*

certain stratum of German society is quite appalling, though Fassbinder stoutly denied that the story was necessarily homosexual in its context. However its significance is read, it was seen as a gay movie by millions who had never seen such a thing before, and finally made Fassbinder a name outside the limited art-house circuit.

Its success seems to have had a slightly disorienting effect on Fassbinder, or perhaps

merely confirmed him in a direction he was already going. *Mutter Küsters Fahrt zum Himmel* (1975, *Mother Kuster's Trip to Heaven*) resumed the theme of *Fox* – the betrayal of the proletariat by the bourgeoisie – in another form, with the ruthless exploitation of a working-class heroine by perfidious middle-class politicos. But *Chinesisches Roulette* (1976, *Chinese Roulette*), *Satansbraten* (1976, *Satan's Brew*) and particularly *Despair* (1978), pursued an extravagant aestheticism to the exclusion of much else: *Chinese Roulette*, a melodramatic family tragedy exploring emotional sterility among the promiscuous rich, is at least foolish but fun. But *Despair*, though enlivened by a fine study in suppressed hysteria by Dirk Bogarde as a chocolate manufacturer slowly going mad, suffers from Fassbinder's relative insecurity directing in English. Neither is this helped by an excess of gloss applied to a film already overloaded with a subject from a Nabokov novel and an elaborately over-literate script by Tom Stoppard.

*In einem Jahr mit 13 Monden* (1978, *In the Year of Thirteen Moons*) managed the remarkable feat of making its weird subject – the last agonized days of a transsexual who cannot co-exist with either his/her male lover or ex-wife and teenage daughter – quite stodgy and dull.

*Die Ehe der Maria Braun* (1979, *The Marriage of Maria Braun*) whipped through thirty years of German history wrapped round the vaguely symbolic figure of a separated wife who uses sex to become a business tycoon, all for love of her absent husband. In *Lili Marleen* (1981) Hanna Schygulla sings the song about eighteen times for an ambiguous trip down memory lane in the good old bad old days. *Lola* (1981) combines elements from both films in the person of a cabaret singer who highlights provincial corruption in vamping a civic official and ends up owning the town brothel. *Die Sehnsucht der Veronika Voss* (1982, *Veronika Voss*) concerns a faded film star addicted to drugs and death. After these studies of women, Fassbinder returned to homosexual themes in *Querelle* (1982), adapted from a Jean Genet novel, with a sailor as the vamp. He died in 1982 from a mixture of drink and drugs.

JOHN RUSSELL TAYLOR

*Top left: in* Lili Marleen *Hanna Schygulla plays the singer. Top: bizarre adventures of a sham writer (Kurt Raab) in* Satan's Brew. *Above: in* The Marriage of Maria Braun *a wife (Hanna Schygulla) uses her beauty and brains to provide luxury for her husband's release after serving a sentence for a murder she had committed*

**Filmography** (including TV films)

**1965** Der Stadtstreicher (short) (+sc; +act). **'66** Das kleine Chaos (short) (+sc; +act). **'67** Tony Freunde (actor only). **'68** Der Bräutigam, die Komödiantin und der Zuhalter (actor only) (USA/GB: The Bridegroom, the Comedienne and the Pimp). **'69** Fernes Jamaica (short) (actor only); Liebe ist kälter als der Tod (+sc; +ed; +co-des; +act) (GB: Love Is Colder Than Death); Alarm (actor only); Katzelmacher (+sc; +ed; +des; +act); Al Capone im deutschen Wald (actor only). **'70** Baal (actor only); Götter der Pest (+sc; +ed; +act) (USA/GB: Gods of the Plague); Das Kaffeehaus (video) (+sc); Warum läuft der Herr R. amok? (co-dir; +co-sc; +co-ed) (USA/GB: Why Does Herr R. Run Amok?); Frei bis zum nächsten Mal (actor only); Die Niklashauser Fahrt (co-dir; +co-sc; +co-ed; +act); Der amerikanische Soldat (+sc; +co-des; +lyr; +act) (USA/GB: The American Soldier). **'71** Rio das Mortes (+co-sc); Pioniere in Ingoldstadt (+sc); Mathias Kneissl (actor only); Whity (+co-sc; +co-ed; +act); Der plötzliche Reichtum der armen Leute von Kombach (actor only) (GB: The Sudden Fortune of the Poor People of Kombach); Warnung vor einer heiligen Nutte (+sc; +co-ed; +act) (GER-IT) (USA/GB: Beware of a Holy Whore). **'72** Der Händler der vier Jahreszeiten (+sc; +act) (USA/GB: The Merchant of Four Seasons); Die bitteren Tränen der Petra von Kant (+sc from his own play; +des) (USA/GB: The Bitter Tears of Petra von Kant); Acht Stunden sind kein Tag (5 parts) (+sc); Wildwechsel (+sc) (USA: Jail Bait; GB: Wild Game); Bremer Freiheit (video) (co-dir; +sc; +act). **'73** Super-Girl (actor only); Zärtlichkeit der Wölfe (prod; +act. only) (GB: Tenderness of the Wolves); Welt am Draht (2 parts) (+co-sc). **'74** Nora Helmer (video) (+sc); Angst essen Seele auf (+sc; +des; +act) (USA: Ali: Fear Eats the Soul; GB: Fear Eats the Soul); Martha (+sc); Fontane Effi Briest (+sc; +narrator) (USA/GB: Effi Briest); 1 Berlin-Harlem (actor only). **'75** Wie ein Vogel auf dem Draht (video) (+co-sc); Faustrecht der Freiheit (+co-sc; +act) (USA/GB: Fox/Fox and His Friends); Mutter Küsters Fahrt zum Himmel (+co-sc) (USA: Mother Kusters Goes to Heaven; GB: Mother Kuster's Trip to Heaven); Angst vor der Angst (+co-sc). **'76** Schatten der Engel (co-sc from his own play; +act. only) (SWIT-GER); Ich will doch nur, dass ihr mich liebt (+sc); Satansbraten (+sc) (USA/GB: Satan's Brew); Chinesisches Roulette (+sc) (GER-FR) (USA/GB: Chinese Roulette). **'77** Bolwieser (2 parts) (+sc); Frauen in New York. **'78** Deutschland im Herbst (ep only) (+sc; +act) (USA/GB: Germany in Autumn); Despair/Eine Reise in Lichts (GER-FR); In einem Jahr mit 13 Monden (+sc; +photo; +ed) (USA: In a Year of 13 Moons; GB: In the Year of Thirteen Moons). **'79** Bourbon Street Blues (short) (actor only); Die Ehe der Maria Braun (+co-sc; +act) (USA/GB: The Marriage of Maria Braun); Die dritte Generation (+sc; +photo) (USA/GB: The Third Generation). **'80** Berlin Alexanderplatz (13 parts) (+sc) (GER-IT). **'81** Lili Marleen (+co-sc; +act); Lola (+co-sc). **'82** Die Sehnsucht der Veronika Voss (+co-sc; +act) (GB: Veronika Voss); Querelle (+co-sc) (GER-FR); Theater in Trance (doc) (+comm); Der Bauer von Babylon (doc) (appearance as himself only) (GB: The Wizard of Babylon)

# FEAR EATS THE SOUL 'AA'

### A FILM BY RAINER WERNER FASSBINDER

WITH BRIGITTE MIRA AND EL HEDI BEN SALEM

INTERNATIONAL CRITICS AWARD, CANNES FESTIVAL

GERMAN DIALOGUE – ENGLISH SUBTITLES

COLOUR    RELEASED BY CINEGATE LTD.

" ... the most consistently entertaining as well as the best film currently to be seen ..." *THE TIMES*

" ... an engrossing film ..." *SUNDAY TELEGRAPH*

" ... a genuinely potent parable." *THE GUARDIAN*

" ... a moving and beautifully judged work." *FINANCIAL TIMES*

" ... very provocative ... wonderfully well acted in all parts." *DAILY TELEGRAPH*

---

**Directed by Rainer Werner Fassbinder, 1974**
**Prod co:** Tango Film. **sc:** Rainer Werner Fassbinder. **photo:** Jürgen Jürges. **ed:** Thea Eymès. **prod des:** Rainer Werner Fassbinder. **mus:** archive selections. **sd:** Fritz Müller Scherz. **ass dir:** Rainer Langhans. **prod man:** Christian Hohoff. **r/t:** 92 minutes. German title: *Angst essen Seele auf.* Released in USA/GB as: *Fear Eats the Soul.*
**Cast:** Brigitte Mira (*Emmi Kurowski*), El Hedi Ben Salem (*Ali*), Barbara Valentin (*Barbara*), Irm Hermann (*Krista*), Rainer Werner Fassbinder (*Eugen*), Karl Scheydt (*Albert*), Elma Karlowe (*Mrs Kargus*), Anita Bucher (*Mrs Ellis*), Gusti Kreissl (*Paula*), Walter Sedlmayer (*grocer*), Doris Mattes (*grocer's wife*), Elisabeth Bertram (*Frieda*), Liselotte Eder (*Mrs Münchmeyer*), Marquard Bohm (*Gruber*), Hannes Gromball (*restaurant waiter*), Katharina Herberg (*girl in the bar*), Rudolf Waldemar Brem (*bar patron*), Peter Moland (*chief garage mechanic*), Margit Symo (*Hedwig*), Peter Gauhe (*Bruno*), Helga Ballhaus (*Yolanda*).

*Fear Eats the Soul*, winner of the Critics' Prize at the Cannes Film Festival in 1974, was the first of Rainer Werner Fassbinder's films to gain international acclaim. It emphasizes a theme that Fassbinder often investigated – the callousness and hypocrisy of post-war urban society in Germany. It is the Moroccan immigrant who speaks the words of the German title – *Angst essen Seele auf* – whose ungrammatic form is lost in the English translation. When Emmi automatically corrects Ali ('Angst *isst* Seelen auf') she is instantly fearful lest pulling him up in this way might be interpreted as superiority – and she asks him if it is a Moroccan expression. He, not understanding her, replies that all Moroccans speak like that.

Fassbinder laces what could have been a sentimental love story of an odd couple with a sharp irony which he locates not only in the behaviour of Emmi's dangerously hostile circle of aquaintances, but even in the minutely observed decor. When Emmi invites her family to meet Ali, one of her sons puts his foot through the prominently placed television set –

clearly an indication of what he would like to do to Ali if only he dared. And when they go to a restaurant, the couple sit there as if pilloried, encircled by empty chairs, with the waiter gazing at them from a distance as if they were freaks in a side-show.

Perhaps the most searing irony of all resides in the fact that it is Emmi's pride in Ali and society's eventual, simulated acceptance of their liaison that causes the rift in their marriage: she cannot resist parading him like some rare pet, completely unaware that she is administering an obscure but deadly wound to his male pride. When he leaves her to return to the sleazy bar with his work companions and the cheap whores, he is at least returning to a world whose pitfalls and treacheries he understands; transplanted into the devious *petit bourgeois* society of Emmi's relatives, he is completely at a loss.

Basically, Fassbinder's film concerns two lonely people who can provide each other with all that they require as long as they do not expose themselves to the society around them. The resentment they encounter is not unmixed with

covert jealousy on the part of Emmi's female friends – for Ali, though seemingly unaware of the fact, is a strikingly sexual creature (a fact that Fassbinder underlines by presenting him naked on two occasions) – and with primal animosity on the part of the men.

It is on Emmi and Ali's return from their holiday that Fassbinder makes his most spleenful comments on middle-class society and its values. The simple, good-natured Emmi has proved herself too willing to act as a baby-sitter or general handy-woman; her social indiscretion in taking an Arab lover can be overlooked when weighed against her value as an unpaid help. There is additional irony in the fact that Emmi herself was formerly a member of the Nazi party and that, despite her own experience with Ali, she allows herself to be enlisted by her fellow chars in the persecution of a young Yugoslav worker. But lethal though Fassbinder's depiction of the entrenched racial prejudices of the German middle-class may be, his condemnation of it is never shrill, his compassion for the victims never mawkish.

The camerawork supports this cool, almost formal presentation of facts, enabling the director to involve the audience in his characters' plight, but at the same time making it acutely, constantly aware of the tawdry world it lives in. The role of the elderly charwoman was played to perfection by Brigitte Mira and the Moroccan by El Hedi Ben Salem, a Berber (and a non-professional actor) who, it was claimed, had already experienced a similar situation in real life.

Fassbinder found the original inspiration for his film in *All That Heaven Allows* (1955). In this Hollywood melodrama directed by

Emmi, a good-natured 60-year-old charwoman living in Munich, takes refuge in a bar frequented by Moroccan immigrant workers and whores. She encounters Ali, one of the Moroccans, who invites her to dance (1). His compatriots and Barbara – the virulent, sexy barmaid – poke fun at him but, nevertheless, Ali offers to walk Emmi home. She invites him into her flat (2) and they spend the night together.

Accustomed to the German hostility towards Moroccan immigrants, Ali finds himself more and more drawn to the friendly charwoman and they eventually marry (3) – celebrating afterwards at a posh Italian restaurant (4) where Hitler used to eat. Their marriage provokes the disgust of Emmi's three grown-up sons, the eldest of whom shows his anger by kicking in the TV (5), the local tradesmen (6) and her fellow chars, who ostracize her. To escape the pressure around them, Emmi and Ali take a holiday abroad. When they return, they find the situation changed: Emmi's services have been missed, whether as baby-sitter or as a good customer, and her union with Ali finds a hypocritical social acceptance. But Emmi cannot resist displaying her exotic, much younger husband to her friends (7) and – his masculine pride wounded – he leaves her and takes up with the barmaid (8).

When Emmi visits Ali at his work (9) to plead with him to come back to her, he refuses. One night she returns to the bar and they are reconciled – but Ali collapses on the dance floor. In the hospital, Emmi learns that he is suffering from the chronic stress to which the immigrant workers are prone and that there is little hope of permanent cure. Emmi resolves otherwise (10).

Douglas Sirk, a film-maker held in high regard by Fassbinder, a bourgeois woman (Jane Wyman) commits the social indiscretion of falling in love with her gardener (Rock Hudson), thus incurring the deepest resentment of her family and friends. In Sirk's film a television set also serves as a key prop – an offering by her children as a replacement for her low-born lover Fassbinder's original intention was to have Ali kill Emmi and be hunted by the police, but he discarded this in favour of a hospital scene similar to the ending of *All That Heaven Allows*.

Fassbinder's film finds an even closer thematic link with an earlier work of his own, *Katzelmacher* (1969), the title of which is Bavarian slang for an immigrant worker who is considered a menace because of his suspected unnaturally high sexual potency. The roots of fascist and racist prejudices are located in sexual jealousy – an aspect of intolerance that is certainly evoked, among others, to even more subtle effect in *Fear Eats the Soul*.

DEREK PROUSE

1

2

3

4

5

6

7

8

9

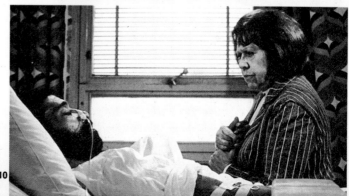

10

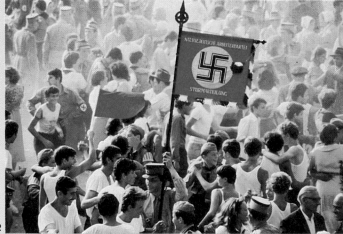

1

2

The Tin Drum is probably the best-known novel in post-war German literature and the one that elevated its author, Günter Grass, to international fame. But Grass's reputation was established in the Sixties when there was hardly any German cinema to speak of. As the 'New German Cinema' began to emerge in the Seventies, Grass received numerous offers to adapt The Tin Drum for the screen; however, it was not until he was approached by the director Volker Schlöndorff and the producer Anatole Dauman that he felt satisfied enough to accept.

Volker Schlöndorff had been involved from the start with the movement towards a new German cinema, and among his early films Der Junge Törless (1966, Young Törless) testified to his understanding of the pre-Nazi period of German history. Furthermore, his historical drama Der plötzliche Reichtum der armen Leute von Kombach (1971, The Sudden Fortune of the Poor People of Kombach) showed the kind of insight into a peasant community that was to stand him in good stead for The Tin Drum.

Grass himself collaborated on the adaptation of his novel for the screen, but many new ideas emanated from Jean-Claude Carrière, a regular screenwriter for the director Luis Buñuel, who brought his own surrealistic perspective to the story. The central theme of both novel and film is the decision of the boy Oskar not to grow up – his refusal to accept 'adult' society in all its bizarre behaviour. And Schlöndorff frequently offers the audience Oskar's viewpoint (for instance much of the film is shot from knee-level), thus translating the world of 'grown-ups' into a bizarre pantomime of sexual and political exploitation that sometimes reaches grotesque proportions. He succeeds in creating an image of the world which is peopled by grotesque marionettes with overblown ambitions and inflated desires. In the same way, the touring circus act which Oskar joins during World War II offers a commentary on wartime events that is all the more telling for being 'distorted' or parodied by dwarfs.

In this context, the style of the film emerges as more mythological

OSCAR AWARD
WINNER
BEST FOREIGN
LANGUAGE FILM

the Tin Drum
X

Produced by FRANZ SEITZ, VOLKER SCHLONDORFF and ANATOLE DAUMAN
Directed by VOLKER SCHLONDORFF Based on "THE TIN DRUM" by GUNTER GRASS
Screenplay by JEAN-CLAUDE CARRIERE, VOLKER SCHLONDORFF
and FRANZ SEITZ in collaboration with GUNTER GRASS
© 1979 Franz Seitz Film-Bioskop Film-Artemis Film-Argos Films
(German Dialogue with English Subtitles)

than the easy blend of nostalgia and naturalism normally associated with films about this period. When Oskar disrupts a Nazi rally by beating his drum, the scene also functions on the level of fantasy. Similarly the compelling opening sequence in which the fugitive soldier hides beneath the woman's skirts conveys both the 'legend' of Oskar's parentage and the earthy realism appropriate to the location and period. Yet although The Tin Drum may look as if it is structured solely around a number of striking and potent images – most memorably the horse's head that is pulled out of the sea, crawling with live eels – it is nonetheless an impressively coherent narrative, especially considering the daunting task of adapting a book of just under six hundred pages.

As for the performances, there can be no doubt that David Bennent's portrayal of Oskar is unique. Schlöndorff knew that the part could not be played by a dwarf if audiences were to achieve the vital sense of empathy and hostility towards the character. Moreover Grass was insistent that Oskar should not be seen as a dwarf but simply as a child who had ceased to grow. A child actor was the only solution and when Schlöndorff discovered that the actor Heinz Bennent, (with whom he had worked before) had a son of 12 whose facial features were years in advance of the rest of his body, the casting problem was solved. Ironically the arrested development that David Bennent genuinely suffers from rendered it impossible for him to play Oskar as a mature adult in

post-war Germany and Schlöndorff had to abandon his original plan of following the novel right through to its conclusion.

Apparently very satisfied with the film's successful transition from book to screen, Günter Grass has gone on to enjoy a revival in popularity, assisted by the fact that the film won the Best Foreign Film Oscar for 1979. The re-creation of Grass's native city of Danzig (now Gdansk) is a fine testament to Igor Luther's photography (making effective use of strong autumnal light in his exteriors) and to the art direction of Bernd Lepel. Visually the film is breathtaking and the occasional appearance of present-day features in the landscapes only serves to underline the contemporary relevance of the film's message.    MARTYN AUTY

3

4

5

6

7

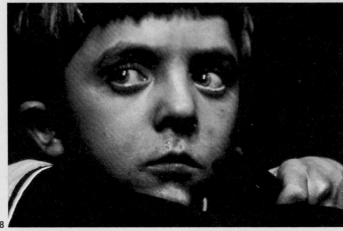

8

**Directed by Volker Schlöndorff, 1979.**
**Prod co:** Franz Seitz Film/Bioskop-Film/GGB 14 KG/Hallelujah-Film/Artemis Film/Argos Film/in association with Jadran Film and Film Polski. **exec prod:** Anatole Dauman. **prod:** Franz Seitz. **sc:** Jean-Claude Carrière, Franz Seitz, Volker Schlöndorff, from the novel by Günter Grass. **photo** (Eastman Colour): Igor Luther. **ed:** Suzanne Baron. **prod des:** Nicos Perakis. **art dir:** Bernd Lepel. **mus:** Maurice Jarre. **ass dir:** Branco Lustig. Alexander von Richthofen, Wolfgang Kroke, Andrzej Reiter, Richard Malbequi. **r/t:** 142 minutes. German title: *Die Blechtrommel*. Released in USA and GB as *The Tin Drum*.
**Cast:** David Bennent (*Oskar*), Mario Adorf (*Alfred Matzerath*), Angela Winkler (*Agnes Matzerath*), Daniel Olbrychski (*Jan Bronski*), Katharina Thalbach (*Maria Matzerath*), Heinz Bennent (*Greff*), Andréa Ferreol (*Lina Greff*), Fritz Hakl (*Bebra*), Mariella Oliveri (*Roswitha Raguna*), Tina Engel (*Anna Koljaiczek as a young woman*), Berta Drews (*Anna Koljaiczek as an old woman*), Roland Teubner (*Joseph Koljaiczek*), Tadeusz Kunikowski (*Uncle Vinzenz*), Ernst Jacobi (*Gauleiter Lobsack*), Werner Rehm (*Scheffler, the baker*), Ilse Pagé (*Gretchen Scheffler*), Kate Jaenicke (*Mather Truczinski*), Helmuth Brasch (*Heilandt*), Wigand Witting (*Herbert Yruczinski*).

At the turn of the century in Poland, a peasant shelters a fugitive beneath her skirts and later gives birth to Agnes. After World War I, Agnes marries a Danzig grocer, Alfred Matzerath, but maintains her affair with her cousin Jan who may be the father of her son, Oskar.

At the age of three, Oskar resolves to stop growing. He becomes very attached to his toy drum (1), letting out a high-pitched scream capable of shattering glass if anyone tries to remove it.

In the city of Danzig, political upheaval is followed by the rise of the Fascist brownshirts (2). At a family outing (3) Alfred buys some eels that have been caught using a dead horse's head for bait, and later forces Agnes to eat them.

Agnes, pregnant by Alfred or Jan, loses the will to live and dies shortly afterwards. Oskar crawls for comfort beneath his grandmother's skirts (4). Alfred takes a young girl, Maria, to be his housekeeper and mistress, and then marries her (5).

Oskar leads Jan into the Polish post office which is under fire from the Germans (6). Jan is captured and executed. Through his friendship with midget somnambulist, Roswitha (7), Oskar joins a circus which tours Europe performing for the Nazi top brass.

After the liberation, Oskar returns to Danzig where Alfred is shot as a collaborator. He resolves (8) to start growing again.

# A face to conjure with

# Klaus Kinski

Although his film career began in the Forties, Klaus Kinski has only recently become a recognized name – a name that as often as not stands for all that is dangerous and decadent

*Above: exercising his taste buds – Nosferatu, the Vampyre and his victim (Isabelle Adjani). Above right: Kinski as the pharmaceutical manufacturer searching for the solution to eternal life in Lifespan (1975). Right: as a Jew escaping from Sweden with the help of a supposed Nazi (William Holden) in The Counterfeit Traitor (1962). Centre right: as Aguirre, Wrath of God. Far right: as a man caught up in a web of intrigue and death in the Bond lookalike La Peau de Torpedo (1970, Children of Mata Hari)*

## Filmography
**1948** Morituri (GER). **'55** Ludwig II (GER); Kinder, Mütter und ein General (GER); Hanussen (GER); Um Throm und Liebe/Sarajevo (AUS). **'56** Waldwinter (GER). **'57** Geliebte Corinna (GER). **'58** A Time to Love and a Time to Die (USA). **'60** Der Rächer (GER). **'61** Die Toten Augen von London (GER) (USA: Dead Eyes of London); Bankraub in der Rue Latour (GER); Die Seltsame Gräfin (GER). **'62** The Counterfeit Traitor (USA); Das Rätsel der Roten Orchidee (GER); The Devil's Daffodil/Das Geheimnis der Gelben Narzissen (GB-GER); Der Rote Rausch (GER); Die Tür mit den Sieben Schlössern (GER-FR); Das Gasthaus an der Themse (GER). **'63** Der Schwarze Abt (GER); Der Zinker (GER); Der Schwarze Kobra (GER); Das Indische Tuch (GER); Scotland Yard Jagt Dr Mabuse (GER); Das Geheimnis der Schwarzen Witwe (GER-SP); Piccadilly Null Uhr Zwolf (GER). **'64** Kali-Yug, la Dea della Vendetta (IT-GER-FR); Il Misterio del Tempio Indiano/Kali-Yug II (IT-GER-FR) (amalgamation of Kali-Yug, la Dea della Vendetta and Il Misterio del Tempio Indiano; released in GB as: Kali-Yug, Goddess of Vengeance); Die Gruft mit dem Rätselschloss (GER); Der Letzte Ritt nach Santa Cruz (AUS-GER); Wartezimmer zum Jenseits (GER); Winnetou II (GER-FR-IT-YUG) (USA/GB: Last of the Renegades); Das Geheimnis der Chinesischen Nelke (GER). **'65** Traitor's Gate (GB-GER); The Pleasure Girls (GB); Neues vom Hexer (GER); Estambul 65/L'Homme d'Istanbul (SP-FR-IT) (USA/GB: That Man in Istanbul); Doctor Zhivago (USA). **'66** Per Qualche Dollaro in Più (IT-SP-GER) (USA/GB: For a Few Dollars More); Our Man in Marrakesh (GB) (USA: Bang! Bang! You're Dead); Gern Hab' Ich die Frauen Gekillt (AUS-IT-FR). **'67** Das Geheimnis der Gelben Mönche (AUS-IT) (GB: Target for Killing); Quien Sabe? (IT) (USA/GB: A Bullet for the General); Die Blaue Hand (GER); Sumuru (GB) (USA: The Million Eyes of Su-Muru); Circus of Fear (GB) (USA: Psycho Circus); Jules Verne's Rocket to the Moon (GB) (USA: Those Fantastic Flying Fools); Ad Ogni Costo (IT-SP-GER) (USA/GB: Grand Slam); Five Golden Dragons (GB). **'68** L'Uomo, l'Orgoglio, la Vendetta (IT-GER); Coplan Sauve Sa Peau (FR-IT) (GB: Devil's Garden); Ognuno per sè (IT-GER) (USA: The Ruthless Four); Due Volte Giuda (IT); I Bastardi (IT-FR-GER) (GB: Sons of Satan); Sigpress contro Scotland Yard/Mister Zehn Prozent – Miezen und Moneten (IT-GER); Il Grande Silenzio (IT-FR). **'69** Sartana (IT-GER); Cinque per l'Inferno (IT) (GB: Five for Hell);

In the Seventies Klaus Kinski's startli... became known through the films of ... Herzog. But just as Herzog is the least ... tional of the new German directors, ... has to be understood as a loner, a ... pirate and an extremist. A glance ... confirms all this. Its intensity speaks ... ation and the ordeal of survival; its ... comes from a life so threatened that ego ... and will have carried it close to madness. ... is a beautiful face too, especially intrig... because of the way it slips from cruel... gentleness, from conquistador to visiona... is among the great faces of modern cin... and yet Klaus Kinski is in his fifties. Where... he before Herzog thought to put a helmet... the one face that might justify the sub-title ... *Aguirre, der Zorn Gottes* (1973, *Aguirre, Wrath ... God*)?

## Nurtured on nightmare

Born Nikolas Nakszynski in Poland in ... is difficult to describe his early life ac... Kinski himself disparages, forgets a... facts, and in his autobiography, *Crever ... Vivre*, he prefers to present himself as ... helpless but enthralled victim in a phantas... goria. His father — a failed opera singer — ... driven to stealing, and as the son of a br... impoverished family, Kinski became a... vagrant, impossible to teach, tame or re... He was forced into the German army at t... of sixteen, and eventually taken priso... the British. Both at the front and in p... camps he sometimes feigned insanity w... witnessing horrors and disasters that might ...

...old Kins... ...have the face of a child, but your ... ...on is brutal at the same time. It ...

...er the y... ...ed down ...olini and Visconti in favour of ...lood-curdling horrors that emerged from the depths of European co-production.

## Sons of Satan

Then came the chance to work with Herzog. The two men fought and argued, but they were fellow-extremists who understood and stimulated one another. *Aguirre, Wrath of God* required a special kind of strutting stardom; without Kinski, the film might have slipped into implausibility. And who else could have put over the warped, sexual sensitivity in *Nosferatu: Phantom der Nacht* (*Nosferatu, the Vampyre*), or felt the nightmare of the victimized soldier in *Woyzeck* (both 1979)? In three films, director and actor substantially extended the cinema's sense of compulsive personality.

At last Kinski was noticed in America, and in the late Seventies he went to Hollywood. Too late to be a great star – even if he could tolerate all the compromises necessary, or be polite long enough – he is not too old to make a name for himself as a great movie actor. But he is not too proud or settled to give up the wandering life, and he could as easily revert to trash.

DAVID THOMSON

Marquis de Sade: Justine/Justine, ovvero le Disavventure della Virtù (GER-FT) (GB: Justine and Juliet); A Qualsiasi Prezzo (IT-GER); A Doppia Faccia/Double Face/Das Gesicht in Dunkeln (IT-GER); Il Dito nella Piaga (IT); Paroxismus (IT-GER-GB) (USA: Venus in Furs); La Legge dei Gangsters (IT). '70 . . . E Dio Dissi a Caino (IT) (GB: And God Said to Cain); La Peau de Torpedo (FR-IT-GER) (USA: Children of Mata Hari; GB: Pill of Death); Sono Sartana, il Vostro Becchino (IT) (GB: I'll Dig Your Grave); Appuntamento col Disonore (IT-YUG); Mir Hat es Immer Spass Gemacht (IT-GER); La Belva (IT); Wie Kommtein so Reizendes Mädchen Zu Diesem Gewerbe?/How Did a Nice Girl Like You Get Into a Business Like This? (GER). '71 Per una Bara Piena di Dollari (IT); El Conde Dracula (SP-GER-IT) (USA: Count Dracula; GB: Bram Stoker's Count Dracula); I Leopardi di Churchill (IT-SP) (GB: Commando Attack); Prega il Morto e Ammazza il Vivo (IT); Nella Stretta Morsa del Ragno/Les Fantômes de Hurlevent/Dracula in Schloss des Schreckens (IT-FR-GER); Il Venditore di Morte (IT); La Bestia Uccide a Sangue Freddo/Das Scholss der Blauen Vogel (IT-GER) (GB: Blooded Beast); Black Killer (IT). '72 La Vendetta è un Piatto che si Serve Freddo (IT). '73 Lo Chiamavano King (IT-SP); Aguirre, der Zorn Gottes (GER) (USA/GB: Aguirre, Wrath of God); L'Occhio del Ragno (IT-AUS). '74 Il Mio Nome è Shanghay Joe (IT) (USA: Shanghai Joe; GB: To Kill or Die); La Mano Spietata della Legge (IT) (GB: The Bloody Hands of the Law); La Morte ha Sorriso all'Assassino (IT); L'Important C'Est d'Aimer (FR-IT-GER) (USA: That Most Important Thing: Love). '75 Le Orme (IT); Lifespan (NETH); Un Genio, Due Compari, Un Pollo/Un Genie, Deux Associés, Une Cloche/Nobody ist der Grösste (IT-FR-GER). '76 Der Netz (GER); Jack the Ripper (SWITZ); Nuit d'Or (FR). '77 Operation Thunderbolt (IS); Madame Claude (FR) (USA: The French Woman); Mort d'un Pourri (FR). '78 Zoo-Zéro (FR); La Chanson de Roland (FR-IT). '79 Nosferatu: Phantom der Nacht (GER-FR) (USA/GB: Nosferatu, the Vampyre); Woyzeck (GER). '80 Haine (FR); Schizoid (USA). '81 Love and Money (USA); Venom (GB); Buddy, Buddy (USA). '82 Fitzcarraldo (GER); Android (USA).

*Since Kinski's work in low-budget European co-productions is poorly documented, this filmography almost certainly omits a number of titles from the busiest period of his career.*

'I see the cinema as a guerilla operation. Guerilla against everything that is fixed, defined, established, dogmatic, eternal. It's not irrelevant that the cinema should be at war, because eventually everything is connected. Hollywood is Wall Street and the Pentagon. In the cinema too we must create two, three, an infinity of Vietnams, that's certain. But that doesn't mean that the cinema must *serve* the revolution: the revolution has no need of servants. Everyone has to make his own revolution . . .'

'Godard has placed himself at the *service* of the revolution. I don't want to serve . . . I think that only in fighting with the cinema, through our movies, for a freer, more authentic expression, with weapons that can include *joie de vivre* and comedy, we are waging the same war as those who fight on the barricades. It's always the same job of freeing yourself from authority, of breaking down rigid structures, of opening up doors, opening up paths; in short to create a free open world where every individual can be himself.'

With *WR – Mysteries of the Organism* the guerilla activities of Dušan Makavejev's cinema reached their peak. It was, in its spirit, a supremely international film, and a film for its moment. At the time it was made the Vietnam War was still on, the events of 1968 in West and

1

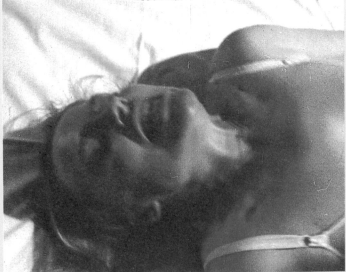

2

5

A merry tool is best!

6

Eastern Europe were still vivid in the memory and the sexual revolution was at its height. Makavejev struck out wildly, gaily, poetically, philosophically in every direction, and made firm enemies on both sides of the Iron Curtain.

Born in Belgrade in 1932, Makavejev graduated in philosophy before enrolling in the Belgrade Academy of Film, Theatre, Radio and Television. A number of short student films already demonstrated his sharply ironic viewpoint. In 1966 he made his first feature, *Čovek Nije Tica* (Man Is Not a Bird), in which his use of cinéma vérité, jokes, investigative asides already showed his belief that;

'We can use everything that comes to hand, fiction, documents, actualities, titles. "Style" is not important. You must use surprise as a psychological weapon . . .We can even use material taken from the enemy.'

The same principles were developed in *Ljubavni Slučaj ili Tragedija Službenice PTT* (1967, *Switchboard Operator*) which originated in a bold newspaper story about a girl who was thrown down a well by her lover; and *Nevinost Bez Zaštite* (1968, *Innocence Unprotected*), a reworking, with additions and commentary, of the first Serbian feature film, a bizarre but touching primitive work made during World War II by a professional

strong man, featuring himself and his stunts – the kind of oddity irresistible to Makavejev's idiosyncratic humour.

*WR – Mysteries of the Organism* is richly, bawdily, outrageously comic. It is also poetic, moral and deeply philosophical. *Joie de vivre* at the ready, Makavejev is at his barricades. But the real innovation of the film is that its intention is therapeutic rather than informative. Makavejev himself said of it that:

'We've tried to make a film which has social effects, because so many people are repressed. If the process of repression developed each day in so many situations, then it must be possible to make counter-repression. In fact comedy is a mechanism of counter-repression; truth is a weapon of counter-repression; joy, every sort of happiness and creation have an anti-repressive action. There are always creative people who make the people around them expand and provoke social changes. Why not, I thought, try to make a film which can provide a point of departure? Be such an initiation? Help a lot of people to find their own creativity?'

With its multiplicity of levels, *WR – Mysteries of the Organism* is, above all, the assertion of a free man. Politically it is unaligned, except with revolution. If it attacks the East, the West can take no

comfort from the fact, nor claim it as their own. If, however, there is a bias, an indication that Makavejev is a Marxist and a Leninist, it is in the fact that in the American scenes it is the whole capitalist system which is under attack: in the Soviet

scenes, it is the perversion and corruption of the socialist ideal for which he reserves his scorn and irony.          DAVID ROBINSON

*Quotations are taken from an article by David Robinson, published in 1971 in* Sight and Sound.

**Directed by Dušan Makavejev, 1971**

**Prod co:** Neoplanta/Telepool. **sc:** Dušan Makavejev. **photo** (Eastman Colour): Pega Popović, Aleksander Petković. **ed:** Ivanka Vukasović. **art dir:** Dragoljub Ivkov. **mus:** Bojana Makavayev. **r/t:** 86 minutes. Original title: *WR – Misterije Organizma*.

**Cast:** Milena Dravić (*Milena*), Jagoda Kaloper (*Jagoda*), Ivica Vidović (*Vladimir Ilyich*). Zoran Radmilović (*Zoran*), Miodrag Andrić (*soldier*), Tuli Kupferberg (*US soldier*), Jackie Curtis (*herself*), the ghost of J. V. Stalin.

A free essay, or a set of variations on the basic theory of the German psychologist and biologist Wilhelm Reich, that social and political oppression has direct connections with sexual frustration. An elaborate collage brings together documentary records of Reich's career and work using old news films and photographs including pictures of his arrest on technical charges (1) – he died in prison in Pennsylvania – interviews with former colleagues and examples of his theories of sexual therapy (2); various scenes from the American sexual Underground including Jackie Curtis (3), the transvestite star of Paul Morrissey's *Flesh* (1968), and the

editor of the magazine *Screw* having his private parts cast in plaster; footage from old Soviet socialist-realist films (4), deifying a white-clad heroic Stalin; a fictional story of a young Yugoslav girl (5) whose efforts to bring sexual enlightenment to a Soviet skating star (6, 7) result in her decapitation on the edge of his ice skates (8). At the end of the film her severed head continues gaily preaching, while the plastic Soviet hero sings the Underground poet Bulat Okudjava's 'Ode to François Villon' an exhortation to God to give mortals what they need: 'And God, please don't forget me!'

*Some scenes shot in black and white*

3

4

7

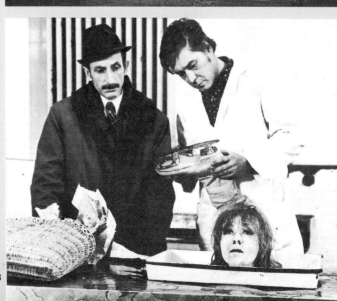

8

In *Rough Treatment* Andrzej Wajda leads his hero on an eventually fatal odyssey through the spiritual wilderness that is Poland in the late Seventies. At the time the film appeared the leading Polish filmmakers had clearly and aggressively constituted themselves as the moralists of the nation. It was striking that, more than a year before the great eruptions that began in the shipyards of Gdansk, all the sources of dissatisfaction and anger that stirred the founding of the Solidarity trade-union movement throughout Poland were already being openly discussed in film after film. A prominent critic, Jacek Fuksiewicz, very clearly laid out the themes of these new films in an article published in *Polish Perspectives* in August 1979:

'The list will include, as well as familiar and diagnosed elements, which social policy is attacking, ones which are still embryonic and only glimpsed or sensed by literature and the cinema: examples of loss of moral sensibilities and bearings, of consumer attitudes developing into acquisitiveness, self-seeking and careerism, of instrumental and manipulative treatment of people, of inability to adjust to the advances in the democratization of our life, of emergence of pseudo-élites arrogating special privileges, of hypocrisy, cynicism and opportunism. . . .'

New directors emerged with films attacking corruption, cynicism, opportunism in socialist society: Agnieszka Holland (the writer of *Rough Treatment*) with *Aktorzy Prowicjonalni* (1979, Provincial Actors); Feliks Falk with *Wodzirej* (1978, Top Dog) and *Szansa* (1979, Chance); Janusz Kijowski with *Kung-Fu* (1979). One of these new directors, Krzysztof Kieślowski won the Grand Prix at the 1979 Moscow Festival with his third feature film, *Amator* (1979, *Camera Buff*), a shrewd comic exposé of censorship.

The essential inspiration of the new directors and this new critical mood, however, was the example of the two established and acknowledged major Polish film artists, Andrzej Wajda and Krzysztof Zanussi. Wajda was President of the Association of Film Makers and artistic director of one of the main production units through which film production in Poland is organized, Unit X. Zanussi's great influence is reflected in his appearance as himself in *Amator*. More importantly, films like Wajda's *Człowiek z Marmuru* (1976, *Man of Marble*), which found uncomfortable parallels between abuses of workers in the early Fifties and more recent events, and Zanussi's *Barwy Ochronne* (1977, *Camouflage*), exposing corrupt and mendacious academic attitudes, fired the fearless first shots of the new era of social criticism through film.

As it happened, both these films encountered severe official disapproval during a period of particularly oppressive cultural policy, but Wajda, as the more senior figure, was made to feel the keener sting.

## Shown at the Cannes, New York and London Film Festivals

**Directed by Andrzej Wajda, 1978**
**Prod co:** Zespoły Filmowe Unit X. **exec prod:** Barbara Pec-Ślesicka. **sc:** Agnieszka Holland, Andrzej Wajda, Krzysztof Zaleski. **photo** (colour): Edward Kłosiński. **ed:** Halina Prugar. **art dir:** Allan Starski, Maria Lubelska-Chrolowska. **set dec:** Maria Osiecka-Kuminek, Magdalena Dipont. **mus:** Jerzy Derfl, Wojciech Mylynarski. **cost:** Wiesława Starska, Anna Włodarczyk. **sd:** Piotr Zawadzki, Malgorzata Lewandowska. **r/t:** 114 minutes. Polish title: *Bez Znieczulenia*. Released in GB as: *Rough Treatment*.
**Cast:** Zbigniew Zapasiewicz (*Jerzy Michalowski*), Ewa Dalkowska (*Eva Michalowska*), Andrzej Seweryn (*Jacek Rosciszewski*), Krystyna Janda (*Agata*), Emilia Krakowska (*Dr Wanda Jackowicz*), Roman Wilhelmi (*Bronski*), Kazimierz Kaczor (*editor-in-chief*), Iga Mayer (*Eva's mother*), Aleksandra Jasieńska (*Ola Michalowska*), Marta Salinger (*Kookie Michalowska*), Stefania Iwińska (*housekeeper*), Halina Golanka (*Eva's sister*), Jerzy Stuhr (*Eva's lawyer*), Maria Teresa Wójcik (*Jerzy's lawyer*), Danuta Balicka-Satanowicz (*judge*), Jolanta Kozak-Sutowicz (*Stenia*), Zygmunt Kestowicz (*features editor*).

To a degree, *Rough Treatment* was certainly inspired by his experiences of the subtle humiliations and deprivation of privilege that officialdom in the late Seventies had in store for those who stepped out of line – a line which still favoured the Soviet-approved 'socialist realist' principle that the artist should depict the world not as it is, but as it should be.

The bitter and brilliant screenplay was by Wajda himself in collaboration with Agnieszka Holland, who, as the daughter of a prominent Jewish politician whose life had ended with a fall from a window, had herself a keen awareness of the realities of recent political life.

Wadja was working with familiar and well-tried collaborators: the cinematographer Edward Kłosiński who had also shot *Man of Marble*; a fine actor Zbigniew Zapasiewicz, whose gallery of modern intellectuals included the cynical college teacher in Zanussi's *Camouflage*; and the actress Krystyna Janda, who played leading roles in

Wajda's preceding *Man of Marble* and subsequent *Dyrygent* (1980, *The Conductor*), although in the past Wajda had rarely used the same actress in more than one film.

In the early scenes of *Rough Treatment*, Jerzy is cocky and truculent. As his self-confidence – his whole personality indeed – is gradually stripped away, our sympathy for him grows, and the viewer begins to share his own exasperation, bewilderment and disillusionment at the possibility that in a superficially idealist and egalitarian society the scope for such individual and inhuman persecution is limitless. It is attitudes of mind – those listed in Fuksiewicz's article – that turn people into instruments of such oppressive machinery. And of all the attitudes, the most dangerous is that cynicism of which Jerzy has himself, perhaps, in his time been guilty. 'How are you going to prove what isn't true?' he asks his wife's lawyer. 'Proof', the man answers, 'is never a problem.'

DAVID ROBINSON

Jerzy Michalowski, a man in his middle forties (1), is a successful and popular journalist, specializing in international affairs. Confident of his privileged position, he talks freely in a television interview about comparisons between Poland and western European societies. His criticisms of the system do not go unnoticed. . . .

Returning to his office, he begins to sense small and then growing encroachments on his position. He no longer receives his regular *Newsweek* and other western publications. His personal jobs are usurped. His office is re-allocated to someone else. Eventually, he finds himself without work. His forthcoming series of lectures at the University is inexplicably cancelled (2).

At the same time that his professional life is being dismantled by forces he cannot precisely identify or challenge, his fifteen-year old marriage to Eva (3) breaks up, and he subsequently seeks advice from a dentist friend (4). He remains on his own, declining into alcoholism which is the subject of gossip (5). Bitterest of all, his wife's new lover (6) turns out to be an objectionable young opportunist and Party hard-liner, with whom Jerzy finds himself in professional rivalry.

At the divorce trial, his belief in justice is shattered as his wife, prompted by her advisers, assails him with false evidence. Demoralized, he finds some consolation with a beautiful but enigmatic young student (7). He is alone in his flat, however, on the day that a gas explosion of unexplained origin ends his broken life.

74

1

2

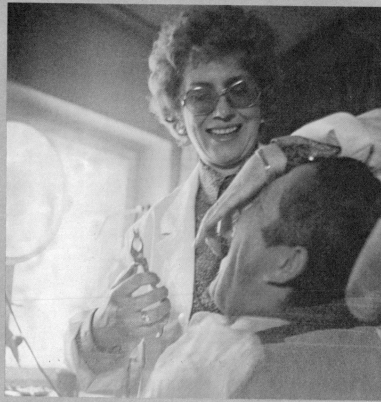

3

4

7

# Ken Loach and the price o

**Each of Ken Loach's films is a stark social comment. With fearless honesty he reveals the problems of unemployment, insanity, poverty and the class structure. But tackling such taboo subjects has meant that this high-calibre director has always had problems finding the cash for his movies**

When Ken Loach, with many dazzling television achievements and a powerful cinema film behind him, was trying to get *Kes* (1969) off the ground, he was turned down by almost all the major film companies. 'It's about a boy and a bird', his producer Tony Garnett explained to a potential backer. 'Wrong kind of bird', was the reply when it became clear that the love of the boy's life was a kestrel hawk.

Having battled away for the relatively low budget needed to make *Kes*, Loach and Garnett had to do battle all over again to get it screened. It lay on the shelf for nearly two years.

'Nobody will pay to see a film without sex or violence' was one of the reasons given. 'The dialogue won't be understood south of Sheffield' was another. But behind these specious arguments there were probably objections to the film's radical implications. 'People go to the pictures to escape their worries, not to be faced with them on the screen', is how one top-level film man put it.

## Taking flight

Only after a vigorous campaign by critics who had seen the film privately was *Kes* finally shown to the public – not, however, with the usual London premiere and nationwide release, but in a few northern cities where it was billed as a children's film. But the public response was overwhelming and *Kes* has since become internationally known as a major British film.

*Below: after her back-street abortion goes wrong Rube (Geraldine Sherman) is helped by friends Sylvie (Carol White) and Eileen (Vickery Turner) in* Up the Junction. *Right: Carol White again in* Cathy Come Home

*Far left: Loach with Grace Cave and Sandy Ratcliff – mother and disturbed daughter in* Family Life *and (above) Ratcliff and Malcolm Tierney in a scene from the film. Left: Carol White and Terence Stamp in* Poor Cow

Its success, however, did not open a magic door for its extraordinarily gifted director, who has had to fight for the simple right to make the films of his choice in his own way. Following *Kes*, Loach had to abandon a cherished project about a Durham coal-strike in the Twenties because nobody would back it. He then offered several ideas to MGM-EMI, who after much indecision gave the go-ahead for him to make *Family Life* (1971) – not because they were excited over a film about a schizophrenic girl but, Loach believes, because it featured a teenage girl.

During the Seventies he made a number of powerful and controversial television dramas, culminating in the brilliant four-part *Days of Hope* (1975), about family and political loyalties in the ten years leading up to the General Strike of 1926. It was some time, however, before he was able to start putting together his next cinema film. Another bitter and painful experience was his struggle for backing for *Black Jack* (1979), a children's adventure film about a young Yorkshire apprentice and a French highwayman. Money might have been forthcoming for a lavish production with a big-name star. But this would have operated against the film's deglamorized presentation of eighteenth-century town and country life,

and, indeed, against Loach's entire creative approach. Eventually the National Film Finance Corporation put up nearly 100 per cent of its extremely low budget.

Loach had yet more struggles to face over *The Gamekeeper* (1980) and *Looks and Smiles* (1981), the latter of which probes deeply and sadly, but with great affection, into the lives of three unemployed youngsters. The public availability of both of these highly significant films, which like *Kes* were scripted by the novelist Barry Hines, has been severely restricted by television ramifications.

## Radical realism
Ken Loach's work is a highly individual development of the long-standing tradition in British cinema for social realism, a tradition which reached a major peak in the 'New Wave' of the Fifties. By the mid-Sixties, the 'New Wave' had receded against the rising tide of Americanization, and it was television, then in one of its most fertile periods, that offered the best creative opportunities.

It was in this atmosphere that Loach (b. 1936), who had joined the BBC in 1961 after studying law at Oxford University and had had a brief career as an actor, was able to team up with Tony Garnett for a series of dynamic

television presentations about pressing social problems. Their first major breakthrough was *Up the Junction* (1965), a startling evocation of the life-style of women workers in a south London factory. A year later, *Cathy Come Home* rocked the nation with its agonizing account of the gradual disintegration of a young working-class couple made homeless through no fault of their own.

With a fusion of documentary and drama-fiction techniques, Loach achieved an urgent, on-the-spot style of presentation which looked and felt like real life. This gave rise to accusations from some quarters that he was deceiving the public by blurring the line between fact and fiction. He has also been accused of indulging in 'mere' naturalism. But an analysis of his work reveals the fine artistry and deep social insight that has gone into achieving the naturalistic effect. For instance, beneath the close-to-life surface of his first cinema film, *Poor Cow* (1967), lies a carefully designed structure that emphasizes the gap between life as it is and life as it should be, as it deals with a young working-class mother rising above the grimness and deprivation of her circumstances through the memory of a short-lived, idyllic romance. *Kes*, the story of a scraggy little schoolboy who finds self-fulfilment through rearing and training a kestrel hawk, is a purer and more poetic development of a similar theme. In scene after scene – engaging, funny, exhilarating or infinitely sad – Loach shows how home, school and future prospects are totally at odds with the boy's true aspirations.

## Country life
Underlying the plea in *Family Life* for a more humane and environmental approach to the treatment of mental illness is a bitter attack on both the destructiveness of conventional family morality and on the ethics of society. *The Gamekeeper*, on the surface, is a random report of a year on a country estate. But something very complicated and highly organized is going on underneath, provoking fundamental questions about property ownership and class divisions and about male domination within the family. Much of this emerges through the contradictory and amusing

*Above: a production shot shows Billy (David Bradley) being beaten up in* Kes. *Left: Tom Matthews (Cliff Kershaw) returns from the war in* Days of Hope. *Below left: unemployed Mick (Graham Green) with his girlfriend Karen (Carolyn Nicholson) in* Looks and Smiles

personality of the gamekeeper – a menial to his aristocratic employer, a tyrant to his family and his former workmates at the steel-works nearby. But, although his behaviour can provoke laughter or criticism, audiences cannot help warming to him as they watch him struggling between the opposing class ideologies in which life has so neatly trapped him.

Ken Loach, unlike most politically motivated film-makers, puts people first. His characters are not mouthpieces, his political themes flow naturally – with only a very occasional dialogue contrivance – from the individuals he creates. His intense care and affection for people draws a response from a wide-ranging audience – bridging the gap between 'mass' and 'minority' filmgoers.

It is a sad comment on the health – and sanity – of the British film industry that it has for so long and in so many ways been erecting barriers between the public and one of its most cherished directors.           NINA HIBBIN

**Filmography**
1964 Diary of a Young Man (TV); Tap on the Shoulder (TV). '65 Three Clear Sundays (TV); The End of Arthur's Marriage (TV); Up the Junction (TV); The Coming Out Party (TV); Wear a Very Big Hat (TV). '66 Cathy Come Home (TV). '67 In Two Minds (TV); Poor Cow (+co-sc). '68 The Golden Vision (TV). '69 The Big Flame (TV); Kes (+co-sc). '71 After a Life Time (TV); Rank and File (TV); Family Life (film version of In Two Minds) (USA: Wednesday's Child). '75 Days of Hope (TV). '77 The Price of Coal (TV). '79 Black Jack (+sc). '80 The Gamekeeper (TV); Auditions (TV). '81 A Question of Leadership (TV); Looks and Smiles. '83 The Red and the Blue (TV); Questions of Leadership (4 TV docs, produced but not transmitted in 1983).

# NEWLY IN VIEW

Many smaller countries emerged from cinematic obscurity to make a new and exciting challenge for international attention in the Seventies

For a while at the beginning of the Seventies, it looked as if the cinema emerging from countries such as Switzerland, Canada and Algeria might become really competitive with the already established major cinemas of the world. It did not quite happen, for a variety of reasons, but it was certainly very exciting when it looked as if it might – when a Canadian crowd-pleaser, *The Apprenticeship of Duddy Kravitz* (1974), could win the Grand Prize at the Berlin Film Festival and an Algerian epic, *Ahdat Sanawouach El-Djamr* (1975, *Chronicle of the Years of Embers*), could take the Grand Prize at the Cannes Film Festival; when an actress from a Swiss film, Isabelle Huppert in *La Dentellière* (1977, *The Lacemaker*), could capture the British Film Academy Most Promising Newcomer of the Year Award and unknown directors from Spain, Iran, Belgium and Senegal could attract international attention and audiences.

At the beginning of the Seventies, the newly subsidized Canadian and Swiss cinemas were poised for international acclaim, the repressed Spanish cinema was about to emerge from the Franco era, the continent of Africa was waking up to the possibilities of film-making and from Belgium to Iran 'new waves' of film-makers were rolling forward. At the major international film festivals – Cannes, Berlin, Venice and London – where such developments are first noticed, it looked like the dawn of a new era as commercial distribution followed critical acclaim. The face of international cinema seemed to be changing.

By the early Eighties, the 'new waves' of the emergent cinemas of the Seventies had receded and the changes were rather less than had been hoped. Politics, economics and diminishing cinema audiences adversely affected many of these new cinemas. Some were nearly dead, like Iran's; others survived in a very different form, like Canada's.

Long a cultural dependent of the USA, Canada had no feature film-making of importance before the Sixties. The National Film Board was the basis of Canadian film culture and helped to spark off the *cinéma-vérité* movement in Canada that led to such films as *Pour la Suite du Monde* (1964, *The Moontrap*) by Michel Brault and Pierre Perrault and *Warrendale* (1967) by Allan King. The real launching for Canadian cinema came when the new Canadian Film Development Corporation began to finance feature films in 1968. First to win praise was the Quebec cinema and especially the films of Gilles Groulx, Claude Jutra, Gilles Carle, Denys Arcand and Jean-Pierre Lefebvre. These French-language film-makers had the advantage of not having to compete directly with the American cinema; to gain equal attention, the English-language film-makers had to become distinctively 'Canadian'.

Allan King developed an intimate documentary technique, having his biggest success with *A Married Couple* (1969). Robin Spry, after gaining acclaim for *Prologue* in 1969, created an acidic investigative style in such films as *One Man* (1977), about pollution, and *Drying Up the Streets* (1978), about drugs. Other film-makers utilized avant-garde techniques, the most influential being Michael Snow with *Wavelength* (1967), ⟷ (1969, also known as *Back and Forth*) and *La Région Centrale* (1971, The Central Region). David Cronenberg combined science fiction with anti-sexuality in *Stereo* (1969) and *Crimes of the Future* (1970), and then created a series of bizarre personalized horror films: *The Parasite Murders* (1975, released in Britain as *Shivers*), *Rabid* (1977), *The Brood* (1979) and *Scanners* (1981). His disturbing vision of the world has few parallels in the Canadian cinema.

The first English-language director to please both audiences and critics was Donald Shebib with *Goin' Down the Road* (1970), which had a nice, relaxed Canadian quality of its own. Unfortunately, none of his later films has had as much impact, though

*Above left: in* The Apprenticeship of Duddy Kravitz, *Duddy (Richard Dreyfuss) involves his Christian girlfriend Yvette (Micheline Lanctôt) in negotiating a land deal when the owners will not sell to a Jew; he finally gets the land but loses the girl. Above: hired gunman Jay Mallory (Donald Sutherland) is much concerned at* The Disappearance *of his estranged wife (Francine Racette) and follows her trail from Canada to England, only later discovering her connection with a murder plot*

*Between Friends* (1973) was widely shown. The greatest international success was Ted Kotcheff's screen version of Mordecai Richler's novel *The Apprenticeship of Duddy Kravitz*, a wryly comic tale of ambition in Montreal that became a box-office hit after winning the Grand Prize at Berlin. Kotcheff, who returned to Canada to make this film after a career in England, did not repeat this success in Canada but went on to Hollywood.

Many of the most successful Canadian directors, including Norman Jewison, Arthur Hiller, Sidney Furie and Daryl Duke, are not thought of as Canadian, though some returned from Hollywood when the international production era of the late Seventies provided an opportunity. The same was true of a Canadian-born star, Donald Sutherland, who came back for such 'Canadian' co-productions as *The Disappearance* and *Les Liens de Sang/ Blood Relatives* (both 1977). Even stars produced by the Canadian cinema itself, Geneviève Bujold, for example, eventually felt the necessity of moving on to Hollywood. The native Canadian industry was virtually swamped in the late Seventies by the trend to international film production, and not one genuinely Canadian English-language film was released in 1980.

The Swiss cinema that emerged in the Seventies was more impressive than its Canadian counterpart, despite a financial crunch at the end of the decade that partially crippled it. Swiss cinema hardly existed before the Sixties; its roots were in Fifties Britain – Alain Tanner and Claude Goretta were both associated with the Free Cinema movement and made the short *Nice Time* together in 1957. State finance and television money finally got the Swiss feature industry under way in the late Sixties and, as in Canada, it was the French-language film-makers who made the initial running, notably Alain Tanner with *La Salamandre* (1971, *The Salamander*), Michel Soutter with *Les Arpenteurs* (1972, The Surveyors) and Claude Goretta with *L'Invitation* (1973, *The Invitation*). All were founding members of the Group of 5 production company, which helped to make the Swiss cinema a viable international force. Tanner was interested in socio-political investigation, especially in *Le Retour d'Afrique* (1973, *Return from Africa*) and *Jonas: Qui Aura 25 Ans en l'An 2000* (1976, *Jonah Who Will Be 25 in the Year 2000*). Goretta was the explorer of human frailty, especially in his masterpiece *The Lacemaker*.

The Geneva-based French-language directors had a rather delicate Alpine-airy quality in their films, a stark contrast to the heavier work of the German-language directors who emerged from Zürich in the middle of the decade. Thomas Koerfer was the most intellectual, with such intensely Brechtian films as *Der Tod des Flohzirkusdirektors oder Ottacaro Weiss reformiert seine Firma* (1973, *The Death of the Director of the Flea Circus*), highly theatrical in style, and *Der Gehülfe* (1976, The Assistant). Daniel Schmid was more operatic and style-conscious, as he demonstrated in *La Paloma* (1974) and *Schatten der Engel* (1976, Shadows of Angels). Rolf Lyssy put Swiss society under a critical microscope in *Konfrontation* (1975, *Konfrontation: Assassination in Davos*) and *Die Schweizermacher* (1978, *The Swissmakers*).

The biggest disappointment of the Seventies was the new Spanish cinema. At the beginning of the decade, a group of young film-makers headed by Carlos Saura seemed certain to give birth to a major new cinema as Franco's hold on Spain weakened. Good films were produced and new directors did appear but the new freedom did not lead to the expected breakthrough.

Spanish cinema has a long tradition, but Luis

Buñuel was the only important director to come out of pre-World War II Spain. The modern Spanish cinema, after the disaster of the Civil War, grew up in the Fifties with Luis Berlanga's *Bienvenido, Mr Marshall* (1953, *Welcome, Mr Marshall*) and Juan Bardem's *Muerte de un Ciclista* (1955, *Death of a Cyclist*). The combination of Italian director Marco Ferreri and Spanish writer Rafael Azcona brought a Buñuelesque feeling back to Spanish cinema through grotesque films such as *El Cochecito* (1959, *The Wheelchair*). Buñuel himself returned to make *Viridiana* (1961) in Spain – it was banned as soon as it was finished. The obsessions of Carlos Saura became central to Spanish cinema in such films as *La Caza* (1966, *The Hunt*), *Peppermint Frappé* (1967), *Cría Cuervos* (1976, *Raise Ravens*) and *Deprisa, Deprisa* (1981, Quickly, Quickly).

The best Spanish film of the Seventies was Victor Erice's *El Espíritu de la Colmena* (1973, *The Spirit of the Beehive*); few other films were able to reflect the psychological state of Spain with such accuracy and effectiveness. Two of the finest talents to develop during the Seventies were José Luis Borau with *Furtivos* (1975, *Poachers*) and Jaime Camino with *Las Largas Vacaciones del 36* (1976, *The Long Holidays of 1936*). Pilar Miró's *El Crimen de Cuenca* (1980, The Cuenca Crime) depicted the Civil Guard as being less than angelic; it was totally banned in Spain and a military court ordered all copies destroyed. The death of Franco had not changed Spain as much as had been hoped.

Belgium, like Canada and Switzerland, is a country divided along linguistic lines, and this makes its already small population almost too fractional to support a native film industry. In effect, there was none until the Sixties. Top talents, such as director Jacques Feyder and writer Charles Spaak, emigrated to France; and it was left to the documentarists, notably Henri Storck, to keep Belgium's film reputation alive. Belgium's breakthrough year was 1967, when André Delvaux' *De Man Die Zijn Haar Kort Liet Knippen* (1966, *The Man Who Had His Hair Cut Short*) won the British Film Institute's Sutherland Trophy as the most original and imaginative film of the year, and Jerzy Skolimowski's *Le Départ* (1967, The Departure) won the Grand Prize at Berlin.

Harry Kümel made an outstanding debut in 1968 with the Dutch co-production *Monsieur Hawarden*, a baroque fantasy of ideas. A similar approach worked less well in such later films as *Malpertuis: Histoire d'une Maison Maudite* (1972, *Malpertuis*) and *Het Verloren Paradijs* (1977, The Lost Paradise). André Delvaux had more success with his later films, working in both French and Flemish. His finest achievement was an epitome of poetic ambiguity, *Rendez-vous à Bray* (1971, *Rendezvous at Bray*); but he has continued to excel in such films as *Belle* (1973) and *Une Femme Entre Chien et Loup* (1979, *Woman in a Twilight Garden*).

The second wave of Belgian directors emerged from the avant-garde in the early Seventies, led by the highly original Chantal Akerman, whose *Jeanne Dielman, 23 Quai du Commerce, 1080 Bruxelles* (1975) was a deliberately paced but powerful piece of intensely feminist cinema, over three-and-a-half hours long. Her later films, including *Les Rendez-vous d'Anna* (1978, Anna's Rendezvous), increased her reputation. Jean-Jacques Andrien made a strong impact in 1975 with his hallucinatory *Le Fils d'Amr Est Mort* (Amr's Son Is Dead). One of Akerman's associates, Samy Szlingerbaum, became a director himself in 1980 with the sensitive Yiddish-language *Bruxelles – Transit* (Brussels – Transit).

The Netherlands has always had close links with Belgium in film production because of the language

*Left: The* Woman in a Twilight Garden *is divided between a collaborator husband and a lover in the Resistance. Far left: Theodor Angelopoulos (right) directs his* O Megalèxandros, *set in 1900. Above far left:* Des Morts *(1978, Of the Dead) is a blood-soaked Belgian documentary on death and funeral rites around the world. Top far left: a supermarket cashier (Miou-Miou) is jailed for undercharging in* Jonah Who Will Be 25 in the Year 2000. *Centre top: Piccadilly Circus is where people search for a* Nice Time *on a Saturday night. Top right: the Spanish* Camada Negra *(1977, Black Brood) is an outspoken political film about a group of right-wing terrorists masquerading as a choir and was made soon after Franco's death. Above: a little girl (Ana Torrent) believes she has befriended Frankenstein's monster in* The Spirit of the Beehive

*Above:* Chronicle of the Years of Embers *shows the part played by one family from 1939 to 1954 in the events leading up to the Algerian struggle for independence from France.* Top: To Proxenio tis Annas *(1972, Anna's Engagemaent) is a touching Greek tale of a maid (Anna Vaguena) whose engagement to an eligible young man (Stavros Kalarogiou) is arranged and then broken off.* Top right: The Herd *won the British Film Institute Award in 1979 as the most original and imaginative film shown at the National Film Theatre*

situation – Flemish and Dutch are very similar. These co-productions have sometimes been of key importance – for example, the documentary *Borinage* (1933) and Fons Rademakers' commercial success *Mira* (1971) – and they can call on governmental sources in each country for funds, which is some compensation for the problems caused by the two languages.

Greece was another country with remarkable achievements during the Seventies, mostly through the work of one man. The country has a film production history going back to 1912, though its industry did not effectively get started until after World War II. It began to get international attention in the Fifties, especially the work of Michael Cacoyannis, including *Kyriakatiko Xypnima* (1954, *Windfall in Athens*), *Stella* (1955) and *Electra* (1962), probably the best screen adaptation of Greek tragedy, with fine camerawork by Walter Lassally, excellent music by Mikis Theodorakis and a superb central performance by Irene Papas. Cacoyannis had his biggest commercial success with *Zorba the Greek* (1964). The other major hit was American Jules Dassin's *Pote Tin Kyriaki* (1959, *Never on Sunday*), which made Melina Mercouri into an international star and helped to erase the HUAC blacklist stain from Dassin's film career.

Strict controls of content affected the young Greek film-makers in the Seventies as commercial production began to drop and audiences slipped away to television. The major film-maker who emerged was Theodor Angelopoulos, whose *Anaparastassis* (1970, Reconstruction) was a critical hit at the 1971 Berlin Festival. Angelopoulos seemed to have borrowed stylistically from Miklós Jancsó for his second, more overtly political film *Meres Tou 36* (1972, Days of 36); but the borrowings were fully absorbed in his third film and masterpiece *O Thiassos* (1975, *The Travelling Players*), perhaps the greatest film in the history of Greek cinema. His more recent films, also long and epic in style, are *I Kinigui* (1977, The Hunters) and *O Megalèxandros* (1980, Alexander the Great), mixing history and myth with political and cinematic awareness in long, continuous shots.

Greece's neighbour, Turkey, produced nearly two hundred films in 1979, but is mainly known around the world for the work of Yilmaz Güney, who began as a star actor and went on to writing and directing, taking his popular audience with him. His criticisms of injustice aroused the animosity of officialdom and he was imprisoned on

political grounds. Later, he received a 19-year sentence for shooting a judge and had to make films from prison, directed on his behalf by his associate Zeki Ökten. *Sürü* (1979, *The Herd*) and *Düsman* (1980, The Enemy) were made in this way.

The development of the continent of Africa as a film-making centre in the Seventies was capped by the Cannes prize won by Algeria in 1975 for Mohammed Lakhdar Hamina's *Chronicle of the Years of Embers* and reinforced by the festivals of African films in Tunisia and Upper Volta. Actually the African cinema was split into two segments, divided by geography and other characteristics. North Africa is as much part of Arabic as of African cinema, as can be seen by the festival set up in Carthage with strong participation from Egypt, Tunisia, Algeria and Morocco. The other African countries, although divided linguistically by their backgrounds as French or English colonies, united to create the Black African Festival in Ougadougou.

## Film festivals were show-cases and useful markets for small nations

These festivals became meeting grounds for the exchange of ideas and co-operation.

In North Africa, the obvious leader in the Seventies should have been Egypt, the 'Hollywood of the Nile', with a long-established film industry producing over fifty features a year. In fact, Egypt failed signally to give a lead; Algeria and, in black Africa, Senegal set the pace. But Egypt's top directors, Youssef Chahine and Salah Abu Seif, already established by their earlier work, continued to develop in the Seventies, often in co-productions with other North African countries. The best-known film of the period was Shadi Abdelsalam's *El Mumia* (1970, *The Night of Counting the Years*), but this director made no further films in the Seventies, a reflection on the state of the Egyptian industry.

Algeria, on the other hand, full of revolutionary fervour, became inspired around the time of Italian Gillo Pontecorvo's magnificent co-production *La Battaglia di Algeri* (1966, *Battle of Algiers*). Ahmed Rachedi directed *L'Aube des Damnés* (1965, The Dawn of the Damned) and this was followed in 1967 by Mohammed Lakhdar Hamina's small masterpiece *Le Vent des Aurès* (Wind From the Aurès). Hamina's Cannes prize winner was not at all the

only notable Algerian film of the Seventies.

Tunisia, with slightly less fervour, also produced interesting films, including the Grand Prize winner of the 1980 Carthage Film Festival, *Aziza*, Abdellatif Ben Ammar's fine study of a young girl. Ben Ammar's earlier films, *Une Si Simple Histoire* (1970, A Very Simple Story) and *Sejnane* (1974) were also worthwhile, as was Ridha Bahi's attack on speculative tourist development, *Soleil des Hyènes* (1977, Hyena's Sun) and Naceur Ktari's slick *Assoufara* (1976, The Ambassadors). Morocco, like Tunisia, did not really develop a film industry but still turned out some valuable films, including Ahmed El Maanouni's *Alyam Alyam* (1978, Oh the Days) and Ben Barka Souhel's *Mille et une Mains* (1974, Thousand and One Hands). Unfortunately the best films were not always popular in their own countries.

The films of black Africa were made from a genuinely new viewpoint. Black African cinema began in Senegal where the first all-African film, *Afrique sur Seine* (1955, Africa on Seine), was made in French by Paulin Vieyra. The first film made in a black African language, Wolof, was Ousmane Sembene's fine *Mandabi* (1968, The Money Order). Sembene has become the leader of African cinema, not only for his inspiration but because of the quality of his films. His *Emitaï* (1972) and *Ceddo* (1977, Outsiders) can bear comparison with the best cinema of any other country. Other directors have made films in Senegal and in such countries as Nigeria, Mauritania, the Ivory Coast and Niger. African cinema showed considerable promise as it moved into the Eighties.

Regrettably the same cannot be said of the brilliant cinema that developed in Iran in the Seventies. By 1980, it was virtually dead, with most of its major directors living outside the country and film production practically at a standstill, compared with an output of over a hundred films a year in the late Sixties. This was a real loss, in quality as well as quantity, since the Iranian cinema had produced four directors of international stature during the Seventies. The first to be noticed was Daryush Mehrjui, whose *Gav* (1968, The Cow) attracted attention at the film festivals of Venice and London in 1971. The attention paid to *The Cow* soon changed the face of Iranian cinema; by 1973, when Mehrjui helped to found the New Film Group, the Iranian cinema was a creative force of originality and strength. Mehrjui himself had commercial as well as critical success with *Postchi* (1972, The

Postman); but he ran into enormous censorship problems from the medical establishment over *Dayereh Mina* (1975, The Cycle).

Bahram Beyzai attracted attention at the first Teheran International Film Festival in 1972 with *Ragbar* (Downpour) and then made a terrific impression with the mysterious *Gharibeh-va-meh* (1974, The Stranger and the Fog). His *Tcherikeh Tara* (1980, The Ballad of Tara) was the last major film to come out of the new Iranian cinema of the Seventies, shot partially before and finished after the revolution. The third major director was Bahman Farmanara, whose *Shazdeh Ehtejab* (Prince Ehtejab) won the Grand Prize at the 1974 Teheran Festival and whose ambitious *Saiehaieh Bolan de Bad* (Tall Shadows of the Wind) came out in 1979.

Farmanara and Beyzai both had strong elements of mysticism in their work; the fourth major Iranian director appeared, at least on the surface, to be a pessimistic realist. Sohrab Shahid Saless, one of the most important directors to appear anywhere in the world during the Seventies, began his career with the bleak but beautiful *Yek Ettefaghe Sadeh* (1973, A Simple Event), about a poor child, and *Tabiate Bijan* (1974, Still Life), about an old couple. He then went to Germany to make a study in alienation, *In der Fremde* (1975, Far From Home), and became a film-maker in exile, creating a unique, quiet style of desperation that expressed Seventies *angst* in the way that Ingmar Bergman's films had depicted Fifties anguish. Saless has continued to work in Germany and to make outstanding films, including the startling *Ordnung* (1980, All in Order), a reflection on the meaning of madness.

Finally, the Philippines, the second biggest film-producing country in the world (251 features in 1971), has come into the limelight of world cinema after long being neglected, despite its prizes gained at Asian festivals. By a quirky chance, the first director from the Philippines to attract attention in Europe was the naive, self-taught Kidlat Tahimik, whose *Mababangong Bangungot* (1977, The Perfumed Nightmare) appeared like a work of primitive art at that year's Berlin Film Festival and won the Critics' Prize. However, the first director from the Philippines who seemed able to achieve international stature was Lino Brocka. His *Insiang* was shown at Cannes in 1978, to be followed by *Jaguar* in 1980. In 1981, his earlier film *Maynila, Sa Mga Kuko Ng Liwanag* (1975, Manila: In the Claws of Darkness) became the first Filipino film to get commercial distribution in Britain.           KEN WLASCHIN

*Top: Youssef Chahine's Askndrie . . . Lie? (1979, Alexandria . . . Why?) is an Egyptian–Algerian co-production set in the British-occupied port city during World War II; the main character is a young man (Mohsen Mohiedini) who wants to go to California to train as an actor and does so after the war. Above: a poor man (Mamadou Guye) and his wives (Ynousse N'Diaye and Issa Niang) are only further impoverished by The Money Order sent to him by his nephew*

Claude Goretta's *The Lacemaker* follows the tenets of the British Free Cinema movement of the Fifties with which the director was closely associated. It is documentary-like in style, with unobtrusive camerawork, concentrating on the revealing details of behaviour in a methodical fashion that made the film seem slow to some critics. It expresses the social responsibilities of the artist, concerns itself with the dignity and well-being of ordinary people in society, and stresses the significance of everyday events.

In particular, *The Lacemaker* skilfully explores some divisive elements in civilized society that normally receive scant attention. The timid Pomme and the insecure François would seem well-suited to each other, but their relationship is not a balanced one. Pomme is only too anxious to please François, but he cannot resist dominating her and trying to change her. She is content with her humble job and her friendship with the shallow, extrovert Marylène. He wants her to improve herself to fit in with his circle of friends, and he drops her when the gap in their education and intellect seems to him too great.

Adding to this cultural divide is the social handicap of Pomme's working-class background, shown up on the visit to the country estate of François' well-off parents. François quickly changes the conversation when Pomme's line of work comes up and she – probably only because of nervousness – chokes on her food. Later, François' mother can only find in Pomme's favour that 'she seems very decent'.

After François ends the affair, another student accuses him of having treated Pomme like an employee whom he has then fired. Yet Pomme was happiest playing the role of servant – ironing François' clothes, cooking his food. In fact, *The Lacemaker* explores not only a sociological problem – the intolerance of the intelligent person towards the more simple-minded – but a psychological one peculiar to Pomme. Whereas Marylène externalizes her grief at the end of an affair and gets it out of her system, Pomme is shattered by the outcome of her first sexual relationship and withdraws into herself, succumbing to anorexia and mental breakdown.

4

5

# The LACEMAKER

Goretta subtly indicates some of the other reasons for Pomme's collapse. She has lacked a father and meant too much to her mother, who still thinks of her as a child. Pomme behaves in the immature way of a 13-year-old – scoffing food, looking for shells on a beach – and lacks social skills. She can neither swim nor dance and she retreats from groups. Marylène, though recognizing that Pomme is 'fragile', is ultimately more concerned with her own happiness, as is François who uses Pomme to bolster his own ego by sexual conquest.

François certainly makes Pomme happy, as is clear from her radiance on the beach the day after their first night together, but he will not accept lasting responsibility for her. It seems unreasonable to expect that he should, although Goretta argues: 'We are always responsible for somebody else, but we don't know it sometimes – that we are responsible for the other,' and seems to regard the problem as only one of incommunicability because Pomme and François have different ways of expressing themselves, rather than seeing them as ultimately incompatible.

Goretta puts his view in words at the end, quoting the Pascal Lainé novel on which the film is based:

'He came close to her, very close to her, but did not see her. Because she was one of those people who never reach out but who must be

7

patiently sought, whom one must know how to see. In bygone days, a painter would have chosen her for a genre painting. She would have been a seamstress, a water-bearer, or a lacemaker.'

Isabelle Huppert has said of her role:

'She's not a passive character really. She has a very strong interior life . . . you realize she feels within herself a passion, what a tragic heroine would feel, something really huge in herself, and you couldn't see it.'

Perhaps this gulf between inner feelings and actions indicates a sickness rather than hidden depth of character. . . . Certain shots of

Pomme suggest a blankness, a lack of inner feelings, a need for outside stimuli to bring her to life.

At any rate, Pomme's final prolonged stare into the camera – as though posing for a portrait by Vermeer, one of whose paintings of working-women gives the film its title – invites each spectator to look beyond external appearances and to judge how they would have responded to her. It certainly seems true that Pomme would have been happier in a less complicated age. Her condition is both tragic and moving, whether or not society and François can be held responsible for the causes leading to her final breakdown.           ALLEN EYLES

**Directed by Claude Goretta, 1977**
**Prod co:** Action Films/FR3 (Paris)/Citel Films (Geneva)/Filmproduktion Janus (Frankfurt). **exec prod:** Yves Peyrot. **prod:** Yves Gasser. **assoc prod:** Klaus Hellwig, Lise Fayolle. **sc:** Pascal Lainé. Claude Goretta, from the novel by Pascal Lainé. **photo** (Eastman Colour): Jean Boffety. **ed:** Joëlle van Effenterre, Nelly Meunier, Martine Charasson. **art dir:** Serge Etter, Claude Chevant. **mus:** Pierre Jansen. **sd:** Pierre Gamet, Bernard Chaumeil, Alex Pront, Claude Villand. **sd eff:** Jérôme Levy. **prod man:** Bernard Lorain. **ass dir:** Laurent Ferrier, Patrick Grandperret. **r/t:** 107 minutes. French title: *La Dentellière*. Released in GB as *The Lacemaker*.
**Cast:** Isabelle Huppert (*Béatrice, known as Pomme*), Yves Beneyton (*François Beligne*), Florence Giorgetti (*Marylène Thorent*), Anne Marie Düringer (*Pomme's mother*), Renata Schroeter (*Marianne*), Michel de Ré (*Gérard*), Jean Obé (*M. Beligne*), Monique Chaumette (*Mme Beligne*), Anne Deleuze, Rosine Rochette (*voices*).

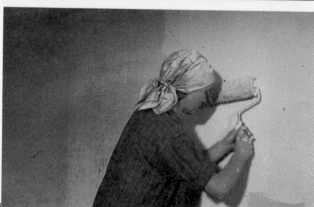

Pomme works as a trainee in a Paris hairdressing salon (1) and lives with her mother. Her friend Marylène helps them celebrate Pomme's 18th birthday. Pomme watches Marylène's emotional outburst when her protracted affair with a married man is terminated (2) and accompanies her on an end-of-season holiday in the Normandy seaside resort of Cabourg (3). Marylène moves in with an American she meets and leaves Pomme to her own devices.

Eating ice-cream, Pomme is befriended by a student, François. They become inseparable (4) and François tests her trust in him by having her close her eyes and follow his directions to the edge of a clifftop (5). He later presses her into sleeping with him.

Back in Paris she moves in with him and starts redecorating his flat (6), but feels out of place when a group of students hold a philosophical discussion (7). Introduced to François' parents, Pomme chokes on a fishbone and embarrasses her lover (8). At the flat, he grows unresponsive to her advances and later tells her they are not suited to each other (9).

She leaves him, becomes chronically ill and collapses in the street. Months later, François visits her in a sanatorium (10) and she tells him about an imaginary trip to Greece. He leaves, upset, and she resumes her knitting (11).

*Sunday Too Far Away*, the feature debut of Ken Hannam (who had previously worked as a director for BBC television on such series as *Z-Cars* and *Dr Finlay's Casebook*) was perhaps, on the basis of its screening at the 1975 Cannes Film Festival, the film that did more than any other to put Australia on the international movie map.

Its impact lay partly in its lack of pretension: here was a film prepared to treat the direct experience of everyday life without being either slick or patronizing. It is true that *Sunday Too Far Away* is set back in the Fifties – and this fact in itself possibly helped to heighten for overseas audiences the sense of journeying into an uncharted terrain, making the film a discovery in time as well as a discovery in place. But the period background is always unobtrusively drawn and its *relative* recentness allows the movie a quality of immediacy notably different from the perhaps self-indulgent evocation of a more distant historical past in several subsequently admired Australian films – such as Peter Weir's late Victorian piece *Picnic at Hanging Rock* (1975), perhaps the best-known example, and also Hannam's second feature, *Break of Day* (1976), which is set in the Twenties.

*Sunday Too Far Away* offers, in fact, a kind of paradox. The style of presentation has a novelistic and debatably 'old fashioned' transpar-

'Friday night too tired,
Saturday night too drunk,
Sunday too far away.'
THE SHEEP SHEARERS WIFE'S LAMENT

...concluding ...cteristically ...claims, 'It ...it was the ...s to make the ...'privileged' ...upon the ...ned dignity ...heir taking ...ultim... resolution in victory for the strikers is not dramatized but

...dence over the pr... criptive demands of mere plot. This quality of open-endedness makes a link between Hannam's film and the work of John Ford, as more than one critic commented when *Sunday Too Far Away* first appeared. A Fordian robustness is certainly in the air in the elaborately orchestrated bar-room punch-up between strikers and blacklegs which ends the film. It is present, too, in the wryly affectionate delineation of the rituals of 'mateship' among the disparate shearers.

But there is also a terser, even perverse, edge to the film which is perceptibly different from the romantic vision of Ford. It emerges in the scenes of Foley's breakdown, as well as in the black humour of the episode in which the disrespectful undertaker who brings a van rather than a hearse is forced to drive away with Garth's body macabrely propped up in the passenger seat.

A matter-of-fact refusal to romanticize the material extends to Hannam's treatment of the expansive landscapes against which much of the action takes place. Truthfulness to the perceptions of the down-to-earth protagonists prevents the

settings from taking on a spurious grandeur.

More than anything, it is this confident sense of proportion – a readiness to engage with the subject matter and let it dictate its own human terms – that marks *Sunday Too Far Away* as typical of the Australian 'New Wave' for which it was an early standard bearer.

The film also served as a principal introduction to international audiences for Jack Thompson, an actor who has since been seen in a fairly bewildering variety of roles – including a missionary in *The Chant of Jimmie Blacksmith* (1978) and a Boer War officer in *Breaker Morant* (1980), but whose air of stolid independence has never been better utilized than in Hannam's film. And the fact that, while Thompson is the leading man, he impresses (for all his virility and humour) as essentially a character player rather than as a star is altogether consonant with that sense of teamwork which is thematically central to *Sunday Too Far Away* and also a function of its craftsmanship.

TIM PULLEINE

**Directed by Ken Hannam, 1975**
**Prod co:** South Australian Film Corporation. **exec prod:** Gil Brealey. **sc:** John Dingwall. **photo** (Eastman Colour): Geoff Burton. **ed:** Rod Adamson. **art dir:** David Copping. **mus dir:** Patrick Flynn, Michael Carlos. **mus:** Patrick Flynn. **title song:** Patrick Flynn, Bob Ellis, sung by Jack Thompson. **sd ed:** Greg Bell. **sd rec:** Peter Fenton, Barry Brown. **shearing advisers:** Doug Limou, Laurie Rankin. **stunt and fight arr:** Ian Jamieson. **ass dir:** Malcolm Smith, Geoff Simpson, Mandy Smith. **prod man:** Matt Carroll, Malcolm Smith. **r/t:** 95 mins.
**Cast:** Jack Thompson (*Foley*), Phyllis Ophel (*Ivy*), Reg Lye (*Old Garth*), John Charman (*barman*), Gregory Apps (*Michael Simpson*), Max Cullen (*Tim King*), Ken Shorter (*Frankie Davis*), Robert Bruning (*Tom*), Jerry Thomas (*Basher*), Philip Ross (*Dawson*), Laurie Rankin (*station hand*), John Ewart (*Ugly*), Sean Scully (*Beresford*), Peter Cummins (*Black Arthur*), Graeme Smith (*Jim the Learner*), Ken Weaver (*Quinn*), Lisa Peers (*Sheila Dawson*), Hedley Cullen (*mailman*), Wayne Anthony (*undertaker*).

Timberoo, Australia, 1955. Despite having vowed to change his occupation, veteran sheep shearer Foley (1) finds himself, after surviving a car crash, helping contractor Tim King (2) to shanghai (3) seven shearers to make up a team to work at the station owned by Dawson.

The shearers (4), who include veterans like Ugly and the novice Jim, are made to shear stud rams (5), and Dawson's consequent nervousness leads to his being barred from the shed. The shearing becomes competitive – with the mysterious Black Arthur (6) threatening Foley's supremacy (7). The oldest shearer, the alcoholic Garth (8), drinks himself to death in a fit of despair. Later Foley fails to beat Black Arthur's total (9) and loses all his pay in a gambling bout.

The men learn that the government is to withdraw the 'prosperity' bonus they were awarded the year before, and a strike is called. Blacklegs are drafted in and when Foley learns that their leader is an untried shearer who had previously queried his own prowess, he joins his fellows in fighting off the incomers in a big brawl (10). A caption states that the strike was ultimately successful.

*The black-and-white shots are production stills*

# THEIR BRILLIANT CAREERS

## 'New Wave' Australian Film-makers

**Considering the long period between 1940 and 1970 when locally produced feature films were so few and far between, the rebirth of home-grown cinema in Australia has been phenomenal. Helped by government funding, a number of talented young directors proved that there was a real possibility of making internationally successful, quality films . . . down under**

In 1971 the Australian Government began to make available money to support a feature film industry, and a long cinematic drought was at last over. Perhaps it is not surprising that the initial films produced were almost all comedies . . . and broad 'ocker' comedies at that. Tim Burstall made *Stork* (1971), adapted from a play by David Williamson, whose ear for contemporary Australian vernacular had already earned him a secure place in the history of Australian theatre; now his racy dialogue and outrageous situations were able to keep cinema audiences laughing too. *Stork* is the story of a *ménage à quatre*, and its tall, gangling hero, Stork (Bruce Spence) is an endearing mixture of loud-mouthed extrovert and insecure virgin.

Burstall was the only one of the new directors of the Seventies who had, in fact, already made a feature film; as an energetic enthusiast he directed children's films and documentaries during the previous decade, and, in 1969, an extremely ambitious feature – *2000 Weeks*. This was a semi-autobiographical plea to people of talent to stay and work in Australia rather than flee to what at the time were seen

as the greater cultural attractions of Britain; the culture drain had reached epidemic proportions, and Burstall's film courageously dealt with the problem. Unfortunately, *2000 Weeks* was attacked by those very film critics who had all along been pressing for an indigenous movie industry. The attacks were certainly unjustified, for, though not a complete success, *2000 Weeks* was a breakthrough of considerable proportions.

Burstall rallied in the Seventies, and turned his back on the cultural credentials and aspirations of his past, preferring to make a series of commercial entertainments which proved popular at the box-office. He followed the success of *Stork* with the less ambitious *Alvin Purple* (1973), which merged 'ocker' comedy with soft-core sex inspired by Danish 'family porno' movies. The mixture proved a bonanza at the box-office, but the script (by Alan Hopgood) was weak and predictable. Two screenplays by David Williamson subsequently provided the basis of two of Burstall's best films – *Petersen* (1974) and *A Faithful Narrative of the Capture, Suffering and Miraculous Escape of Eliza Fraser* (1976). It was

*Petersen*, a comic drama set on a university campus, which made a star of Jack Thompson, perfectly cast as a labourer trying to improve his prospects with a belated education and becoming involved with the wife (Wendy Hughes) of his professor.

Less successful was *End Play* (1975), a somewhat predictable whodunnit scripted by Burstall himself, but he was back on form with *The Last of the Knucklemen* (1979), an excellent adaptation of a popular play by John Powers. Tim Burstall's style is punchy and sometimes unsubtle, and he has been accused of male chauvinism: after *Alvin Purple* he retaliated by sending up the women's movement in *Petersen*, which predictably attracted even more hostile criticism. He has an ambivalent love-hate attitude to his fellow film-makers, professing to scorn those who try to make 'personal' as opposed to avowedly commercial films, but he is generally respected as a battler who, after a serious early reverse, went on to prove he had his finger on the pulse of what the mass audience in Australia wanted to see.

### Uniquely ocker

Meanwhile another 'ocker' hero – that stereotype uncouth, beer-drinking Australian male – had been created by Barry Humphries for the English anti-Establishment satirical magazine *Private Eye*. The immortal Barry McKenzie then emerged in two bawdy films by Bruce Beresford – *The Adventures of Barry McKenzie* (1972) and *Barry McKenzie Holds His Own* (1974) – both about the grotesque misadventures of a 'typical' Aussie in Pommyland. A film buff from his school-days, Beresford had made amateur films in Sydney before becoming film editor for the Nigerian Government's

directors set about remedying the omission. Michael Thornhill's *Between Wars* (1974) was a key early example: with a thoughtful screenplay by Frank Moorehouse, the film followed the career of an outspoken non-conformist (Corin Redgrave) from the end of World War I up to the outbreak of World War II.

The post-war theme would be taken up, with even more assurance, by Phillip Noyce in his remarkable debut film *Newsfront* (1978), which explores the career of another vociferous rebel – this time a newsreel cameraman (Bill Hunter) – betw... Australia b...

*Left:* The Devil's Playground *explores the moralistic indoctrination of adolescent seminarians.* Above: *another side of repressed sexuality, in Bruce Beresford's butch, swaggering, broad comedy* Don's Party. *Above right: Beresford's* Breaker Morant; *historical subjects are still much favoured by 'New Wave' directors. Below right: the eerie* Picnic at Hanging Rock

...rock in the Victorian countryside. This was one of the first quality films to win international recognition, and director of photography Russell Boyd won the 1977 British Film Academy Award for Best Photography for his visual contribution.

Peter Weir, who was to become one of the most impressive of the new film-makers in Australia, started his professional career in a humble capacity at a Sydney television station, and made his first films to entertain the station's staff at their annual Christmas party. His quirky sense of humour was much in evidence in his first feature – *The Cars That Ate Paris* (1974) – about the inhabitants of a small town who scavenge the cars they have deliberately caused to crash, but in his later films he tended to play down the humour in favour of a disturbing feeling that nature was somehow conspiring against mankind.

production unit and, in 1966, head of film production for the British Film Institute. He made the Barry McKenzie films largely because of his friendship with Barry Humphries, and the first of these was extremely successful. As a result, Beresford was able to direct the screen version of one of David Williamson's most popular plays, *Don's Party* (1976). Since then he has deliberately tried different genres, though *The Getting of Wisdom* (1977), set in a girls' boarding-school in 1900, was a long-cherished project. Certainly, it stands in complete contrast to his subsequent thriller *Money Movers* (1978). In 1980 Beresford produced two very successful films: the award-winning *Breaker Morant* and an amusing version of yet another Williamson play, *The Club*. Based on an incident during the Boer War, *Breaker Morant* – though very ambivalent towards its three 'heroes', accused by the British of atrocities against Boers – was widely praised for its acting and the tension of its court-room scenes.

Modest to a fault, Bruce Beresford is a quiet worker who deliberately tries to extend himself with each new film. He prefers a regular team of collaborators (Don McAlpine as director of photography, Bill Anderson as editor) and is highly respected as an economical, conscientious film-maker with an astringent sense of humour. Actors find working with Beresford particularly rewarding, and several have given their best performances in his films.

## Back to the outback
For a time it seemed as though film-makers wanted to avoid contemporary subjects altogether, and more and more films were set in the past. Australian audiences had been denied seeing their history on film until now, and

Weir and Boyd collaborated again on *The Last Wave* (1977) in which water became a sinister force, firstly in the torrential rain that deluged the city of Sydney almost continuously through the film, and secondly in the vision of a giant tidal wave conjured up in the mind of the protagonist (Richard Chamberlain). Although *The Last Wave* was also a success in the United States, especially in California, Weir was only able to make a television feature – *The Plumber* (1979) – during the next three years. However, in 1981 he was able to realize his long-cherished ambition to make a film about the young Australians who took part in the Dardanelles campaign during World War I – a film called, simply, *Gallipoli*.

Weir is a master at creating cinematic tension, of making the ordinary seem extraordinary; he has deservedly become the most individualistic of the new Australian directors.

## Digging up history

There have been two other splendid recreations of turn-of-the-century Australia, for both of which Don McAlpine's photography has been widely praised: Beresford's *The Getting of Wisdom* and Gillian Armstrong's *My Brilliant Career* (1979). Both were adapted from autobiographical books by young women who had been forced to assume male pseudonyms so as to be able to have their work published in the first place. *My Brilliant Career* – the first theatrical feature made by a woman since the Thirties – was an enormous success all over the world with its sensitively told story of a feisty young woman who chooses a career in preference to a safe marriage; leading players Judy Davis and Sam Neill deserve particular mention.

Other period films traced Australian history in other areas. Ken Hannam's very underrated *Break of Day* (1976) was about life in a small town decimated by the loss of its menfolk as a result of World War I; it was set at the time of the first Anzac Day in 1920. Hannam, whose background was radio before he worked for the BBC directing television series, had started his feature film career with *Sunday Too Far Away* (1975), about the lives of sheep-shearers, and one of the best films of the Seventies. While those two were admirable, Hannam had less success with subsequent films – *Summerfield* (1977), a thriller, and *Dawn!* (1979), a biography of swimming champion Dawn Fraser.

Donald Crombie, who scored an immediate success with his first feature *Caddie* (1976), had worked at Film Australia on a series of accomplished documentaries. *Caddie*, with its luminous performance from Helen Morse, dealt with a family crisis, this time set in the Depression and written by a former barmaid who, as a single parent, had to struggle to bring up two children during that period. Some critics compared Crombie's sensitive direction with that of John Ford, a comparison further underlined in his second feature – *The Irishman* (1978) – about the impact of industrial changes on a small town (again set in the Twenties) and the resulting break-up of a family. A third feature, *Cathy's Child* (1979), about a Maltese woman's attempts to reclaim the baby kidnapped by her own husband, further underlined Crombie's concern with family situations, and confirmed his talent as a sensitive director of actresses.

Another director concerned mainly with social themes is Fred Schepisi, who entered the industry through newsreels, documentaries and commercials. His magnificent first film, *The Devil's Playground* (1976), is strongly autobiographical in its study of the repressive life of boys in a Catholic seminary in the Fifties. Schepisi also made one of the most important historical Australian films with *The Chant of Jimmie Blacksmith* (1978), an angry indictment of the mistreatment of the Aboriginal people. Though it was praised by all the critics, it apparently proved too threatening, for audiences stayed away wherever it was shown.

## Out of the bush

Other film-makers emerged from different backgrounds and unexpected sources: Jim Sharman is a theatre director whose innovative stage productions of *Hair* and *Jesus Christ Superstar*, as well as *The Rocky Horror Show*, gained him an international reputation. In Australia he is also known for his excellent theatre productions of plays by Patrick White, and indeed his most satisfying film to date has been from a White script – *The Night The Prowler* (1978) – about an apparent rape in a bland environment and the degenerates lurking in self-satisfied suburbia. Sharman's most famous film, however, is *The Rocky Horror Picture Show*, which he made in 1975.

Contemporary themes have been dealt with in other interesting features: Michael Thornhill's *The FJ Holden* (1977) about the alienation of young people in Sydney's outer suburbs; John Duigan's treatment of a similar disenchantment in Melbourne, *Mouth to Mouth* (1978); Esben Storm's accomplished romantic drama *In Search of Anna* (1978) about a young man just out of prison; Steven Wallace's powerful *Stir!* (1980), based on the events leading up to a prison riot. And George Miller, who was a medical doctor before turning to film-making, made a violent thriller – *Mad Max* (1979) – which turned out to be very popular.

*Above: in* Newsfront *a cameraman (Bill Hunter) finds his assistant (Chris Haywood) drowned. Below: Richard Chamberlain in* The Last Wave. *Below Right:* The Picture Show Man *travels to outback towns with Freddy (John Ewart) and Larry (Harold Hopkins)*

It is encouraging to be able to say that, in general, films that have tried to be 'international' by importing foreign talent and adapting local themes to please some nebulous transatlantic audience have failed on every level. Overall, the most interesting aspect of the Australian revival of the Seventies is that so many films of quality were actually made. Considering the fact that there had been virtually no possibility of working in feature

*Top right: Sam Neill and Judy Davis in* My Brilliant Career. *Right:* Stir! – *part of the trend towards social concern. Bottom right:* The Chant of Jimmie Blacksmith – *Gilda (Angela Punch) is married to an Aboriginal (Tommy Lewis) striving to join white society*

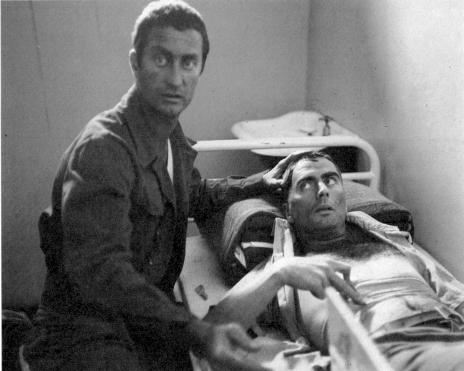

films for so many years, the standard of the work produced when the money *did* become available seems astonishingly high. Whether that quality can be sustained through the Eighties is very much a moot point, as tax incentive schemes – which look fine on paper – threaten to change the kind of film Australians can make. But, whatever the future, the Seventies proved to be an exhilarating decade for cinema down under. DAVID STRATTON

# FINCHIE

**Claimed by Britain as a product of British cinema and regarded by Australians as an Australian actor, Peter Finch developed ultimately as an international cinema star. He retained the rare distinction throughout his 42 years as an actor of being regarded within the profession as an unusually gifted artist**

Winner of five British Academy Awards, plus Russian and German awards, Peter George Frederick Ingle Finch (1916–77) is the only actor up until now to have been awarded a Hollywood Oscar (for Best Actor) posthumously. As many critics on both sides of the Atlantic agree, this was possibly not so much for his bravura performance in *Network* (1976) as Hollywood's tacit accolade for an entire, at times brilliant and often underrated career. Easygoing, gregarious and very friendly on the surface, there was a withdrawn, spiritual side, a secret self in Finch that confided in nobody.

The paradox of Peter Finch, a man of rare and unrealized potential, was an innate fecklessness that was part of an amazing, almost gipsy gift which affected his acting, his painting and his writing. As a screen actor he was able to develop a spontaneous natural ability to achieve perfection on the first take, and this – in true gipsy fashion – could tarnish with too much repetition. In a close observation of his many films, one characteristic emerges that has seldom, if ever, been commented on by any critic: his natural facility to merge perfectly with any landscape against which he may be playing; the skin tones and hair always seemed to blend harmoniously with the colours of nature. He was a man who felt at ease in primitive surroundings, and who felt a deep affinity with every aspect of nature.

He remained to the end of his life an unpredictable 'loner', lacking single-minded dedication as an actor. He opted for the natural primitive existence, as his attempts to settle and farm in Jamaica show. He always yearned to be free of possessions and possessive ties. As much a natural gipsy as he was a natural actor, his quest for freedom determined the pattern of his career. He loved his solitude, but detested loneliness and the thought of old age, and from these he would try to escape back among acquaintances, with a woman, or through drink.

In many ways Peter Finch remained immature until his death, but he retained that state of constantly *wanting* to learn, and of growing more aware, that is perhaps a subtler aspect of maturity. Though amusing, and marvellous company at his best, he was not at all what so many hoped to find and this often left them sadly deluded. Love, for example, was 'undiscovered country' for him, and a terrain of experience that he was always seeking. However, the man in search of his own identity and inner truth was in perpetual conflict with himself.

The mystical against the material; that little bit of guile; the sensitivity, ruthlessness and vulnerability; evasiveness and drunken bravado; irony and romanticism – those contradictory characteristics that often go to make the true artist, all made a kaleidoscopic pattern within his personality. These were what women found so attractive in Peter Finch, and what they wished to hold and possess and strangle eventually. He escaped, of course, always, as he once explained: '. . . like Kipling's Cat who went back through the Wet Wild Woods waving his wild tail, and walking by his wild lone.'

He wanted to feel that the acting profession merited respect. His professional life began with a solid training in Australian radio, vaudeville, theatre and the Australian cinema of the Thirties and Forties. As an actor and potential director on his arrival in England from Australia in 1948, he hoped to work in both Paris and London, and to expand in every

*Top left: Finch played a POW finally re-united with his lover in* A Town Like Alice. *Above: in Ealing's* The Shiralee *a cuckolded husband (Finch) takes his small daughter (Dana Wilson) on the road. Below:* No Love for Johnnie *charts the career of a Labour MP*

direction. But the lure of the cinema and all its involvements became too great for him. In many ways the cinema created a pattern of existence in his private life which gave him freedom and money but no real fulfilment or peace of mind. He was an actor's actor and a director's actor: many great directors who worked with Finch praised him as one of the most gifted they had ever directed. In this he seems to have evoked a similar response to Robert Donat and Gérard Philipe, and like both he was deeply respected and loved by the general public. Yet Peter Finch was often passed over by casting directors and producers in favour of lesser talents. For three of his award-winning films he was not even the director's first choice for the part.

Was he then – as some have suggested – a gifted chameleon who personified absolutely the roles he created? And among the ~~...~~ Joe Harman, the Aussi~~...~~ *Alice* (1956), Captair~~...~~ Spee in *The Battle*~~...~~ Oscar Wilde in *The*~~...~~ Johnnie Byrne, ~~...~~ (1961), Dr Daniel Hirsch in *Sunday, Bloody Sunday* (1971). Or was Finch, as Fred Zinnemann (who directed him in *The Nun's Story*, 1959) described him: '. . . a man with a kind of magic which emanates from the screen'?

In *The Shiralee* (1957) Finch plays Jim Macauley – a swagman who tramps through the Australian countryside looking for work and burdened with a cross of his own making (his lonely child wrested from a faithless wife). It was a role in which Finch found a character of his natural choice. He identified completely with the hard-fisted, laconic Aussie loner whose embittered philosophy of marriage – 'why should I put my saddle on one filly when I have the freedom of the paddock?' – nearly cost him his child's life.

When it came to *The Trials of Oscar Wilde* Peter Finch was considered very unlikely casting as Victorian London's most fashionable playwright and wit. Yet his sensitive portrayal of genius, the unwilling victim of a predilection for sodomy, torn between his infatuation for Bosie (Lord Alfred Douglas) and the shame of his betrayal as husband and father, won him immediate international acclaim.

*No Love for Johnnie*, which was based on the true life story of Wilfred Fienburgh – a brilliant north of England Labour MP killed in a car crash – was an extremely difficult challenge for Finch, who always remained basically uncommitted politically. The character of Johnnie Byrne emerges as a shallow, charming, ruthless, very astute politician able to manoeuvre his way to the top in British politics as Assistant Postmaster General. Able to identify absolutely with the personality, he managed to get everything that existed in Fienburgh onto the screen in a performance which won him his third British Film Academy Award and the Silver Bear Award at the Berlin Film Festival in 1961.

The part for which he may well be best remembered, however, was provided by *Sunday, Bloody Sunday*, the story of a triangular love relationship between a young sculptor (Murray Head), an embittered woman (Glenda Jackson) and a homosexual Jewish doctor in his early forties (Peter Finch) which progresses over ten consecutive days from Friday to Sunday. The disturbed emotional

*Above: John Schlesinger's* Far From the Madding Crowd *(1967) in which Boldwood (Finch) attacks Sergeant Troy (Terence Stamp). Below: a stormy affair with a young artist (Murray Head) in* Sunday, Bloody Sunday

balance of all three, in what is conveyed rather than spoken, is the underlying theme of the film. Finch's award-winning characterization of the anguished, introverted and ultimately rejected Dr Hirsch, finally willing to accept the compromise of shared love, is rated by many as

his finest. Penelope Gilliatt, who wrote the scenario, remembers a rehearsal with the three lead actors when Finch had this to say about a line he found ambiguous in one of his scenes:

'Don't give me a line reading, don't give me an inflexion or anything I can mimic. Just tell me why I'm doing it and then I can do it. I simply need the spark, the *reason* for which I'm saying the line.'

Sidney Lumet's *Network* was the penultimate feature film he made before an untimely

written. As a result of this role Finch was rocketed to total American stardom . . . only to burn out like a meteor.

One of Finch's great qualities, never exploited on the screen, was his sublime sense of the ridiculous. Drinking in a bar, he could lose in a second the dark 'olive-soaked' voice and become utterly unpretentious and non-theatrical. He was never given the opportunity as an actor to make fun of his own particular kind of pretentiousness and importance, although he was a master of self-mockery. His only contribution to the cinema as a writer and director is *The Day* (1960), a 26-minute black-and-white film shot on Ibiza, which shows Finch's visual flair for capturing with a painter's eye the essence of Spanish peasant life. Everything is suggested, nothing is overstated. With virtually no dialogue it is a work full of beautiful comic touches that shows, with rare simplicity, reality as seen through the eyes of a Spanish child. A shot of a scarecrow and then the shot of an old peasant woman standing in the fork of a tree on a lonely roadside immediately assume the fantasy of a Goya painting in the imagination of the little boy Antonio, who – suddenly terrified – sees her as a sinister scarecrow against the stark trees.

In an instant Finch evokes both the true and imagined terror of early childhood. The little boy filling his hat with water to give his donkey a drink, his attempts to reach the large door-knocker just out of reach, his collision with the artist's easel which he sends flying down a long flight of steps and his quick decision to put the canvas back . . . but only up one step as a frightened token gesture of apology: every comic detail shows the inventive mind of a born cinema director.

The story is simple: on a farm, far across the salt flats a child is about to be born, so the little boy Antonio must go – for the first time alone – with the donkey and cart to gather his uncles, aunts and cousins from the town. As a director, Finch perfectly captures a childlike quality in his visual narrative, together with a humour that is completely Spanish, ironical and satirical. *The Day* reveals more of his true character than any of his film performances. *The Day* is the man behind the actor's mask of Peter Finch.

TRADER FAULKNER

*Top left: the undistinguished* Bequest to the Nation *(1973) from Terence Rattigan's play about Lord Nelson. Top right: as Queen Christina's beloved cardinal in* The Abdication *(1974). Above: as the newsman threatening suicide on the* Network *– a fitting climax to Finch's own charismatic career on the screen*

death in 1977. Paddy Chayefsky's script evolves on the screen as a twentieth-century Hogarthian satire on the evils of what commercial television could become in the United States. Finch, an 'anchor-man' on the fictitious UBS network, facing dismissal for the steady decline in his ratings, unintentionally wins top rating in his final appearance by lampooning his employers and threatening TV suicide. In an explosive bravura performance as Howard Beale – 'mad prophet of the air waves' – Peter Finch released within himself a force, a terrible rage which suddenly seemed to be using him. The force releasing itself through him was of a far greater dimension than the conception of the character as it had been

## Filmography

**1935** Magic Shoes (AUS) (unreleased). **'38** Dad and Dave Come to Town (AUS) (GB: The Rudd Family Goes to Town); Mr Chedworth Steps Out (AUS). **'41** The Power and the Glory (AUS). **'43** Red Sky at Morning (AUS). **'44** Rats of Tobruk (AUS); South West Pacific (AUS); Jungle Patrol (short) (narr. only) (AUS). **'46** A Son Is Born (AUS); Indonesia Calling (short) (narr. only) (AUS); Native Earth (short) (narr. only) (AUS). *All remaining films GB unless otherwise stated*: **'49** Eureka Stockade (+2nd ass. dir; +cast. dir) (USA: Massacre Hill); Train of Events *ep* The Actor. **'50** The Wooden Horse; The Miniver Story. **'52** The Story of Robin Hood and His Merrie Men/Robin Hood. **'53** The Story of Gilbert and Sullivan (USA: The Great Gilbert and Sullivan); The Heart of the Matter. **'54** Father Brown (USA: The Detective); Elephant Walk (USA); Make Me an Offer! **'55** Passage Home; The Dark Avenger (USA: The Warriors); Josephine and Men; Simon and Laura; The Queen in Australia (doc. short) (narr. only) (AUS); Melbourne, Olympic City (doc. short) (narr. only) (AUS). **'56** A Town Like Alice (USA: The Rape of Malaya); The Battle of the River Plate (USA: Pursuit of the Graf Spee). **'57** The Shiralee; Robbery Under Arms; Windom's Way. **'59** Operation Amsterdam; Children of Korea (narr. only); The Nun's Story (USA). **'60** Kidnapped (USA); The Trials of Oscar Wilde (USA: The Man With the Green Carnation/The Green Carnation); The Day (short) (dir; +prod; +sc. only); The Sins of Rachel Cade (USA). **'61** No Love for Johnnie. **'62** I Thank a Fool. **'63** In the Cool of the Day. **'64** Girl With Green Eyes; First Men in the Moon (guest); The Pumpkin Eater. **'65** Judith (USA). **'66** The Flight of the Phoenix (USA); 10.30 PM Summer (USA). **'67** Come Spy With Me (uncredited) (USA); Far From the Madding Crowd. **'68** The Legend of Lylah Clare (USA). **'69** The Greatest Mother of Them All (unfinished). **'70** Krasnaya Palatka/La Tenda Rossa (USSR-IT) (USA/GB: The Red Tent). **'71** Sunday, Bloody Sunday; Something to Hide. **'73** Lost Horizon (USA); England Made Me; Bequest to the Nation (USA: The Nelson Affair). **'74** The Abdication. **'76** Network; Raid on Entebbe (USA TV film shown in cinemas abroad).

# COUNTRY AND WESTERNS

**The twanging of banjos or the thunder of gunshots enlivened the soundtracks of films about the rural South and West – country-music movies and Westerns**

Country-and-western music grew up with the movies, but the success of Robert Altman's film *Nashville* (1975) made people aware of how strong the country connection had become. Country songs were heard on the soundtracks of films as different as *Bonnie and Clyde* (1967), *Five Easy Pieces* (1970), *The Last Picture Show* (1971) and *Deliverance* (1972); country songs were turned into such successful movies as *Ode to Billy Joe* (1976), *Convoy* and *Harper Valley PTA* (both 1978); and movie stars with country orientation and country music in their films moved to the top of the popularity polls, most notably Burt Reynolds and Clint Eastwood. By 1980, country music was the most popular form of music in the USA after rock and had become part of the movie mainstream. In 1981, the Best Actress Academy Award went to Sissy Spacek for her impersonation of country singer Loretta Lynn in the box-office hit *Coal Miner's Daughter* (1980).

Country-music films had, however, been around since the beginning of sound, made by small studios. Then a country song sung by a country singer, Tex Ritter, won the Academy Award as the Best Film Song of the year in *High Noon* (1952). The success of the film, and of the song, helped to restore the popularity of theme-songs in movies; and country music slowly began to move away from the B-picture studios towards the big time. It took a while, and the main breakthrough did not come until the Seventies.

It started off with Johnny Cash. After featuring in an excellent documentary *Johnny Cash – The Man, His World, His Music* (1969), he provided the songs in John Frankenheimer's *I Walk the Line* and Sidney J. Furie's *Little Fauss and Big Halsy* (both 1970), then turned actor, playing opposite Kirk Douglas in Lamont Johnson's *A Gunfight* (1971). Despite his powerful screen presence, it was not Cash but a relative unknown who was the first modern country-music singer to become a major movie star – always excepting Elvis Presley, whom country buffs also claim.

This was a former Rhodes Scholar turned Nashville janitor, Kris Kristofferson, who established himself as a top country songwriter in 1970 with 'Me and Bobby McGee', followed by 'Help Me Make It Through the Night'. He played a small role in Dennis Hopper's *The Last Movie* (1971) and then starred in Bill Norton's *Cisco Pike* (1971), in which he sang four of his songs and portrayed a songwriter-singer who gets involved with drugs and a crooked policeman (Gene Hackman). His voice was on the soundtrack of John Huston's *Fat City* (1972), and next he sang and acted in *Blume in Love* (1973) as the rival in love of a divorce lawyer (George Segal). He then gained international prominence playing Billy the Kid in Sam Peckinpah's *Pat Garrett and Billy the Kid* (1973). He was the suitor of Alice (Ellen Burstyn) in Martin Scorsese's *Alice Doesn't Live Here Anymore* (1974), in which he also sang a little. In the second remake of *A Star Is Born* (1976), matching charisma with Barbra Streisand, he portrayed a country singer on the way down,

through booze and ego, as she rises, and he did it well enough to avoid unfavourable comparisons with his earlier counterparts Fredric March and James Mason. In Michael Ritchie's tongue-in-cheek *Semi-Tough* (1977) he teamed up with another major country-orientated star, Burt Reynolds, and they milked some gags out of the music of old-time B-movie cowboy star Gene Autry, which provided most of the music soundtrack of the film. *Convoy*

*Top: Loretta Lynn (Sissy Spacek), persuaded to appear with a local band in* Coal Miner's Daughter, *goes on to singing success. Above: Barbara Jean (Ronee Blakley) about to break down on stage in* Nashville, *an incident based on a real-life event in the career of Loretta Lynn*

saw him reunited with director Sam Peckinpah in the film version of a country song, scripted by Bill Norton, and featuring country songs by half the hit-makers of Nashville. Truckers had become the new country heroes, the new cowboys, and the Nashville songwriters had rushed to help create the legend. Kristofferson's career to date reached a climax of sorts when he starred in a colossally expensive failure, Michael Cimino's brilliantly directed but faultily scripted Western *Heaven's Gate* (1980) – it had some good country fiddling, too.

Another country-music star who began a Hollywood career was the ageless hippie Willie Nelson. He provided a few songs for films, such as the Roy Rogers comeback picture *Mackintosh & TJ* (1975), but his real start was a good supporting role as the manager of an ex-rodeo star (Robert Redford) in *The Electric Horseman* (1979). He sang five songs

brilliantly, turning out to have remarkable screen presence despite his age and style. In his next film he was the central figure, a country singer not unlike himself on tour in Jerry Schatzberg's *Honeysuckle Rose* (1980). Based rather surprisingly on the old Ingrid Bergman love story *Intermezzo* (1939), with Willie Nelson in the Leslie Howard role of a man divided between wife and musically talented mistress, it showed once again how powerful his screen presence could be, and gained him an Oscar nomination for his hit song 'On the Road Again'.

The other new Hollywood face in the Eighties fresh from Nashville belonged to Dolly Parton, a highly intelligent singer-songwriter whose extravagant blonde wigs and emphatic bust disguised an acute publicity awareness. Her role opposite Jane Fonda and Lily Tomlin in *9 to 5* (1980) and her impressive hit song from that film seemed to mark the beginning of a major film career.

The non-singer Burt Reynolds retained a strong bias towards country-music-related films as he climbed to top position among American stars in the late Seventies, according to the annual poll of exhibitors. *Deliverance* made a hit out of 'Duelling Banjos' as played by Eric Weissberg and Steve

*Left: Jeannie C. Riley's 1968 hit song told of a mother who fights the Parent-Teacher Association. Bottom left: Burt Reynolds as a band promoter and hold-up man in WW and the Dixie Dancekings*

Above: Kris Kristofferson as a drug pusher and Gene Hackman as a crooked cop in Cisco Pike. Below: Ode to Billy Joe, based on Bobbie Gentry's 1967 hit song, was about a boy's mysterious suicide

Mandel in 1972. In 1973 Reynolds made the first of his moonshine chase films, *White Lightning*, directed by Joseph Sargent, in which he played a dealer in illicit alcohol; the 1976 sequel was *Gator*, in which he directed himself and country-music star Jerry Reed. He perfected his delightful persona as a charming con-man and gave it a purely country-music setting in John G. Avildsen's *WW and the Dixie Dancekings* (1975), the story of how a confidence trickster turns a no-talent group into Grand Ole Opry stars. Told with verve and style, it also featured country stars Don Williams and Jerry Reed.

Reynolds' major hits were *Smokey and the Bandit* (1977) and its sequel *Smokey and the Bandit II* (1980), released in Britain as *Smokey and the Bandit Ride Again*): they respectively appeared as 23rd and 57th in *Variety*'s 1984 listing of all-time box-office hits. *Smokey and the Bandit*, directed by stunt coordinator Hal Needham as his first picture, was another chase film about bootleggers, but it came up fresh as new paint with songs and acting by Jerry Reed and a superb performance by Jackie Gleason as the sheriff. *Smokey and the Bandit II*, again directed by Needham, told a similar story but was more varied and interesting in its country-music accompaniment, provided by artists including the Statler Brothers, Tanya Tucker and even Roy Rogers as well as Jerry Reed.

Not to be outdone as a 'good ole boy' on the country scene, Clint Eastwood was diverted from his usual hard-line violence to country monkey-tricks in *Every Which Way But Loose* (1978), directed by James Fargo. Eastwood played a fighting trucker whose best friend is an orang-utan and whose best girl is a country-music singer. The soundtrack was as big a hit as the film, with the Eddie Rabbitt title song very popular and other music by the likes of Hank Thompson, Mel Tillis and Charlie Rich. The sequel *Any Which Way You Can* (1980), directed by Buddy Van Horn with not much variation in story, had another good soundtrack that featured Clint Eastwood singing with Ray Charles. In between, Eastwood himself directed a far superior film, the contemporary Wild West fantasy *Bronco Billy* (1980), with an outstanding score mostly performed by country stars Merle Haggard and Ronnie Milsap; Eastwood joined Haggard on one duet, 'Barroom Buddies'.

Some of the best country films of the Seventies had little in the way of star value but a good deal of hard-edged plot. Particularly fine was Daryl Duke's *Payday* (1973), with Rip Torn portraying an ageing country star still trying to make the big time. Gus Trikonis' *Nashville Girl* (1976), made for Roger Corman, starred Monica Gayle as a 16-year-old girl trying to break into the Nashville music world, even at the price of her own self-respect.

Possibly the most effective films in getting people to listen to country songs and singers without being conscious of it were those that used country music primarily for mood and characterization. The delightful banjo music in Arthur Penn's *Bonnie and Clyde*, 'Foggy Mountain Breakdown' played by Lester Flatt and Earl Scruggs, was superbly integrated into the narrative and the car chases. The vulnerable waitress Rayette (Karen Black) in Bob Rafelson's *Five Easy Pieces* would not have been what she was without her reliance on the sentiments of Tammy Wynette songs. Texas in the Fifties could not have been so clearly evoked in Peter Bogdanovich's *The Last Picture Show* without the constant background of Hank Williams, Bob Wills and His Texas Playboys, Lefty Frizzell and the other country musicians of the period. Good ole hillbilly music was making a comeback at last.

KEN WLASCHIN

The Seventies began with the greatest of all Western stars, John Wayne, receiving a long-awaited Oscar in April 1970 for his performance in Henry Hathaway's *True Grit* (1969). It ended with his death in June 1979.

The years in between can be regarded as the period in which the Western was dragged kicking and screaming into the twentieth century. The genre's characteristic tone of affirmation or elegy, expressing a nineteenth-century confidence about the future, was transformed into a new tone of cynicism and despair, born of a distinctly modern feeling of helplessness and unease. When the USA bicentenary came along in 1976, the Western – the form which, above all, celebrates the triumphant emergence and civilization of America – could not rise to the occasion. The most typical responses came from Robert Altman, with *Buffalo Bill and the Indians . . . or Sitting Bull's History Lesson*, and Arthur Penn, who directed *The Missouri Breaks*. The former shows one of the country's national heroes (played by Paul Newman) as a slow-witted and self-deluding clown; the latter presents as its embodiment of law and order a fat, transvestite sadist (an extraordinary creation by Marlon Brando), who specializes in killing from a distance.

It is perhaps not surprising that the Western should go into a phase of irony and self-criticism. John Ford, the doyen of Western directors and the one who had celebrated the pioneering spirit on film in its purest form, had died in 1973. Other great veteran directors of the genre were to die within the following few years – Howard Hawks in 1977, Raoul Walsh in 1980. After *El Dorado* (1967),

## In the Seventies the conventional Western hero rode off into the sunset – perhaps for good

Hawks did manage one more variation on his classic *Rio Bravo* (1959), this time called *Rio Lobo* (1970). Significantly, it is one of his darkest films, evoking a world where chivalry between hero and antagonist no longer exists and which seems to be discovering pleasure and sophistication in sadism.

Even Sam Peckinpah was quiet. It seemed the harrowing vision he had presented in *The Wild Bunch* (1969), a film whose nightmarish violence was to reverberate influentially through other directors' Westerns, had exhausted his sensibilities. His major contribution was the distinguished *Pat Garrett and Billy the Kid* (1973), a study of cynical pragmatism and of adjustment to encroaching civilization. Garrett's pursuit of the Kid takes on an obsessive air as if, by destroying him, he can eradicate his own dubious past and live to grow old with the country.

The death or conversion of the gunfighter so that civilization might prosper is a common theme in Sixties Westerns, expressed most poignantly in Ford's *The Man Who Shot Liberty Valance* (1962). There were numerous Westerns at this time about men whose prowess with a gun has helped to tame the country but who, at the point of transition, have to be rejected for their special skill has become both unnecessary and threatening to the new society. It is a theme that recurs in later Westerns, such as Don Siegel's *The Shootist* (1976) and William Wiard's *Tom Horn* (1979), although the inflection tends to be different. The Sixties had accepted this change as painful, but inevitable and necessary. Seventies films seem more bitter. Tom Horn, for example, is framed, tried and condemned for murder by a society that has no further use for him and fears him. Steve McQueen's performance as Horn, in his penultimate film, was masterly.

During the Seventies the Western suffered the fate of all genres – it became self-conscious. The previous decade had been preoccupied with reflections on the West – on the gap between fact and legend – and the Western hero who was becoming older and more tired. But it then became absorbed with itself as a form – how a Western is constituted, what its main elements are and mean, and how they have been relayed to mass audiences. This self-consciousness appears in several forms. There is the broad comic parody of Mel Brooks' *Blazing Saddles* (1974), an irreverent spoof on basic Western situations. Michael Crichton, the writer and director of *Westworld* (1973), blends cowboy and science fiction in an ingenious tale about programmed robots in a mock frontier town who start killing holidaymakers. In particular, the new films allude to screen history, referring not to the myth of the West but to the mythology of the Western film. Thus, *The Shootist*, which stars John Wayne as an ex-gunfighter dying of cancer, opens with a montage of scenes from earlier Wayne films, blurring the distinction between the specific character he is playing and the general screen persona he had built up over his career. The film becomes an elegy for Wayne himself, who invests the part with enormous dignity. Both Clint Eastwood's *High Plains Drifter* (1973) and *The Missouri Breaks* play on the audience's recognition of the classic Western hero of George Stevens' *Shane* (1953), whose knightly behaviour is mocked and demonized by the two mysterious heroes in both these modern films who also ride in from nowhere to save threatened communities but leave chaos in their wake. Shane (Alan Ladd) was a kind of saviour, an inspirer of men; Eastwood's satanic protagonist in *High Plains Drifter* is an embodiment of what men fear in themselves.

The Seventies Western tends to be short of conventional heroes. With the exception of Eastwood, there was no actor really identifiable as a natural Western star. Indeed, one of the major themes is the decline of heroism, the absence of charisma. This is true even of Westerns that have the names of the central characters in their titles, such as Robert Altman's *McCabe and Mrs Miller* (1971) and Richard Lester's *Butch and Sundance – the Early Days* (1979). In both films the heroes have increasing difficulty in making their presence felt to people busying themselves with the growth of community. And both stage superb gunfights, which are striking precisely because so little notice is taken of them: the townsfolk are too preoccupied to pay much attention to such outmoded confrontations.

The more sceptical and ironical attitude to heroism was probably a response to the infection of cynicism derived from the political traumas of the decade. The influence of the Watergate affair can be felt in a Western such as *Posse* (1975), with Kirk Douglas directing and starring in a sharp little tale about a ruthlessly opportunistic marshal with political ambitions and a mastery of the publicity machine, who is eventually abandoned by supporters (the posse of the title) even more unscrupulous than he is. Vietnam is a ghostly and disturbing shadow through a number of films. Ralph Nelson's *Soldier Blue* and Arthur Penn's *Little Big Man* (both 1970) both recreate the massacre of Indian villages by the US Cavalry as an analogue to the My Lai massacre.

Indeed, the Vietnam experience might explain why so many Seventies Westerns are interested in the years immediately following the American Civil War and the difficulties men find adjusting to post-

war society. In *The Outlaw Josey Wales* (1976), Clint Eastwood directed himself as a man whose quest for revenge (after the murder of his family during the war) is ultimately less important than his desire for peace and healing. On the other hand, two remarkable films about the Jesse James and Cole Younger gangs, Philip Kaufman's *The Great Northfield Minnesota Raid* (1972) and Walter Hill's *The Long Riders* (1980), remain abrasive and disillusioned, presenting characters whose war experience makes it hard for them to put down roots, to conform to a new era of materialism.

A number of Seventies Westerns offer interesting variations on modern social themes. Reflecting a contemporary moral malaise, they often draw little distinction between heroes and villains. John Huston's *The Life and Times of Judge Roy Bean* (1972) makes a hero of the hanging judge. In Robert Benton's *Bad Company* (1971) the outlaws are presented as comically endearing even at their most bestial, and the development of the innocent young hero is an inexorable progress towards crime. In the two Westerns he has made for the director Sydney Pollack, *Jeremiah Johnson* (1972) and *The Electric Horseman* (1979), Robert Redford has used the form to proclaim his particular ecological interests, both films employing the majesty of the landscape and the later one, set in the modern day, showing how a resourceful Westerner can outsmart and humiliate big business. William Fraker's *Monte Walsh* (1970) is concerned with the issue of unemployment in the old West, what happens to cowboys when their skills are superseded by technology: some drift into crime; Monte Walsh himself (Lee Marvin) is offered a job as a circus performer. Turning the offer down, he comments: 'I'm not gonna spit on my whole life.'

Nevertheless, this is one of only two outlets for the Seventies Western hero. The Wild West Show – the aestheticizing and anaesthetizing of frontier adventure – is handled with affectionate respect in Clint Eastwood's *Bronco Billy* (1980); but it is treated savagely in *Buffalo Bill and the Indians . . . or Sitting Bull's History Lesson*, which is concerned not with the West as history or legend but as theatre. The film's iconoclastic proposition is that the West does not represent the heart of American adventurism but the origins of American showbiz.

The other outlet is the rodeo, the modern cinema's arena for the activities of those who still have 'Westering' in their blood. The films with this background – including Cliff Robertson's *J.W. Coop* (1971), Stuart Millar's *When the Legends Die* and Sam Peckinpah's *Junior Bonner* (both 1972) – play

*Left: the face of the future Western hero? If so, it is a face that unscrews – Yul Brynner as a robot gunslinger in* Westworld. *Above left: Kirk Douglas as the self-seeking marshal whose political ambitions are wrecked in* Posse. *Top left: heading for the last round-up – Monte (Lee Marvin, squatting, centre) and Chet (Jack Palance, kneeling to his left), two cowboys whose time has passed in* Monte Walsh. *Top: the sun goes down on rodeo-rider J.W. Coop (Cliff Robertson). Top right: civilization encroaches on the world of* Bronco Billy, *in which the Wild West Showman (Clint Eastwood) briefly turns train-robber. Above right: revenge-seeking orphan Mattie (Kim Darby) enlists the help of Rooster Cogburn (John Wayne) in* True Grit. *Above: the runaway boys (Jeff Bridges and Barry Brown) of* Bad Company

alternately witty and moving games with the concept of the cowboy in modern civilization. The humour comes from the incongruity of detail, such as the modern cowboy's having to transport his horse by truck in *Junior Bonner*; or the cowboy capitalist in *J.W. Coop* arriving at the rodeo in a jet, pausing only to ask a fellow passenger if he will kindly pass on a message to his broker. When J.W. Coop himself attempts to emulate this champ's life-style and become one of the new jet-propelled whiz-kids of the Wild West circuit, he finds that a cow has nibbled away some of his flying machine.

The conventional Western movie was, then, thoroughly revised in the Seventies. Indeed, *Little Big Man* turned the genre inside out for, as the title suggests, the film is all about paradoxes and contraries. American history is seen through the eyes of an Indian (who is actually a white man); the US Cavalry are referred to as 'savages' and the Indians as 'Human Beings'; an Indian scout offers advice which, as he knows it will be, is reversed by General Custer, a judgment that culminates in the Battle of the Little Big Horn – the classic instance of a soldier advancing his men when they should be retreating. Several of the major characters in the film are shot in the back (they are, it is inferred,

facing the wrong way round), and *Little Big Man* generally is a marvellous inversion of all the old legends, even if it does not go so far as to present the Indian culture through authentically Indian eyes.

It was inevitable that the tragedies of recent American history should feed a retrospective doubt into the legends of its pioneering past. The romantic mode of the Western diminished in the Seventies, being replaced by a visual and verbal realism and brutality that was coupled with a moral ambivalence about the place of violence in American society. Latterday Westerns invariably ask how did America get to this present from that past? Such a question informs their presentation of history, and issues of 'goodies and baddies' take second place to themes such as the growth of racism and capitalism, or the origins of legitimized violence in the American psyche. But the romantic Western myth – the eradication of evil by brave, good and active men – still has the power to stir the imagination. Does it enshrine basic truths, or perpetuate dangerous over-simplifications? The development of the genre unfortunately came to a temporary halt during the early Eighties with the huge box-office disaster of *Heaven's Gate* (1980) and the failure of *Barbarosa* (1982).                                    NEIL SINYARD

# THE LAST HARD MEN

In the movie world a well-established means of gaining promotion from featured player to star is to win a reputation for thoroughgoing nastiness. What did the trick for Robert Ryan and Richard Widmark in the Forties and for Ernest Borgnine in the Fifties, subsequently did it for several others in the Sixties and Seventies – especially for Lee Marvin, James Coburn and Charles Bronson.

## Lee Marvin's rising star
Lee Marvin, who was born in 1924, built his career gradually over more than a decade. Following his screen debut in 1951, he made his impact in *The Big Heat* (1953), where his playing of a gangland chief's brutal henchman – who throws scalding coffee into the moll's face – is the epitome of slobbish menace. His hick-town thug in *Bad Day at Black Rock* (1955) is a rural version of the same theme, and over the next few years he created a gallery of varied but invariably unpleasant characters ranging from out-and-out 'baddies', such as the bank robber in *Violent Saturday* (1955), to unsympathetic 'straight' roles like the corrupt colonel in *Attack!* (1956).

This trend reached its apogee when John Ford cast him as the unmitigatedly evil outlaw Valance in *The Man Who Shot Liberty Valance* (1962). With this whip-wielding blackguard, Marvin seemed to reach a dead end in villainy and decided to try his hand at comedy. In Ford's next film, *Donovan's Reef* (1963), he appears as a kind of overgrown schoolboy in a whimsical joke about American sailors 'gone native' in the South Seas. Playing, as he had in *The Man Who Shot Liberty Valance*, against the formidable John Wayne, Marvin holds his own in bouts of gargantuan drinking and farcical fisticuffs, even taking time out to play with a toy train set.

It was this humorous vein that ultimately led to Marvin's acquiring star status – plus an Oscar – in the comedy-Western *Cat Ballou* (1965). Here he plays a dual role as both a

*Opposite page: Charles Bronson (top) as the gun-toting bank robber in* Machine Gun Kelly. *Bottom left: Lewton Cole (James Coburn) finds himself in a spot of bother after a stolen wallet leads to a duel and a murder charge in* Waterhole #3 *(1967). Bottom right: hewn from granite –* Lee Marvin *in* The Big Red One

black-hearted hired killer and his boozed-up ex-gunslinger brother – whose gestures toward machismo tend to be undercut by the frequency with which his pants fall down, but who pulls himself together sufficiently to vanquish his sibling in the climactic showdown. This could be seen to symbolize Marvin's farewell to his villainous past, for from then on – with his name safely above the title – his career proceeded along new lines.

On the one hand he periodically returned to the whiskery, eye-rolling eccentricity of *Cat Ballou* – most unexpectedly, perhaps, in the musical *Paint Your Wagon* (1969), from which his raspingly melancholic rendition of the song 'Wandering Star' became a surprise popular hit – but to contrast with the extravagance of performances such as these, Marvin has also (to rather more notable effect) offered a series of functionally pared-down portraits of pragmatic men of action. Those figures can be moral (the righteous soldier of fortune in *The*

*Above left: rivals (Montgomery Clift and Lee Marvin) photo-finish at the* Raintree County *(1957) Fourth of July race. Above: Dwayne Hickman, Tom Nardini, Michael Callan, Jane Fonda, John Marley and Marvin in* Cat Ballou

*Professionals*, 1966) or wholly amoral (the avenging hit-man of *Point Blank*, 1967), but they are united by the way in which their physical assertiveness is offset by an unsettling impassivity.

It was as the mission leader in the war movie *The Dirty Dozen* (1967), a character at once both martinet and iconoclast, that this distinctive blending found itself a forceful and popularly acclaimed niche. More recently, Marvin's most fruitful appearances have been as the laconic Southern law officer in *The Klansman* (1974) and – edging further into abstraction as he gets older – as the sergeant, a granite-like eternal soldier, at the centre of *The Big Red One* (1980).

## Cool, calculating James Coburn
If Marvin has been seen to best advantage in 'non-character' roles, the opposite tends to be true of James Coburn, whose lanky frame is reminiscent of Marvin's even if his personality has leaned more toward the debonair.

Coburn, born in 1928, first received recognition as the knife-throwing member of *The Magnificent Seven* (1960). He had several good small roles over the next few years, notably in *Charade* (1963) as a latter-day cowboy stomping incongruously around Paris in threatening pursuit of Audrey Hepburn, and more sympathetically, as the grizzled cavalry scout in *Major Dundee* (1965).

He finally achieved star billing as one of the rather Jolly Rogerish pirates in *A High Wind in Jamaica* (1965), a performance that characteristically combines a light-hearted demeanour with a hint of underlying pessimism. But the starring vehicles then contrived for him proved to be unrewarding additions to the then prevalent secret-agent cycle – *Our Man Flint* (1965) and its sequel *In Like Flint* (1967). Playing a stereotyped super-spy of such multi-faceted talents that he is enlisted as a ballet master in his few moments of spare time, Coburn was thrown back on a somewhat mechanical display of cool charisma.

Quite a few of Coburn's subsequent movies

proved indifferent or unpopular (in some cases both), but *The President's Analyst* (1967) utilizes his capacity for bemused comedy better than the Flint films. By contrast *Hard Contract* (1969), casting him as a professional assassin, exploits his grimmer side quite effectively. However, Coburn's most memorable role during the past decade has been that of Garrett in Sam Peckinpah's *Pat Garrett and Billy the Kid* (1973). Here Coburn eloquently and economically brings out the implications of Garrett's being a man divided against himself, and destroying himself as surely as his erstwhile friend and eventual quarry, Billy the Kid.

*The Last Hard Men* (1976) is not a particularly distinguished Western – in fact, it is an inferior Peckinpah imitation – but at least it provided Coburn with a meatily villainous role as a murderous train robber, and with a worthy adversary in Charlton Heston as the veteran peace officer who manages to put paid to his activities.

## James Coburn: filmography

**1959** Ride Lonesome; Face of a Fugitive. **'60** The Magnificent Seven. **'62** Hell Is for Heroes. **'63** The Great Escape; The Murder Men (compiled from *eps* of TV series: Cain's Hundreds); Charade; The Man From Galveston (orig. pilot for TV series: Temple Houston). **'64** The Americanization of Emily. **'65** Major Dundee; A High Wind in Jamaica (GB); The Loved One (guest); Our Man Flint. **'66** What Did You Do in the War, Daddy?; Dead Heat on a Merry-Go-Round. **'67** In Like Flint; Waterhole #3; The President's Analyst. **'68** Duffy (GB); Candy (USA-IT-FR). **'69** Hard Contract; The Last of the Mobile Hot-Shots (re-released as: Blood Kin). **'72** Giú la Testa (IT) (USA: Duck! You Sucker; GB: A Fistful of Dynamite); The Honkers; The Carey Treatment. **'73** Una Ragione per Vivere e una per Morire (IT-FR-SP-GER) (USA/GB: A Reason to Live, a Reason to Die; video rel. title: Massacre at Fort Holman); The Last of Sheila; Pat Garrett and Billy the Kid; Harry in Your Pocket. **'74** The Internecine Project (GB-GER). **'75** Bite the Bullet; Hard Times (GB: The Streetfighter). **'76** Sky Riders; The Last Hard Men; Midway (GB: Battle of Midway); White Rock (doc) (appearance as narr. only). **'77** Cross of Iron (GB-GER). **'78** Convoy (2nd unit dir. only); Circle of Iron (co-sc. only) (GB: The Silent Flute); Private Eye (compiled from TV series: The Dain Curse); California Suite (guest). **'79** Firepower (GB); The Muppet Movie (guest); Goldengirl. **'80** The Baltimore Bullet; Mr Patman/Patman/Midnight Matinee (CAN); Loving Couples. **'81** Looker; High Risk.

*Opposite page: the sublime (Coburn as leader of a German battalion in* Cross of Iron, 1977) *and the ridiculous (spy extraordinaire in* In Like Flint). *Bottom: a prizefighting team – Coburn and Bronson in* Hard Times

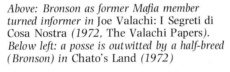

*Above: Bronson as former Mafia member turned informer in* Joe Valachi: I Segreti di Cosa Nostra *(1972,* The Valachi Papers). *Below left: a posse is outwitted by a half-breed (Bronson) in* Chato's Land *(1972)*

## Charles Bronson: man of action

In more relaxed vein, Coburn was certainly impressive as the manager of a bare-knuckle fighter in *Hard Times* (1975), a film in which the role of the enigmatic fighter provided one of the best recent opportunities for another leading screen tough guy, Charles Bronson. Born in 1921, Bronson's screen career started at the same time as Marvin's: both made their debut with bit parts in the comedy *You're in the Navy Now* (1951). However Bronson, who until 1954 used his Lithuanian family name Buchinsky, remained longer in minor roles (one of the most striking was as Vincent Price's assistant in the horror film *House of Wax*, 1953). It wasn't until the late Fifties that he found himself promoted to leading parts in B pictures, among them Roger Corman's *Machine Gun Kelly* (1958). The quizzical air of latent brutality attached to Bronson's early screen persona lent itself forcefully to the film's lurid view of a psychopath.

In the Sixties Bronson's progress quickened: he graduated to lead heavy in big-budget films, notably as the flamboyant villain of the Western *Four for Texas* (1963); he appeared in 'non-violent' roles in films such as *The Sandpiper* (1965) where, somewhat surprisingly, he plays a 'beat generation' sculptor; and in *The Dirty Dozen* his upward mobility within the star system was signified by the fact that he not only plays a largely sympathetic character but is also actually allowed – unlike most of the rest of the cast – to remain alive for the end titles.

However, it was in Europe that the seal was set on Bronson's career. In a string of foreign-made Westerns and crime thrillers, especially in *C'Era una Volta il West* (1968, *Once Upon a Time in the West*), Bronson – despite, or possibly because of, his craggily unconventional physique – became a top box-office draw on the continent.

On the strength of this newly-won prestige,

Bronson returned to the US and a run of starring vehicles, several of them in tandem with his wife, British actress Jill Ireland. Most of these were routine action films, relying heavily on the foreign market to turn in the profits. However, one or two were more interesting, notably *Hard Times* with its spare and rigorous setting in Depression-era New Orleans.

*Death Wish* (1974) quite cleverly rings the changes on Bronson's screen image, presenting him in its early stages as a quiet professional man, model husband and father, who is then transformed into a one-man army, waging war against Manhattan's muggers after his wife and daughter are raped and murdered. And *Breakout* (1975) is an enjoyable adventure story, exploiting the easier-going side of Bronson's personality by casting him as a jack-of-all-trades prevailed upon to spring a fellow-American from a Mexican jail.

Though sometimes cast in an ambiguous light, Bronson has essentially remained on the side of the angels in recent years. It would be nice to think, however, that beneath the surface of his rehabilitated screen character there still lurks – as with other ostensibly reformed ex-heavies like Marvin – a little of the old anti-social impulse.        TIM PULLEINE

---

**Charles Bronson: filmography**
**1951** You're in the Navy Now/USS Teakettle; The People Against O'Hara (retitling for USA TV: The Sweet Smell of Failure); The Mob (GB: Remember That Face). **'52** Red Skies of Montana/Smoke Jumpers; The Marrying Kind; My Six Convicts; Pat and Mike; Diplomatic Courier; Bloodhounds of Broadway; The Clown. **'53** House of Wax; Crime Wave (GB: The City Is Dark); Miss Sadie Thompson. **'54** Tennessee Champ; Riding Shotgun; Apache; Drum Beat; Vera Cruz. **'55** Big House, USA; Target Zero. **'56** Jubal; Explosion (short) (orig. *ep* of TV series: Warner Brothers Presents). **'57** Run of the Arrow. **'58** Ten North Frederick; Showdown at Boot Hill; Gang War; Machine Gun Kelly; When Hell Broke Loose. **'59** Never So Few. **'60** The Magnificent Seven. **'61** Master of the World; A Thunder of Drums; X-15. **'62** Kid Galahad; **'63** The Great Escape; Four for Texas. **'64** Guns of Diablo (compiled from *eps* of TV series: The Travels of Jaimie McPheeters); This Rugged Land (compiled from *eps* of TV series: Empire). **'65** Bull of the West (compiled from *eps* of TV series: The Virginian); The Sandpiper; Battle of the Bulge. **'66** This Property Is Condemned. **'67** The Dirty Dozen. **'68** La Bataille de San Sebastian (FR-MEX-IT) (USA/GB: Guns for San Sebastian); Villa Rides!; Adieu l'Ami (FR-IT) (GB: Farewell, Friend); C'Era Una Volta il West (IT) (USA/GB: Once Upon a Time in the West). **'69** Twinky (GB) (USA: Lola). **'70** Le Passager de la Pluie (FR-IT) (USA/GB: Rider on the Rain); You Can't Win 'em All (GB); Città Violenta (IT-FR) (USA: The Family; GB: Violent City). **'71** De La Part des Copains (FR-IT) (USA/GB: Cold Sweat); Quelqu'un Derrière la Porte (FR-IT) (USA: Someone Behind the Door; GB: Two Minds for Murder); Soleil Rouge (FR-IT-SP) (USA/GB: Red Sun). **'72** Chato's Land (GB); The Mechanic (re-released in GB as: Killer of Killers); Joe Valachi: I Segreti di Cosa Nostra (IT-FR) (USA/GB: The Valachi Papers). **'73** Valdez il Mezzosangue (IT-SP-FR) (USA: Chino; GB: Valdez the Halfbreed); The Stone Killer. **'74** Mr Majestyk; Death Wish. **'75** Breakout; Hard Times (GB: The Streetfighter). **'76** Breakheart Pass; St Ives; From Noon Till Three; Raid on Entebbe (orig. TV). **'77** The White Buffalo; Telefon. **'79** Love and Bullets. **'80** Cabo Blanco (USA-SP); Borderline. **'81** Death Hunt. **'82** Death Wish II. **'83** Ten to Midnight.

# Robert Altman

Apart from making Donald Sutherland and Elliott Gould into world stars, and Major 'Hot Lips' Houlihan (Sally Kellerman) into a national monument, *M\*A\*S\*H* exhibited Altman's naturalistic overlapping dialogues for the first time, and an editing technique that audaciously mixed realism with parody, leaving the viewer uncertain which was which. It was a *tour de force* of film-making, a signal to the world that a major American talent had at last found his wings – even the essential glibness of thought seemed not to matter at the time.

## Finding new wings

Convinced now that he would be taken seriously, Altman made *Brewster McCloud* (1970) which, as one critic has said:

'. . . touched on everything from the Icarus myth to the red shoes Margaret Hamilton never got to wear in *The Wizard of Oz*.'

The story of a young man preparing to fly like a bird in the depths of the Houston Astrodome, with the assistance of a bird-woman mentor, the film was poorly received but remembered with affection. Certainly, its swingeing satire of anything and everything

# and the Movies ... or Hollywood's History Lesson

**Ever since *M\*A\*S\*H*, Hollywood and the American film establishment have had a love-hate relationship with this remarkably resilient director. He is loved because he became, astonishingly late in life, the prodigal son of the 'new' Hollywood and darling of the counter-culture. He is hated because he seems to make movies the way other people pour coffee – with none of the anticipatory hype that is generally considered par for the course**

Robert Altman's greatest break was the huge success of *M\*A\*S\*H* in 1970. It was a financial triumph that instantly made him a bankable director, inspired a very long-running television series and forced Hollywood to move in radically different directions. Yet Altman was 45 when he made *M\*A\*S\*H*, and its producer, Ingo Preminger, suggested that he would not have had the opportunity if those who hired him had seen his previous work, which they afterwards watched with some horror.

What is worse, he has never had another financial hit like *M\*A\*S\*H*, though his more recent *Popeye* (1980) did much better than was expected by those who first saw it. He has had an astonishing career over the last decade or so, influencing many of the best young American film-makers, but never really convincing the business side of the industry that he gives a damn about it. He is an enigma to many, and possibly even to himself.

## Many\*Americans\*Seem\*Hostile

Altman was born in Kansas City, Missouri, in 1925, the son of an insurance salesman who was also an inveterate gambler. He was raised a Roman Catholic and studied mathematics at college. After serving as a World War II bomber pilot, he took a job directing industrial films for the Calvin Company in Kansas, which eventually led to his directing and producing *The Delinquents* in 1957 and *The James Dean Story* later that year. These two not very remarkable films led to a long stint in televi-

sion, directing episodes of *Alfred Hitchcock Presents*, *Bonanza*, *Whirlibirds* and many other popular series. If he formed a style in those days, it is not now readily apparent. What the experience could have taught him was how to work fast and knit together as competently as possible material that would not disturb the brains of a flea. This, he now says, is exactly what he did not want to learn.

His next feature film was the Warner Brothers science-fiction epic *Countdown* in 1967, followed two years later by *That Cold Day in the Park* (1969) which was somewhat better reviewed and had about it an atmosphere and technical dexterity that eventually became two of the hallmarks of his later projects. His evocation of the Canadian scene was more striking than the psychodrama between its schizophrenic heroine Frances (Sandy Dennis) and the new man in her life (Michael Burns).

But, whatever the estimation of that film, which some regard as a real beginning, no-one was prepared for what Altman made of the Mobile Army Surgical Hospital in *M\*A\*S\*H*. Ring Lardner Jr's screenplay had been offered to well over a dozen other directors before Altman, who decided that they had all missed a golden opportunity to go for bust. The ribald, irreverent comedy he made of it went even further than Lardner had hoped in deflating official hypocrisy about the war in Korea. Nothing was sacred, not even the blood of the heroic wounded. But, more important, the film was technically daring, too.

Far left: Robert Altman wielding his own
clapperboard on the set of Nashville. Above: the
wild humour of M*A*S*H – now almost a
byword for anti-government satire – was a
brilliant send-up of military pride

Below: The Long Goodbye attempted to
transpose detective Philip Marlowe (Elliott
Gould) to the offbeat modernity of Hollywood.
Bottom right: Warren Beatty as McCabe, the
defeated pioneer in McCabe and Mrs Miller

American still looks shrewd, if ill organized.

Altman had thus gone from box-office
smash hit to minority cult film within the
space of a year. *McCabe and Mrs Miller* – made
in 1971 and later voted by a plethora of critics
one of the ten best films of the decade – was
intended to steer a middle course. It was not a
satire, except in a few incidentals, but a true
story of the Old West, counteracting and
subverting most of the usual Hollywood
clichés, Pauline Kael called it:

'. . . a beautiful pipe-dream of a movie – a
fleeting, almost diaphanous vision of what
frontier life might have been.'

The story of a little man (Warren Beatty)
who builds a community with the help of a
clever madam (Julie Christie) only to lose it to
more powerful people, it is Altman's sharpest
visualization of the corruption of the American
Dream. It is also about optimists who are born
losers, and gamblers who never really expect
to win. Above all, it is a supremely beautiful
movie, and the next year Altman went on to
make another.

*Images* (1972), though, was magnificent
only on its surface and fairly pretentious
underneath. The story – set in a misty, ghostly
Ireland – concerns a schizophrenic woman
(Susannah York) through whose perceptions
is constructed an argument about what is real
and what is false. If *Images* made some think
that Altman was intent on becoming a European art director, *The Long Goodbye* (1973),
*Thieves Like Us* and *California Split* (both 1974)
put him securely back in his own natural
territory. All three films made comments specifically about America; the first two about
American films as well.

By now, Altman had gathered around him a
group of actors and technicians who formed a
kind of stock company in opposition to the

established order, and who knew what he was about. He had an organization he could trust, and who trusted him. *The Long Goodbye* was perhaps the most considerable of these films: a highly original up-dating of Raymond Chandler, with Elliott Gould as a puzzled and far from omnipotent Philip Marlowe, no longer wandering the dark city streets of yore, but tramping the bright boulevards of Los Angeles.

*Thieves Like Us* was virtually a remake of Nicholas Ray's *They Live by Night* (1948), and was taken from the novel which inspired the Ray film. But its portrait of ignorant robbers pushing their luck to extremes and then taking the consequences, in a decaying, ramshackle South, is not as striking as either Arthur Penn's *Bonnie and Clyde* (1967) or Terrence Malick's *Badlands* (1973).

*California Split* goes back to California, gambling and a view of American men chasing women but finding real friendship only with each other. The resonances, though, are patchy and fail to make an entirely convincing whole.

*Nashville* (1975) was a different matter altogether, weaving a score of characters into a cinematic tapestry that achieves both shape and purpose. This film is in the top ten American movies of the Seventies (Altman is the only director mentioned twice in this critics' poll) and fully deserves its accolade. Pauline Kael termed it 'an orgy' and saw, in its depiction of the Nashville country-music scene, an allegory about the whole of America. Others were more circumspect – 'Let Us Not

Praise *Nash[...]*
essay whic[...]
ambitious i[...]
his only a[...]
of arbitr[...]
watchers[...]
just the v[...]
looked ou[...]
seen and[...]

**Rapid [...]**
After *Na[...]*
. . . *or Sit[...]*
Paul Ne[...]
Altman's [...]
De Laure[...]
it is, at l[...]
well as r[...]
ican my[...]
as the n[...]
1977. A[...]
*Three W[...]*
preten[...]
mation[...]

*A W[...]*
(both 1[...]
in qui[...]
achiev[...]
some [...]
fiction[...]
hacke[...]
politic[...]
of th[...]
financ[...]
cartoo[...]

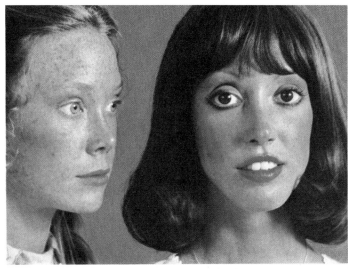

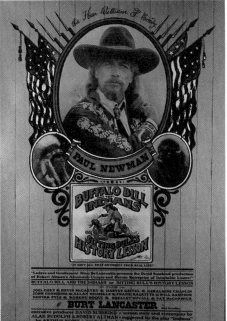

*Above left: Shelley Duvall and Louise Fletcher in* Thieves Like Us. *Above right: a strange girl (Sissy Spacek) and her friend (Duvall) are two of the* Three Women. *Left: Altman shows the Wild West hero as just a showman. Below: Duvall as Olive Oyl, Robin Williams as* Popeye

of McCabe and made on a giant set which was, like that of *McCabe and Mrs Miller*, almost a world in itself. And Altman is now reaching yet another turning-point in his career.

His company, Lion's Gate, which has enabled him to make his own films comparatively cheaply with first-class technical facilities, is no longer operating. There was no possibility of its continuing to support young film-makers or those who cannot get money anywhere else – like Alan Rudolph who made *Welcome to LA* (1976) and Robert Benton with his *The Late Show* (1977). But there seems, however, no prospect of Altman himself drying up. He has the priceless ability to move from one project to another before profits or losses are finally counted, and to inspire confidence in people who usually play safer than they do with him.

In a way, Altman is a legend in his own

lifetime, a creator among artisans and the very antithesis of the conveyor-belt director. He is universally admired for his independent spirit and originality, even by those who do not regard his work that highly. Among those who value it greatly, he is cherished as the one mature outpost of sanity in an insane system that often seems intent on self-destruction. 'Like a lot of Americans, I'm ambivalent about America. I love it and hate it.'

That seems to be America's reaction to him, particularly Hollywood Americans who want recognizable heroes in their films, not characters like Brewster McCloud, Buffalo Bill and McCabe who refuse to fit preconceptions. In hard times, anyone dealing with uncertainties rather than certainties is deeply suspected. And this perhaps is Robert Altman's chief concern – to look out of windows and see the passing scene differently. His is surely a worthier aim than that of nine out of ten film-makers. As he insisted years ago:

'I'm trying to reach toward a picture – I don't think I'll ever succeed but somebody else will if I start the ball rolling – that's totally emotional, not narrative or intellectual, where an audience walks out and can't tell anything about it except what they feel.'

DEREK MALCOLM

**Filmography**
1947 The Secret Life of Walter Mitty (actor only). '48 Bodyguard (co-sc. only). '54 The Builders (doc. short). '57 The Delinquents (+sc); The James Dean Story (doc) (co-dir; +co-prod; +co-ed). '64 Nightmare in Chicago (orig. TV; retitling for TV: Kraft Suspense Theatre: Once Upon a Savage Night). '67 Countdown. '69 That Cold Day in the Park (USA-CAN). '70 M*A*S*H; Brewster McCloud. '71 McCabe and Mrs Miller (+co-sc). '72 Images (+sc) (EIRE). '73 The Long Goodbye. '74 Thieves Like Us (+co-sc); California Split (+co-prod). '75 Nashville (+prod; +co-song); Russian Roulette (actor only). '76 Buffalo Bill and the Indians . . . or Sitting Bull's History Lesson (+prod; +co-sc); Welcome to LA (prod. only). '77 The Late Show (prod. only); Three Women (+prod; +sc). '78 A Wedding (+prod; +co-sc); Remember My Name (prod. only). '79 Quintet (+prod; +co-sc); A Perfect Couple (+prod; +co-sc); Rich Kids (exec. prod. only). '80 Health (+prod; +co-sc); Popeye. '82 Come Back to the 5 & Dime Jimmy Dean, Jimmy Dean; Precious Blood (TV); Rattlesnake in a Cooler (TV). '83 Streamers. '84 The Ugly Monstrous Mind-Roasting Summer of O.C. and Stiggs.

# ENTER LAUGHING

**As the old guard of comedy faded out, a new generation was emerging in the late Sixties and the Seventies to keep the laughter flowing**

As the Seventies began, the continuity of Hollywood comedy appeared to have been ruptured, with virtually all the top-line comedians and most of the leading directors associated with the genre for many years now vanished from the screen. The triumphant survivor among directors was Billy Wilder. But even his output became sporadic, and after the commercial failure of the delightful Italian-set romantic comedy *Avanti!* (1972), he ran for cover with a raucously lively but fairly conservative remake of the old Broadway warhorse *The Front Page* (1974).

The intermittently brilliant ex-cartoonist Frank Tashlin, who died in 1972, had directed the last starring vehicle of Danny Kaye, *The Man From the Diner's Club* (1963). Tashlin concluded his career with *The Private Navy of Sergeant O'Farrell* (1968), one of the brighter spots in the generally disappointing later work of another veteran comic, Bob Hope, who made his most recent appearance in *Cancel My Reservation* (1972).

Jerry Lewis remained active as both performer and director throughout the Sixties, but the quality of his work showed evident signs of decline as the decade wore on. After an uninspired war comedy *Ja Ja Mein General! But Which Way to the Front?* (1970), he retreated into silence, apparently beset by personal difficulties, not to re-emerge until *Hardly Working* (1980), about an unemployed circus clown who pretends to be a variety of characters; the film scored a cult critical success in France but has been less well received elsewhere.

The one comic performer who remained a sure-fire box-office proposition during the Seventies was Peter Sellers in the guise of the bumbling Inspector Clouseau, centrepiece of a string of spin-offs from *The Pink Panther* (1963). These films, including *The Return of the Pink Panther* (1975) and *The Pink Panther Strikes Again* (1976), were elegantly directed by Blake Edwards, who later notched up a success of a different sort with the sex comedy *'10'* (1979), featuring his wife Julie Andrews, later to bare her bosom in his Hollywood satire *S.O.B.* (1981).

Sex comedy, if of a generally rather cautious and compromised kind, proved one of the staples of Hollywood humour in the Seventies. Typical were *The Owl and the Pussycat* (1970), with George Segal exercising his rumpled charm as a timid bookshop assistant caught up with Barbra Streisand's eccentric call-girl, and *A Touch of Class* (1973), with Segal again, this time as an untimid insurance man, partnered by Glenda Jackson as the business-woman with whom he indulges in an extra-marital affair. Segal starred, too, in *Blume in Love* (1973), an engaging film in which director Paul Mazursky consolidated the instinct he had shown in *Bob & Carol & Ted & Alice* (1969) for sympathetic and inventively funny examinations of modern sexual customs, a talent he was subsequently to develop in *An Unmarried Woman* (1978), starring Jill Clayburgh.

It was the enormous popularity of *The Graduate* (1967), the story of a young man's first encounters

with sex and love, that really gave impetus to 'permissive' comedy, while the scale of its success also turned director Mike Nichols into a prestigiously hot property. His blockbuster anti-war satire *Catch-22* (1970), adapted from Joseph Heller's supposedly unfilmable cult novel of the previous decade, was followed by *Carnal Knowledge* (1971), which, scripted by cartoonist Jules Feiffer, traces the amorous rakes' progress of two erstwhile college boys. Perhaps Nichols' best-achieved film, however, was his least ambitious, *The Fortune* (1975), a knockabout farce set in the Twenties, with Jack Nicholson and Warren Beatty as a pair of incompetent would-be killers.

Nichols initially made a gilded reputation partnering Elaine May, first in nightclubs, then on Broadway, in a series of fashionable satirical sketches. Elaine May was herself to venture into the cinema, as actress and later as director, notably of *A New Leaf* (1971), an acidly amusing little fable about an unprepossessing heiress (May) whom a penniless upper-class loafer (Walter Matthau) seeks to marry for her money.

In the theatre, Nichols directed two plays by the writer who, since the early Sixties, has dominated mainstream humour on Broadway, and increasingly in Hollywood, too – Neil Simon (though, perhaps strangely, Nichols has never directed Simon's work for the cinema). Simon's name rapidly became a byword for profitability, and virtually all his plays have been converted into movies. Simon himself scripted the adaptations of *Barefoot in the Park* (1967), *The Odd Couple* (1968), *The Prisoner of Second Avenue* (1974) and *The Sunshine Boys* (1975), among others. He also branched out into original screenplays, for conventional situation comedies such as *The Out-of-Towners* (1970), and for two ingenious spoofs of detective fiction, *Murder by Death* (1976) and *The Cheap Detective* (1978). Simon's work can sometimes seem hollow and predictable (as in *Plaza Suite*, 1971) but he retains an uncanny instinct for giving the public

*Above: Freddie (Stockard Channing) is an heiress, Nicky (Warren Beatty) is her lover and, for convenience, Oscar (Jack Nicholson) is her husband; both men want to murder her for her money – but, since it is a comedy, they do not succeed. Below: God (George Burns) enlists a disciple (John Denver) and even testifies for him in court when he is sued for slander after passing on God's opinion of a mercenary revivalist preacher*

*Above: in his* History of the World – Part One *(1981), Mel Brooks plays several parts. As Moses, he drops one of the three tablets of stone and, luckily for sinners, announces only ten instead of fifteen commandments. Top: Sonja (Diane Keaton) reluctantly marries her cousin Boris (Woody Allen) when he unexpectedly survives a duel in* Love and Death, *a witty parody of Tolstoy with a dash of Ingmar Bergman. Top right: Michael Palin as a cured leper and Graham Chapman as Brian, who accidentally becomes a prophet, in* Monty Python's Life of Brian, *which departs radically from the cinema's usual cautiously reverent treatment of religious themes*

what it wants.

Simon's pre-Broadway apprenticeship was served as television writer and gagman, notably for the Sid Caesar programme *Your Show of Shows*, on which his fellow employees included no fewer than three other men who were to become key figures in the cinema – Carl Reiner, Mel Brooks and Woody Allen.

Reiner, who also appeared in the Caesar show, went on to become the creator of the hit series *The Dick Van Dyke Show*, and after writing a couple of nondescript movies (*The Thrill of It All*, 1963; *The Art of Love*, 1965) assumed the mantle of film director. His first feature, *Enter Laughing* (1967), derived from his semi-autobiographical novel, was a somewhat forcedly comic account of a young man's attempts to break into show business, while *The Comic* (1969), his second film, was a falteringly off-beat vehicle for Dick Van Dyke as an unlikeable silent-screen comedian. But in the late Seventies, Reiner was responsible for two extremely popular comedies showcasing contrasted personalities. *Oh, God!* (1977) is a whimsical joke in which veteran funny-man George Burns essays the role of the Almighty, whilst *The Jerk* (1979) casts Steve Martin in a picaresque farce about an ex-foundling trying without conspicuous success to make good in life. Reiner's best film, though, remains *Where's Poppa?* (1970), a distinctive black comedy featuring Ruth Gordon as a senile Jewish momma and George Segal as her harassed son.

Mel Brooks, formerly a comedy artist in nightclubs and on television, as well as the creator of several television series, including *Get Smart*, burst on to the movie scene as writer-director of the

hilariously tasteless *The Producers* (1967). Then, during the Seventies, he turned out a succession of zany send-ups of established film genres, starting with the immensely profitable parody-Western *Blazing Saddles* (1974), full of genially lunatic invention. Brooks progressed to *Young Frankenstein* (1974), filmed in black and white and actually utilizing the laboratory props from the original Universal Frankenstein movies, and to *High Anxiety* (1977), an affectionate parodic homage to Alfred Hitchcock – to whom it is dedicated.

The star of various Brooks movies has been Gene Wilder, a comic actor with a considerable flair for the absurder aspects of neurotic vulnerability, who has twice functioned as writer-director of vehicles

## Modern Hollywood comedy often depends on star performers who are also writers and directors

for himself. *The Adventure of Sherlock Holmes' Smarter Brother* (1975) has some appealing semi-surrealist touches, though *The World's Greatest Lover* (1977) is a mainly misfiring farce about Hollywood in the Twenties, the background also of Brooks' *Silent Movie* (1976). And Marty Feldman, who played a featured role in *Young Frankenstein*, turned director for yet another genre spoof, the largely misconceived *The Last Remake of Beau Geste* (1977).

Undoubtedly the outstanding comic talent of the modern cinema belongs to Woody Allen. Ex-cabaret performer and playwright (*Play It Again Sam*, filmed 1972), Allen began his directorial career in the cinema – having earlier written and appeared in *What's New, Pussycat?* (1965) – with modestly-budgeted, almost revue-like movies centred round himself, such as *Take the Money and Run* (1969) and *Bananas* (1971). But then, with the delightful Diane Keaton as his co-star, he moved on to the elaborately-formulated comedy of *Sleeper* (1973) and *Love and Death* (1975), and thence to the considerable ambition of such overtly personal, thoughtful but still dazzlingly funny works as *Annie Hall* (1977) and *Manhattan* (1979).

In Britain, humour on the big screen has tended to draw on what has already been done on television. At one end of the scale, this has simply meant that numerous television situation comedies were adapted as movies, usually with dispiriting results. Even when the original television shows were above average, as with *The Likely Lads* (filmed 1976) or *Rising Damp* (filmed 1980), the adjustment to a different medium tended to be problematical.

Then again, admired television performers gravitated to the cinema, notably Peter Cook and Dudley Moore, once ubiquitous satirical presences on the domestic screen. But they were none too lucky with their material: Stanley Donen's *Bedazzled* (1967) was a lame updating of the Faust legend, while Paul Morrissey's *The Hound of the Baskervilles* (1978) was an embarrassingly silly parody of the Conan Doyle story about Sherlock Holmes. Moore, however, fared better in Hollywood, where he took the male lead in *'10'* and *Arthur* (1981).

The principal humorous success on British television in the early Seventies was *Monty Python's Flying Circus*, a weird pot-pourri of satire, whimsy and aggressive eccentricity, which – along with its regular performers, who included John Cleese, Eric Idle and Graham Chapman – soon acquired cult status and a huge following. Inevitably the cinema beckoned. *And Now for Something Completely Different* (1971) was a rather cautious beginning, merely a rehash of their television routines. But *Monty Python and the Holy Grail* (1975) was notably more ambitious, complementing the random gag-making with a visually imaginative creation of a mock-medieval landscape. In a comparable vein, but this time deliberately courting controversy, *Monty Python's Life of Brian* (1979) was nothing less than a manic alternative version of the New Testament.

Uneven as they may be, these films stand in stark contrast to most other recent British comedies. As the Carry On series gradually faded away during the Seventies, it was replaced by the Confessions movies, to equally styleless but considerably less welcome effect. Starring the simpering Robin Askwith, these low-budget productions, which included *Confessions of a Window Cleaner* (1974) and *Confessions of a Pop Performer* (1975), were sold on the strength of nothing but unremitting coarseness.

With equal coarseness, West Germany churned out a seemingly endless string of soft-core sex romps, featuring pot-bellied, cigar-smoking lechers and feather-brained damsels ready to throw off their clothes at any (or no) provocation. The Italian studios also purveyed a fair amount of broadly comparable fare. But at least there were also some Italian comedies of a more rewarding kind, often directed by such veterans as Luigi Comencini and Dino Risi. Old-time matinée idol Vittorio Gassman starred in Risi's *Profumo di Donna* (1975, *That Female Scent*), a quite stylish black comedy about the love-life of a blinded cavalry officer.

In France, another Italian star, Marcello Mastroianni, figured in Italian director Marco Ferreri's *La Grande Bouffe* (1973, *Blow-Out*), a bizarre satire about a quartet of well-heeled gourmets who decide to gorge themselves to death. An eyebrow-raising French comedy was Bertrand Blier's scabrous *Les Valseuses* (1974, *Making It*), depicting the amorous and criminal adventures of a couple of slobs. The same director later scored a widespread popular hit with the more sentimentally inclined *Préparez Vos Mouchoirs* (1977, *Get Out Your Handkerchiefs*), which concerned a man trying to find his girlfriend a new lover.

An even bigger boulevard hit, however, subsequently to become one of the biggest-grossing French films ever shown in the USA, was Edouard Molinaro's *La Cage aux Folles* (1978, *Birds of a Feather*), a stagy but smartly-timed comedy of homosexual manners. This spawned a sequel, the less amusing *La Cage aux Folles II* (1980). Earlier, Molinaro directed an effectively sharp little black comedy *L'Emmerdeur* (1973, *Pain in the A\*\**), which neatly contrasted the personalities of Lino Ventura, as an underworld hit man, and Jacques Brel, as the dejected salesman whose suicide attempts constantly get in the way of the killer's professional obligations.

This film, or at least the play from which it derives, provided the basis for Billy Wilder's *Buddy Buddy* (1981), starring Walter Matthau and Jack Lemmon. Perhaps, after all, there is more continuity in present-day cinema comedy than might appear to be the case.　　　　TIM PULLEINE

*Below:* National Lampoon's Animal House *(1978) celebrates the unruly life of a college fraternity house, whose members are considered the blight of the campus, back in 1962. 'Bluto' (John Belushi, centre of group) is one of the chief troublemakers. Bottom: in* La Cage aux Folles, *Renato (Ugo Tognazzi) owns a homosexual nightclub and Albin (Michel Serrault), known as 'Zaza', is his star drag artist as well as his lover. Bottom left:* Airplane! *(1980) parodies those chronicles of in-flight disaster that make flying seem like a bad dream instead of a means of quick transport*

# Woody Allen

Woody Allen's first films were broad satires. In his later work he has opted for an increasingly baleful – and autobiographical – view of the world, one where love and sex become more and more impossible and death emerges as the biggest single fact of life. He directs movies in which he plays pained misfits possessed of a lacerating, self-deprecating wit and surrounded by hopelessly neurotic women. No other film-maker so readily associated with comedy has presented such a despondent and pessimistic vision of relationships and adult behaviour in modern bourgeois America

# Films about love and other neuroses

In his nightclub act, Woody Allen tells about once being offered a fortune to make some vodka advertisements and not knowing whether to accept or not. 'I needed the money,' he laments, 'but I feel that drinking intoxicating beverages is immoral.' Wracked by indecision, he seeks trustworthy advice – from his psychiatrist, his bank manager, finally his rabbi. 'Don't do it!' cries God's spokesman. 'Vodka is evil! Refuse the money!' He does, and immediately feels a better man for it. Later, he sees one of the ads he has righteously turned down. It shows Senta Berger in a skimpy bikini reclining on a sun-drenched beach holding a cool vodka and tonic. Her lips are provocatively parted, her eyes smoulder with desire for the man beside her. The man is Allen's rabbi.

There, in angstful and Talmudic miniature, is the key to Woody Allen's vision and popular appeal as a film-maker. Critics have called his work undisciplined, confused, emotionally self-indulgent, psychologically and artistically dishonest. But audiences composed largely of the educated middle and upper classes have nevertheless come more and more to identify with the nerve-wracking little fables he builds upon his view of the world, and to agree, wryly, that modern urban life really is plagued by the treachery, false counsel, neurotic insecurity and pandemic philistinism he portrays.

Since 1966, when *What's Up, Tiger Lily?* was released, Allen has made or starred in approximately one film a year – and while none has been a box-office smash to the same degree as the films of Mel Brooks or Neil Simon (Hollywood's other two major comedy film-makers of the Seventies), all have earned money, nearly all go on being shown and re-shown in big-city cinemas around the world, and many are already considered comedy classics.

Born Allen Stewart Konigsberg in New York in 1935, he dropped out of university and began to write for television and top American comedians before working as a dramatist and stand-up comic himself. Allen's early films are, in fact, more like nightclub routines than proper movies – gags strung together around a theme with no serious attempt at organic cinematic composition. *What's Up, Tiger Lily?* is really the old game of putting funny captions to familiar pictures – in this case an English soundtrack to a Japanese samurai thriller – producing verbal pyrotechnics like, 'Heathen Pig! Saracen Dog! Spanish Fly!' *Take the Money and Run* (1969), in which Allen plays Virgil Stockwell, an underprivileged *schlemiel* chasing the American Dream (or Nightmare) who tries cello first, then bank robbery, and ends up getting life, is an episodic documentary send-

up of 'committed' sociological problem films complete with voice-over, psychoanalytic asides and comments from Jewish parents disguised in funny noses. *Bananas* (1971) stars Allen as Manhattan drop-out Fielding Mellish in a banana-republic revolution and is a topical bistro act – with palm trees – satirizing television ads, radical politics and New York culture snobbery.

## Sex and the single sheep

*Everything You Always Wanted to Know About Sex, But Were Afraid to Ask* (1972) is a series of revue sketches built loosely around the title of Dr David Reuben's pop sexology best-seller. Leaning hard on one-liners, innuendo, and a lot of ridiculous libidinal props, it is especially notable for one finely directed sequence featuring Gene Wilder as an hysterical psychiatrist who falls in love with a sheep, loses all, and ends up on Skid Row swigging Woolite. *Play It Again, Sam*, made by Herbert Ross in 1972 from Allen's Broadway play, is the story of a romantic creep-hero possessed by the spirit of Humphrey Bogart. The film is

111

important for Allen's first clearly defined performance as the 'little man' victimized by his own fears and self-loathing – the now familiar Allen persona – and for introducing Diane Keaton as his leading lady (she co-starred in four of his next six films). *Sleeper* (1973), Allen's fourth directorial outing and the first with a tight enough script to begin looking like a proper movie, is a parody of a science-fiction thriller taking a backwards look at Sixties and Seventies mid-cult American absurdities.

*Love and Death* (1975), a fondly observed parody of *War and Peace* and perhaps the best conceived of Allen's comedies, is his tribute to the classical literature that seems to play so important a role in his own vision of himself. Dealing with the themes of the title that will become steadily more important in his later films (at times insufferably so), the film ends with a hallmark sequence (reminiscent of the vodka joke) in which Allen, as Boris Grushenko, condemned to death for attempting to assassinate Napoleon (of *course* he failed), is solemnly promised by an angel that God means to spare his life – following which he is promptly and hitchlessly executed. Martin Ritt's *The Front* (1976) is the first film starring Allen to abandon a specifically funny format, and it serves as a bridge to the films that follow. An exposé of the McCarthyist persecution of film and television writers in the Fifties, it features Allen as Howard Prince, small-time hustler and pontificating 'front' for the scripts of blacklisted writers, who eventually finds some principles in himself, takes a stand against the Red-baiters and wins back the girl he loves as a reward.

## Panic in New York

Beginning with *Annie Hall* in 1977, Allen abruptly shifted tone in his films, dropped the earlier improbable formats, became nearly autobiographical, and began using humour as a counterpart to stories he deliberately intended as small, poignant tragedies of New York city life. The old worries still persist in the films that follow – the philistines still hedge him in, eliciting more wounded stares and painful, self-annihilating jokes – but new, more profound worries appear, too: a gnawing, almost panic-stricken doubt about the value of his own celebrity, and attached to that doubt, as if by handcuffs, the harrowing question of women and their power to save or destroy him. In *Annie Hall*, *Manhattan* (1979) and *Stardust Memories* (1980), the dominant

issue is the hero's failure to sustain a relationship with a woman, each time caused by his obsessive insecurity about his creative integrity and the real value of his work. In *Annie Hall*, Allen's insecurity takes the form of Pygmalion-playing. Alvy Singer, successful New York Jewish comedian and all-in masochist, already 16 years in analysis, meets Annie (Diane Keaton), mixed-up Midwestern WASP, decides he's in love, and immediately starts trying to turn her into somebody she isn't – somebody as bright, culturally-hip, guilt-ridden and insecure as he is – so he won't have to risk something 'permanent' is the apparent underlying psychology. Eventually, of course, it works. Annie discovers life with Alvy isn't fun anymore, leaves him and goes out to Hollywood – the ultimate betrayal – where, as Allen not altogether inaccurately observes, 'the only cultural advantage is that you can make a right turn on a red light'. They remain friends, but Annie has failed her test, and Alvy can safely retreat back to the lonely land of the misunderstood – where, presumably, he feels most comfortable.

*Interiors* (1978), Allen's first 'serious' film as director, is consecrated to this same brand of gratuitous suffering in such unbalanced excess that it comes dangerously close to self-parody. Publicly proclaiming *Interiors* as his first 'important' film, Allen democratically divides his private insecurities this time among several characters (but doesn't appear himself). The performances are uniformly good. The film

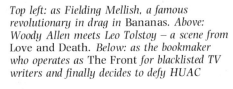

*Top left: as Fielding Mellish, a famous revolutionary in drag in* Bananas. *Above: Woody Allen meets Leo Tolstoy – a scene from* Love and Death. *Below: as the bookmaker who operates as* The Front *for blacklisted TV writers and finally decides to defy HUAC*

*looks* superb, and was obviously planned with great care. But because it was made in self-conscious imitation of the films of Ingmar Bergman (one of Allen's heroes and an unparalleled master of controlled mood), the script's excesses stand out against the carefully modulated background like something meant deliberately to shock, embarrass and ultimately be laughed at. It is arguable that if Allen had been less preoccupied with Bergman's style he might have made a better film of *Interiors* – except that, free of Bergman's

112

woman, is trying two new women: 17-year-old Tracy (Mariel Hemingway), who loves him, and Mary (Diane Keaton), his best friend's temporarily defected mistress, who does not. Eventually Isaac opts for Mary, occasioning a moving scene in which he must convince the tearful Tracy that she is wasting her life with a man twice her age and should go to London where a place in an acting school has been offered her. Tracy, heartbroken, agrees to leave him. Isaac only realizes Tracy was right for him all along when Mary announces she is leaving, too. But whether the realization grows from Isaac's actually having learned something about himself, or merely from panic at being suddenly left with no woman at all, is never properly explored, a serious shortcoming in an otherwise excellently observed story, which leaves Isaac a pathetic, rather despicable figure at the end.

passion, excitement, intelligence and an immediate understanding of his own dilemma. Daisy (Jessica Harper), a young musician Sandy meets at the resort hotel where he is attending a retrospective festival of his own films (which he despises), symbolizes innocence, a fresh start, and like Tracy in *Manhattan*, unconsidered allegiance. Isobel (Marie-Christine Barrault), a Frenchwoman with two children who has recently left her husband, represents wisdom, maturity, patience, home, stability. All three relationships fail, but the failures seem right in this film, consistent with the figure Sandy knows he has become: a player of old love scenes, still hopeful but running short of illusions and, apparently, time.

Almost indistinguishable now from his own private hang-ups, Allen's dramatized masochism becomes the essential glue that holds *Annie Hall*, *Interiors*, *Manhattan* and *Stardust Memories* together. He *has* to suffer from crippling self-doubt, he *has* to lose in love, otherwise his films won't work – and neither, presumably, will his life. At the beginning of *Annie Hall*, Alvy tells the famous joke about Groucho Marx always insisting that he would never join a club that would have him as a member. Recast, that joke states the issue perfectly: 'I need love,' Alvy is saying. 'Without love, creatively meaningful or not, my life is empty. But how can I possibly have faith in any woman who would love somebody like me?' The dilemma is not imagined. Woody Allen really does need love. That's why he imitates his film-maker heroes. And he really is worried about not yet having made a great film himself.

GEORGE ROBERT KIMBALL

*Above right: fruit of the future? Woody in* Sleeper. *Below: a rare moment of warmth between Renata (Diane Keaton) and Joey (Marybeth Hurt) in* Interiors. *Below right: Sandy greets his French mistress (Marie-Christine Barrault) in* Stardust Memories

influence, he almost certainly would not have made the film at all. For if there is one thing Allen has always stood against, it is pretentiousness in art, and *Interiors*' greatest single failing is that it is pretentious.

With *Manhattan*, Allen returned to New York realism and the proven path blazed by *Annie Hall* (winner of the 1977 Oscars for Best Picture, Best Director, Best Script and Best Actress). This time Allen is Isaac Davis, a successful television-comedy writer in mid-life crisis who, having lost his wife to another

*Stardust Memories* – a dream-like time-wandering, film-within-a-film imitation of Fellini's *Otto e Mezzo* (1963, $8\frac{1}{2}$) – is another creative *crise-de-coeur*, this time delivered by Sandy Bates (Allen), enormously popular maker of insignificant comedy movies, who, suffocated by his sycophantic fans and undeserved celebrity, longs to rid himself of 'upbeat endings' and do something meaningful with his life before it's too late. Death fills his dreams and visions, and there is a persuasive desperation about the character, lacking in the previous films, that makes his need for a woman's love more convincing. Now there are three, a universal triumvirate, who represent for Allen the three possible roads to salvation. Dorie (Charlotte Rampling), a neurotic actress plagued by jealousy and her own creative uncertainties, embodies the contemporary woman, Allen's female counterpart, and offers

**Filmography**
**1965** What's New, Pussycat? (sc; +act. only). '66 What's Up, Tiger Lily? (add. dir; +assoc. prod; +co-sc; +act. on re-ed. and dubbed version of Japanese film: Kizino Kizi, 1964). '67 Casino Royale (actor only) (GB). '69 Take the Money and Run (+co-sc; +act); Don't Drink the Water (orig. play only). '71 Bananas (+co-sc; +act). '72 Play It Again, Sam (sc. from own play; +act. only); Everything You Always Wanted to Know About Sex, But Were Afraid to Ask (+sc; +act). '73 Sleeper (+co-sc; +act; +mus). '75 Love and Death (+sc; +act). '76 The Front (actor only). '77 Annie Hall (+co-sc; +act). '78 Woody Allen: An American Comedy (doc) (appearance as himself; +narr. only); Interiors (+sc). '79 Manhattan (+co-sc; +act). '80 Stardust Memories (+sc; +act); To Woody Allen, From Europe With Love (doc) (appearance as himself only). '82 A Midsummer Night's Sex Comedy (+sc; +act). '83 Zelig (+sc; +act). '84 Broadway Danny Rose (+sc; +act); The Purple Rose of Cairo (+sc).

# With the greatest of ease
# Burt Reynolds

Somewhere inside Burt Reynolds' hirsute, hunky frame there lurkes an intelligent, warm, sensitive soul just waiting to break out and express itself. Indeed, the delicious irony is that his intentions seem sincere. To watch a reasonably gifted actor fight against the values placed on him by the movie industry is a neat reversal, for a man usually finds himself trapped by definitions of sexuality that generally work to suppress women.

Reynolds' name is synonymous with tough, knockabout action, and his employment prior to becoming an actor was excellent training: he had been a halfback for Florida State University's football team, had tried his hand at general athletics and was briefly a nightclub bouncer. His first parts were for television, in such all-action series as *Riverboat* (begun in 1959), *Hawk* (begun in 1966) and *Dan August* (begun in 1970). He finally broke into movies with a collection of straightforward macho roles of a disposable nature, also doubling as a stuntman. During the Sixties it seemed that his chesthair-count mattered more than anything else.

## Delivering the goods
In 1972 Reynolds (b. 1935) put his image to intelligent and ironic use in what is still one of his most interesting films. As befitted the Seventies, with its steadily developing feminism, John Boorman's *Deliverance* is a delirious expression of male sexual paranoia. The film skirts cautiously, but adventurously, around the theme of homosexuality while depicting four men whose canoeing trip turns into a

**The macho, swaggering man-about-town is the decoy; the charming, *risqué* clown is the public image; but when both are combined with a natural sense of comic timing and panache, the man becomes Burt Reynolds, superstar**

*Above: about to fall down on the job in* Shamus, *a private-eye thriller involving a millionaire, a murder and some stolen jewels. Left: a group of men canoeing down a perilous river find that their fellow man is far more dangerous in* Deliverance

114

nightmare when they are attacked by local hillbillies. The men are seen to form attachments among themselves and to utilize hunting skills – signs of virility – as a means of impressing each other. External forces come to mirror these forbidden desires in the form of enforced male seduction by the sexuality rapacious marauders.

That same year Reynolds risked his 'popular' image by appearing as the first-ever male centrefold in the April issue of Cosmopolitan. It was an event that underlined certain pertinent facts regarding male stars, for in the cinema the male is largely defined by actions and the female by looks. 'Real' men must never exist primarily as sex objects, that is for women – or foreigners such as Rudolph Valentino, Ramon Novarro, Fernando Lamas. When Reynolds submitted his unadorned form for erotic delectation he was overstepping certain firmly marked boundaries, and it was perhaps this transgression that cost him the Oscar nomination for Deliverance.

A similarly 'confused' image continues to run through his films, manifesting itself in various twists and turns of his labyrinthine career. He has, for instance, continued in his accustomed role as the action hero, perhaps most typically as an extremely athletic private eye in Shamus (1973), and as a moonshiner out to gain revenge for a drowned brother in White Lightning (1973). The curious melodrama of the latter and the off-beat nature of The Man Who Loved Cat Dancing (1973) – with Sarah Miles as a runaway wife who takes up with outlaws – illustrate that even in action movies Reynolds often seeks out an element of the bizarre. However, veteran director Robert Aldrich utilized the harsher side of Reynolds'

image in The Longest Yard (1974), in which a jailed professional footballer plays dirty against the warden's team, and Hustle (1975), the story of a Los Angeles cop and a classy hooker who try to make the big-time. both films bring out the strident adolescent in Reynolds, and both films have little respect for any woman the 'hero' comes into contact with.

## Smoke screens

In recent years Reynolds has become identified with a particular style of adventure comedy filled with stunts and larger-than-life characterizations. Smokey and the Bandit (1977), Hooper (1978), Smokey and the Bandit II (1980), (released in Britain as Smokey and the Bandit Ride Again) and The Cannonball Run (1981) are all films aimed at a male audience, stressing macho values, the philosophy of action and all revolving around the traditionally masculine world of automobiles (much in the manner of many a Steve McQueen movie). Smokey and the Bandit is an attractive combination of direct simplicity, with the joyous inventiveness of many a silent chase comedy. Hooper, the tale of an ageing stuntman who reluctantly gives way to younger blood, has a good line in the gentle art of demolishing pretensions (the leading character irresistibly recalls Reynolds' own background) and marvellously utilizes its film-world milieu. However, from here on, the adventure comedies rush swiftly downhill. Smokey and the Bandit Ride Again lacks even freshness and The Cannonball Run represents the very nadir of this type of car-comedy in its crassness of humour and its aimlessness.

In action movies and comedies alike Reynolds remains likeable, with a gentleness that is stubbornly on show throughout all his dust-

*Above: hanging around in* Navajo Joe *(1967). Below: as an adventurer smuggling liquor into America in* Lucky Lady

raising heroics. He likes to think that he is a latter-day Cary Grant, and even if it is difficult to see any significant resemblance the wish itself says much. In defiance of the image that has made him a star, Reynolds has involved himself in a whole series of movies calling more on his powers of sensitivity and charm than on muscle-bound smugness. *Lucky Lady* (1975), involving a Thirties' booze-smuggling *ménage à trois*, failed to justify the employment of such talents as Reynolds, Gene Hackman and Liza Minnelli, and *At Long Last Love* (1975) was a brave if tragic attempt to re-create the Thirties' musical. Still intent on recalling the past and echoing the debonair Grant, Reynolds went on to star in Peter Bogdanovich's *Nickelodeon* (1976), a yarn about the early days of movie-making. It was not well received critically, but Bogdanovich has a way with soft, deft characterization, and Reynolds' role as a star whose fame is short-lived reveals a great deal of hidden talent.

More substantial are the abrasive comedies *Semi-Tough* (1977) and *Starting Over* (1979). *Semi-Tough*, as the title might suggest, does not treat its footballing heroes with too much reverence and even subjects them to Jill Clayburgh's forceful personality head on. Reynolds' role – which, as in *Hooper*, again has

Action: an aggressive Reynolds in the Western The Man Who Loved Cat Dancing *(above)*; as the stuntman Hooper *(left)*, he needed no stand-in; about to 'get his' as the convict footballer in The Longest Yard *(below)*

definite associations with his own background – was met with a certain incredulity by both critics and fans; its subtle, oblique satire (of human relationships, virility rituals and the like) seemed to be the wrong vehicle for Reynolds. In fact, he, Clayburgh and Kris Kristofferson work beautifully as a team. If *Semi-Tough* was deemed inappropriate for Reynolds, then *Starting Over* provided the final challenge to both critics and box-office. Looking very much like a male version of *An Unmarried Woman* (1978), the film's dark edges and 'masculine' position seem diametrically opposed to the trajectory of Reynolds' career. He feels particularly bitter about the fact that what he rightly considers to be one of his best roles was ignored that year in favour of his co-stars Candice Bergen and Jill Clayburgh, who each received Oscar nominations.

## Never say die

His general dissatisfaction with the course that his career was taking led Reynolds inexorably towards direction. His first effort was *Gator* (1976), a reasonably popular sequel to *White Lightning* but a film that did little to challenge the 'rut' in which Reynolds found himself. *The End* (1978) was a quite different matter, a radical departure from the image. In this black comedy on the subject of death he plays a terminally-ill character intent on suicide as a speedy release. Reynolds again acknowledges the passing years with a middle-aged role, and the film has an engagingly bizarre zaniness that is Reynolds' forte.

There is a tedious element of intellectual pretension in Reynolds' wish to be Cary Grant and win Oscars, but this should not blind anyone to the basic facts of his career. As the later Seventies saw a series of stronger, more positive roles for women, so images of men reflected the changing status of sexual identity. Packaged within a hulking frame, encouraged to act rather than feel, Reynolds twists and turns in confusion under the arc lamps. His case is comparable to that of Clint Eastwood, another hero of the macho-school. In films such as *Every Which Way But Loose* (1978) Eastwood's image takes a certain amount of punishment, especially at the hands of a hairy-chested orang-utan. Yet Eastwood, while tending to mellow as the years go by, somehow always remains recalcitrantly intact. Reynolds' image is shot through with more genuine self-doubt, softness and charm than Eastwood could ever allow to slip through.

MARTIN SUTTON

### Filmography
1961 Angel Baby; Armoured Command. '65 Operation CIA. '66 Un Dollaro a Testa (IT-USA). '67 Navajo Joe (IT-SP). '68 Fade In. '69 Sam Whiskey; Impasse; 100 Rifles; Shark (MEX-USA). '70 Skullduggery. '72 Fuzz; Deliverance; Everything You Always Wanted to Know About Sex But Were Afraid to Ask. '73 Shamus; The Man Who Loved Cat Dancing; White Lightning. '74 The Longest Yard (GB: The Mean Machine). '75 WW and the Dixie Dancekings; At Long Last Love; Lucky Lady; Hustle. '76 Silent Movie; Gator (+dir); Nickelodeon (GB-USA). '77 Smokey and the Bandit; Semi-Tough. '78 The End (+dir); Hooper. '79 Starting Over. '80 Rough Cut; Smokey and the Bandit II (GB: Smokey and the Bandit Ride Again). '81 The Cannonball Run; Paternity; Sharky's Machine (+dir). '82 The Best Little Whorehouse in Texas; Best Friends. '83 The Man Who Loved Women. '84 Stick.

*Top: a group of shady characters and a child (Tatum O'Neal) experience the dangers inherent in the setting up of their own* Nickelodeon

*Above: the mid-life crisis coming to a head in* Starting Over *with Jill Clayburgh. Below:* Smokey and the Bandit Ride Again

# Louis Malle Making it look like child's play

'The ideal audience for me is children . . . not adolescents or young people but children. I like the way children look at the world, with open eyes and without references. As a film-maker, I wish people could look at my work without reference'                                           Louis Malle, 1978

AC-17

Not so long ago there sprang up a new vogue among French film-makers for expiating the nation's collective guilt by making films about collaborationism during World War II or the occupation of Paris by German forces. From *Les Portes de la Nuit* (1946, *Gates of the Night*) to *Le Dernier Métro* (1980, *The Last Métro*), from the old tide to the *nouvelle vague* , directors have been trying to convince a nation that there was nothing to be ashamed of.

No doubt Louis Malle has been accused of jumping through the same hoops with his film of collaborationist southern France, *Lacombe Lucien* (1974), but it is only one of a series of films of memory, of recalling and exorcising truths painful to both the characters and the films' audiences – tinged, as ever, with the fertile irony of the seasoned documentarist. *Lacombe Lucien* marked a long-deserved high point for Malle's works of fiction – he had already found notoriety with *L'Inde Fantôme* (1969, *Phantom India*), a documentary series made for television – as the film received considerable international critical acclaim (Best Film at the British Academy Awards and Italian Critics Association; Oscar nomination for Best Foreign Film).

## Rags to reichs

*Lacombe Lucien* follows the rise to arrogant supremacy of a country-boy, Lucien (expertly

*Above right: the jacket marks the spot – Malle on location for* Atlantic City USA. *Below: maternal love takes over – Jeanne Moreau as a wife with two lovers in* The Lovers. *Below right: Madame Lacombe (Gilberte Rivet) takes a 'message' to* Lacombe Lucien *(Pierre Blaise)*

played by Pierre Blaise, a non-actor and himself of peasant origin) who drifts unintentionally into the French Nazi police. Being given a gun, smart clothes and money helps him to discover a certain temporary identity which – undisturbed by the subsequent loss of friends and family – is troubled only by his love for a rich Jew's daughter, whom he finally rescues from deportation.

However, despite being only mildly sadistic rather than downright violent, the film managed to upset its native audience with its sympathetic, though ignorantly-fascist hero and its suggestions that a degree more subservience and obsequiousness could have helped the French win the war. To redress the balance, Malle added a sobering coda to the film, but he has since – though not for this reason alone – made his films in America.

Louis Malle had himself been a child in Occupied France: born into a wealthy family of sugar manufacturers from northern France on October 30, 1932, he was evacuated to a Carmelite college at Fontainebleau where some Jewish children were hidden, their parents being either deported or dead. One day German soldiers invaded the school, removed the principal, took away the Jewish children and closed down the building. So, at a highly susceptible age Malle was deeply scarred by such brutal observations, and later by his encounters with the Resistance movement when he was a refugee in central France.

Many memories of his rebellious schooldays came to be fictionalized as the common-stock of his films about adolescence, and indeed it must have been his own heart complaint and images of convalescence with an English

nanny that helped fill in the inner adolescent secrets so charmingly encapsulated in *Le Souffle au Coeur* (1971, *Dearest Love*). For Malle, this was his 'first' feature, since it involved no collaboration and he wrote the screenplay himself; until then his career had seen many switches in direction.

After impatiently leaving the *Institut des Hautes Etudes Cinématographiques* (IDHEC) with the feeling that little in the French film industry would appeal to him, he joined Jacques Cousteau's team as a probationer on a three-year voyage, learning various jobs including underwater camerawork, editing and codirecting. His collaboration with Robert Bresson on *Un Condamné à Mort s'Est Echappé* (1956, *A Man Escaped*) then gave him the confidence to prepare his first feature film – *Ascenseur Pour l'Echafaud* (1958, *Lift to the Scaffold*), a psychological thriller which owed something to Hitchcock – when he was only 24. a film that won the Louis Delluc award for outstanding merit. After four months hectic

118

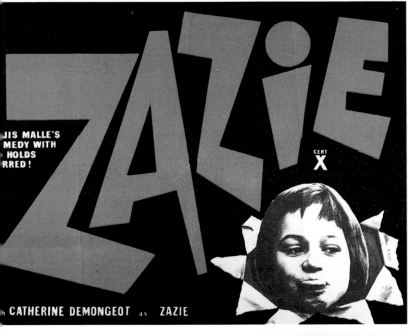

CATHERINE DEMONGEOT as ZAZIE

*Above: the world as seen through the innocent eyes of a cheeky child. Above right: Moreau and Brigitte Bardot in* Viva Maria! *Right: a dream/fantasy scene from* Black Moon *(1975) that contrasts with the film's other theme – war*

preparation, Malle then teamed Jeanne Moreau and Jean-Marc Bory in the Fifties' most controversial film, *Les Amants* (1958, *The Lovers*), a joyful paean to a bourgeois woman's adultery with a young student. But it was with his third solo film – *Zazie dans le Métro* (1960, *Zazie*) – that there began to appear some less commercially successful ideas. *Zazie*, from Raymond Queneau's novel about a little girl visiting her transvestite uncle in Paris and discovering that the world is a crazy and chaotic source of amusement, was perhaps ahead of itself in the experimental use of time and manic games.

## Passages to India
After *Zazie* Malle returned, with ever-increasing assurance, to the 'innocent eye'

style in both documentary and fiction films, and his career took a remarkable upturn after an impulsive personal decision. He had made *Vie Privée* (1962, *A Very Private Affair*), a semi-biographical look at Brigitte Bardot, and decided thereafter to make documentaries and features simultaneously; these latter included *Le Feu Follet* (1963, *A Time to Live and a Time to Die*), a despairing study of the last days of a 30-year-old man behaving like an adolescent and realizing that the only way to avoid adulthood is suicide. Thus, Malle initiated his passion for revealing the darker side of man's estate, despite going on to try a light-hearted female version of the buddy movie genre – *Viva Maria!* (1965) – which necessitated an unhappy attempt to pair Brigitte Bardot and Jeanne Moreau. By this time his disillusionment with the French film world meant not only a divorce from his wife, but also a move to India where he spent four months filming his impressions of that country.

The forty-odd hours of unscripted film were shot in three weeks with Etienne Baker (camera) and Jean Laureux (sound), and subsequently edited into eight parts with Malle

narrating. *Calcutta* (1969) is probably the best known of the *Phantom India* cycle and merited considerable censorious comment from the Anglo-Indian middle-class and the Indian government. Claiming, in a somewhat patronizing way, that his enchantment with India lies in the country's traditional social structures and varieties of religious forms so far untouched by the uniforming power of Western industrialized society, Malle was nevertheless hailed as an unconventional observer of the religion, politics, caste system and people of a land striving to update itself. He expressed his desire to avoid working within preconceived ideas by using the camera as:

'. . . an instrument through which one registered emotions – surprise, shock . . . . We developed a special style of "machine gun" filming to achieve this – you'd stand in the middle of something and shoot a burst in one direction, a burst in the other, just to try and catch as many facets as possible.'

From then on his work has seemed dogged by realism, and Malle acknowledges that he learned 'precision, discretion and . . . a taste for truth and authenticity' from Bresson. But

*Left: André Gregory and Wallace Shawn in* My Dinner With André. *Above left: a day out for the ladies and* Pretty Baby (*Brooke Shields, centre*). *Above right: the mobster (Burt Lancaster) is delighted to be able to help the widow (Susan Sarandon) in* Atlantic City USA

from Jacques Tati he also discovered the importance of an acute sense of observation and a very personal use of dialogue that is kept to a minimum. *Le Souffle au Coeur* mixes professionals and Malle's preferred non-professionals to bring to life dreams of a teenage boy's incestuous sexual fantasies about his mother, and it is this subject-matter that caused it to be withdrawn from entry in the Cannes Film Festival. Profoundly ambiguous when it is realized that the gestures and actions of love-making are the same as maternal love and love for a mother, Malle's technique separates the world into child and adult: the adult world is one of hypocrisy and preconceived values; in the eyes of the child (often filmed looking directly into the camera) lies a judgment of the adult's decadence. Malle's taste for the indefensible is carried over into the ambiguity of *Lacombe Lucien* where, filmed exclusively around the boy in a cold, documentary way (achieved with hand-held camera), the absence of moral judgments and the notion that not all fascists are monsters led to attacks from the Left and the Right.

## Locking up his daughter

In fact, Malle occasionally gives the impression that he is protecting the defunct values of the middle class, and once again he found himself at the centre of controversy with *Pretty Baby* (1978). His despair with French cinema at the

end of the Seventies, his love of jazz, and later his love of actress Susan Sarandon had all demanded a move to America, where this time the problems would be with censors and distributors. *Pretty Baby* acquired notoriety even before its release: Violet (Brooke Shields), a young girl brought up in a brothel by her prostitute mother (Susan Sarandon), is exploited both as a child and as a woman – something Malle admits would horrify him if it happened to any child of his. After the earlier mother-son relationship, he turns his attention to the father-daughter incest fantasy, or its alternative, the young girl raped by her stepfather. Malle had read about the New Orleans photographer E.J. Bellocq, who had worked in the Storyville whorehouses around 1910; in the film, Bellocq (Keith Carradine) lives for a time with Violet, but the relationship is not developed and most of the action is shot in the whorehouse, a location allowing Malle to exclude scenes of explicit sex as an activity to be taken for granted instead of shown.

Since America represented a definite uprooting for Malle he decided to stay on and do some more work there. After all, he had never been classed as one of the *nouvelle vague*, despite being part of their generation, and felt free to use Canadian money, American actors and the very American story of a dying East Coast resort's artificial rejuvenation with the building of tourist-attracting casinos. *Atlantic City USA* (1980) is rather an unexpected offering from the man who once said that he found contemporary themes unsatisfying and chaotic, but it still has its gaze firmly fixed on the past and its mystifying dislocation with the present. Burt Lancaster (often filmed in the familiar Malle close-up) was deliberately chosen, as an ageing actor, to portray an ageing, supposed ex-mobster befriending a young widow (Susan Sarandon) in an old town long past its glory. Opening as a modern psycho-drama, the film itself changes direction halfway, becoming an ironic, amused pastiche of the *film noir*, one of whose optimistic plots it could easily be following. Reality, thankfully,

finally seems to have slipped Malle's grasp.

## The Americanization of Louis

Malle has since married Candice Bergen and adopted self-imposed exile, but he is adamant that if he is to go on working in English, it must be in an English or American situation. Like the ironies accompanying the characters' individualist choices in his earlier films (Lucien falling in love with a Jewess, Bellocq displaced by a stepfather). Malle worked on a documentary about immigrants in Minnesota. He directed the stage version of Wallace Shawn's *My Dinner With André*, a two-handed discussion about creativity set in a restaurant. It was then filmed in 1980, no doubt refusing – like all Louis Malle's films – to fit easily into any category of content or form. DAVID ROPER

**Filmography** (including TV films)
**1955** La Fontaine de Vaucluse (doc. short) (+photo; +ed); Station 307 (doc. short) (+photo; +ed) (GB). **'56** Le Monde du Silence (doc) (co-dir; +co-photo) (GB: The Silent World); Un Condamné à Mort s'Est Echappé (tech. ass. only) (GB: A Man Escaped). **'58** Ascenseur Pour l'Echafaud (+co-sc) (USA: Frantic; GB: Lift to the Scaffold); Les Amants (+co-sc) (USA/GB: The Lovers). **'60** Zazie dans le Métro (+prod; +co-sc) (USA/GB: Zazie). **'62** Vie Privée (+co-sc; +act) (FR-IT) (USA: A Very Private Affair); Le Combat dans l'Ile (sup. only); Vive le Tour (doc. short) (+co-photo). **'63** Le Feu Follet (+sc) (FR-IT) (USA: The Fire Within; GB: A Time to Live and a Time to Die). **'64** Bons Baisers de Bangkok (TV doc). **'65** Viva Maria! (+co-prod; +co-sc; +co-mus) (FR-IT). **'66** Der Junge Törless (sup. only) (GER-FR) (USA/GB: Young Törless). **'67** Le Voleur (+prod; +co-sc) (FR-IT) (USA: The Thief of Paris; GB: The Thief). **'68** Histoires Extraordinaires *ep* William Wilson (+co-sc) (FR-IT) (USA: Spirits of the Dead; GB: Tales of Mystery). **'69** Calcutta (doc) (+prod; +sc; +narr); L'Inde Fantôme (7-film doc. TV series) (+prod; +sc; +narr) (GB: Phantom India); La Fiancée du Pirate (actor only) (USA: A Very Curious Girl; GB: Dirty Mary). **'71** Le Souffle au Coeur (+sc) (FR-IT-GER) (USA: Murmur of the Heart; GB: Dearest Love). **'74** Lacombe Lucien (+co-sc); Place de la République (doc); Humain, Trop Humain (TV doc) (GB TV: A Human Condition). **'75** Black Moon (+co-sc) (FR-GER). **'78** Pretty Baby (+prod; +co-sc) (USA). **'80** Atlantic City USA (CAN-FR) (USA/GB: Atlantic City); My Dinner With André (USA). **'82** Invitation au Voyage (actor only). **'84** Crackers (USA).

# BRIEF ENCOUNTERS

**By the Seventies, love and marriage were no longer happy endings but problems – and they continued to give trouble well into middle age**

Statistics on divorce rates only emphasize that the last two decades have seen the erosion and near-collapse of marriage and of all the shibboleths and taboos designed to keep it in place, such as monogamy, heterosexuality, fidelity, self-sacrifice and 'till death us do part'. Male and female roles once thought immutable are gone with the wind. To this amazing turn of events, movies offer ample testimony. In *Kramer vs Kramer* (1979) the husband (Dustin Hoffman) discovers the joys and trials of taking care of his small son, while the wife (Meryl Streep) fumbles towards some sort of professional fulfilment. In *The Turning Point* (1977), in a reversal of the laws of movie mythology, it is not the 'career woman', the ballerina Emma (Anne Bancroft) who has regrets, but the housewife Deedee (Shirley MacLaine) who thinks she may have made the wrong choice in giving up dance for marriage. In film after film – *Girlfriends*, *An Unmarried Woman* (both 1978), *My Brilliant Career* (1979) – heroines turn their backs on conventional roles or seductive men for the uncharted seas of self-sufficiency and being single.

Many of the most interesting film-makers of the Seventies – Woody Allen and Paul Mazursky, Robert Altman and John Cassavetes, Ingmar Bergman in *Scener ur ett Äktenskap* (1973, *Scenes From a Marriage*), Claude Chabrol in *Une Partie de Plaisir* (1974, *A Piece of Pleasure*) and Marco Ferreri in *L'Ultima Donna* (1976, *The Last Woman*) – bore witness to a new era of sexual anxiety, an era of increasing awareness on the part of women and a corresponding panic on the part of men.

If romantic love had been, as Swiss author Denis de Rougemont suggests, a relatively recent development in western civilization, entering with the thirteenth-century troubadours and their lyrical love-songs, then perhaps its death-rattle was now being heard. The fragile balance between a man and a woman, resting on their shared deference to the ideal of male courtship and female acquiescence, of man as provider and woman as nurturer, had finally given way. A new kind of film, appropriately elliptical and fragmented, often clinical, often chaotic, emerged to record the disintegration.

Sometimes it was the howl of a housewife who saw her days dribbling out in the dishwasher's cycles. Carrie Snodgress acted out an upper-crust Park Avenue version of matrimonial disenchantment in *Diary of a Mad Housewife* (1970), while Gena Rowlands, in *A Woman Under the Influence* (1974), played a lower-class woman having a nervous breakdown. Men felt boxed in, too, by the suburban routine – a fate from which John Cassavetes briefly rescued three of them (played by Ben Gazzara, Peter Falk and himself) in sending the heroes of his *Husbands* (1970) on one last adolescent spree. But then, adolescent bonding could also be a prison – the philandering Jonathan (Jack Nicholson) in *Carnal Knowledge* (1971) suffers from a case of arrested development because of the womanizing, boozing, college-fraternity ethic that the Cassavetes characters embrace.

How to grow up, how to relate, or why bother? Husbands and wives had awakened to find that they did not know, had never really known, each other. In *Such Good Friends* (1971), Otto Preminger's film from the Lois Gould novel, the heroine (Dyan Cannon) is stunned to find that her dying husband has left behind a diary chronicling the sexual adventures he has had with her good friends – all without her knowledge.

With more options, there was more room for confusion and misunderstanding. The sexes and generations were at cross-purposes, comically and poignantly, in *Lovers and Other Strangers* (1970), adapted from the Renee Taylor-Joseph Bologna play. Family members and friends, old and young, bride and groom – all the participants in this socially mixed marriage talk in a liberated fashion. They end up talking to themselves. Amidst these lurchings towards liberation, the stalwart Italian parents of the groom, Bea and Frank Vecchio

*Above: in George Cukor's* Pat and Mike, *Mike (Spencer Tracy) is a brash sports promoter who decides to build up Pat (Katharine Hepburn) as an all-round woman athlete; but his interest in her gradually becomes more than professional. Below: a shipboard romance in* Now, Voyager *brings together the neurotic Charlotte (Bette Davis) and a married man, Jerry (Paul Henreid); though they must soon part, Charlotte is later able to help Jerry's unhappy daughter*

(Beatrice Arthur and Richard Castellano), provide a touching foil. They represent a generation and a class in which husband and wife did not expect to have open life-styles, matching orgasms or mutual revelations of anything more intimate than preferences in pasta. They accept, resignedly, the burden of unshared secrets, and the mutual strangeness of husband and wife. 'Don't look for happiness,' Bea says to Richie (Joseph Hendy), another son, who is on the brink of divorce, 'it'll only make you miserable.'

But happiness, in a civilization that had satisfied most of its material wants and sent its children to college, was the only thing left to want. The concept of happiness had become vast and amorphous, taking in all the requirements of the newly-expanded, over-analysed self.

People expected, and thought they deserved, more than their parents had had out of life. They were asking for more but felt they were getting less, and the sense of disillusionment was often played out against the backdrop of old Hollywood films. Where was the dream of one man and one woman, perfectly matched for all eternity? It had been promised in those delirious close-ups of Ingrid Bergman and Gregory Peck in *Spellbound* (1945) or the witty interplay of such couples as Lauren Bacall and Humphrey Bogart in *To Have and Have Not* (1944) and Katharine Hepburn and Spencer Tracy in *Adam's Rib* (1949). A recurring image in later films was that of modern, 'realistic' characters viewing the old movies on television. For instance, the movie-addict wife (Jean Simmons) in *The Happy Ending* (1969) has her head full of unfulfillable romantic dreams from this source. In *Lovers and Other Strangers*, Wilma (Anne Meara) lies panting and unsatisfied while her 'Italian lug of a husband' Johnny (Harry Guardino) watches *Spellbound* for the seventh time. The kids in *Summer of '42* (1971) go to the cinema to see *Now, Voyager* (1942) and are bowled over by the scene in which Jerry (Paul Henreid) lights two cigarettes together and hands one of them to Charlotte (Bette Davis). The film critic Allan Felix (Woody Allen) is fixated on Bogart

---

## The old movies had presented a fascinating image of love that belonged to a world of fantasy

---

in *Play It Again Sam* (1972). Alice Hyatt (Ellen Burstyn), in *Alice Doesn't Live Here Anymore* (1974), is lured into fantasies of becoming a singer by identifying with film star Alice Faye.

The illusions of the old films, with their shimmering black-and-white photography, studio sets and dream people, seemed to contrast with the 'superior realism' of the new films, with their grainy colour photography, authentic locations and aggressively unglamorous characters. The self-pitying Woody Allen protagonists, the messy, soulful slobs of Cassavetes, the quirky native birds of Altman's aviary were a conscious renunciation of what an Altman film of 1979 ironically called *A Perfect Couple*.

But there had always been a distance between fantasy and reality for the audience, a sense that only in the never-never land created by Hollywood were people who looked like Carole Lombard and Jimmy Stewart going to eke out their lives in a tenement; and only in screenplays perfectly pitched between the masculine and the feminine, would Hepburn and Tracy find the equilibrium they achieved in *Adam's Rib* and *Pat and Mike* (1952), written by the husband-wife team of Garson Kanin

and Ruth Gordon.

Audiences understood intuitively the fabulous quality of these love stories and the conventions that allowed men and women to challenge each other for about ninety or a hundred minutes – through song, through the thrust and parry of dialogue, through the kiss and kill of melodrama – and reach, or fail to reach, a romantic truce before the final fade-out. Love was a power struggle, and antagonism was an essential element in attraction. Hero and heroine could even trade sexual roles over the safety net of their fixed identities as man and woman.

But once these roles were called into question, once everyone no longer subscribed to the notion of there being something called 'man's work' or 'a woman's world', none of the conventions applied. The prohibitions and taboos – against divorce, against infidelity – had been lifted. Everyone was free to revolve in his own orbit, without any mutually understood imperatives of behaviour and with no common court of appeal.

Paul Mazursky's *Blume in Love* (1973) was an extraordinarily moving picture of marital bafflement. It depicted the uncertainty of a husband (George Segal) who has strayed but continues to love his estranged wife (Susan Anspach), a conventionally trendy Californian welfare officer whose identity is so little fixed that she invents her self each day anew. Unable to get through to her, Blume finally takes her by force. The divorced husband and his ex-wife end up together in Venice, Italy,

*Above: clasping his son, Gérard (Gérard Depardieu) tells his new girlfriend Valérie (Ornella Muti) about the phallic superiority of the male in* The Last Woman. *Above left: Tina Balser (Carrie Snodgress) is overwhelmed by the domestic routine in* Diary of a Mad Housewife; *she is constantly nagged for her inefficiency by her husband and her daughters. Top left: Isaac Davis (Woody Allen) shares a moment of uncomplicated happiness with his teenage girlfriend Tracy (Mariel Hemingway) in* Manhattan

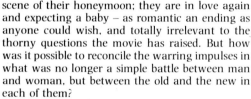

scene of their honeymoon; they are in love again and expecting a baby – as romantic an ending as anyone could wish, and totally irrelevant to the thorny questions the movie has raised. But how was it possible to reconcile the warring impulses in what was no longer a simple battle between man and woman, but between the old and the new in each of them?

Men no longer had the edge, *qua* men, and it was a blow to their ego that European directors understood immediately and confronted more honestly than did their American and British counterparts. In Marco Ferreri's stunning and disturbing *The Last Woman*, Gérard Depardieu plays a sexualized version of the old-style tough guy, the last in the line. Unable to relate to women except through sheer physical dominance, he ends by taking a knife and slashing his penis, betraying emblem of the supremacy he can no longer establish. No less devastating was Claude Chabrol's *Une Partie de Plaisir*, in which a man is completely shattered by a show of independent will from the long-time mistress who lives with him and has borne his child. Her subservience had been the last remaining prop of his dwindling self-esteem.

In *Scenes From a Marriage*, Ingmar Bergman used the format of a six-part television series to conduct a marathon investigation into that phenomenon known as the 'happy marriage' (ending in divorce), with Liv Ullmann as the wife, Marianne, and Erland Josephson as the husband, Johan. The reduced cinema version, still nearly three hours long,

became a 'couples' picture', spurring analytic arthouse patrons to perform auto-critiques of their own marriages.

Bergman shows two people who have become a habit to each other, who know each other too well and too little. As in *Blume in Love*, the crisis is provoked by the husband's infidelity; but Johan seems to be fleeing from his wife's massive, all-encompassing *understanding* rather than from coldness or indifference on her part. As usual, Bergman's sympathies are more with the woman than the man: she is capable of growing and questioning, while he acts out of pure desperate reflex. But a faintly critical note creeps into Bergman's portrayal of Marianne as a creature completely and almost irritatingly in tune with herself. That alliance with nature that Bergman has envied and worshipped in his women can become, in the shrunken bourgeois world of the film, a force of smugness and complacency.

The dilemma of Johan, the phenomenon that came to be known as the 'male menopause', was linked in its own way to the dissolving ties of marriage. There was no longer any pride or dignity in growing old together, and consequently old age itself came to be regarded as a dread disease, to be held at bay by the desperately youthful strategy of a last fling. William Holden, weather-beaten and soulful in *Breezy* (1973) and *Network* (1976), was a champion in the male menopause sweepstakes – a man who could court a girl over twenty or thirty years his junior and not seem ridiculous.

*Top left:* A Perfect Couple *consists of zany rock singer Sheila Shea (Marta Heflin) and staidly respectable Alex Theodopoulos (Paul Dooley), a classical-music enthusiast who becomes a groupie with her band. The unlikely pairing resulted from the director Robert Altman's wish to use the actors again after they had played smaller roles in* A Wedding *(1978). Top: in* Alice Doesn't Live Here Anymore. *Alice (Ellen Burstyn) briefly fulfils her ambition to become a singer when she gets a job at a bar in Phoenix, but she has to flee the city when her love-life gets too difficult. Above: two sides of an unusual triangle in* Sunday, Bloody Sunday *(1971) – Alex (Glenda Jackson) and the bisexual Bob (Murray Head)*

with Diane Keaton, including *Annie Hall* (1977). The lovers were young, really young – in their teens or twenties – while it was the adults, the character actors, who showed what happened after the first bloom of romance had faded. There was, then – contrary to the purely sentimental myth of old movies propagated in Seventies films – a place for disenchantment: it was simply taken on by the character actors, the boozing husband and nagging wife, or Mom and Dad who were not remotely interested in their continued growth as 'full human beings'. And they *looked* old – the parents of Andy Hardy (Mickey Rooney) in the MGM series of the late Thirties and early Forties look like a couple out of a Grant Wood painting, closer in age to grandparents than parents.

Nowadays the seekers after love and the disenchanted have become one and the same, and considerably older than their romantic counterparts in the past. The characters played by Renee Taylor and Joseph Bologna in *Made for Each Other* (1971), Gena Rowlands and Seymour Cassel in *Minnie and Moskowitz* (1971), Jill Clayburgh in *An Unmarried Woman, Starting Over* (1979) and *It's My Turn* (1980), Burt Reynolds as the divorcé in *Starting Over* are all looking for love and fulfilment long past what was once considered the age of stability.

A breaking down of old forms runs through other categories as well. The present-day film-maker no longer identifies exclusively with one sex. The critic and novelist George Orwell once remarked on D. H. Lawrence's ability to get inside the thoughts and feelings of other sensibilities – women, children, even animals. This was considered remarkable at the time, but it is simply part of the baggage of the modern artist. The unlimited options now opened up provide opportunities to be welcomed as well as perils to be faced. Despite the difficulties in creating characters and plausible love affairs on the modern screen, no-one would really want to go back to the straighter and narrower confines of the Thirties and Forties Hollywood film.

If the rules and rituals of romantic antagonism can no longer be precisely defined, it is because the modern sensibility can no longer remain smugly identified with one sex against the other. Films such as *It's My Turn* and *Atlantic City USA* (1980) seem to have arrived at a new kind of equilibrium between the sexes. In Claudia Weill's *It's My Turn*, Kate (Jill Clayburgh) is torn between her wittily unpossessive lover Homer (Charles Grodin) and an old-fashioned ex-baseball player, Ben (Michael Douglas). Louis Malle's *Atlantic City USA*, a portrait of the gambling mecca, centres on the glossily cynical-sensual pairing of Burt Lancaster's ex-con and Susan Sarandon's lady croupier. In both films there is an awareness that love is, after all, a trade-off – and no less romantic for that.      MOLLY HASKELL

But the partnering of an older man and a younger woman, so long considered 'normal' in a society that viewed the older-woman-younger-man twosome as grotesque, was given a comical and slightly more critical perspective in '10' and *Manhattan* (both 1979). As George (Dudley Moore) pursues the perfectly-proportioned beach goddess Jenny (Bo Derek) in '10', writer-director Blake Edwards suggests that 40 is a dangerous age, precisely because it is more at home with fantasy than reality. George is no more in tune with this free spirit of the 'sexual revolution' than is Isaac Davis (Woody Allen) with his high-school girlfriend Tracy (Mariel Hemingway) in *Manhattan*. There was a brilliant, and perhaps widely misinterpreted, scene where the two of them are watching television and Tracy, in all the fresh, unknowing cruelty of adolescence, announces that she will never, ever have a facelift. Far from being a putdown of the women who do have facelifts, the remark seems to be Allen's way of indicating the brutal barrier separating youth and age in contemporary society, and it is with his own age group that Isaac throws in his lot.

In the older movies, people stuck with their age groups because there was a certain dignity and propriety in doing so. Youth went with youth, beauty with beauty; the man was several inches taller than the woman – another shibboleth that Woody Allen shattered in his various partnerships

*Above: George (Dudley Moore) with his regular girlfriend Sam (Julie Andrews) and the tempting Jenny (Bo Derek), whom he rates '10' on his scale of beauty. Below: Lou (Burt Lancaster), who makes his living in illegal gambling, tries to impress trainee croupier Sally (Susan Sarandon) in Louis Malle's Atlantic City USA*

# The Odder Half

Walter Matthau

**In his mastery of the double-take, Walter Matthau is without equal; in his exaggerated expression of pain, surprise, truculence and gloomy misanthropy, he is unsurpassed; that he remains infinitely lovable is his shining triumph**

Walter Matthau is large, round-shouldered and tending to flab, like a prize-fighter gone to seed. By no means an athletic figure, he nevertheless gives an impression of stealth, walking with a stoop that might precipitate a slow run. His putty-like face moulded into a perpetual scowl, he is easily piqued and often loses control of his voice – although he mostly talks in a flat drawl that implores respect while hinting at insincerity. He is both rogue and comedian, often at the same time.

Matthau has perfected the art of being an unmitigated slob: in *The Fortune Cookie* (1966) he stalks a hospital corridor and places a dime in a charity box, fishing it out again when no one is looking; in *The Odd Couple* (1968) he deals out sandwiches like playing cards, shedding bread and pastrami all over the floor, and allows an entire dish of linguini to form a mould on his kitchen wall; as a Hollywood sex symbol in *The Secret Life of an American Wife* (1968) he lives amidst a forest of dirty glasses, curling canapés and brimming ashtrays whilst his minions replenish his sexual appetite and pay homage to his ego; *The Front Page* (1974) sees him as an unscrupulous newspaper editor who tries to prevent his ace reporter's marriage by informing the girl that her fiancé is a child molester and sexual exhibitionist; in *The Sunshine Boys* (1975) he trades insults like a man permanently suffering from a bad attack of dyspepsia.

Yet Matthau, for all the festering garbage and character assassinations, has made slob-bishness and misanthropy a winning combination, much like Wallace Beery and W. C. Fields before him. As the director Billy Wilder said during an interview in 1981: 'Matthau is a unique star. When you write a screenplay for him – or for Jack Lemmon – there is no possible alternative to him.' It was Wilder who first recognized Matthau's true filmic potential and

*Above: publicity shot for* Hello, Dolly! *Right: having married Henrietta (Elaine May) for money, Henry Graham repents of his plan to leave her to drown in* A New Leaf

provided the role for which he had been waiting more than ten years. *The Fortune Cookie* also provided Matthau with the Academy Award for Best Supporting Actor and made him an 'overnight' star. It was certainly about time.

## Not a man most likely to

He was born in 1920 to a family of poor Russian-Jewish immigrants in New York's Lower East Side. He started work as a sports instructor and became a radio operator during World War II. After the war he joined the Dramatic Workshop of New York and played in summer stock before making his Broadway debut in 1948. He quickly earned a reputation as an accomplished actor whose misfortune it was to appear in short-runs, and like many Broadway actors he went to Hollywood to pay the bills.

Some of Matthau's early films were very good indeed, but his roles scarcely stretched him or offered him many opportunities to create a lasting impression – he was either killed off too early or appeared too late. His Hollywood debut was in *The Kentuckian* (1955),

125

fighting a duel with whips against the film's star and director, Burt Lancaster. He played another villain later that year in *The Indian Fighter* opposite Kirk Douglas, and was the friend of the cortisone-addicted 'hero' (James Mason) in Nicholas Ray's classic melodrama *Bigger Than Life* (1956). He was the cynical reporter in Elia Kazan's *A Face in the Crowd* (1957) and supported Elvis Presley in *King Creole* (1958). Between Broadway assignments, where he won a Tony Award in 1961, he directed his first and only film, *Gangster Story* (1959), a B picture that was never released in Britain.

Matthau's cinematic fortunes improved in the early Sixties, a factor greatly helped by his increasing stage prestige. In *Lonely Are the Brave* (1962) he gave an outstanding performance as the county sheriff who reluctantly tracks down his prey (Kirk Douglas). In *Fail Safe* (1964) his marvellous psychotic scientist urging a nuclear attack on Russia was unfortunately overshadowed by *Dr Strangelove, Or How I Learned to Stop Worrying and Love the Bomb* – released in the same year – but *Fail Safe* is nevertheless a shrewd evocation of Cold War fever.

Stanley Donen's stylishly Hitchcockian *Charade* (1963) provided Matthau with his best part to date. As the dark side of Cary Grant's charm, he is the villain who earns the trust of a gullible female (Audrey Hepburn) by posing as an American embassy official. In 1965 he returned to Broadway to star in Neil Simon's *The Odd Couple* for which he won immediate acclaim. But despite being just about the hottest star on Broadway, Matthau was still only a supporting actor in movies.

It was then that Wilder stepped in with *The Fortune Cookie*. Matthau plays a shyster lawyer who exploits a modest injury sustained by his client (Lemmon) in order to swindle the insurance company. With its incipient paranoia and bugging devices, *The Fortune Cookie* was strangely prophetic of the Richard Nixon/Watergate era and Matthau's superb performance en-

*Right: detectives Larsen (Bruce Dern) and Martin (Matthau) trail a killer in* The Laughing Policeman *(1973). Below right:* The Front Page *has to wait for its editor and ace-reporter (Jack Lemmon). Below: partners in fraud – with Lemmon in* The Fortune Cookie

capsulates the ethics of greed and the art of deviousness with extraordinary precision. But Wilder was careful not to present Matthau's Willie Gingrich as wholly repugnant – his ingenuity, acute resentment of corporate power and tireless energy compared to his client's immobility made him an almost heroic figure. In fact Matthau usually invests his 'good guys' with more misanthropic zeal than the evil that motivates his 'villains'.

## Odder things have happened
The film version of *The Odd Couple* confirmed Matthau's new star status. Again paired with Jack Lemmon, he plays a divorcee sharing an apartment – with disastrous results. For all its intense theatricality and anonymous direction it is an acting *tour de force*. Since then both Matthau and Lemmon have become closely associated with New York-based light comedy, Matthau playing the quintessential urban American male prone to sexual anxiety, ulcers, hysterical daughters and overbearing wives. His roles in *Plaza Suite* (1971), in which he stars in three different episodes about the occupants of a hotel suite; *The Sunshine Boys*, as half a vaudeville act; *The Secret Life of an American Wife*, where he is seduced by a bored housewife; *Cactus Flower* (1969), in which

*Left: as an over-the-hill baseball coach, Matthau resorts to eccentric tactics to the astonishment of the Bears' leader (Tatum O'Neal, left) in* The Bad News Bears. *Above left: building a cot for a young couple's baby proves to be therapeutic for a depressed widower in* Kotch. *Above: Matthau on the set of* Buddy, Buddy *with Billy Wilder and crew*

he is a dentist falling for his secretary; and *A New Leaf* (1971), the story of a bankrupt playboy's acquisition of a wealthy wife, have been largely formulary 'odd couple' routines dependent on the quality of the script. Matthau has coasted through them all with great style.

## The sky's the limit

Happily, Matthau has not allowed himself to be trapped within this genre. Apart from a few curious choices such as *Hello, Dolly!* (1969), in which he is totally becalmed by Barbra Streisand, and *Earthquake* (1974) – where he props up a bar and performs under the pseudonym of Matuschanskayasky – Matthau has appeared in several more challenging and often more dramatic roles, adapting his persona whilst retaining his insolent demeanour and his immense facility for the wisecrack and the slow-burning fuse of audience collusion.

He was very moving as a 72-year-old widower in *Kotch* (1971), directed by Jack Lemmon, and a bibulous baseball instructor in

The Bad News Bears (1976), a film that was a huge commercial success. As Walter Burns in *The Front Page* he became a latter-day Mephistopholes in a further round with Jack Lemmon that never stopped to draw breath.

His two best dramatic performances are in *Charley Varrick* (1973) and *The Taking of Pelham 1 2 3* (1974). In the former he is a crop-duster – with a sideline in robbing banks – who runs up against the Mafia but manages to outwit them all the way. There is something chilling about the way Varrick incinerates his wife's corpse after a bungled robbery, but his battle against 'the mob' eventually makes a hero of him. Matthau was far more restrained in *The Taking of Pelham 1 2 3*, brilliantly working against the essential hysteria of the subject – the hijack of a New York subway train. As the transit authority cop, he builds up a richly detailed character living and breathing the city's stench and decay. The familiar stoop and quizzical eyes of Matthau are respectively uncoiled and blazing, turning him into a man of action who saves the day before disappearing into grey anonymity. It is a remarkable performance and a rare demonstration of

Matthau's versatility.

Matthau worked again with Wilder and Lemmon on *Buddy, Buddy* (1981), a farcical 'odd couple' movie in which he plays a Mafia assassin who becomes entangled with a neurotic (Lemmon). It is a rogue-comedian part that only Matthau can play so sinisterly and yet so endearingly.
ADRIAN TURNER

### Filmography
**1955** The Kentuckian; The Indian Fighter. **'56** Bigger Than Life. **'57** A Face in the Crowd; Slaughter on Tenth Avenue. **'58** King Creole; Voice in the Mirror; Ride a Crooked Trail; Onionhead. **'59** Gangster Story (+dir). **'60** Strangers When We Meet. **'62** Lonely Are the Brave; Who's Got the Action? **'63** Island of Love; Charade. **'64** Ensign Pulver; Fail Safe; Goodbye Charlie. **'65** Mirage. **'66** The Fortune Cookie (GB: Meet Whiplash Willie). **'67** A Guide for the Married Man. **'68** The Odd Couple; The Secret Life of an American Wife; Candy (USA-IT-FR). **'69** Cactus Flower; Hello, Dolly! **'70** King: A Filmed Record . . . Montgomery to Memphis (doc) (narr. only). **'71** A New Leaf; Plaza Suite; Kotch. **'72** Pete 'n' Tillie. **'73** Charley Varrick; The Laughing Policeman (GB: An Investigation of Murder). **'74** The Taking of Pelham 1 2 3; Earthquake (as Walter Matuschanskayasky); The Front Page. **'75** The Gentleman Tramp (doc) (narr. only); The Sunshine Boys. **'76** The Bad News Bears. **'78** Casey's Shadow; House Calls; California Suite. **'80** Little Miss Marker (+exec. prod); Portrait d'un Homme à 60% Parfait: Billy Wilder (doc) (as himself) (FR); Hopscotch. **'81** Buddy, Buddy. **'82** The First Monday in October; I Ought to Be in Pictures. **'83** The Survivors.

**In the Seventies women began to be seen as human beings able to think, work and take care of themselves; the watchword – independence. On the screen this trend was portrayed by a new and exciting breed of actress, demanding tough films to match**

The film industry is still a male-dominated system. For every female screenwriter (Eleanor Perry), director (Claudia Weill), producer (Barbra Streisand), film editor (Marcia Lucas) and production designer (Polly Platt) there is an army of male counterparts. The power, money and ultimate decisions in films are still largely in the hands of men. But the female voice *is* heard, however muffled by patriarchy, in the realm of acting.

Forties Hollywood was the era when certain actresses reached dizzy heights of strength and independence seldom seen since. Figures like Katharine Hepburn, Joan Crawford, Barbara Stanwyck and Bette Davis, with their fierce self-confidence and boundless energy, were far from the conventional screen image of women. The self-satisfied smugness of the Fifties saw a complete change both in actresses and the roles they played, and the Swinging Sixties did not do much to remedy the situation despite endless attempts to come to terms with the 'sexual revolution' and the pill.

The Seventies proved a confusing muddle from which it is difficult to draw any coherent pattern. On the whole, however, the movies provided actresses with deeper roles to tackle, a factor largely due to the impact that feminism had made upon the cinema. Indeed, the decade saw 'pop feminism' as the actual subject of films such as *Alice Doesn't Live Here Anymore* (1974), *L'Une Chante, L'Autre Pas* (One Sings, the Other Doesn't), *The Turning Point, Julia* (all 1977) and *An Unmarried Woman* (1978). Hollywood found box-office potential in the revival of the 'woman's film', the emphasis being on then current trends in women's liberation. The results were sometimes fascinating, sometimes just patronizing confections, but it was always the women stars who galvanized the audience.

The Seventies certainly saw an impressive turn-out of actresses projecting a determined, resourceful and self-reliant image. Besides the obvious figures of Jane Fonda and Vanessa

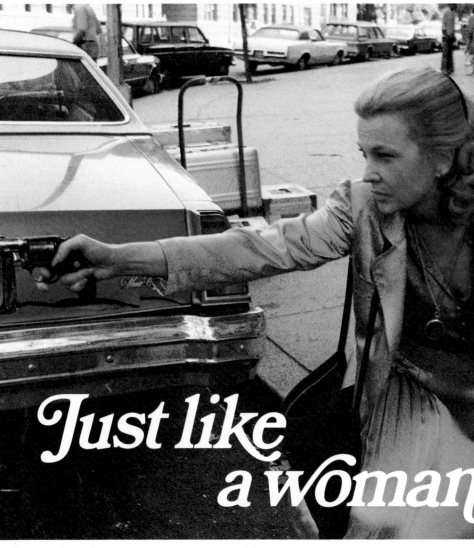

*Just like a woman*

Redgrave, stars such as Faye Dunaway, Ellen Burstyn, Barbra Streisand, Gena Rowlands, Sissy Spacek, Katharine Ross, Geneviève Bujold, Glenda Jackson and Jill Clayburgh are remarkable for the forcefulness of their screen presence, even when the role is none too promising.

### Alice comes of age

Ellen Burstyn (b. 1932) plays a middle-aged widow in search of lost childhood dreams and money to feed her young son in *Alice Doesn't Live Here Anymore*, one of the earliest feminist-

inflected Hollywood roles and, in retrospect, just about the most interesting. The tendency – even in this kind of film – has been to see a woman's life in the context of her relationships with men, but *Alice Doesn't Live Here Anymore* concentrates on the heroine's personal dreams

*Right: Caterina Silveri (Jill Clayburgh) at her husband's grave in* La Luna. *Below: looking for love or trouble? Richard Gere and Diane Keaton in* Looking for Mr Goodbar. *Below left: the end is near for Holly (Sissy Spacek) after a trail of destruction in* Badlands

*Left: Gloria (Gena Rowlands) operating her own 'protection' racket to save Phil (John Adames) from the Mafia. Above: Ellen Burstyn in* Alice Doesn't Live Here Anymore

and new relationship with her son. Burstyn injects her role with just the right balance of determination and vulnerability. She won an Academy Award for her performance, but the mere handful of roles she has been given in the Seventies is possibly a sign of the confusion in which Hollywood finds itself when faced with such an unclassifiable and individual female talent. However, she added considerably to the brave if old-fashioned *Same Time Next Year* (1978) in which she plays one half of an adulterous pair who spend a weekend each year together for 26 years.

## A woman alone

Another star of the new 'woman's film' is Jill Clayburgh (b. 1944). She is vivacious and irrepressible in all her roles, but her image is that of an open, racy woman who beds Gene Wilder in the comedy-thriller *Silver Streak* (1976), and makes short work of her two footballing suitors, Burt Reynolds and Kris Kristofferson, in the comedy *Semi-Tough* (1977). The role that really made her a leading female star of the decade was that of the heroine in *An Unmarried Woman*. In this, and the later feminist offering *It's My Turn* (1980), she portrays women trying to find their feet and cope with new life-styles outside marriage. They are both glossy, 'radical chic' essays on liberation, and focus too much on the woman's relationship to men while overdoing the kooky quality of Clayburgh's image in order to suggest how untogether and vulnerable her characters really are. Nonetheless, Clayburgh is wonderfully alive and controlled enough to make them both memorable portraits. Similarly, she salvaged the incestuous opera-singer role in *La Luna* (1979, *Luna*) and is an unforgettable presence as the woman that hero Burt Reynolds turns to after a failed marriage in *Starting Over* (1979) – a fascinating male equivalent to *An Unmarried Woman*.

Someone who projects a less brittle and middle-class image than Clayburgh is the increasingly splendid Sissy Spacek (b. 1949). Her appealingly plain and waiflike appearance belies a tough-minded independence. She made her debut as the victim of a prostitution racket in *Prime Cut* (1972), a film that explores few of her talents, whereas *Ginger in the Morning* (1973), the story of a lonely salesman who picks up a sassy girl hitch-hiker, is clearly suited. However, it was in *Badlands* (1973), in which she plays a schoolgirl on the run with a romantic garbage-collector who has murdered her father, that she was first noticed. This dreamlike movie establishes a delicate and affectionate relationship of equality between the two and is one of the delights of Seventies cinema. Also remarkable were her performances in *Three Women* (1977), a bizarre story of a relationship between two workers in a convalescent home and an older woman, and *Coal Miner's Daughter* (1980), a biographical account of the determined struggle to fame of country-and-western star Loretta Lynn and her resultant marital upsets. Spacek's characterization in the latter represents her most perceptive acting to date.

## Allen and after

Meryl Streep (b. 1951) and Diane Keaton (b. 1946) have both touched briefly upon portrayals of the sensitive but determined woman. Keaton seems to find it difficult to break away from the image of Woody Allen's offbeat sidekick, the touching, uncertain projection of his fantasies and insecurities. Her one commercially viable appearance outside an Allen movie is as the teacher cruising late-night singles bars for sexual encounters in *Looking For Mr Goodbar* (1977). It is a film as uncertain of its direction as the confused heroine, and her murder at the hands of an offended closet homosexual opened up more questions about sex beyond the marriage-bed than it could cope with. Meryl Streep also played opposite Woody Allen – as his former wife now into a lesbian relationship – in *Manhattan* (1979). It says more about Allen's sexual insecurities than lesbianism, but Streep's utterly unstereotypical and human performance saves the character from becoming just one more debauched decadent. She effects another

129

Above: stalemate in Manhattan – Meryl Streep and Woody Allen. Above right: Susan Wheeler (Geneviève Bujold) after bodies in Coma. Right: British stars Oliver Reed, Alan Bates and Women in Love – Glenda Jackson, Jennie Linden, Eleanor Bron

salvage job in her most famous role as the ex-wife fighting for the custody rights of her child in *Kramer vs Kramer* (1979). Although the film lacks objectivity, condemning what appears to be an independent woman as an unsuitable parent, Streep commands sympathy for her calm and discriminating interpretation.

## Women against the world

Geneviève Bujold (b. 1945) and Gena Rowlands (b. 1934) will be remembered for their involvement in a new kind of Seventies action film, one where it is the woman who initiates the action and is the centre of the film. Previously this had only happened, and to a lesser extent, in various Roger Corman crime thrillers and prison dramas, as well as in the early female Western *Johnny Guitar* (1954). *Coma* (1978) and *Gloria* (1980) were two movies that continued the trend and their relative success indicated the possibility of further offerings in similar vein. As a junior surgeon uncovering a mysterious and illegal international human spare-part market, Bujold's role in *Coma* called for unhysterical authoritativeness in order for the audience to identify with a responsible woman up against a world of male 'protector-guardians'. Gena Rowlands has frequently played interesting roles for John Cassavetes (her husband), but none are as uncompromisingly plucky as *Gloria*. *Gloria* presents the stunning vision of a woman with a gun standing up to and confounding the power and organization of New York's Mafia.

## Romance and an English woman

One actress of the decade who has never really found her niche is Glenda Jackson (b. 1936). Part of the problem is possibly her attraction to literary and theatrical projects that are then treated in too respectful a manner for the medium of cinema. More importantly, Jackson's obvious toughness, intelligence and eroticism have been too much of an embar-

rassment to cinema; instead of harnessing her qualities to good effect, male directors have perverted her talents cruelly, none more so than Ken Russell. In *Women in Love* (1969) and *The Music Lovers* (1971), her sexuality is re-morselessly parodied as threatening nympho-mania and her intelligence becomes mere bitchiness. Even in the promising *Sunday, Bloody Sunday* (1971), in which she shares her bisexual lover with a man, the Jackson charac-ter is made to pay for her liberated ways by seeming tragic and confused. Nonetheless, there is something of the delightful Katharine Hepburn-Spencer Tracy association in her

collaboration with George Segal, especially in the comedy on adultery *A Touch of Class* (1973) – even if the film ultimately seems too man-nered and dated.

## Little women

With regard to the actress, the Seventies will certainly be marked as the decade that pro-duced some of the most memorable child stars since the Thirties. But the 'new' child stars – such as Linda Blair, Jodie Foster and Brooke Shields – project images of childhood and femininity that are post-Freudian and feminist influenced. Linda Blair (then 14 years old)

Above left: Shelley Duvall (b. 1950) with Bud Cort in her debut Brewster McCloud (1970). She has since starred in many Robert Altman pictures. Above: Sally Kellerman (b. 1938) in A Little Romance (1979). She shot to fame as 'Hot Lips' in M*A*S*H (1970). Right: Geraldine Chaplin (b. 1944), a 'star' since the Sixties, is an avenging ex-wife in Remember My Name (1978). Below: Karen Black (b. 1942) during filming for Nashville (1975). She exploded into movies with Easy Rider (1969) and Five Easy Pieces (1970)

plays a 12-year-old possessed by the devil in *The Exorcist* (1973). The real horror of the film resides in its vision of childhood sexuality, a suggestion it regards as unspeakably ~~...~~ Childhood sexuality again sizzled ~~...~~ ~~... two stories involving ...~~

innovations for quick profit, Hollywood opened up new possibilities for actresses, with some unknown and some older faces coming ~~...~~ to answer the challenge. If there was a ~~...~~ women – and actresses intelligent ~~...~~ ough made the best of any ~~... scenarios~~ – there was also ~~... inst~~ them in a series of ~~...~~ women were the ~~...~~ ks. It is a pity that ~~...~~ e shadow of titles ~~...~~ (1979), *He Knows* ~~...~~ s *Dressed to Kill* ~~... M~~ARTIN SUTTON

# Last Tango in Paris

*Last Tango in Paris* was Bernardo Bertolucci's first popular and commercial success. Unlike his previous films, it is located in the present and is not explicitly political. Despite the publicity surrounding it as a sex film and its prosecution in Italy under the obscenity laws, it is, as the director himself has stated, not an erotic film, merely a film about eroticism.

Although *Last Tango in Paris* is most memorable for its depiction of the vital and basic sexual relationship between 19-year-old Jeanne and the 45-year-old Paul, there are two subsidiary relationships which provide an important counterpoint to the central theme. Jeanne is engaged to Tom, a young film-maker. They are in love and envisage the perfect future together as a conventional bourgeois couple. Jeanne refers to it as the 'pop' marriage that smiles down from the advertisements on the billboards. Paul's wife, Rosa, has recently committed suicide, and his examination of the failure of their life together provides another level to the argument of the film. Through these three entangled affairs, Bertolucci develops a strong analysis of the family and sexuality, a powerful indictment of romantic love and a study of the nature of illusion, reality and cinematic truth.

The film opens with Paul and Jeanne separately walking through the streets of Paris towards an apartment they are both independently interested in renting. Jeanne is young, attractive and alive, full of hope about what life holds in store for her. But Paul comes to the apartment with a history. He is middle-aged and pained by the recent death of his wife. His future is uncertain. Gradually, the film reveals that Paul failed at the one stable relationship in his life – he failed to satisfy his wife, either emotionally or sexually because he never came to terms with who she was. He never really knew her. Later in the film, as he sits by her corpse, he becomes angry at the make-up plastered on her face. He violently wipes it off, complaining that she never wore the stuff. It is as if her suicide forced him to realize their marriage was illusory and not based on the real foundation of mutual knowledge.

But Paul also has a second history that is equally important to the film – the history of Marlon Brando, perhaps the last great Hollywood star, however rebellious, in the classical tradition. The maid recalls the police description of Paul:

'You know he was a boxer. Then he was an actor, then a bongo player. A revolutionary in Mexico, a journalist in Japan. One day he embarks in Tahiti, wanders around, learns French . . .'

Paul represents what Brando represents: a star whose romantic and rebellious image belongs to another age. Jeanne is a member of the younger generation whose dreams are shaped by the old illusion but who has no place for romantic heroes in the contemporary world.

If Jeanne's relationship with Paul is a commentary on past film culture, her relationship with Tom comments on the radical alternatives in cinema in the Sixties. Tom is a film-maker committed to a kind of political *cinéma vérité*. He and his crew follow Jeanne around, filming her romance with him and her preparations and thoughts surrounding the forthcoming marriage. For Tom, life is cinema and cinema is life. He is incapable of living without the voyeuristic framework that his film-making provides. His resulting distance from reality traps him into the same conventional, bourgeois notion of love and marriage. Tom is played by Jean-Pierre Léaud (star of François Truffaut's autobiographical films), a choice which further intertwines Bertolucci's critiques of film-style and life-style.

It seems at first as if Paul and Jeanne's relationship can provide an alternative. Paul is looking for sex to heal his pain, and Jeanne, though looking for love, is sexually excited by Paul's animal attraction. Cocooned in their big, empty apartment, cut off from the outside world they agree to tell each other nothing about themselves. Thus, sex becomes a new, more basic method

communi... ...tudes
more d... ...fami
rul...

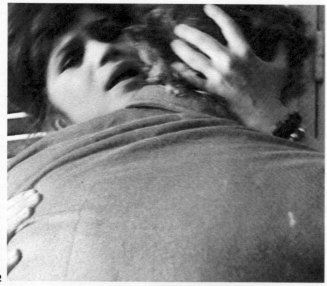

**Directed by Bernardo Bertolucci, 1972**
**Prod co:** PEA Cinematografica/Les Artistes Associés. **prod:** Alberto Grimaldi. **sc:** Bernardo Bertolucci, Franco Arcalli. **photo** (Technicolor): Vittorio Storaro. **ed:** Franco Arcalli. **art dir:** Ferdinando Scarfiotti. **prod des:** Maria Paola Maino, Philippe Turlure. **mus:** Gato Barbieri. **sd rec:** Antoine Bonfanti. **prod man:** Mario Di Biase, Gérard Crosnier. **ass dir:** Fernand Moszkowics, Jean-David Lefèbvre. **r/t:** 129 minutes. Italian title: *Ultimo Tango a Parigi*. Released in GB as *Last Tango in Paris*.
**Cast:** Marlon Brando (*Paul*), Maria Schneider (*Jeanne*), Jean-Pierre Léa (*Tom*), Darling Legitimus (*concierge*), Catherine Sola (*TV script gi* Mauro Marchetti (*TV cameraman*), Dan Diament (*TV sound engine* Peter Schommer (*TV assistant cameraman*), Catherine Allégret (*Ca* erine), Marie-Hélène Breillat (*Monique*), Catherine Breillat (*Mouche* Stéphane Kosiak, Gérard Lepennec (*removal men*), Maria Michi (*Ros* mother), Veronica Lazare (*Rosa*), Luce Marquand (*Olympia*), Mic Delahaye (*Bible salesman*), Laura Betti (*Miss Blandish*), Massimo Gir (*Marcel*), Giovanna Galetti (*prostitute*), Armand Ablanalp (*prostitut* customer), Gitt Magrini (*Jeanne's mother*), Rachel Kesterber (*Christir* Mimi Pinson (*president of tango jury*), Ramon Mendizabal (*orchest* leader).

love of her hero; her only option is to kill him.

The final scene is a masterly combination of Brando's acting and Bertolucci's direction which coalesces the conclusion of the life and myth of Paul/Brando. Jeanne shoots Paul; he crumples slowly and cleanly without blood. As he dies, he removes a piece of chewing-gum from his mouth, plac-

ing it neatly under the railings, finally falling to the floor, dead. It is an ending which, like the film itself, is ambiguous. Paul's death can indicate the impossibility of escaping the bounds of romantic love, or the hope of a more realistic future. Jeanne holds that future in her hands, and killing off the past myths is a necessary part of regeneration in politics.            SALLY HIBBIN

**Paul and Jeanne meet while viewing a vacant apartment in Paris (1). They enjoy a brief, wordless sexual encounter (2). Paul returns to the seedy hotel where his wife Rosa has recently killed herself with a razor. Jeanne goes off to meet her fiancé, Tom a young film-maker. Their meeting is filmed by his intrusiv crew (3).**

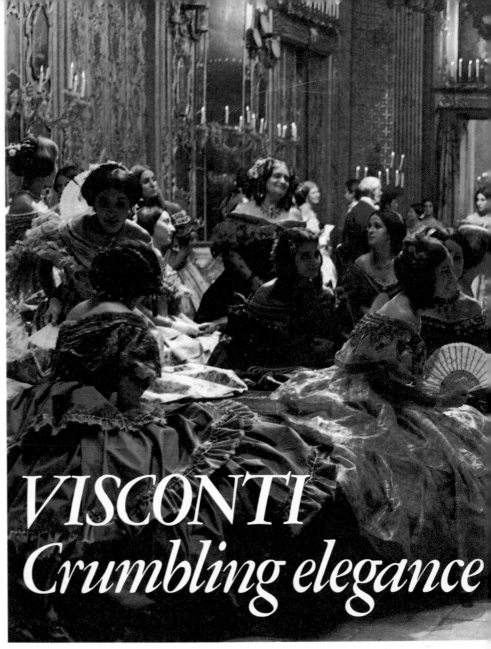

# VISCONTI
## Crumbling elegance

**The decadence of the bourgeoisie, the destructive tensions of family life and the death-throes of the Italian aristocracy are the themes that run through Luchino Visconti's later work. Yet each frame of his films is a strikingly beautiful composition, contrasting starkly with the decaying life-styles he portrays so meticulously**

decades of his career
s one of the giants of
is reputation was
number of films
ms, including
ilms, and 14
d more than
opera pro-
Ironically,
the face of
hostility to
national fes-
his work (or
distributors.
Visconti had
any other,
cel Proust's
Temps Perdu,
ver a decade
ause of prob-

ought Proust's
as Visconti. Its
n throughout
ng of the past
on the present,
ch a decadent
ted siege by
ent. Writer
nd in itself
ained the
elements

### Realism and melodrama

From his early films such as *Ossessione* (1942, Obsession) and *La Terra Trema* (1948, The Earth Trembles), Visconti gained a reputation as a realist, indeed as one of the fathers of neo-realism. However, seen through the prism of his entire work, those early films take on another coloration. They are melodramatic in the truest sense of the term, operatic in style. Other themes also now seem to be at least as important as those common to neo-realistic films: the power of the past, the destructive elements of sexual passion, and the deterioration of basic social units, particularly the family. All of these could well be used to describe Visconti's much later work.

When he began to pursue the melodramatic-operatic style and to develop these themes, Visconti was attacked as 'a betrayer of neo-realism'. This began as early as *Senso* (1954, *The Wanton Countess*), a sensuously rich study of the destructiveness of sexual passion set against the background of the *risorgimento*. In the Venice of 1866, the Countess Livia Serpieri falls in love with the Austrian Lieutenant Franz Mahler, finally betraying not only her husband but the Italian Resistance and the lieutenant as well. The film analyses Italian

history and class structure, with both the decaying ruling class and the revolutionary class passing away as the decadent middle-class maintains its position despite the revolution. None of this is treated 'realistically' but is handled rather like the Verdi opera that begins the film and in which the action and characters are larger than life.

*Le Notti Bianche* (1957, *White Nights*), an adaptation of Dostoyevsky, posed the aesthetic question of a choice between reality and fantasy within the narrative of a man attempting to woo a woman away from her romantic dreams. The woman's dream comes true and the 'realistic' lover is rejected. Visconti heightens the film's preference for romanticism through the purposely artificial sets.

### Sicilian subjects

*Rocco e i Suoi Fratelli* (1960, *Rocco and His Brothers*) recounts the misadventures of a Sicilian family come to Milan to work. It has a realistic base in the problems of Southern families seeking to better themselves in a hostile Northern city. Giuseppe Rotunno's imaginative camerawork captures the 'real' Milan, its streets, its marshes, in realistic if carefully composed fashion. The disintegration

return to the period of *Senso*, with the action removed to Sicily. Instead of centring on an obsessive love affair, however, the plot concerns the ageing prince Don Fabrizio attempting to come to terms with the inevitable disappearance of his class, the aristocracy, either through revolution or through intermarriage. His nephew, Tancredi (Alain Delon), seems in his way the agent for both, first as a soldier for Garibaldi and then as the new husband of the daughter of the bourgeois Don Sedara. Like Visconti himself, the prince is an aristocrat, but his sympathies are with the revolution. The final sequence, almost without dialogue, as the prince walks through the rooms of a palace during one of the last parties given by his class, amounts to a review of the ideas and emotions of the entire film. The feeling is one of nostalgia for the world of the aristocrat but a final acceptance that it should be swept away.

In *The Leopard* Burt Lancaster's performance ... unequalled in his career until ... lar role in *Gruppo di Famiglia in* ... 5, *Conversation Piece*). This was ... most personal film in a decade. The ... has locked himself away from life, collecting paintings of English family groups. Suddenly into his world break the wife of a fascist industrialist, her politically active leftist lover, her son, and her son's (and lover's) young mistress. At first horrified by their 'corruption' and 'bad taste', he learns to love Konrad, the activist, and to understand the others. He also learns finally to reject the past, and 'art', and to live in the present, with people. Visconti uses both decor and costume to underscore character and emotion, from the cluttered museum-like apartment of the professor, to the horrendously garish modern mélange of the 'love nest' upstairs, to the overly elegant gowns in which Silvana Mangano as Bianca, the industrialist's wife, sweeps into his life.

## Families under threat

Between *The Leopard* and *Conversation Piece* there were five feature films which are problematic to all save the most devout admirers of Visconti. *Vaghe Stelle dell'Orsa* (1965, *Of a Thousand Delights*) is again concerned with the break up of a family and the effect of the past on the present. Sandra must come to terms with her past – a mother who she thinks has betrayed her father to the Fascists, a brother with whom she may have had an incestuous affair – in order to be fully able to accept her husband. The film is elegantly made, but cold. Furthermore, Claudia Cardinale is unable to suggest the ambiguous, distant, haunted quality that is necessary to the central role.

*Above: Visconti re-creates the sumptuous surroundings of the Sicilian aristocracy in* The Leopard. *For its British and American release, the film was badly dubbed and printed on inferior colour stock, losing much of its impact. Below: Rocco (Alain Delon) and Nadia (Annie Girardot) – the ill-fated lovers of* Rocco and His Brothers. *Rocco wants to end the affair after Nadia has been raped by his elder brother, Simone. Below right: in* The Stranger, *Meursault (Marcello Mastroianni) is condemned to death for a senseless murder*

of the Pafundi family when confronted with foreign values can be seen as a continuation of neo-realist social analysis and the temptations confronted by each of the brothers as symbolic of social pressures. Yet the tone, the characters, and even the casting of the film make it clear that those are but side issues for Visconti. The power of *Rocco and His Brothers* comes from the internal explosion of the family and the tension between fraternal fidelity and sexual obsession.

*Il Gattopardo* (1963, *The Leopard*) was a

*Top: disturbed, the professor remembers the past and his mother (Dominique Sanda) in* Conversation Piece. *Top right: Helmut Berger as the demented German king,* Ludwig. *Above: the decadence of the Nazi SA helped bring about its downfall by the more militarized SS in* The Damned. *Below: Tadzio (Björn Andresen), the unwitting charmer of* Death in Venice

*Lo Straniero* (1967, *The Stranger*) perhaps came 25 years too late, based as it was on the novel by Albert Camus whose own ideas had subsequently developed further. It was also perhaps too faithful to the novel, for indifference and a lack of action are difficult to turn into film.

With *La Caduta degli Dei* (1969, *The Damned*), the themes of family disintegration, the fall of a class and sexual obsessions are set against the rise of Nazism in Germany. While many of the set-pieces are extremely well handled the constant hysteria in tone, the excessive acting and decor, and the ultimate trivialization of political and social ideas into sexual ones make the film crudely sensational.

## Personal flaws

*Morte a Venezia* (1971, *Death in Venice*) succeeds on the level of decor and historical recreation, on the level of theme (the source novelist Thomas Mann's notion of the northerner going south and being destroyed through contact with corruption, primarily sexual), and on the level of basic casting (particularly Dirk Bogarde as the northerner who becomes sexually obsessed with a young boy). Alas, however, the central figure – and thus the obsession – does not work. By casting the role of the boy, Tadzio, with a young actor (Björn Andresen) more feminine in appearance than not, Visconti forces us to accept his hero's newborn homosexual desires on faith. Because Tadzio is something of a coy flirt instead of the unconscious object of erotic obsession, the audience is left with a rather tiresome tale of unrequited love.

The five-hour *Ludwig* (1973) also suffers from an error in central casting. This time it is brought about by Visconti's own personal obsessions. Ludwig is made less a figure of grand and glorious madness with a vision too grandiose for a king to make real than a rather pouty young man who likes fancy dress, his cousin, big castles and young artists.

Visconti returned to full creative power with *Conversation Piece*, but his health then rapidly declined. He had almost finished *L'Innocente*, (1976, *The Innocent*), based on Gabriele D'Annunzio's novel, when he died, and the film was finished by other hands. Still, what there is of Visconti is impressive and the themes of sexual attraction and family disintegration within a melodrama are treated with romantic discretion.

Few directors deserve to be called *auteurs*, but Visconti certainly does. He had a firm hand in every aspect of his films, from choice of subject and development of script to the placing of objects on the set. Of those directors who began in Italy before the war, only he and Roberto Rossellini kept faith with their basic aesthetic and cultural ideas no matter how misunderstood and rejected those ideas were at various points in their careers. All that is of value in the modern Italian cinema sprang from these two giants. DAVID OVERBEY

### Filmography
1936 Une Partie de Campagne (uncred. ass. dir) (FR). '37 Les Bas-Fonds (uncred. ass dir) (FR) (USA/GB: The Lower Depths). '40 La Tosca (ass. dir; +co-sc). '42 Ossessione (+co-sc). '45 Giorni di Gloria (doc) (co-dir only). '48 La Terra Trema (+sc; +mus. arr). '51 Bellissima (+co-sc); Appunti su un Fatto di Cronaco (doc. short). '53 Siamo Donne *ep* Anna Magnani (USA: Five Women/Of Life and Love; GB: We, the Women). '54 Senso (+co-sc) (GB: The Wanton Countess). '57 Le Notti Bianche (+co-sc) (USA/GB: White Nights). '60 Rocco e i Suoi Fratelli (IT-FR) (USA/GB: Rocco and His Brothers). '62 Boccaccio '70 *ep* Il Lavoro (+co-sc) (IT-FR) (GB: The Job). '63 Il Gattopardo (+co-sc) (USA/GB: The Leopard). '65 Vaghe Stelle dell'Orsa (+co-sc) (USA: Sandra; GB: Of a Thousand Delights). '67 Le Streghe *ep* La Strega Bruciata Viva (IT-FR) (USA: The Witches); Lo Straniero (+co-sc) (IT-FR-ALG) (USA/GB: The Stranger). '69 La Caduta degli Dei (+co-sc) (IT-GER) (USA/GB: The Damned). '71 Morte a Venezia (+prod; +co-sc) (USA/GB: Death in Venice). '73 Ludwig (+co-sc) (IT-FR-GER). '75 Gruppo di Famiglia in un Interno (+co-sc) (IT-FR) (GB: Conversation Piece). '76 L'Innocente (+co-sc) (IT-FR) (GB: The Innocent).

# Ermanno Olmi

## Camera of

'Our culture has no place for the old or for the very young, it's a place for sterile people who don't know how to communicate any more. That's why I am happy to return to the people in the mountains.'

Ermanno

Though Olmi has often been called a pessimist because he depicts the bleakness of life so vividly and implies that Christian resignation will console the sufferer for everything he must bear in this world, this is a very schematic and indeed dogmatic way of looking at the content of his cinema. Ermanno Olmi is really an optimist; he believes that life's mystery lies with the old and the very young. Nothing is more expressive in poetic terms of his vision of the world than the scene in *L'Albero Degli Zoccoli* (1978, *The Tree of Wooden Clogs*) which shows the complicity between the old man and the little girl to whom he explains how he will get his tomatoes to ripen before everyone else's. It is an act of rebellion against nature

itself, and the girl is wonderstruck wh[en] has proof that he was right. It is a fa[...] without sleeping beauties and magic [...]

In the same film, Olmi shows anoth[er] rebellion: a peasant's son is sent to sc[hool] those years – the end of the last century – and in that part of Italy, peasant children did not go to school. It just wasn't considered necessary. One day the boy's clog breaks as he is running out of school, and he has to trudge home barefoot across several miles of rough country road. To provide him with new clogs, the father goes out late one night to cut down a poplar tree belonging to the owner for whom he works as a sharecropper. With the wood he carves out the new clogs so that the boy can go

*Top:* Time Stood Still *was Olmi's first feature, which started life as a documentary about an old man and a youth in isolation while guarding a dam. Above: on location in a rubbish dump – Olmi shooting* The Scavengers. *Left:* Tre Fili Fino a Milano *(1958) – an example of Olmi's desire 'to talk about the reality of the times in which I live'*

to school as usual the next day. Later, when the father's theft is discovered, he is sacked by the landowner; the family have to pack their meagre belongings onto a cart and leave the community. The boy is clutching his satchel with his school-books. It may be some time before he can go to school again, but knowledge is one of the privileges in life that he has conquered, even if his father can do nothing about losing his job.

These are examples of how Olmi believes that films should have a close connection with the reality waiting for us outside in the streets, one that does not make us rub our eyes with disbelief as we come out of the darkened cinema into the light of day. Ermanno Olmi was born in 1931 in one of the most clerical regions of Northern Italy – the Bergamasco, the frontier between Lombardy and the Veneto. Olmi's father was an engine driver who was sacked from the state railways because he was a socialist and wouldn't join the Fascist Party. Olmi had spent his early childhood in Bergamo living in the working-class railwaymen's council houses near the station. When his father lost his job they moved to Milan, where Ermanno went to school. During the summer holidays he would visit his peasant grandmother and would listen to stories about life in the country – the world that he was to depict in *The Tree of Wooden Clogs*.

His father had succeeded in getting a job with the Edison-Volta electrical firm in Milan, and when he died during the war, first Olmi's mother and then he himself found jobs with the same firm. His teenage interest in theatricals turned towards films when at Edison they gave him a 16mm camera and let him make shorts, at first about company outings and activities, and then documentaries which gradually won him a reputation. Then he persuaded his employers to let him make a long documentary that in fact turned into a feature. This was *Il Tempo si è Fermato* (1959, *Time Stood Still*), made in black and white but in 'Scope, about the human relationship between a mature man of mountain peasant stock and a young student from the city who spend a winter together as watchmen over a half-built dam.

Olmi was to return later to the theme of a relationship between an older man and a youth in *I Recuperanti* (1970, *The Scavengers*) in which the bizarre, anarchistic Toni teaches a young unemployed veteran just back from the war how to make a living scavenging for scrap metal in the valleys of the Asiago Altopiano where many of the battles of World War I had been fought. The old man not only teaches him how to dig for metal and if possible avoid being blown to pieces by the buried shells, but also a philosophy of life that has a lot to do with Olmi's eternal belief in the virtues of the land and the peasant life. Though in the end the young man chooses a less dangerous job as a bricklayer, Toni's final song about the joy and freedom of the open air was a prelude to Olmi's own flight from Milan and its urban nightmares. He was to build a home in Asiago where he still lives today.

That was not to be until the Seventies. In the meantime, Olmi established his professional reputation as a creative film-maker in Milan – only being tempted once towards the alluring Roman film scene. Even this was something very much according to Olmi's vision of things:

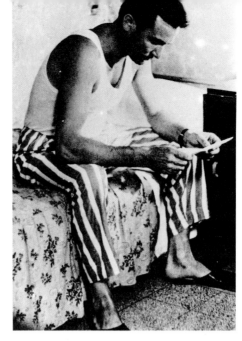

*Above left and right: romance by correspondence;* The Engagement *is an observation of the emotional complexities in a long-distance relationship. As with much of Olmi's work, the film examines the way man's employment adversely affects his personal life*

*Below: like many other neo-realist film-makers, Olmi shows a deeply humanitarian concern for people denied the means to voice their discontent.* The Tree of Wooden Clogs *reveals the desperate hardship of a peasant's life at the turn of the century*

a film about Pope John XXIII who, like Olmi, had been born in the Bergamasco peasant fringe. The film – *E Venne un Uomo* (1965, *A Man Named John*) – produced by Harry Saltzman, was not a success. Partly it was because Olmi let himself be convinced for the first and only time to use a professional actor, Rod Steiger, who was quite out of place, even if the idea of telling the Pope's story through a contemporary intermediary was interesting. Pasolini – who loved Olmi's work – was to reproach Olmi for having ignored the contradictions in Pope John and behaving as if there were only 'one tone' in his life.

Olmi ventured south in only one film, his third feature *I Fidanzati* (1963, *The Engagement*). This was to Sicily where his hero, a welder from a Milan factory, had been transferred with a good contract, though obliged to leave behind his fiancée. There is a New Year's party at which the two fail to communicate; by

now Olmi's technique has become sophisticated – the sequence is seen in flashback by the man in his loneliness in Sicily. Whereas Italian films usually refer to the Southerners' feeling of being outcasts in northern cities, this is the Northerners' reply.

Olmi's most mature films before *The Tree of Wooden Clogs* were his trilogy on bourgeois Milan, whose economic miracle he himself had lived through, seeing the balloon burst before the hopeful Sixties exploded in violence and dissent. The best of the three is *Un Certo Giorno* (1969, *One Fine Day*) – as delicate and sorrowful a film as *Il Posto* (1961, *The Job*) but with perhaps a much stronger feeling for characterization. Another of his non-professionals, Brunetto De Vita (on whom Olmi moulded the character), plays the advertising executive who is about to get a promotion. An accident – the man runs over a worker on the side of a street as he is speeding to the airport – causes

him to reassess his values and relationships.

In *Durante L'Estate* (1971, *During the Summer*) Olmi allowed the whimsical in his nature to take the upper hand. Yet this story of a rather odd map designer with a passion for heraldry was full of charm and showed another aspect of Milan from that of the drudgery of work. There is a splendid sequence in the gardens beside Lake Como when the 'professor' decides to name a rose after the girl whom he has elevated to Princess, and is chased by policemen and flower lovers.

In 1974 he made *La Circostanza* (*The Circumstance*) – a cold and rather over-written story again about a car accident that changes people's lives. In this case it is a well-off bourgeois woman who runs into a boy on his bike and then tries to lavish on him some of the affection she is no longer able to give to her own children, who are all going their own way in life. Olmi's deep feelings for the peasant virtues and the consoling graces of the family once again come to the forefront when they are all reunited.

Four years later Olmi was to make *The Tree of Wooden Clogs*. Thanks to Italian television he had been able to keep on working during the lean years between films. As well as the features produced for RAI (Italian state-owned television) he had made documentaries and series on young people's problems and on religious subjects. The success of *The Tree of Wooden Clogs* at Cannes gave him a wide audience in Italy for the first time, and he was at last unanimously accorded the stature of one of the country's leading film artists. The film had cost 300 million lire (£100,000 in 1978) and Olmi earned only £12,000 for his effort despite its being sold to almost every country in the world. RAI also produced Olmi's subsequent film, *CamminaCammina* (1983, Walk, Walk) with a slightly more generous budget – though still a shoestring one by comparison to most contemporary productions. For the first time, Olmi tackled an allegorical subject set in no definite epoch. Filmed in Tuscany in the area around the Etruscan city of Volterra, it is the story of a journey by a group of travelling players who believe that a phenomenon has occurred in a distant city. When they get there, they find that nobody knows anything about it. The film did not repeat the success of its predecessor.

JOHN FRANCIS LANE

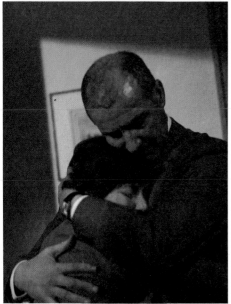

*Olmi used professional actors for the first time in* A Man Named John *(top), although he reverted to non-professionals for* One Fine Day *(above). Below: Gianni (Andreino Carli), the younger of* The Scavengers. *Below right:* CamminaCammina – *an historical allegory*

### Filmography

**1954** La Diga del Ghiacciaio (doc. short); La Pattuglia di Passo San Giacomo (doc. short). **'55** Buongiorno Natura (doc. short); Cantiere d'Inverno (doc. short); L'Energia Elettrica nell'Agricoltura (doc. short); La Mia Valle (doc. short); Il Racconto Della Stura (doc. short); Società Ovesticino-Dinamo (doc. short). **'56** Costruzioni Meccaniche Riva (doc. short); Fertilizzanti Complessi (doc. short) (sup. only); Manon: Finestra 2 (doc. short); Tesatura Meccanica Della Linea 220,000 Volt Santa Massenza-Cimego (doc. short) (sup. only); L'Onda (doc. short); Pantano d'Avio (doc. short) (sup. only). **'57** Bariri (doc. short) (sup. only); Campi Sperimentali (doc. short) (sup. only); Fibre e Civiltà (doc. short) (sup. only); Michelino 1 B (doc. short); Progresso in Agricoltura (doc. short) (sup. only); Peru, Istituto de Verano (doc. short) (sup. only). **'58** Giochi in Colonia (doc. short); Colonie Sicedison (doc. short) (sup. only); Il Frumento (doc. short) (sup. only); Il Pensionato (doc. short); Tre Fili Fino a Milano (doc. short); Venezia Città Moderna (doc. short). **'59** Alto Chiese (doc. short) (sup. only); Cavo ad Olio Fluido 220,000 Volt (doc. short) (sup. only); El Frayle (doc. short) (sup. only); Fertilizzanti Prodotti Dalla Società del Gruppo Edison (doc. short) (sup. only); Natura e Chimica (doc. short) (sup. only); Il Tempo si è Fermato (+sc) (GB: Time Stood Still). **'60** Il Grande Paese d'Acciaio (doc. short); Po: Forza 50,000 kW (doc. short) (sup. only); Le Grand Barrage (doc. short) (sup. only); Il Pomodoro (doc. short) (sup. only). **'61** Un Metro è Lungo Cinque (doc. short); Il Sacco in Plypac (doc. short) (sup. only); Il Posto (+sc; +ed) (USA: The Sound of Trumpets; GB: The Job). **'62** Una Storia Milanese (prod; + act. only) (GB: A Tale of Milan). **'63** I Fidanzati (+co-prod;+sc) (USA: The Fiancés; GB: The Engagement); La Rimpatriata (co-prod. only); I Ragazzi che si Amano (co-prod. only); I Basilischi (co-prod. only) (GB: The Lizards); Il Terrorista (co-prod. only). **'65** E Venne un Uomo (+co-sc) (USA: And There Came a Man; GB: A Man Named John). **'69** Un Certo Giorno (+sc;+ed) (GB: One Fine Day). **'70** I Recuperanti (+co-sc;+photo;+ed) (GB: The Scavengers) (shot as TV film but shown in cinemas). **'71** Durante L'Estate (+co-sc; +photo; +ed) (USA/GB: During the Summer) (shot as TV film but shown in cinemas). **'74** La Circostanza (+sc;+photo;+ed) (USA/GB: The Circumstance) (shot as TV film but shown in cinemas). **'78** L'Albero Degli Zoccoli (+sc;+photo;+ed) (USA/GB: The Tree of Wooden Clogs). **'83** CamminaCammina (+prod; +sc; +photo; +ed); Milano 83 (doc) (+sc; +phot; +ed).

Starting with Gradisca, a local beauty, lighting a torch and setting a bonfire ablaze to roast the 'winter witch' and usher in the spring, and ending with the wistful farewell she bestows a year later on the randy teenage boys at her wedding while sadly tossing away her bridal bouquet, the small-town life celebrated by *Amarcord* is above all one of community rituals and seasonal changes. Within this basic rhythmic pattern of eternal recurrence, dreams and other fantasies play as much of a role as precise recollections.

*Amarcord* means 'I remember' in the regional dialect of Rimini (Fellini's own home town), and even

though the director has been at pains to disclaim any specific autobiographical intent in this episodic caravan of burghers and small-town events, it is clear enough in Fellini's work as a whole that fact and fancy are never very far apart. *Amarcord* is Fellini's thirteenth feature as a director, made 20 years after his first treatment of male adolescence in *I Vitelloni* (1953, *The Spivs*), and the distance he has travelled since is largely a matter of the extent to which he has learned to trust imagination over 'realistic' observation. Thus the strange white fluffy substance that drifts through the province every spring is neither less magical nor less ordinary than

the mysterious local snowfall, which can easily beat the cinema as an evening's main attraction. And the pomp and circumstance so inextricably intertwined with the ceremonies of church and state – funerals, weddings and public rallies – are carried over into the less formal, local pastimes which sometimes merely involve standing around and gawking.

Unavoidably, the rites of puberty and the spectacle of politics – climaxing in the ecstatic figures of the blonde nymphomaniac Volpina or the charismatic Mussolini – testify to the same tortured libidos. It is worth noting that the privileged sector of Fellini's poetic kingdom, like that of Jacques Tati, is always the town square and public forum where diverse personalities are allowed to pass and mingle. Privacy scarcely seems to exist at all in a community ruled by gossip, rumour and myth, yet it is precisely the domain of privacy that the town's collective dream-life feeds upon – sexual extravaganzas that, like the cinema itself, seem to rely on intimacies denied to most citizens.

Some critics have objected to the vulgar directness of the scatological and sexual humour in *Amarcord*. The latter includes such moments as the brief encounter between Titta and Luccia, the tobacconist who invites him to suck her enormous breasts after he has demonstrated his youthful prowess by lifting her hefty body several times . . . until she proves too much for him. Yet Fellini's bawdy – tied in this case to his background as a cartoonist – is merely the reverse side of his sense of pathos, which comes to the fore with Titta's mad Uncle Teo, who climbs a tree and refuses to budge because he doesn't have a woman at all.

It is typical of Fellini's style, sup-

ported by Nino Rota's bitter-sweet score, that his characters always seem to wind up with too much or too little – perpetually stuck, as it were, between the mud and the stars. Subjective memory can distort, flatten, contract or expand, whilst, at the same time, recollection remains in innocent awe of spectacles as diverse as an ocean liner at night (the magisterial *Rex*, framed by beautifully backlit sets), and a Fascist rally.

*Amarcord* was the fourth of his features to win an American Academy Award for best foreign film,

## Directed by Federico Fellini, 1973

**Prod co:** F. C. Produzioni (Rome)/PECF (Paris). **prod:** Franco Cristaldi. **prod sup:** Alessandro Gori, Gilberto Scarpellini. **sc:** Federico Fellini, Tonino Guerra. **photo** (Technicolor): Giuseppe Rotunno. **ed:** Ruggero Mastroianni. **art dir:** Danilo Donati. **mus:** Nino Rota. **mus dir:** Carlo Savina. **cost:** Danilo Donati. **sd:** Oscar De Arcangelis, Mario Maldesi. **tech adv:** Jean Paul De La Motte. **prod man:** Lamberto Pippia. **ass dir:** Maurizio Meino. **r/t:** 123 minutes.
**Cast:** Pupella Maggio (*Miranda Biondi*), Magali Noel (*Gradisca*), Armando Brancia (*Aurelio Biondi*), Ciccio Ingrassia (*Uncle Teo*), Nandino Orfei (*Il Patacca*), Luigi Rossi (*lawyer*), Bruno Zanin (*Titta Biondi*), Gianfilippo Carcano (*Don Baravelli*), Josiane Tanzili (*Volpina*), Maria Antonietta Beluzzi (*tobacconist*), Giuseppe Lanigro (*Titta's grandfather*), Stefano Proietti (*Oliva*), Carla Mora (*maid*), Gennaro Ombra (*Pinwheel*), Aristide Caporale (*Giudizio*), Ferrucio Brembilia (*Fascist leader*), Antonio Faa' Di Bruno (*Count Lovignano*), Gianfranco Marrocco (*Count Poltavo*), Alvaro Vitali (*Naso*), Bruno Scagnetti (*Ovo*), Bruno Lenzi (*Gigliozzi*), Fernando de Felice (*Ciccio*), Francesco Vona (*Candela*), Donatella Gambini (*Aldina Cordini*), Franco Magno (*Zeus, school principal*), Mauro Misul (*philosophy teacher*), Armando Villella (*Fighetta*), Dina Adorni (*math teacher*), Francesco Maselli (*physics teacher*), Mario Silvestri (*Italian teacher*), Fides Stagni (*history teacher*), Marcello Bonini Alos (*gym teacher*), Domenico Pertica (*blind man*), Fausto Signoretti (*coachman*), Fredo Pistoni (*Colonia*), Mario Liberate (*proprietor of the Fulgor*), Mario Nebolini (*secretary of city hall*), Vincenzo Caldarola (*beggar*), Fiorella Magalotti, Marina Trovalusci (*Gradisca's sisters*), Milo Mario (*photographer*), Antonio Spaccatini (*federal officer*), Bruno Bartocci (*Gradisca's bridegroom*), Marco Laurentino, Riccardo Satta, Carmela Eusepi, Clemente Baccherini, Mario Del Vago, Marcello Di Falco.

1

4

7

140

and it is not hard to see why. The garrulous lawyer who intermittently serves as the film's narrator and local guide reminds us that much of what we see is peculiar neither to this time nor to this town; the film charts the lot of provincial dwellers everywhere, and Fellini has been true to this principle by fashioning a movie *for*, as well as about, his home-town cronies. Refugees of small towns – as well as those who still live in them – will find parts of their experience writ large in Fellini's earthy sketches.

JONATHAN ROSENBAUM

In a small Italian coastal resort during the Fascist period, the arrival of spring is signalled by the appearance of *manine*, white puffballs that blow through the province. Aurelio Biondi berates his teenage son Titta (1) for not working, and his wife Miranda sends Titta off to the local priest for confession. Here, a query about masturbation evokes erotic memories and fantasies – including ones that involve Volpina, a whore (2).

After a Fascist rally is held to greet a visiting dignitary (3), the police exhibit some brutality towards certain local citizens, including Aurelio, a Socialist. At the swank Grand Hotel, legends still persist of a tryst between a glamorous hairdresser named Gradisca (4) and a visiting prince, and a pushcart merchant who gets invited into the suite of a visiting harem (5).

When the Biondis collect Titta's Uncle Teo from a nearby insane asylum for a family picnic, he climbs a tree and demands a woman until a dwarf nun from the asylum coaxes him back down again. Back in town, the people go out to sea in boats to catch fleeting glimpses through the fog of the *Rex*, a luxury liner (6). Titta is allowed to suck the nipples of the chubby tobacconist once he has managed to lift her huge body several times (7).

After a heavy snowfall, Miranda Biondi dies in hospital and is buried by her family. In the springtime, as the *manine* once again come to town, Gradisca marries a policeman, and a festive outdoor banquet celebrates the event (8).

2

3

5

6

8

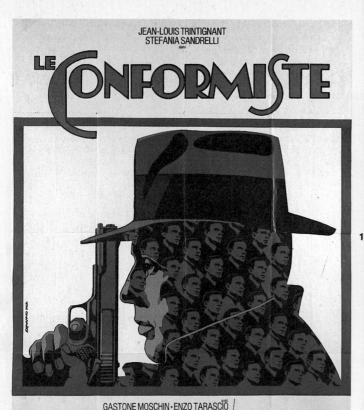

JEAN-LOUIS TRINTIGNANT
STEFANIA SANDRELLI dans

# LE CONFORMISTE

GASTONE MOSCHIN · ENZO TARASCIO avec
FOSCO GIACHETTI · JOSE QUAGLIO
avec DOMINIQUE SANDA dans le rôle de ANNA
et la participation de
PIERRE CLEMENTI

Producteur associé GIOVANNI BERTOLUCCI
Produit par MAURIZIO LODI-FE
Réalisé par BERNARDO BERTOLUCCI
D'après le roman de ALBERTO MORAVIA
TECHNICOLOR
Une production MARS FILM PRODUZIONE S.p.A. ROME · MARIANNE PRODUCTIONS PARIS
Distribué par CINEMA INTERNATIONAL CORPORATION

# The Conformist

*Above: French poster for this Italian/French/German co-production*

The Conformist was Bernardo Bertolucci's most ambitious and elaborate film to date on its release in 1970, and it introduced him to a far wider audience than his works had previously reached. Up until then Bertolucci's films had been relatively intimate in scale and scope, although they were not without their elaborate and impressive set-pieces: the riverside elegy, Unità rally and premiere of Verdi's *Macbeth* in *Prima della Rivoluzione* (1964, *Before the Revolution*); and the most extraordinary experiments and flourishes that fairly overflowed in *Partner* (1968), Bertolucci's most Godardian film.

However, *The Conformist* showed Bertolucci as having cast off the Godardian mantle. At the same time the re-creation of Fascist Italy provided him with a broad canvas on which to create a whole series of quite breathtaking and vertiginous cinematic *tours de force*: the Parisian dance-hall scene, complete with sly and suggestive reference to Laurel and Hardy, in which Anna and Giulia dance an erotic tango; the sleeping-car honeymoon, a richly coloured echo, perhaps, of the make-believe train-ride in Max Ophuls' *Letter From an Unknown Woman* (1948); the bleak, deadly car journey along wintry roads, climaxing in the murders in the eerie, snow-covered forest; and so on. As Bertolucci admits, 'the point of departure was cinema, and the cinema I like is Sternberg, Ophuls and Welles', three directors who, like Bertolucci, are masters of style but for whom style is never an end in itself. Thus in *The Conformist* the lyrical flourishes are not simply spectacular or decorative, they are also dramatically significant.

In all his films Bertolucci attempts to relate the psychological and personal to the political and social, making them interesting amalgams of Marx and Freud. In *The Conformist*, the theme of fascism cannot be divorced from unresolved psychological and familial tensions, particularly those revolving around father-son relationships. Indeed, it is these relationships that are the key to all Bertolucci's films and the basis from which their more obvious political concerns arise, just as the patriarchal family is the basis of patriarchal society. As Bertolucci put it when questioned about his relationship with his father:

'My own father was anti-fascist, but obviously I feel that the whole bourgeoisie is my father. And fascism was invented by the petit bourgeoisie.'

In *The Conformist* Marcello's latent, unacknowledged homosexuality – and thus his compensatory desire to conform (which in Italy at that time meant conformity to fascist ideals) – is perhaps the result of his failure to identify with both his real father and the father substitutes, Quadri and Italo. It is his failure to pass beyond the Oedipal phase that is the source of his hostile relationships with his actual father and his shifting, ambiguous attitudes towards Quadri and Italo.

The personal significance of the film's various father-son relationships is emphasized by the fact that Quadri's Parisian address and telephone number actually belong to Jean-Luc Godard! Obviously Bertolucci is implying that *The Conformist* marks a break with his own mentor and father-figure, and with the radical aesthetic and political ideas to which Godard was committed at that time. As Bertolucci ironically put it:

'*The Conformist* is a story about me and Godard . . . I'm Marcello and I make fascist movies and I want to kill Godard who's a revolutionary . . . makes revolutionary movies and is my teacher.'

Indeed, the film was denounced as fascist by sections of the Left: Bertolucci was accused not simply of selling out to Paramount but also of reducing fascism to a purely psychological phenomenon and of equating fascism and homosexuality. However, this is precisely what he doesn't do: rather he demonstrates that Marcello's unresolved sexual problems lead to an almost pathological desire to conform. Thus he conforms to fascism while it represents the acceptable norm, but rapidly changes his tune after the Liberation – witness his denunciation of Italo. Nor does Bertolucci represent fascism in purely psychological terms, instead he recognizes and portrays the complex interpenetrations of the sexual and the social.

JULIAN PETLEY

**Directed by Bernardo Bertolucci, 1970**
**Prod co:** Mars Film (Rome)/Marianne (Paris)/Maran (Munich). **prod:** Maurizio Lodi-Fè. **assoc prod:** Giovanni Bertolucci. **sc:** Bernardo Bertolucci, from the novel by Alberto Moravia. **photo** (Technicolor): Vittorio Storaro. **ed:** Franco Arcalli. **art dir:** Nedo Azzini. **set dec:** Fernando Scarfiatti. **cost:** Gitt Magrini. **mus:** Georges Delerue. **r/t:** 108 minutes. Italian title: *Il Conformista*. Released in GB as: *The Conformist*.
**Cast:** Jean-Louis Trintignant (*Marcello Clerici*), Stefania Sandrelli (*Giulia*), Gastone Moschin (*Manganiello*), Enzo Tarascio (*Quadri*), Pierre Clémenti (*Lino Seminara*), Dominique Sanda (*Anna Quadri*), Christian Alegny (*Raoul*), José Quaglio (*Italo*), Milly (*Marcello's mother*), Giuseppe Addobbati (*Marcello's father*), Yvonne Sanson (*Giulia's mother*), Fosco Giachetti (*colonel*), Benedetto Benedetti (*minister*).

2

3

5

6

7

Marcello Clerici, a Fascist agent in Mussolini's Italy, recalls his past while on a mission to kill Professor Quadri, one of his former teachers and now an active anti-fascist in Paris.

He remembers how, as a boy, he had killed Lino, a chauffeur who had tried to seduce him (1). Escaping detection he had attempted to expiate his guilt by becoming as conformist as possible.

In 1938 he becomes engaged to the suitably petit-bourgeois Giulia (2), and involves himself with the Fascist group OVRA (3), offering to spy on Quadri while honeymooning in Paris. However, he is ordered to assassinate the professor, and on arriving in Paris he takes Giulia to visit his future victim and his wife Anna (4), to whom he is instantly attracted. She, meanwhile,

attempts to seduce Giulia (5).

Marcello arranges for Quadri to be ambushed the next day during a journey out of Paris, and he tries to persuade Anna not to accompany her husband on the journey. Failing (6), he is forced to watch helplessly as both are killed by OVRA agents deep in a wintry forest (7).

Some years later Marcello is wandering among the crowds celebrating the end of the Mussolini regime in Rome, when he meets Italo, a dedicated Fascist and his one-time mentor. He then spots Lino, very much alive and in the process of picking up a young male prostitute (8). Hysterically he denounces both Italo and Lino as Fascists, homosexuals and murderers, but finds himself unable to take his eyes off the object of Lino's attentions. . . .

8

# Passions, Politics &

Pasolini's cinema refuses easy, conventional critical definitions and consequently has been frequently misunderstood. Lacking – indeed rejecting – the superficial stylistic and thematic continuities so beloved of the critical consensus, its contradictions have been vaguely dubbed as Christian-Marxist. However, this does isolate an aspect of Pasolini's cinema: namely, that it is particularly deeply embedded in Italian cultural and political life with all its conflicting traits and elements, the most important of which is the opposition between the two commanding ideologies of Catholicism and Communism.

Born in 1922 in Bologna, northern Italy, Pier-Paolo Pasolini came from a social background for which there is no real English equivalent:

'My origins are fairly typical of petit-bourgeois Italian society. I am a product of the Unity of Italy. My father belonged to an old noble family from the Romagna, while my mother comes from a Friulan peasant family which subsequently became petit bourgeois.'

He admitted 'an excessive, almost monstrous love' for his mother, and that he lived 'in a state of permanent, even violent tension' with his father – a Fascist supporter, tyrannical and overbearing. Pasolini grew up with a dislike of institutionalized religion (his father was a non-believer who made the family go to church for social reasons) and was not a practising Catholic; however, he also admired his mother's 'poetic and natural' sense of religion and admitted in himself a tendency towards mysticism: 'I see everything in the world, objects as well as people and nature, with a certain veneration.'

## Poet and peasant
At seventeen Pasolini began to write poetry in the Friulan dialect. Significantly, Friuli was not only his mother's native area, it also represented a regionalism of which his father – as both a Fascist and an inhabitant of central Italy – strongly disapproved. But Pasolini's interest in peasant dialects does not simply relate to his family, it also attests to a somewhat backward-looking, romantic, idealized

**It was a cruel irony that Pier-Paolo Pasolini's death – in brutal and mysterious circumstances – should resemble a legend worthy of one of his own films. His early work had been about delinquency, and contained searching political allegory, and although often condemned as obscene, his poetic interpretations of classical stories could be said to have created myths for the modern world**

vision of the peasantry as a source of 'true, natural values' which is as prevalent in his cinematic as his literary works. This early penchant for obscure dialect poetry was also connected with the current vogue for literary aestheticism – the idea that the language of poetry is absolute and sufficient unto itself. This cultivation of form for its own sake returns in Pasolini's cinema, representing a vigorous and stimulating attack on outworn forms of naturalism such as neo-realism, as well as a tendency towards extreme impenetrability.

Pasolini's favourite authors were deemed degenerate by the Fascists, and so, fuelled by hatred for his father, Pasolini developed a visceral anti-Fascism and turned towards Marxism. After the war, his Marxist leanings were reinforced at the University of Bologna, and he actually joined the Communist Party briefly in 1947–8. However, as he admits, his Marxism was emotional, aesthetic and cultural rather than directly political, and was strongly linked to his attachment to the (largely Catholic) peasantry. Indeed, Pasolini displayed only the sketchiest awareness of the works of Marx and Lenin, and none of his films could be said to adopt a rigorous, coherent and thoroughgoing Marxist point of view.

## Cinema Roma
In 1950 Pasolini came to Rome, both the political capital of Italy and the home of Cinecittà, and thus an ideal place for someone interested in both film and politics. Here he became a scriptwriter, working mainly on would-be artistic low-life films – the last dying gasps of neo-realism – though he also had a hand in Fellini's *Le Notti di Cabiria* (1957, *Nights of Cabiria*) and Bertolucci's *La Commare Secca* (1962, *The Grim Reaper*).

Pasolini's work on Roman underworld films fitted perfectly with his interest in the Roman sub-proletariat, that was for him the urban equivalent of the Friulan peasantry. His earliest novels and films are set in this sector of society rather than among the organized, industrial proletariat. His first film *Accattone* (1961) is the chronicle of a small-time hustler, which, for all its employment of seemingly neo-realist devices (fragmentary narrative, non-professional actors, seedy locations, etc.), is significant precisely for its departures from the genre.

Though the film may be set among the sub-proletariat, it is not *about* them as a class and does nothing to elucidate their social condition. In this respect Pasolini's use of dialect here is less 'realistic' than a hermetic formal device which, as in his poetry, draws attention to the sounds of the words themselves. Similarly, the film's fractured structure, in which many shots appear to fulfil no clear narrative function, is less a 'realist' feature than the filmic equivalent of poetic language: metaphorical, connotative and largely self-referential.

*Accattone*, like so much of Pasolini's work, operates not on the level of the psychological and the social, but on that of fable and myth. His second film – *Mamma Roma* (1962) – is the story of an ex-prostitute who tries unsuccessfully to give her son a 'respectable' bourgeois background. It introduces another key Pasolini theme, and one that is exposed more fully in *Teorema* (1968, *Theorem*): the unacceptable face of the modern bourgeois and petit-bourgeois worlds.

## Of Marx and myth
With *Il Vangelo Secondo Matteo* (1964, *The Gospel According to St Matthew*) Pasolini

# Pasolini

*Top far left: Franco Citti as Accattone, the young pimp operating in Rome's delinquent quarters. Top left: Judas (Otello Sestili) gives the kiss by which Jesus (Enrique Irazoqui) is betrayed in* The Gospel According to St Matthew. *Above: freely reworking Sophocles,* Oedipus Rex *overflowed with grandeur*

took an already much mythologized subject. Clearly influenced by Rossellini's *Francesco, Giullare di Dio* (1950, *Flowers of St Francis*), Pasolini almost reverses the trajectory of *Accattone* by moving from the mythical and sacred to the everyday. Generally read as an attempt to pull Christianity back to its popular, primitive roots, it was largely this film which earned him the 'Christian-Marxist' tag. However, it could also be argued that the representation of the various 'modern' accretions to the Gospel demonstrates that the Bible possesses no one fixed meaning, but various different meanings which have come to it over centuries of social usage. Ultimately the film expresses a belief in the virtues of the people independent of social classes, while its view of history is too cloudy

and romanticized to be considered properly materialist. In line with Pasolini's reverence for what he calls the sacred, the miracles are allowed to retain their sense of mystery.

Coinciding with the upsurge in left-wing political activity in the late Sixties, Pasolini retreated increasingly into the creation of a largely mythical universe, with films such as *Edipo Re* (1967, *Oedipus Rex*), *Teorema, Porcile* (1969, *Pigsty*) and *Medea* (1970). It was hardly surprising that he should be attracted by the Oedipus legend, not only in *Oedipus Rex* but throughout many of his films in which its presence (though not always immediately obvious) acts as a structure of images and ideas informing the whole. *Oedipus Rex* is framed by a contemporary prologue and epilogue, set in

the Friulan countryside and Bologna respectively. The main action occurs not in an historically specific ancient Greece, but in a seemingly timeless pre-historical North Africa, a world of primitive drives and desires. This is presented as deliberately strange and distanced, like someone else's dream, affording the spectator no possibility of involvement and identification.

## Before the Fall
Like many Pasolinian figures Oedipus inhabits

*Above left: the convent gardener in one of* The Decameron *tales has to fertilize more than his flowers. Above: Pasolini's pessimistic and bestial comparison of destructive societies*

### Filmography

**1955** La Donna del Fiume (co-sc. only) (IT-FR) (USA/GB: Woman of the River). **'56** Il Prigioniero della Montagna (co-sc. only). **'57** Le Notti di Cabiria (co-sc. only) (IT-FR) (USA: Nights of Cabiria: GB: Cabiria). **'58** Marisa la Civetta (co-sc only) (IT-SP); Giovani Mariti (co-sc. only) (IT-FR). **'59** La Notte Brava (co-sc. only) (IT-FR) (GB: Night Heat); Morte di un Amico (co-sc. only) (GB: Death of a Friend). **'60** Il Bell'Antonio (co-sc. only) (IT-FR); La Lunga Notte del '43 (co-sc. only); Il Carro Armato dell'Otto Settembre (co-sc. only); La Giornata Balorda (co-sc. only) (IT-FR) (USA: From a Roman Balcony; GB: A Day of Sin); Il Gobbo (actor only) (IT-FR) (GB: The Hunchback of Rome). **'61** La Ragazza in Vetrina (co-sc. only) (IT-FR) (GB: The Woman in the Window);

Accattone (+sc). **'62** La Canta delle Marane (short) (co-sc. only); Mamma Roma (+sc); La Commare Secca (co-sc. only) (GB: The Grim Reaper). **'63** RoGoPaG/Laviamoci il Cervello *ep* La Ricotta (+sc) (IT-FR); La Rabbia (first part of doc. compilation only; +sc). **'64** Comizi d'Amore (doc) (+comm; +appearance as interviewer); Il Vangelo Secondo Matteo (+sc) (IT-FR) (USA/GB: The Gospel According to St Matthew). **'65** Sopraluoghi in Palestina (+comm; +co-narr). **'66** Uccellacci e Uccellini (+sc) (USA: Hawks and Sparrows). **'67** Le Streghe *ep* La Terra Vista dalla Luna (+sc) (IT-FR) (USA: The Witches); Edipo Re (+sc; +mus. sup; +act) (USA/GB: Oedipus Rex); Requiescant (actor only) (IT-GER). **'68** Capriccio all'Italiana *ep* Che Cosa Sono le Nuvole? (+sc); Teorema (+sc)

(USA/GB: Theorem); Appunti per un Film sull'India (+sc). **'69** Amore e Rabbia/Vangelo '70 *ep* Il Fiore di Campo (+sc) (IT-FR) (USA/GB: Love and Anger); Porcile (+co-sc) (IT-FR) (USA/GB: Pigsty). **'70** Medea (+sc) (IT-FR-GER); Ostia (co-sc. only); Appunti per un'Orestiade Africana (+sc) (IT-FR) (GB: Notes for an African Oresteia). **'71** Il Decameron (+sc; +act) (IT-FR-GER) (USA/GB: The Decameron). **'72** Dodici Dicembre (anonymous co-dir); I Racconti di Canterbury (+sc; +act) (IT-FR) (USA/GB: The Canterbury Tales). **'73** Storie Scellerate (co-sc. only) (IT-FR) (GB: Bawdy Tales). **'74** Il Fiore delle Mille e Una Notte (+sc) (IT-FR) (USA/GB: Arabian Nights). **'75** Salò o le Centoventi Giornate di Sodoma (+sc) (IT-FR) (USA/GB: Salo or the 120 Days of Sodom).

a pre-moral world, obeying only his basic drives before eventually being forced to enter into knowledge, to understand the significance of his acts and to realize that certain desires are taboo. But by then it is too late and retribution inevitably follows, making many of Pasolini's films akin to pagan versions of the myth of the Fall, set in the realms of the universal and the mythic as opposed to the personal and the psychological. Indeed, his trilogy of tales – *Il Decameron* (1971, *The Decameron*), *I Racconti di Canterbury* (1972, *The Canterbury Tales*), *Il Fiore delle Mille e Una Notte* (1974, *Arabian Nights*) – celebrates a pre-lapsarian world, the invocation of an almost magical past in which innocence is still possible. *Arabian Nights* in particular is a paean to guiltless sexuality, to the naked human body and to frank sexual

*Top: The Canterbury Tales, part of the trilogy of medieval subjects which borrowed from the more erotic stories in Boccaccio and Chaucer. Right: a grotesque pan-sexual travesty of the marriage sacrament in Salo – declared obscene, blasphemous and anti-establishment in the Italian courts, but a virulent attack on fascism*

desire; a film in which, unusually, the male heterosexual vision does not dominate, and male and female beauty and desire are treated in an unconventionally equal manner.

After the relative innocence of the trilogy Pasolini plunged back into the horrors of a twentieth century in the grip of Fascism with *Salò o le Centoventi Giornate di Sodoma* (1975, *Salo or the 120 Days of Sodom*). Transposing the Marquis de Sade's eighteenth-century erotic tales to a castle in northern Italy during

the last days of Mussolini, Pasolini presents an increasingly extreme series of orgies and tortures in order to demonstrate that sex is no longer a means of liberation but simply one more tool of oppression. The point may be debatable, but not the horrifying cruelty and pessimism of this uncannily valedictory work.

Pasolini was battered to death by a teenage youth shortly after completing *Salo* on November 2, 1975, in circumstances that still remain clouded and controversial. JULIAN PETLEY

# PAST GLORIES?

**French and Italian cinema of the Seventies was much preoccupied with the question of popular memory, particularly of World War II**

The links – both economic and aesthetic – between the French and Italian film industries are historically the strongest between any two major film-producing nations. During World War II both countries turned out their share of Fascist or collaborationist films. In the early Sixties, Italian cinema had a revival at the same time as the French *nouvelle vague*; and in 1968, when world events triggered a wave of 'revolutionary' film-making, the student riots and demonstrations in France and Italy served as catalysts for a thoroughgoing revision of cinematic form and content.

The industries should be seen, therefore, as closely connected and both should be assessed in the aftermath of May 1968. In France, thanks largely to Jean-Luc Godard, cinema had discovered a new freedom of expression that was well exemplified in *Le Vent d'Est* (1970, Wind From the East), a film that posed history as a set of problems rather than facts. It seemed to the radical film-makers – Godard in France, Michelangelo Antonioni, Roberto Rossellini, Pier-Paolo Pasolini and Bernardo Bertolucci in Italy – that the innovation and experimentation of the *nouvelle vague* had softened into a smooth, socially palatable style that flattered the bourgeoisie's image of itself as fashionably left-wing and liberated. This spirit encouraged the organizers of the Cannes Film Festival in 1969 to institute a new section – the 'Quinzaine des Réalisateurs' (Directors' Fortnight). Back in Paris, the civil servants running the Centre National de la Cinématographie (National Centre for Cinema) opened their doors to researchers and initiated a programme of state financial aid to young film-makers.

Liberalism was very much the order of the day in Italy too. Relaxation of censorship allowed *Fellini Satyricon* (1969) and Visconti's *La Caduta degli Dei* (1969, The Damned) a relatively troublefree passage despite their 'decadent' settings and depiction of homosexuality. Both these films explored the relationship between power and sexual 'deviance' in different historical contexts and were thus forerunners of a major trend in mid-Seventies movies.

But the most symptomatic Italian film of the immediate post-1968 period was Liliana Cavani's *I Cannibali* (1970, The Cannibals). In this film, a latter-day Antigone is determined to bury the body of her rebel brother after a bloody revolution where the authorities have decreed that the dead will lie in the streets as an example to all. Somewhat over-schematic in its political allegory, the film is nevertheless a powerful moral tale for the Seventies and a chilling vision of the incipient police state which was to provide the thematic basis for many of the finest Italian movies of the next five years.

Typical of such political parables, though distinguished from many by the ingeniousness of its plot and the rigour of Gian Maria Volonté's central performance, was Elio Petri's *Indagine su un Cittadino al di Sopra di Ogni Sospetto* (1970, *Investigation of a Citizen Above Suspicion*), in which a police officer apparently escapes detection for a

crime he has committed because his seniority places him 'above suspicion'.

In France, the impulse of May 1968 was continued with *Camarades* (1970, Comrades), in which director Marin Karmitz challenged the whole basis of trade unionism as a means to workers' power. Jean-Luc Godard, who from 1969 to 1972 formed part of a film-makers' collective named after the Soviet documentarist Dziga Vertov, made a partial return to mainstream cinema, as well as a bitter commentary on the lessons of 1968, with *Tout Va Bien* (1972, All Goes Well), which also criticizes the unions. Trade unions emerge as the cowardly agents of compromise in *Coup pour Coup* (1972, *Blow for Blow*), a film about workers' occupation of a textile factory, made by a collective directed by Marin Karmitz.

Because of the proliferation of tiny multi-screen cinemas on the Left Bank, 'minority' films and the work of unknown directors always enjoyed more

*Above: Trimalchio (Mario Romagnoli), a rich, freed slave, gives his orders at his feast in* Fellini Satyricon; *the predominant red tints express the sensuality of the scene. Fellini shows ancient Rome as a place of orgiastic self-indulgence and arbitrary power. Below: André Halimi's documentary examines the entertainment industry's collaboration with the Germans in wartime France*

Above: knights prepare for battle in Lancelot du Lac, a version of the Arthurian legend. Top: Rose (Isabelle Huppert) with her lover, the hypocritical Judge Rousseau (Philippe Noiret), who is determined to send an insane killer to the guillotine in Le Juge et l'Assassin. The film is set in provincial France in 1893. Top right: Anna Quadri (Dominique Sanda) captivates The Conformist (Jean-Louis Trintignant), a Fascist agent who is plotting to murder her left-wing husband

chance of being seen and written about in Paris than anywhere else in the world. The films that the majority of Parisians (and therefore French moviegoers) went to see were either, at worst, home-grown slapstick comedies or, at best, aesthetically pleasing but politically innocuous films from the established stylists – François Truffaut, Claude Chabrol, Eric Rohmer and Jacques Rivette.

By contrast with what threatened to become a complacent bourgeois cinema in France, the revival of civil and political themes in Italian cinema was refreshing. Two notable films, Damiano Damiani's *Confessione di un Commissario di Polizia al Procuratore della Repubblica* (1971, *Confessions of a Police Commissioner to the District Attorney*) and *L'Istruttoria è Chiusa: Dimentichi!* (1972, The Inquest Is Over: Forget About It!), exposed corruption in the judiciary and the prison system. It was a theme that Francesco Rosi was to amplify in *Il Caso Mattei* (1972, *The Mattei Affair*), in *Lucky Luciano* (1973) and, most impressively of all, in *Cadaveri Eccellenti* (1976, *Illustrious Corpses*).

In Italian political life, the tenuous alliance of Christian Democrats and centrist parties survived from one coalition government to the next in the teeth of strong opposition from the Socialists and the Italian Communist Party (PCI). On the extreme left and right wings were ranged the Red Brigades, who were responsible for kidnapping several govern-

ment ministers and killing ex-prime minister Aldo Moro in 1978, and the Neo-Fascists, whose campaign of terror was marked by the bombing of Bologna railway station in 1980 and other outrages.

One of the most controversial figures to emerge from this confused context was Lina Wertmuller, who mounted a policy of populist cinema that would tackle the major issues of the past and the present. Foregrounding sex and politics in a bold and entertaining manner, Wertmuller was acclaimed in the USA as a cult figure. On the surface, her politics appeared to be left-wing – she professed herself a Socialist supporter in interviews – and her treatment of sex seemed progressive, with dominant, self-aware women calling the shots in the sex war. Her various films include *Mimi Metallurgico Ferito nell'Onore* (1972, *The Seduction of Mimi*), *Film d'Amore e d'Anarchia* (1973, *Love and Anarchy*), *Travolti da un Insolito Destino nell'Azzurro Mare d'Agosto* (1975, *Swept Away by an Unusual Destiny in the Blue Sea of August*) and *Pasqualino Settebellezze* (1976, *Seven Beauties*). To view them is to encounter the shallow sentiments of a social satirist whose special scorn is reserved for the working class and for women. The reaction to her films from the Left and from feminists was most vociferous in the USA, where they were breaking box-office records for Italian films. Depending on viewpoint, Wertmuller's ideas are either too broad to be confined in social or political labels, or so haphazardly thought-out as to be class-bound and sexist.

Insofar as there was an equivalent of this popular political cinema in France, Constantin Costa-Gavras could be said to be the key figure of the decade. *Z* (1969), set in Greece at the time of the Colonels' junta, and *L'Aveu* (1970, *The Confession*), a reconstruction of a Czech show trial, both starred Yves Montand, an actor noted for his left-wing sympathies. Montand's next film with Costa-Gavras was *Etat de Siège* (1973, *State of Siege*), a fictional account of the capture of a CIA agent by Tupamaro guerrillas in South America. Again the style was that of the suspense thriller made to look authentic by filming in a documentary manner.

As he continued to explore the political possibilities of narrative film, Costa-Gavras not only made his boldest film – *Section Spéciale* (1975, *Special Section*), an indictment of the French wartime government's policy of appeasement to the

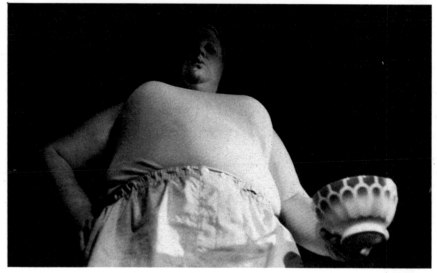

Germans – but he also inspired a whole sub-genre of political thrillers that combined messages for contemporary audiences with all the suspense of action movies. History could be rendered problematic, used to trouble an audience rather than to confirm its safe distance from past events. The cinema could exhume some skeletons from the domestic closet by re-examining events and scandals from the past in France.

Such was the rationale that could be discerned beneath the arty and attractive surface of many French movies in the Seventies. Modishly nostalgic films such as Louis Malle's *Lacombe Lucien*, Alain Resnais' *Stavisky . . .* (both 1974), François Giraud's *Le Trio Infernal* (1974, *The Infernal Trio*), Joseph Losey's *Mr Klein* (1976) and Claude Chabrol's *Violette Nozière* (1978) were a strong draw at the box-office. Yet all these films offered more than mere period charm. They suggested through their re-examination of *causes célèbres* that all was far from well beneath those carefully authentic period costumes and sets.

## History came alive on the screen as film-makers opened the eyes of the people to past realities

This tendency coincided with the coming to power in France of a new bourgeoisie whose figurehead was President Giscard d'Estaing. The Gaullist era, and with it all the fervent oppositions to Pétain's government of collaboration, was discarded. According to the critics of *Cahiers du Cinéma*, a different version of that crucial period of French history could now be written (and screened) in which, for the first time since the war, it could be admitted that France was not so anti-fascist as all that and the myth of the Resistance – so sacred to the Gaullists – was a deception that had kept people from understanding the truth about their nation.

It was in this context that such a film as *Lacombe Lucien*, with its account of how a peasant youth is refused entry to the Resistance and joins the Nazi secret police instead, could be produced and become a *succès de scandale*. The floodgates were actually opened by the documentarist Marcel Ophuls, whose film *Le Chagrin et la Pitié* (1970, *The Sorrow and the Pity*) released many memories and feelings that had

been repressed since the Occupation. Other documentaries that evoked similar responses included *Français, Si Vous Saviez* (1973, Frenchmen, If You Knew . . .) and *Chantons Sous l'Occupation* (1976, Let's Sing Under the Occupation). It became clear that the real struggle in French cinema was to be fought over the question of popular memory – how the people understood their history.

French film-makers, notably André Téchiné in *Souvenirs d'en France* (1975, France's Memories), confronted the problem that to 'rewrite' history required a radically new approach to the way history is represented on film. Some of their subjects were drawn from 'living memory' such as *Stavisky . . .*, the tale of a great financial swindler in the Thirties, or *Violette Nozière*, the young prostitute who, in the Thirties, poisoned both her parents, killing her father, and went on to earn a pardon from de Gaulle after years in prison.

Other subjects were taken from earlier, well-documented cases, such as René Allio's *Moi, Pierre Rivière, Ayant Egorgé Ma Mère, Ma Soeur, Mon Frère . . .* (1976, *Moi, Pierre Rivière*), a young nineteenth-century peasant's account of how and why he killed his mother, sister and brother, or Bertrand Tavernier's *Le Juge et l'Assassin* (1976, The Judge and the Killer), which dealt with a perversion of justice in the pursuit and prosecution of a mass-murderer in rural France. Several 'historical' films,

*Top left: Stavisky . . . (Jean-Paul Belmondo) presides over a meeting as his corrupt financial empire slowly crumbles in the Depression of the early Thirties. Top: in Allonsanfán, set in the Italy of 1816, the aristocratic Fulvio Imbriani (Marcello Mastroianni) is a reluctant revolutionary who finally betrays his comrades and is himself killed. Above: Hilde (Shirley Stoler), a concentration-camp commandant, enjoys humiliating the Italian prisoner who attempts to seduce her in Seven Beauties*

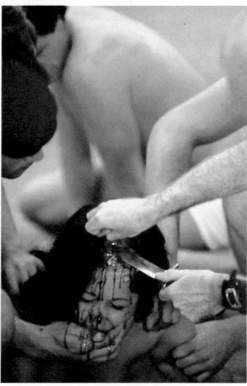

*Above:* Le Dossier 51 *(1978, File 51) concerns an attempt to blackmail a French diplomat into spying for a secret organization; the intrusion on his private life drives him to suicide. Right: four Fascist dignitaries in* Salo *gratify their sadistic tastes by arranging the torture of young girls and boys. Below: in* Illustrious Corpses, *Inspector Rogas (Lino Ventura, right) investigates the politically motivated murders of several judges, part of a right-wing conspiracy that will also result in his own death*

among them Robert Bresson's *Lancelot du Lac* (1974) and Frank Cassenti's *La Chanson de Roland* (1978, The Song of Roland), sought their subjects in medieval legend or in the period before the French Revolution – René Allio's *Les Camisards* (1971, The Camisards), Bertrand Tavernier's *Que la Fête Commence . . .* (1975, *Let Joy Reign Supreme*) and Ariane Mnouchkine's *Molière ou la Vie d'un Honnête Homme* (1978, *Molière*). These films tended to be more lavish and spectacular than the scrupulously documented case histories like *Moi, Pierre Rivière*, but essentially all the films favoured analysis of history over mere story-telling with period backdrops.

Because of the close ties between France and Italy in film production and distribution as much as in criticism and audience taste, the same theme of returning to domestic history dominated serious Italian cinema of the mid-Seventies, though such directors as Dino Risi, Luigi Comencini and Ermanno Olmi continued to refine the arts of social comedy and the drama of contemporary relationships. The decade was, however, dominated by Pasolini (up to his death in 1975), Rossellini (whose major work was for television until he too died in 1977), Fellini and, above all, Bertolucci.

Each of these directors addressed the question of popular memory according to his own individual style: Rossellini in *Anno Uno* (1974, *Italy, Year One*); Pasolini – in terms of myth – in his trilogy that concluded with *Il Fiore delle Mille e Una Notte* (1974, *Arabian Nights*); Fellini most impressively in *Il Casanova di Federico Fellini* (1976, *Fellini's Casanova*); and Bertolucci in *Il Conformista* (1970, *The Conformist*), *La Strategia del Ragno* (1970, *The Spider's Stratagem*) and *1900* (1976). An epic reconstructing the popular memory of the rise and overthrow of Italian Fascism, with outstanding performances from Burt Lancaster, Robert De Niro, Donald Sutherland, Laura Betti and Dominique Sanda, *1900* was certainly Bertolucci's most ambitious as well as his most populist film.

Far less popular in appeal but equally important for its treatment of recent Italian history, Pasolini's last film *Salò o le Centoventi Giornate di Sodoma* (1975, *Salo or the 120 Days of Sodom*) was released to outrage from the Right and confusion from the Left. The film is also concerned centrally with Fascism, but focuses specifically on its relationship to sexuality and sadism. Thus the torture and sadistic abuse of a group of young boys and girls serves not to gratify the audience's depraved voyeuristic impulses – as the more hysterical reviews claimed – but to raise questions of a serious nature about the relations of power to violence and sexuality.

These issues were also present in a number of Italian box-office hits of the period, including Liliana Cavani's *Il Portiere di Notte* (1974, *The Night Porter*), Lina Wertmuller's *Seven Beauties* and Tinto Brass' *Salon Kitty* (1976); but the treatment was so superficial – on the level of sex and jackboots – as to make no contribution to the understanding of Fascism or its exorcism from the collective consciousness of the nation.

Finally, it should be recalled that the debate about history and its representation on film brought to world recognition several directors who already had at least a decade's experience behind them but whose finest work to date was completed in the Seventies. Francesco Rosi has been mentioned but Ettore Scola with two films – *C'Eravamo Tanto Amati* (1975, *We All Loved Each Other So Much*) and *Una Giornata Particolare* (1977, *A Special Day*) – and Paolo and Vittorio Taviani with *Allonsanfán* (1974) and *Padre Padrone* (1977, Father Master) contributed to the ongoing commitment of their native cinema.

MARTYN AUTY

# LET IT BE ROCK

**Electric guitars and resonant drums – the sounds of rock music thundered through many movies of the Seventies, documentaries as well as fiction films**

The Seventies should have been a golden era for rock movies. All the portents were favourable. At the start of the decade, *Easy Rider* (1969) and *Woodstock* (1970) had made fortunes both for their backers and for the record companies which had leased the soundtrack rights. Technical improvements in sound recording ensured that live concerts could be taped and reproduced with near-perfect clarity in the cinema (though admittedly few theatres were equipped to take advantage of this). Besides, the Sixties pop-music boom had enriched any number of rock stars, many of whom looked to the film industry either to invest their new wealth or to expend it.

The teenagers who had purchased pop records in the Sixties in such unprecedented quantities were now reaching their early twenties – the age range that was the most statistically significant in the composition of cinema audiences. This applied equally well to the film-makers themselves; for the first time, films would actually be made by directors who had been part of the rock'n'roll generation.

It was a moment of great promise, then; but such promise would be realized only fitfully. The incontestable achievements were that practically every major rock act did become the subject of a rock movie (Fleetwood Mac and the Beach Boys being exceptions), and that the films that were made spanned a range of territory that adequately reflected the variety of the music itself.

Dennis Hopper's *Easy Rider* was the most commercial film up to that time to have pitted the ideals and aspirations of the counter-culture against the cynicism and violence endemic in American society. The alternative society, drugs and all, was good box-office. Thus cinema audiences suddenly had to stomach a couple of effete student-protest movies, *Getting Straight* and *The Strawberry Statement*, as well as *Joe* (all 1970), a portrait of a foul-mouthed redneck. The depiction in *Joe* of the drug-crazed young was patently absurd, but it was almost redeemed by a performance of massive authority from Peter Boyle in the title role.

Boyle later turned up with Jane Fonda and Donald Sutherland in the appealing comedy *Steelyard Blues* (1973). The film, with a musical score from Paul Butterfield, Nick Gravenites and the late Mike Bloomfield, examined a group of contemporary misfits sympathetically and plausibly, but by then traces of the alternative society were fast disappearing.

There were other films that clearly took their cue from *Easy Rider*: *Two-Lane Blacktop* (1971), with James Taylor and Dennis Wilson, and *Electra Glide in Blue* (1973), for example, as well as *Cisco Pike* (1971), an excellent thriller about drug-dealing which starred Gene Hackman and, making his debut in a leading role, Kris Kristofferson. The post-*Easy Rider* boom produced few films of lasting merit; and in the aftermath of the collapse of Sixties idealism, the film that most accurately anticipated the mood of the young during the Seventies, and cast its long shadow over the events of the decade,

was Stanley Kubrick's ultra-violent *A Clockwork Orange* (1971).

There was one crucial respect in which *Easy Rider* was a pioneer movie – the soundtrack consisted almost entirely of previously released material. This had never been accomplished before in mainstream commercial films; film-makers had adjudged the copyright difficulties to be insuperable, and usually played safe by commissioning an original score, often distinguished for its very lack of originality. *Easy Rider* changed the position completely, although it paid the penalty for its groundbreaking. Contractual problems indeed proved labyrinthine, with the result that the film reached Great Britain several months in advance of its accompanying soundtrack album. Nevertheless, recording and publishing companies subsequently realized that, by over-zealously defending their copyright songs, they were simply denying themselves a potentially lucrative source of extra income. In the long run, the *Easy Rider* breakthrough was decisive, and such directors as George Lucas, in *American Graffiti*, and Martin Scorsese, in *Mean Streets* (both 1973), were able to use more or less the soundtrack material of their choice.

The other major seminal film of the period was *Shaft* (1971). A surprise success itself, it spawned an entire movie sub-genre of superspade thrillers, with original scores fashioned after Isaac Hayes' brilliant prototype. None was very memorable, and only Curtis Mayfield's music for *Superfly* (1972) attained individual distinction.

Much less influential, though much more creditable, was Perry Henzell's *The Harder They Come* (1972), the first Jamaican feature film. Jimmy Cliff

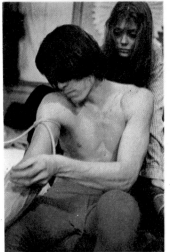

*Top:* Woodstock, *Michael Wadleigh's documentary of the epic rock festival held at Bethnal, New York, in August 1969, condensed '3 days of peace, music . . . and love' into 3 hours of film. Among those who appear are Crosby, Stills, Nash and Young, Joan Baez, The Who, Jimi Hendrix, Joe Cocker, Ten Years After, Santana and half a million hippies. Above: Patrick McDermott as the drug-addicted Frank and Susan Sarandon as his girlfriend in John G. Avildsen's* Joe, *a backlash against hippiedom*

offered himself as star and his own experiences, hustling for work in the island's unsavoury music business, as dramatic inspiration. Such authenticity was appropriately garnished with some of Jamaica's finest reggae music.

The rock movie in the Seventies was re-routed by *American Graffiti*, a film concerned with teenage traumas in small-town Northern California in 1962; the period was re-created exactly, though much of the music used came from the Fifties. The strength of the characterization was no less important than the authenticity of the settings, so that the film succeeded as more than mere nostalgia. *American Graffiti* had a dreamlike quality, capturing adolescence at its moment of extinction, when

### Rock movies never quite lived up to the potential they had boasted at the start of the decade

adulthood beckoned. Its soundtrack was an unqualified joy. The songs were placed in context so meticulously that any audience could appreciate that the director's own sympathies were fully engaged.

Once the hippie dream had corroded, there had been a resurgence of interest in the uncomplicated sounds of early rock'n'roll. Such films as D. A. Pennebaker's *Keep On Rockin'* (1972) and Sid Levin and Robert Abel's *Let the Good Times Roll* (1973) attested to this shift in popular taste. In the wake of *American Graffiti*, such tastes were not simply gratified, they were satiated. There was an *American Graffiti*-type film for blacks in *Cooley High* (1975), there was one for Jews in *Eskimo Limon* (1978, *Lemon Popsicle*) and arguably there was one for the mentally retarded in *National Lampoon's Animal House* (1978). There was also an official follow-up, *More American Graffiti* (1979), directed by Bill Norton, who had made *Cisco Pike*.

*American Graffiti* had included the fondly remembered line, 'Rock'n'roll's been going downhill

ever since Buddy Holly died'. The inevitable biopic, *The Buddy Holly Story* (1978), with Gary Busey in the title-role, succeeded, despite a thorough disregard for factual accuracy, because it achieved a kind of emotional veracity, and because Busey turned in a winning performance.

The British equivalent of *American Graffiti* was *That'll Be the Day* (1973), directed by Claude Whatham from a lively original script by Ray Connolly. This was another evocative film, featuring two sharp central performances by David Essex and Ringo Starr. The Fifties music, however, was used less discriminatingly than it had been in *American Graffiti*. *That'll Be the Day* had a sequel, *Stardust* (1974); but this time the result was a shallow variant of the Beatles' story.

Sixties nostalgia movies on the whole foundered, perhaps because they seemed to be impatient with history, and did not take enough care to reconstruct the Sixties era. The two most notable artefacts of Sixties pop culture were both filmed in the Seventies: they were the Beatles' album *Sgt. Pepper's Lonely Hearts Club Band*, in a catastrophic 1978 version, and the musical *Hair*, limply directed by the respected Miloš Forman in 1979. *Quadrophenia* (1979) boasted a cocky central performance from Phil Daniels as a mod, but little else; its period flavour ranged from the superficial to the nonexistent. Wildly overrated, it should have been criticized for its lack of genuine understanding of adolescent frustration. The condition had been captured most convincingly, most achingly, in a film that slipped out almost unnoticed several years earlier, Barney Platts-Mills' minor masterpiece *Bronco Bullfrog* (1970).

Some films about the Sixties can be exempted from the general condemnation. In particular, there were two powerful films about the legacy of the Vietnam War, *Coming Home* (1978) and *Who'll Stop the Rain* (1978, released in Britain as *Dog Soldiers*), both of which used rock music to establish a sense of period. However, the most beguiling, most affectionate re-creation of the Sixties was *I Wanna Hold Your Hand* (1978), which earnestly recaptured the New York atmosphere at the time of

*Above, far left: Tim Curry as Frank N. Furter, transvestite and modern Dr Frankenstein, who is engaged in building the perfect male sex-object in Jim Sharman's cult classic* The Rocky Horror Picture Show *(1975), an adaptation of Richard O'Brien's spoof horror musical. Above left: drive-in waitresses in George Lucas'* American Graffiti, *which pays nostalgic homage to Saturday night cruisin', juke-box joints, teenage love and rock'n'roll in 1962. Below: more nostalgia, this time for Beatlemania, in Robert Zemeckis'* I Wanna Hold Your Hand, *in which four girls from New Jersey travel to New York to see their idols appear on the Ed Sullivan Show in 1964. The Beatles are heard but not seen*

*Above: Seventies teen idol David Essex (left) as Jim MacLaine with Ringo Starr (centre) as his pal and Billy Fury on the stage in* That'll Be the Day, *a tough and seedy view of England in the early days of rock'n'roll. After dropping out of school Jim drifts through jobs in fairgrounds and holiday camps, casual liaisons with girls and a dead-end marriage until he sees a guitar in a shop window . . . hence the sequel* Stardust. *Above right: Bette Midler, 'the Divine Miss M' herself, as a junkie rock superstar on the skids in Mark Rydell's* The Rose. *Below right:* American Hot Wax *(1978), directed by Floyd Mutrux, tells the story of the late Alan Freed (Tim McIntire), who coined the term 'rock'n'roll'*

the Beatles' first American visit in February 1964.

When looking backwards had first become acceptable, in the mid-Seventies, nostalgia had probably seemed the decent way out. After all, rock itself had entered a kind of electric jackboot phase. There were principally two films – both bizarre, baroque extravaganzas – that tried to grasp the nettle of this new mood, *Phantom of the Paradise* (1974) and *Tommy* (1975). *Phantom of the Paradise* was a grotesque, saturnine fantasy that amply conformed to the first law of rock: nothing succeeds like excess. *Tommy* was vulgar, garish, highly inventive and very loud; in The Who's rock opera, Ken Russell had finally found the ideal outlet for his untamed imagination.

The debacle of *Sgt. Pepper's Lonely Hearts Club Band* had badly dented the form-book of Robert Stigwood, whose previous productions *Saturday Night Fever* (1977) and *Grease* (1978), both of which starred John Travolta, were the two most commercially successful rock movies of the second half of the Seventies. Trying to explain the appeal of

*Grease*, another film about the Fifties, is not altogether easy; certainly its less-than-breathtaking climax – a new hairdo for Olivia Newton-John – does not seem to account for it. *Saturday Night Fever* was at least a genuinely contemporary movie, and it caught the prevailing disco winds perfectly. Its soundtrack double-album became easily the largest-selling record of all time.

Businessmen were not slow to grasp the fact that films and records could achieve a spectacularly commercial symbiosis. Suddenly there were as many films to accompany soundtracks as vice versa. The most renowned of these, by dint of the excellent Steely Dan title-song on the one hand and the fecklessness of the film itself on the other, was *FM* (1978). When the entertainment industry did manage to create another product where the film and soundtrack vied with each other in commercial potency, it was *Urban Cowboy* (1980), yet another Travolta hit.

By the close of the decade, there was a renewed interest in contemporary themes, partly because of *Saturday Night Fever*, and partly because of the emergence of the British punk or 'New Wave' movement. The films concentrating on the new music tended to be made both by the industry, as in the case of Joe Massot's *Dance Craze* (1981), and in spite of the industry – for instance, Don Letts' *Original Punk Rock Movie* (1977). The socio-political invective that accompanied punk found its most eloquent cinematic expression in the Jack Hazan-David Mingay film *Rude Boy* (1980), with the Clash; Derek Jarman found a style to match the new mood of civil disharmony with *Sebastiane* (1976), *Jubilee* (1978) and *The Tempest* (1979).

Of the films that studied the rock business itself, the most effective were *Breaking Glass* (1980), again with Phil Daniels, and *The Rose* (1979), in which the considerable shortcomings of the film itself were easily outweighed by Bette Midler's performance as the quasi-Janis Joplin figure who overdoses on the life-style that rock stars are expected to conform to. The Sex Pistols' own story was pieced together by Malcolm McLaren, in a desultory, tendentious and objectionable fashion, as *The Great Rock'n'Roll Swindle* (1980).

*Woodstock* stands at the head of the documentary films produced during the Seventies; it has secured an indelible place in the history of rock. Directed by Michael Wadleigh, the film was a celebration both of the music and of the mythology that the occasion enshrined; but if the gathering at Woodstock represented the zenith of the hippie life-style, it was all too quickly followed by its nadir, the scary Rolling

Above: John, Paul, George and Ringo – with a little help from their friend Billy Preston on keyboards – play 'Get Back' to London from the roof of their Apple studio in Let It Be; it was the Beatles' final public performance as a group. Top right: another famous foursome was the subject of Julian Temple's film, which begins with effigies of the anarchic punk heroes being burned in the Gordon Riots. The Great Rock'n'Roll Swindle started life as a Russ Meyer project called Who Killed Bambi? – it ended up as a celebration of Sex Pistols manager Malcolm McLaren's ability to manipulate the rock industry. Above right: Bob Dylan in The Last Waltz, the film of The Band's farewell concert at Bill Graham's Winterland in 1976

Stones concert at Altamont, filmed by Albert and David Maysles and Charlotte Zwerin as *Gimme Shelter* (1970).

The other influential film from the start of the Seventies was the Beatles' *Let It Be* (1970). The intention here had been to show them working and recording together as a group. As it happened, togetherness was the characteristic least in evidence, and so the film showed the band actually in the throes of dissolution. Nevertheless, the Beatles had been pioneers in myriad respects, and this was to be no exception. After *Let It Be*, rock's top acts readily agreed to become the subjects of documentary films. In doing so, they were recognizing not only the appeal of the form developed by the Beatles, but also the fact that the old Hollywood notion, of simply building a musical drama around a star name, had happily passed away.

The last person to realize this was Elvis Presley; but he finally did agree to throw away those wretched scripts, and be filmed simply as Elvis in two interesting documentary movies, though neither *Elvis – That's the Way It Is* (1970) nor *Elvis on Tour* (1972) could claim to have lifted the veil on the Elvis persona.

Such documentaries appeared regularly throughout the Seventies. Most have titles that speak for themselves: *Pink Floyd à Pompéi* (1972, *Pink Floyd Live at Pompeii*); *Yessongs* (1973); *Genesis – a Band in Concert*; and *The Grateful Dead* (both 1977). *The Kids Are Alright* (1979) went several steps further by providing a retrospective of all aspects of The Who's 15-year career. A fascinating and carefully compiled film, it ended up as a moving tribute to the

band's drummer, Keith Moon, who had died while it was being completed.

Of the special-occasion concerts that were filmed, two of the best were *Concert for Bangla Desh* (1972) and *The Last Waltz* (1978). It is just coincidence that both of these featured Bob Dylan, although his charisma undoubtedly contributed greatly to both. Unfortunately, his own four-hour film *Renaldo and Clara* (1978) was insufferably pretentious and unspeakably boring. *The Last Waltz*, directed by Martin Scorsese, contains many excellent performances besides Dylan's and that of The Band, whose farewell concert this was. Other celebrities present included Eric Clapton, Van Morrison, Joni Mitchell and Neil Young, and, like Dylan, they all subsequently featured in their own films.

Documentaries were constructed around Clapton and Morrison individually in *Eric Clapton and his Rolling Hotel* and *Van Morrison in Ireland* (both 1980). Mitchell and Young both made their own films: Joni Mitchell's *Shadows and Light* (1980) was made for television rather than the cinema; Neil Young, under the alias Bernard Shakey, directed two films himself – *Journey Through the Past* (1973) and *Rust Never Sleeps* (1979).

The Seventies had thus been a highly productive period for rock movies in terms of quantity alone. There had even been a handful of excellent films – *American Graffiti*, *That'll Be the Day*, *The Harder They Come*, *Bronco Bullfrog*, *The Last Waltz* and others – but overall there was a lingering feeling that, with all the advantages that should have accrued to rock performers, the years had been ones of underachievement.                    BOB WOFFINDEN

# THE WANDERERS

**Odyssey movies concern a quest or search, a journey in which the landscapes mirror the soul of the restless wanderer**

'A man will search his heart and soul, go searchin' way out there.' So claims the ballad that introduces *The Searchers* (1956), generally held to be John Ford's finest Western and a film that can be seen as both the apogee of classic American narrative cinema and the harbinger of a darker, less reassuring strain in popular movie-making. Thus, with hindsight, it seems appropriate that this film should describe a quest that is not only physical but metaphysical, a search for self-fulfilment or, as the ballad puts it, for 'peace of mind'.

Not that there is anything novel in itself about the metaphorical use of the journey or quest in cinematic narrative. It might even be maintained that the experience of watching a movie is as much that of a journey through time as it is akin to the more frequently invoked notion of dreaming. Certainly, in practical terms, a film like Howard Hawks' *Red River* (1948) directly uses the shifting settings of an itinerary to parallel the psychological development of its characters, while a comedy such as Hawks' *Bringing Up Baby* (1938) seems to offer a farcical variation on the same premise. For that matter, one of the first great post-war landmarks of the 'art' movie, Jean Cocteau's *Orphée* (1950, *Orpheus*), deals with a journey out of the imprisoning self by conjuring up a parallel world, the 'Zone', the no-man's land that lies behind the mirror (or, perhaps, behind the screen). It could be claimed that *Orphée*'s depiction of the 'Zone' – with its menacing, monumental bombed ruins – represents a pre-vision of social upheavals to come.

What is unarguable, however, is that by the time *Orphée* was twenty years old, the cinema had undergone great changes and the world had undergone far greater ones. In terms of political realities, as the Sixties ended, the Vietnam War was in full progress, Soviet forces had entered Czechoslovakia and world recession was just around the corner. Prognostications about what might lie 'out there' could hardly be reassuring. Yet during the Seventies a wide assortment of films appeared from sundry quarters of the globe which might loosely be termed 'odyssey' movies. These otherwise disparate works are unified by their thematic use of the journey to confront the nature of the modern world. Some are distanced, some immediate, but taken together they add up on the one hand to a set of meditations, on the other to a report from the frontier of contemporary consciousness.

Two films by Ingmar Bergman, both detailing fights for survival amid assorted calamities, provide a significant comparison. *Det Sjunde Inseglet* (1957, *The Seventh Seal*), the film that established Bergman's international reputation, clearly belongs to the 'Doomsday' literature of the atomic age but is contained within a carefully wrought, exquisitely photographed medieval allegory. But *Skammen* (1968, *Shame*), though set in a nameless war-torn country, is resolutely contemporary in feeling and almost resembles a newsreel. The film ends in desolation with an image of the central couple, their relationship ruptured by the vicis-

situdes they have gone through, helplessly adrift in an open boat. For all its open-ended power and raw-edged effect, however, *Shame* remains a product of the art house.

By contrast, the recent work of Michelangelo Antonioni betrays a fascinating cross-fertilization of 'art' and 'popular' cinema. After making *Blow-Up* (1966), the story of a quest by an English photographer for literal truths amid the manifold illusions of sybaritically Swinging London, Antonioni again gave a youth angle to his subsequent project. This was his first American movie, *Zabriskie Point* (1970), a work no less extraordinary – if, unhappily, less widely popular – than its predecessor.

*Zabriskie Point* begins in the city with college student Mark on the run from police after a protest demonstration. Then, when he steals a light plane, the action moves out into the vast American landscape where he crosses the path of Daria, a

*Above: Mark (Mark Frechette) and Daria (Daria Halprin) make love among the dust dunes of Death Valley in* Zabriskie Point, *just before Daria has her vision of many similar loving couples. Below: The Stalker (Aleksandr Kaidanovsky) pours away The Writer's alcohol as he guides him and The Scientist in the mysterious Zone*

*Below: the journey up-river to Cambodia is the central motif in* Apocalypse Now. *Bottom: David Locke (Jack Nicholson) in* The Passenger *is a television reporter who decides to adopt the identity of a dead man but finds that he has made a fatal error*

disaffected young secretary driving into the desert to the spot where her boss is launching a resort development. This last fact provides a wittily up-to-date twist on the traditional contradiction in Westerns like *The Searchers* between the desert as wilderness and as garden. And the vanished Western past is again invoked in the haunting tableau of Daria's stop *en route* at a skeletal ghost town, where the strains of 'The Tennessee Waltz' echo forlornly from a juke-box over a vista of rusting decrepitude.

It is at Zabriskie Point itself, in the daunting confines of Death Valley, where years before Erich von Stroheim shot the climax of *Greed* (1925), that the most bizarre sequence occurs. This is the mass love-in – Daria's pot-induced fantasy, presented quite directly – with numerous couples writhing in the dust of the desert floor like victims of Pompeii returned to life. Although escape is illusory – Mark is shot down when he tries to give himself up – the film ends with another departure into the imaginary as Daria 'sees' the luxurious house in the desert blown to smithereens and a slow-motion camera abstracts the appurtenances of modern living into so many relics of an alien consumer culture.

Escape is an illusion also in Antonioni's *Professione: Reporter* (1975, *The Passenger*). The locales this time are principally North Africa and Spain, and the framework like that of a mystery thriller. The hero, Locke, is a prominent television figure but a casualty of material success and a man at the end of his tether. Grasping at the chance to start again, he assumes the identity of a man he finds dead in the next room of a shabby hotel in Chad. But this attempted regeneration ultimately proves to be

a death sentence: the person he has become is an arms dealer with enemies to spare, and Locke winds up a corpse in another shabby hotel in Algeciras.

The extraordinary shot, seven minutes in duration, in which the camera seems to float out of the hotel window and around the little town square outside, serves to encapsulate the impulse behind the entire work, fatalistic yet transcendental. In its implied meditation on materiality, it is opposingly complementary to the elaborate montage of the *Zabriskie Point* finale, and in both films identity is ultimately dissolved into landscape. These movies are, in the fullest sense, voyages into the unknown.

Rather the same might be said of the work of the most widely discussed director to emerge from the Soviet cinema in recent years, Andrei Tarkovsky. He was first acclaimed for a film made in 1965 but shelved in the USSR until 1972. This was *Andrei Rublev*, an impressionistic account of the life and (pretty bleak) times of the fifteenth-century Russian icon painter of that name. Shot in black and white, with a concluding sequence that bursts into colour to show the paintings themselves, the film proceeds episodically through a phantasmagoric and frequently brutal evocation of medieval Russia, with Rublev as the wandering outsider gradually caught up in the feudal turmoil. (Another noteworthy – if slighter – Soviet film of 1972, Georgi Shengelaya's *Pirosmani*, also deals with an itinerant artist, in this case the melancholic nineteenth-century Georgian primitive Niko Pirosmanishvili).

If *Andrei Rublev* might broadly be considered Tarkovsky's *The Seventh Seal*, his later work *Stalker* (1979) moves much closer to the world of *Shame*. The premise derives from a science-fiction novel: three men journey into the mysterious and forbidden terrain of the Zone (echoes of Cocteau), which has apparently been created by the fall of a meteorite and contains a secret 'room' where wishes can come true. To some the film is masterly in its pessimistic foreboding, to others it remains pretentious (and it could certainly be objected that the quality of verbal debate does not rise far above platitude). But pictorially *Stalker* is remarkable in the way that Tarkovsky's visualizing of the supposedly future world outside the Zone, as an environment of foggy squalor and industrial dereliction, coincides with the underground vision of exiled Russian novelist Alexander Solzhenitsyn

while The Stalker of the title, with his shaved head and shapelessly shabby garb, cannot but summon up Solzhenitsyn's *The Gulag Archipelago*. In this context, the fact that the vistas within the Zone are in their overgrown way no less despoliated than those beyond it makes the overall effect doubly cheerless, and a concluding snatch of Beethoven's 'Ode to Joy' offers only a token mitigation.

In the New German Cinema, Wim Wenders created in *Im Lauf der Zeit* (1976, *Kings of the Road*) the ultimate 'road' movie and something more besides – a penumbral journey, filmed in harsh black and white, along the borderland of the two Germanies, and a nostalgic recapitulation of the cinematic heritage in which Wenders has been steeped. On the other hand, Werner Herzog has turned for his most interesting work to the areas of history and legend. *Aguirre, der Zorn Gottes* (1973, *Aguirre, Wrath of God*), shot in Peru, deals with Pizarro's band of conquistadores in their search for

## Journeys into the past and into fantasy are characteristic of the more ambitious odyssey movies

the fabled El Dorado. The central figure is an over-reacher, and the fantastic jungle settings provide their own impressive comment on his incipient madness. In the equally majestic *Nosferatu: Phantom der Nacht* (1979, *Nosferatu, the Vampyre*), the inspiration is Bram Stoker's *Dracula*, the journey is a two-way one. Jonathan Harker's foray into Transylvania leads to his enslavement by the blood-sucking count and the unleashing of Dracula's potency; at the very end, now Dracula's devoted acolyte, Harker gallops dementedly away across a vast tract of desert to infect the world at large with his master's plague.

The most obviously ambitious British film of the decade was Lindsay Anderson's *O Lucky Man!* (1973). The director has said that he appended the 'O' to the title to lend it an air of universality. And though the film begins rather in the mode of early Sixties British films with a satirically realistic look at the life of a travelling coffee salesman, it develops into a sort of latterday *Pilgrim's Progress*, almost

visionary in its stylized evocation of the state of Britain. Ranging from suburbia to the northern moors, and from penthouse to doss-house, the film literally boxes the compass in its chapter headings: 'West', 'North', 'South' and finally – with the conclusion of the film hinting at a touch of Zen – 'East'.

*A Touch of Zen* is the English title of *Hsia nü*, probably the most admired Oriental movie of the late Sixties and early Seventies. King Hu's film, made in 1969 though not seen abroad until later, is at one level an expansive adventure story, full of suitably balletic martial-arts combat. But the action spreads itself out in time as well as space, and the long final section of the three-movement story lifts the action onto an overtly spiritual plane. What begins as the elucidation of a practical mystery ends by embracing a transcendent one.

Most of these movies are works on a literally large scale – some are three hours in duration – while the much-discussed *O Thiassos* (1975, *The Travelling Players*), a Greek film directed by Theodor Angelopoulos, runs to nearly four hours. Nobody could claim that this is an easily accessible work, and some would claim that its politics are facile. But there is an undeniably epic scale to the concept, by which a group of itinerant actors serve as the focus of an imaginative reconstruction of Greek political history in the years from 1939 to 1952.

The form of the odyssey has permeated international cinema in any number of ways. From Japan, Kon Ichikawa's *Matatabi* (1973, *The Wanderers*), a striking but uneven account of roaming *toseinin* (petty crooks) in the nineteenth century, was actually likened by one critic to a 'road' movie. In Australia, Nicolas Roeg made in *Walkabout* (1971) a lyrically precise modern version of the myth of the noble savage, set amid the lunar tracts of the outback. In Italy, Paolo and Vittorio Taviani's *Padre Padrone* (1977, Father Master) is a humanistically-felt description of a Sardinian peasant boy's gradual escape through education from the confines of rural oppression.

Such works may be somewhat removed from the mainstream of popular movie-making. However, the end of the Seventies saw the release of two major American commercial films which not only confronted head-on the crucial experience of Vietnam – hitherto hardly explored by Hollywood – but were unabashedly conceived as odysseys in the grandest form. One was *The Deer Hunter* (1978), with its bold tripartite construction, the other *Apocalypse Now* (1979), derived from one of the great literary journeys, Conrad's *Heart of Darkness*. With both, the quest film was decisively returned to the mass audience – and the cinema's restless search for what might lie 'out there' found a kind of apotheosis.                   TIM PULLEINE

*Above, from left to right: Ansell (Malcolm McDowell) is on the run from pursuing soldiers in Joseph Losey's* Figures in a Landscape *(1970); Mick Travis (Malcolm McDowell) is on the run from a sinister medical research establishment in* O Lucky Man!; *an Aborigine (David Gulpilil) on his* Walkabout *meets a lost girl (Jenny Agutter) and her young brother (Lucien John) in the Australian outback;* Aguirre, Wrath of God *(Klaus Kinski) finds that he is left alone on his raft with Brother Gaspar de Carvajal (Del Negro), the chronicler of his disastrous voyage*

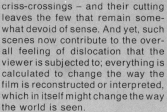

DENNIS HOPPER   BRUNO GANZ   **DER**   LISA KREUZER   GERARD BLAIN

Ein Film von WIM WENDERS **AMERIKANISCHE FREUND** nach ›Ripley's Game‹ von Patricia Highsmith

mit ANDREAS DEDECKE, DAVID BLUE, GERTY MOLZEN, HEINZ JOACHIM KLEIN, AXEL SCHIESSLER    STEFAN LENNERT, RUDOLF SCHÜNDLER, HEINRICH MARMANN, SATYA DE LA MANITOU, ADOLF HANSEN, ROSEMARIE HEINIKEL

als Gäste NICHOLAS RAY, SAMUEL FULLER, PETER LILIENTHAL, DANIEL SCHMID, JEAN EUSTACHE, SANDY WHITELAW und LOU CASTEL    Kamera ROBBY MÜLLER   Musik JÜRGEN KNIEPER   Schnitt PETER PRZYGODDA   Ausstattung HEIDI und TONI LÜDI   Organisation MARTIN MÜLLER, PETER KAISER

Produktionsleitung MICHAEL WIEDEMANN   PIERRE COTTRELL   Herstellungsleitung RENEE OTTO-GUNDELACH   MARGARET MENEGOZ

gefilmt mit ARRIFLEX    Eine Coproduktion der ROAD MOVIES Filmproduktion GmbH, Berlin mit WIM WENDERS Produktion, München, LES FILMS DU LOSANGE, Paris und dem Westdeutschen Rundfunk, Köln · Der Roman ›Ripley's Game oder Regel ohne Ausnahme‹ erschien bei Diogenes

# The American Friend

Wim Wenders is fascinated with roads, journeys, uprooting, with the sense of identity that is attached to having a place to go home to. While travel is strongly a feature of his earlier work, it is also vital to *The American Friend* – all the characters are rootless (Jonathan is Swiss and Ripley is American, though both live in Hamburg), either immigrants or emigrés. And Wenders himself, though German, has an almost obsessive respect and admiration for American movies and the products of British and American pop culture, which in turn he allows to litter his movies.

From the opening shot of Tom Ripley in his stetson and overcoat stepping out of a New York taxi in front of the painter Derwatt's studio, the viewer is deceived – for the next shot shows a Hamburg waterfront . . . and so on, backwards and forwards, through Paris and Munich, though with no discernible change in the general landscape. The world has been reduced to one frighteningly familiar universal city: subway stations, closed-circuit TVs, escalators in airports, nameless hotels, long roads through tunnels, skyscrapers – all the trappings of modern, urban materialism. Even the sacred inner identity has been taken over by the pop songs inside everyone's head – Jonathan, for

example, sings an old Kinks number to himself to help him solve his problems.

In a direct homage to the American cinema Wenders has employed two Hollywood directors as actors – Nicholas Ray and Samuel Fuller – because, as the director himself admits, Europe has found itself psychologically very close to America since Watergate and Vietnam. And, as if it were a metaphor of this, he has chosen the American thriller as a suitable reference frame for a European film-maker. With the appearance of four other directors – Daniel Schmid, Jean Eustache, Peter Lilienthal and Sandy Whitelaw – in gangster roles, Wenders could be accused of a cinéaste's self-indulgence, but he claims that this casting was not intentional. It was just that, never having seen any gangsters, he faced a problem:

'Well, I finally had the idea that I did know some crooks and that they were all directors. They are in fact. They are the only people who force people to do things they don't want, to make them suffer and make people die.'

It was not, however, unintentional that the film contains so many coincidences and scenes of blatant unlikeliness; in its earliest versions there were considerably more

criss-crossings – and their cutting leaves the few that remain somewhat devoid of sense. And yet, such scenes now contribute to the overall feeling of dislocation that the viewer is subjected to; everything is calculated to change the way the film is reconstructed or interpreted, which in itself might change the way the world is seen.

Just as Ripley's *angst* is exacerbated by his inability to feel at home anywhere, so the film has to work in spite of itself to find and keep hold of an identity. Wenders was adamant that the soundtrack should be made in several foreign languages and the dialogue badly spoken, and he has even adapted Patricia Highsmith's original novel so as to render this integral to the subject. *Ripley's Game* had been offered to him in manuscript and he snatched the opportunity to work on it, deliberately choosing to set his film in modern Germany and the world of pornography and films (better known to him than Highsmith's casino settings).

Ray opens and closes the film as a kind of observer, a 'theme' woven deeply into *The American Friend*: Ripley, rather surprisingly for a professional murderer and art swindler, observes himself in his daily memos to his tape recorder, and in one scene, looking and be-

having like a tired Andy Warhol, he 'shoots' himself over and over with a Polaroid. Is he an image, just as Derwatt, the 'dead' painter, lives on in his forgeries of his own work? This notion of identity extends into the character of the whole piece: Jonathan is a picture-*framer* (the film's working title was *The Frame*) whose hobby is ocular devices – praxinoscopes, moving pictures, magic lanterns, the physical manifestations of illusions.

Despite all its multi-layered incidentals, *The American Friend* is a film that manages to keep attention focused constantly on the character of Jonathan, the reluctant and incompetent murderer and the first of Wenders' heroes to have a home and a family – ironically, something that he destroys while trying to protect. The point – so often and so well made by Hitchcock and Agatha Christie – is that a moment's escape from normality can change a whole life, and to emphasize it the whole story is told from Jonathan's point of view. It is a view far removed from the initial impression of narcissistic introspection, and Wenders has not betrayed his leftist roots:

'. . . my films are political simply because they are not about myths, but real people and the possibility of action.'
DAVID ROPER

**Directed by Wim Wenders, 1977**

**Prod co:** Road Movies (West Berlin)/Wim Wenders Produktion (Munich)/Westdeutschen Rundfunk (Cologne)/Films du Losange (Paris). **exec prod:** Michael Wiedemann, Pierre Cottrell. **sc:** Wim Wenders, based on the novel *Ripley's Game* by Patricia Highsmith. **titles:** Sickerts. **photo** (Eastman Colour): Robby Müller. **photo sp eff:** Theo Nischwitz. **ed:** Peter Przygodda. **art dir:** Heidi Lüdi, Toni Lüdi. **cost:** Isolde Nist. **mus:** Jürgen Knieper. **sd ed:** Max Galinsky, Milan Bor. **sd rec:** Martin Müller, Peter Kaiser. **stunts:** Klaus Schichan. **ass dir:** Fritz Müller-Scherz, Emmanuel Clot (Paris), Serge Brodskis. **prod man:** Martin Schäfer, Harald Kügler, Heinz Badewitz, Philippe Schwartz (Paris), Pat Kirk (New York). **prod ass:** Harald Vogel. **r/t:** 123 minutes. Released in USA/GB as: *The American Friend*.

**Cast:** Bruno Ganz (*Jonathan Zimmermann*), Dennis Hopper (*Tom Ripley*), Gérard Blain (*Raoul Minot*), Lisa Kreuzer (*Marianne Zimmermann*), Nicholas Ray (*Prokasch, 'Derwatt'*), Samuel Fuller (*the American*), Peter Lilienthal (*Marcangelo*), Daniel Schmid (*Igraham*), Sandy Whitelaw (*Paris doctor*), Jean Eustache (*friendly man*), Lou Castel (*Rodolphe*), Andreas Dedecke (*Daniel*), David Blue (*Allan Winter*), Stefan Lennert (*auctioneer*), Rudolf Schündler (*Gantner*), Gerty Molzen (*old lady*), Heinz Joachim Klein (*Dr Gabriel*), Rosemarie Heinikel (*Mona*), Heinrich Marmann (*man in train*), Satya de la Manitou (*Angie*), Axel Schiessler (*Lippo*), Adolf Hansen (*Schaffner*).

After a meeting with the painter Derwatt, Tom Ripley (1) returns to his elegant Hamburg mansion with a painting. It later turns up in the workshop of picture framer Jonathan Zimmermann (2), who meets Ripley after it has been auctioned. Ripley learns that Jonathan has a rare blood disease and needs money to support his family should he die.

At home Ripley receives a visit from the gangster Raoul Minot (3), who needs someone to carry out a murder, and reminds Ripley that he owes him a favour. The next day Ripley befriends Jonathan, who gets a telegram warning him that his condition is worsening. Minot then turns up at Jonathan's shop, and Jonathan is tempted by the money he offers him when they discuss the killings on a subway train the following day (4). Minot arranges for Jonathan to have tests done in Paris (5) but he tricks him with false medical reports into thinking he is dying. Shortly afterwards Jonathan follows his victim (6, on right) and murders him in the Metro.

Later Jonathan agrees to kill a Mafia boss on a train from Munich. His wife is now suspicious (7) of his involvement with Ripley. Only when Ripley suddenly appears on the train does Jonathan understand what has been going on; together they manage to kill the gangster and throw his bodyguard (8) out of the carriage. Back at Hamburg Minot breaks into Jonathan's home (9) demanding to know why a bomb has been placed in his flat in Paris. Ripley and Jonathan, by now close friends, wait at Ripley's mansion for a Mafia reprisal. They ambush an ambulance and kill the gangsters inside, then drive it off through the night. At dawn Ripley blows up the ambulance on a deserted beach. Jonathan suddenly roars off with his wife in his own car, abandoning Ripley (10). But the car veers off the road and comes to a halt as Jonathan dies at the wheel.

159

## THESE ARE THE ARMIES OF THE NIGHT.
They are 100,000 strong. They outnumber the cops five to one.
They could run New York City. Tonight they're all out to get the Warriors.

Paramount Pictures Presents A Lawrence Gordon Production "THE WARRIORS"
Executive Producer Frank Marshall Based Upon the Novel by Sol Yurick
Screenplay by David Shaber and Walter Hill Produced by Lawrence Gordon
Directed by Walter Hill [Read the Dell Book]

---

**Directed by Walter Hill, 1979**
**Prod co:** Paramount. **exec prod:** Frank Marshall. **prod:** Lawrence Gordon.
**assoc prod:** Joel Silver. **sc:** David Shaber, Walter Hill, from the novel by Sol
Yurick. **photo** (Movielab): Andrew Laszlo. **sp eff:** Edward Drohan. **ed:** David
Holden. **art dir:** Don Swanagan, Bob Wightman, Fred Weiler. **cost:** Bobbie
Mannix, Mary Ellen Winston. **mus:** Barry De Vorzon, Kenny Vance, Joe
Ferla, Rob Mounsey, Paul Griffin. **songs:** Joe Walsh, Arnold McCuller,
Frederick LaPlano, Mandrill, Genya Raven, Johnny Vastano, Desmond
Child, Rouge, The Mersh Brothers. **sd:** Jack Jacobsen, Al Mian, Tex
Rudloff, Don Mitchell, Richard Cline. **sd eff:** Howard Beals, George Watters
II, Allan Murray, William Andrews, Lee Osborne. **ass dir:** David O. Sosna.
**prod man:** John Starke. **prod co-ord:** Gail Geibel. **r/t:** 94 mins.
**Cast:** Michael Beck (*Swan*), James Remar (*Ajax*), Thomas Waites (*Fox*),
Dorsey Wright (*Cleon*), Brian Tyler (*Snow*), David Harris (*Cochise*), Tom
McKitterick (*Cowboy*), Marcelino Sanchez (*Rembrandt*), Terry Michos
(*Vermin*), Deborah Van Valkenburgh (*Mercy*), Roger Hill (*Cyrus*), David
Patrick Kelly (*Luther*), Lynne Thigpen (*DJ*), Ginny Ortiz (*candy store girl*),
Mercedes Ruehl (*policewoman*), John Snyder (*gas station man*), Dennis
Gregory (*Masai*), Gwynn Press, Jodi Price, Jeffrey Scott, Carl Brown (*prom
couples*).

---

After the Battle of Cunaxa, not far
from Babylon, in September 401 BC,
the Greek prince Cyrus lay dead
after a failed attempt to gain the
throne, and 10,000 Greeks were
faced with surrender to an alien
king or a long march home. Xenophon, a young Athenian, led them
back through 1000 miles of hostile
territory, hounded by barbarians.

Such is the outline of Xenophon's
*Anabasis* – literally. 'The journey
up' – on which Sol Yurick based his
novel *The Warriors*, translating the
Greek mercenaries into a modern
New York street gang desperately

engaged in the tale's ambiguous
kind of warfare. They are running
for their home turf while fighting a
rearguard action against all the
other gangs whose territory they
must cross – it is not exactly a
retreat, but neither is it the kind of
confrontation that the epic usually
glorified. In Yurick's novel, grounded in a solid social-realist context,
Cyrus' conclave in the Bronx
breaks up due to generalized gang
frictions, and the Warriors have
trouble getting back to Coney Island
because they misread the subway
maps! Their exploits *en route* in-

clude stabbing a passer-by for fun
and the subsequent gang-bang of a
passing girl to subdue their excitement over the murder. Their return
return is no triumph, but just another round of deprivation and welfare cheques.

Walter Hill's movie bears virtually no resemblance to the novel
other than the basic framework of
the run home. It opens with a long
shot of the Coney Island ferris
wheel – its name, 'Wonder Wheel',
illuminated brightly against the
deep black of the night; then overhead shots of the snaking subway
trains in electric colours, their
noise subdued by electronic music
on the soundtrack. It is clear from
the start that the movie is a kind of
neon fantasy; a stylized dance
through a subterranean city of the
imagination.

On the rare occasions that the
Warriors surface onto ground level,
the streets are depopulated of 'civilian' life. The Orphans, a bunch of
dispirited 'wimps', are sent scurry-
ing by Swan's petrol-bombing of a
nearby car – to which there is no
local response. A diversionary fire,
set up to delay the Warriors, is
fought by unseen firemen. Indeed,
any signs of 'civilian' life are treac-
herously camouflaged. Ajax suc-
cumbs to the siren voice of a tempt-
ress in the park only to be hand-
cuffed to the bench – she is an
undercover cop. A group of women
who entice three of the gang up to
street level from the Union Square
subway turn out to be the Lizzies – a
lesbian gang of lethal intention, if
less than effective action. The
night-time people rule and the
streets of New York are emptied of
everyday life.

All of which serves to highlight
the film's one confrontation between the gang and 'straight'
people. Some fancily dressed late-
night revellers board the subway
and sit opposite Swan and his girl
Mercy. They all stare at each other
with the blank incomprehension of
aliens. Mercy raises her hand to

adjust her dishevelled hair, and
Swan without a word or even a
glance at her, restrains her hand in
mid-flight. With an understatement
typical of all his films, Hill comp-
resses volumes of social and
psychological comment into the
briefest cinematic gesture.

The film's only other concession
toward social background comes
when the gang finally make it back
to Coney Island as dawn is breaking
over the silent, rainswept funfair;
the 'Wonder Wheel' no longer looks
so very wonderful. '*This* is what we
fought all night to get back to!' says
one of the gang. After that the face-
off on the beach with Luther and the
Rogues is almost perfunctory.
Clearly, what interests Hill is the
race itself, not the prize.

The absolutes of winning and
losing are central to all of Hill's
films, but the main concern is centred on the grace of the sport itself.
As in *The Getaway* (1972) – a film he
scripted for director Sam Peckinpah – and *The Driver* (1978), survival is all and the contender most
likely to attain it is the one who
engages in the struggle with the
most commitment and expertise.

Rarely has the expertise of violent combat been so gracefully
composed as in *The Warriors*.
When they take on the Baseball
Furies in the darkened park, Ajax's
threat – 'I'm going to shove that bat
up your ass and turn you into a
popsicle' – is duly realized in a
sequence which combines all the
energy of a Kung Fu movie with the
controlled precision and style of
modern dance movement. The
rumble in a subway washroom with
the Punks, a gang wearing pre-
teenagers' dungarees and roller-
skates, is similarly orchestrated.

If, finally, the audience is left with
the sneaking suspicion that the
well-fed, photogenic Warriors have
as much street-credibility as the
gangs in *West Side Story* (1961),
there is at least the consolation that
they are far better choreographed.
CHRIS PEACHMENT

160

2

3

4

5

6

7

8

The Warriors, a street gang from Coney Island (1), converge with all the other gangs in New York on a conclave held in the Bronx by Cyrus (2), a black leader who dreams of uniting the gangs into a force that will control the city.

Cyrus is shot by Luther, the psychotic leader of the Rogues and the meeting is broken up by police. In the ensuing mêlée the Warriors are blamed for the shooting. They are pursued by other gangs but make it to the subway at 96th Street.

Due to a fire they are forced to surface onto the street where they encounter the Orphans. The Warriors thrash them but as they return to the subway find they have acquired Mercy, the Orphans' leader's girl, as a companion.

Separated from the rest of the gang by police, Swan the leader, Ajax his lieutenant and two other Warriors beat up the Baseball Furies (3) in a park but Ajax is then arrested by a plain-clothes policewoman. Three other Warriors are enticed by the Lizzies, a lesbian gang, back to their headquarters (4) and narrowly escape being wiped out. The reunion of the Warriors in Union Square leads to another battle in a men's washroom with the Punks (5). The Warriors and Mercy (6) finally make it back as dawn breaks over Coney Island (7), and emerge to find Luther and the Rogues coming for them. In the final showdown on the beach (8), Luther pulls a gun but Swan throws his switchblade into Luther's wrist.

161

KLAUS KINSKI als AGUIRRE DER ZORN GOTTES

Ein Film von
Werner Herzog

mit
Helena Rojo
Del Negro
Ruy Guerra
Peter Berling
Cecilia Rivera
Dany Ades
Armando Polanah

Kamera:
Thomas Mauch

Musik:
Popol Vuh

Werner Herzog
Filmproduktion
Verleih:
Filmverlag
der Autoren
Weltvertrieb:

# AGUIRRE, WRATH OF GOD

*Aguirre, Wrath of God* is Werner Herzog's archetypal tale of a voyage down a jungle river, the final destination of which is ultimate solitude, madness, and death. The film, which was the first to bring Herzog wide international acclaim, although his earlier features had not gone unremarked by some members of the critical community, was also an odyssey for its creators. The making of the film was an adventure at least as exciting as that shown on the screen.

The idea for the film was born when Herzog read, by chance, a dozen lines about Lope de Aguirre in a children's book. After reading what few historical documents still exist, Herzog wrote his scenario in only three days, inventing most of the narrative incidents and characters, although in some cases he used historical figures but gave them ficticious roles:

'Gonzalo Pizarro, the brother of the famous conquistador Francisco Pizarro, died six to eight years before my expedition in 1560. The monk Gaspar de Carvajal existed too, but his name is connected with

another very obscure expedition which had nothing to do with that of Aguirre . . . the rest of the script is pure invention . . . the language isn't realistic, it's more a hallucinatory language, unreal. It's like the ever-slowing movement in the film which becomes immobility.'

Filmed in Peru because Herzog wanted the authentic atmosphere of the jungle, the Amazon, and the presence of the Indians, *Aguirre, Wrath of God* took seven weeks to shoot – after nine months of pre-production organization. It was shot in more-or-less chronological order, partly because Herzog found the film crews' progress down the river directly related to the movement of the voyage in the film, and partly because as the numbers of crew and cast were reduced for the latter part of the film, so it became easier to move them deeper into the jungle.

The relatively low budget did not allow for much in the way of special effects and trickery, the use of which, in any case, Herzog would never have allowed:

'We took a lot of precautions, but

for me the making of a film must be physical. I put my entire body into the making of my films.'

So, the entire cast and crew found itself climbing up the face of a mountain, cutting through jungles and riding dangerous Amazonian rapids on native-built rafts. Even the accidents were written into the script: one night a storm raised the level of water and the violence of the river destroyed a number of rafts. That became part of the story.

Nor were the hazards of river and jungle the only things to be reckoned with. A good part of the exposed footage disappeared half way through the shooting in transit for European laboratories; there was no way it could have been re-filmed, even if there had been the money to do so. Herzog continued filming and the lost cans were later found at Mexico City airport.

The film was shot in English mainly because it was the only common language among the participants – who came from 16 different countries – but Herzog also knew that an English-language version was necessary for the international market. However, the little money that was allocated for post-synchronization left Peru with the man in charge of the process; both

absconded *en route*. This resulted in there being two versions, one in English and the other with a better-quality German soundtrack.

Then there was the 'Kinski affair'. Klaus Kinski, an actor of undoubted ability and owner of a bizarre and fascinating face, is well known for not being the easiest actor in the world to direct and control. Although he is perfect as Aguirre, sliding progressively into madness, he and the director began to have daily scenes of screamed

**Directed by Werner Herzog, 1973**
**Prod co:** Werner Herzog Filmproduktion with Hessischer Rundfunk. **prod:** Werner Herzog. **assoc prod:** Daniel Carino. **sc:** Werner Herzog. **photo (colour):** Thomas Mauch, Francisco Joan, Orlando Macchiavello. **sp eff:** Juvenal Herrera, Miguel Vazquez. **ed:** Beate Mainka-Jellinghaus. **mus:** Popol Vuh. **sd:** Herbert Prasch. **prod man:** Walter Saxer, Wolf Stipetić. **r/t:** 95 minutes. German title: *Aguirre, der Zorn Gottes*. Released in USA/GB as: *Aguirre, Wrath of God*.
**Cast:** Klaus Kinski (*Don Lope de Aguirre*), Cecilia Rivera (*Florès de Aguirre*), Ruy Guerra (*Don Pedro de Ursua*), Helena Rojo (*Inez de Atienza*), Del Negro (*Brother Gaspar de Carvajal*), Peter Berling (*Don Fernando de Guzman*), Daniel Ades (*Perucho*), Armando Polanah (*Armando*), Edward Roland (*Okello*), Daniel Farfan, Alejandro Chavez, Antonio Marquez, Julio Martinez, Alejandro Repullés, and the Indians of the Lauramarca Co-operative.

3

4

7

9

In 1560 a thousand or more Spanish conquerors (including two women and a number of captured Indians) descend from the Andes into the virgin jungle (1) to look for El Dorado, the fabled land of gold. A fever decimates the army and their porters, and the commander Gonzalo Pizarro orders 40 men to explore the river by raft (2). If they fail to return after a week, they will be considered lost.

Don Lope de Aguirre is part of the group led by Don Pedro de Ursua. Early on in the expedition one of the four rafts is trapped in a whirlpool (3) and during the night the men on board are killed by Indians.

Aguirre organizes a revolt against Ursua (4) who is wounded by a gun-shot and nursed by his mistress Inez. Not yet sure of the loyalty of the soldiers, Aguirre proposes Don Fernando de Guzman as ruler of the New World, farcically dethroning Phillip II of Spain. However, Guzman refuses to allow Ursua to be executed.

The troupe begins to suffer from hunger, fever and hallucinations (5) – at one point they 'see' a full-masted ship hanging in the trees – and the jungle is ever more hostile, with daily Indian ambushes (6). They manage to capture one of the Indians, but when he rejects the Bible he is killed. Guzman is finally found dead and the way is clear for Aguirre's plan to found a new dynasty built on the offspring of his sexual union with his own daughter (7).

As the raft continues to drift (8), Ursua is taken into the jungle and hanged; Inez, who alone speaks out against Aguirre's plans, walks into the forest and disappears during an attack on an Indian village (9); and a grumbling soldier is decapitated. Aguirre rules supreme, but his subject soldiers soon perish. His daughter Florès, struck by an arrow, dies in his arms.

At one point Aguirre says 'I am the wrath of God', but the 'wrath of God' alone cannot prevent a horde of monkeys invading the raft as it slowly drifts – directionless – in the river's currents (10).

insults, ending finally in the two threatening to kill one another on the spot. Several years later, when Kinski signed to do two more films with Herzog, he was reminded of the earlier film's problems:

'Yes, it is all true. We seriously would have killed each other. Still, that's a good film, and in this business, you know, one day you can scream "Fuck you! I'm going to kill you!" and mean it, and the next day hug and work well together.'

Still, whatever the problems in its making, from the first image of the almost mystic descent out of the cloud-misted heights to the final circling of the madman left alone on a raft with his 'kingdom' reduced to hundreds of monkeys, *Aguirre, Wrath of God* is one of the director's best films and all he intended it to be: an adventure film having the surface characteristics of the genre, but with something new inside, while at the same time being meant for a large public:

'It has the surface of an adventure film, but it is a very personal film. For me it is alive.'
DAVID OVERBEY **10**

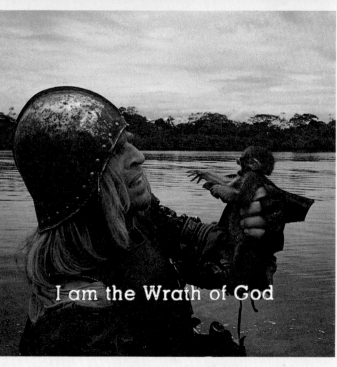

I am the Wrath of God

# Gathering Momentum

# Peter Yates

Opinions on Peter Yates vary widely. Some condemn him for his occasional use of visual gimmickry and a certain lightness of tone; some admire his smooth adaptation to a Hollywood sensibility; many fall somewhere in between. Whatever is the case, as one of the British cinema's migrant directors of the Sixties generation, he has been largely ignored by critics in general who have been more impressed with the likes of John Boorman, Karel Reisz and John Schlesinger.

Yates' devotion to action in his thrillers seems to have developed from his own experience. He was born in 1929 in Aldershot, and was educated at the famous public school, Charterhouse, later graduating from the Royal Academy of Dramatic Art to prove himself to be a competent stage director. He then took to the road for a period as a racing driver, finally inveigling his way into the film industry with some fast-car stunt work. His involvement in film-making deepened and he gained experience as assistant director on films such as the adventure spectacle *The Guns of Navarone* (1961). His directorial debut came with *Summer Holiday* (1963), but in the otherwise forgettable *Robbery* (1967) – based on the Great Train Robbery of 1963 when a British Rail mail train was robbed of vast sums of money – it was the slick forcefulness of the chase sequence which impressed Steve McQueen and finally brought Yates to Hollywood to direct him in *Bullitt* (1968).

## Cars and capers

Although some of the visual trickery of *Bullitt* has dated (a reliance upon the zoom lens, abrupt changes of focus, the laboured use of the 'novel' camera angle), it is nothing like as fatuous as the overworked style-for-style's-sake of the director Norman Jewison's *The Thomas Crown Affair* (1968). Yates effortlessly fell in step with the feel of *Bullitt*'s San Francisco location and the gutsy quality of the cop movie. As in *Robbery*, Yates' fascination with

Speeding cars, hair-raising helicopter rides, daring robberies, high technology, nail-biting suspense – these are all the ingredients of the modern thriller and ones that the director Peter Yates has used to great effect, but as his career has progressed he has also managed to integrate them with an uncanny ability to portray human frailties

precedence.

Action and comedy blended with a certain élan in Yates' subsequent productions *The Hot Rock* (1972), *For Pete's Sake* (1974) and *Mother, Jugs and Speed* (1976). It was here that Yates was able to inject a little more feeling into the action and show more sympathy with the foibles of his characters. *The Hot Rock* is the most successful of these films, a caper movie where inept thieves manage to bungle a thoughtfully planned jewel heist. Technology again features, and a hair-raising helicopter flight through the skyscrapers of downtown Manhattan recalls the distinct feel of the car chase in *Bullitt*. Individual sequences, like a

*Far left: one of cinema's most memorable car chases, through the hills of San Francisco, in* Bullitt. *Left: Peter Yates directs Dennis Christopher as the obsessive cyclist, Dave, in* Breaking Away. *Below: Robert Mitchum in* The Friends of Eddie Coyle

raid on a police station, are beautifully modulated in terms of the comedy-thriller format. *For Pete's Sake*, involving a devoted wife who becomes entangled with various criminal types in an effort to raise money for her cabby husband, suffers from an empty-headed script, even though Barbra Streisand is formidable in the lead, and Yates crafts the chases – especially one with a truckload of cattle – with a great sense of timing. *Mother, Jugs and Speed*, the story of two rival ambulance services in Los Angeles, tries a little too hard to recall the bleak cynicism of *M\*A\*S\*H* (1970). Despite this, it is still highly watchable and Yates directs his cast – especially Bill Cosby and Larry Hagman – with feeling.

## Serious acquaintances

Much less frivolous, and exploring darker areas than he had touched on before, *The Friends of Eddie Coyle* (1973) deals with the Boston underworld and an ageing convict

technology is tinged with cynicism.

Guns kill quickly and make a mess, just as cars are fast, noisy and potentially destructive. The city presents a vision of technology against technology, and in this scheme of things criminal and cop are identified through the methods they use. The trend-setting 11-minute car chase presents so many turnabouts, such a maze of streets, that any identification with Bullitt and his apprehension of the criminal is secondary to the kinetic frenzy of car against car. Bullitt's self-doubt and his girlfriend's fear for his soul are unfortunately left as darker sketches on the edge of the drama, and Steve McQueen's poker-faced acceptance of his duty – it was this film which really launched him to stardom – takes

*Far left: Stanley Baker as the meticulous gang-leader packing away the loot after the daring* Robbery *of a British Rail mail train. Left: Jacqueline Bisset, Nick Nolte and Robert Shaw as divers searching amongst the treacherous wrecks of* The Deep *(1977)*

who, in torment over his family's finances, makes a deal with the law and agrees to become an informer. Yates' feel for the city location is again impressive, and the low-key atmosphere follows on nicely from Paul Monash's script and Robert Mitchum's world-weary performance.

It seems a natural development of Yates' increasingly sympathetic presentation of character that his collaboration with the playwright Steve Tesich should result in two movies where 'human interest' is the presiding factor – *Breaking Away* (1979) and *Eyewitness* (1981, released in Britain as *The Janitor*). These films disprove the critic David Thomson's contention that Yates can only really 'send hub-caps careering round corners' as they allow Yates' preoccupation with emotions to surface.

*Breaking Away* is a comedy of class distinction set in Bloomington, Indiana, centring upon four local teenagers and their battle with the university smart set. Characterization is

motor bike, a fight with a mad dog and a shoot-out in a city stables – are managed with an almost Hitchcockian stylishness, and the city itself is represented as brooding and sinister, bristling with traps for the unwary. But it is the human relationships which take the foreground in the tangle of the hero Daryll's infatuation with Tony, and the latent homosexual feelings that Aldo (James Woods) has for Daryll, his buddy from their days in Vietnam. The film's guarded warmth, so unfashionable for an action thriller, results in a hero (perfectly conveyed in William Hurt's softness) who is capable and idiosyncratic without being stony hard.

Peter Yates' progression from an admiration for pyrotechnic action to probing the more subtle workings of human emotions suggests that critics can no longer afford to pass over this director of ever-increasing potential.

MARTIN SUTTON

*Above: Raquel Welch and Harvey Keitel in* Mother, Jugs and Speed. *Below: William Hurt keeping an eye on things in* The Janitor

taken to extremes, for instance the hero, Dave, is wholly fixated on all elements of Italian culture. Incidents are mounted with a maximum of detail, atmosphere and involvement, especially the dreamy timelessness of swims in the water-filled quarry. The final showdown takes place when bicycle fanatic Dave pits his strength on the side of his town in a race against a team from the university, Yates constructs this action sequence into a veritable *tour de force* of kinetics and bursting emotion.

The script of *The Janitor* falls apart in every way, but particularly in its attempt to unite elements of the political thriller with a study of the bizarre relationship between a female television announcer, Tony, and a janitor, Daryll (played by Sigourney Weaver and William Hurt). In its odd disjunction it remains, though, one of Yates' most fascinating films. The action sequences – a last-minute rescue by

**Filmography**
1960 Sons and Lovers (ass. dir. only); The Entertainer (ass. dir. only). '61 The Guns of Navarone (ass. dir. only); A Taste of Honey (ass. dir. only); The Roman Spring of Mrs Stone (ass. dir. only). '63 Summer Holiday. '64 One Way Pendulum. '67 Robbery (+co-sc). '68 Bullitt (USA). '69 John and Mary (USA). '71 Murphy's War. '72 The Hot Rock (USA) (GB: How to Steal a Diamond in Four Uneasy Lessons). '73 The Friends of Eddie Coyle (USA). '74 For Pete's Sake (USA). '76 Mother, Jugs and Speed (+co-prod) (USA). '77 The Deep (USA). '79 Breaking Away (+prod) (USA). '81 Eyewitness (+prod) (USA) (GB: The Janitor). '83 Krull. '84 The Dresser (+prod).

# THE LAW-ENFORCERS

**The fuzz formed a thin blue line against the final breakdown of law and order in Hollywood's city of eternal night**

As law and order became a top domestic issue in the USA, the cop was the new superstar on cinema and television screens. Between 1968 and 1977, movies with police heroes figured prominently among the American top 20 moneymakers of almost every year, as listed by the New York weekly paper *Variety*: *The Detective* in 1968; *Bullitt* (1968) in 1969; *The French Connection* and *Klute*, both in 1971; *Dirty Harry* (1971) and *The New Centurions* in 1972; *Walking Tall* in 1973; *Magnum Force* and *Serpico* (both 1973) in 1974; *Freebie and the Bean* (1974) in 1975; and *The Enforcer* (1976) in 1977. Cop movies received the industry's acclaim when the Oscars for Best Film of the year went to *In the Heat of the Night* in 1967, and to *The French Connection* in 1971. In addition to these outstanding box-office hits, studios turned out many more movies with police heroes which did not attain the same critical or cash response. Flashing blue lights and screaming sirens also invaded television screens as shows such as *Ironside*, *Columbo*, *Kojak*, *Policewoman* and *Starsky and Hutch* achieved top ratings.

From 1930 to 1967, only three films with police heroes were listed as top moneymakers: *Bullets or Ballots* in 1936; *Detective Story* in 1951; and *Dragnet* in 1954. Each of these does represent a larger cycle of movies with cop heroes, but none achieved the same popularity or significance as the post-1967 cycle.

The new phase of cop movies was spearheaded by Norman Jewison's *In the Heat of the Night* (1967). This portrayed the conflict between the black, highly trained and professionally skilled northern detective Virgil Tibbs (Sidney Poitier) and Bill Gillespie (Rod Steiger, who won the Best Actor Oscar), the prejudiced, vigilante-style police chief of Sparta, Mississippi. True to the film's liberal message, Gillespie is taught to appreciate the superior power of the college degree over the third degree as Tibbs finds the correct solution to a murder case. Arthur Penn's *The Chase* (1966) had already anticipated similar themes in its depiction of honest Sheriff Calder (Marlon Brando) fighting against Southern bigotry, brutality and corruption. Despite some (mixed) critical acclaim, Penn's film was not a popular success and was only indirectly influential.

In 1968 the flood of cop-movies really began in earnest, including the first two police films directed by Don Siegel, *Madigan* and *Coogan's Bluff*, the second of which marked Clint Eastwood's debut as a cop. In addition, also in 1968, sympathetic lawmen were featured prominently in Jack Smight's *No Way to Treat a Lady* (played by George Segal) and Richard Fleischer's *The Boston Strangler* (played by Henry Fonda).

Gordon Douglas' *The Detective* was notable for being the only *urban* film of the cycle to take a consistently liberal stance on the law-and-order debate. Frank Sinatra plays Joe Leland, a dedicated, skilled and honest cop, loyal to 'The Department' (his father was also a policeman) as an abstract symbol and tradition. Leland is generally humane in his methods, but his extraction of a confession to

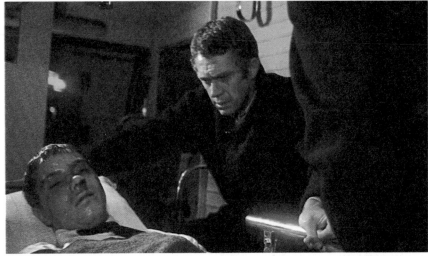

murder from an innocent suspect by psychological pressure eventually brings about his downfall. The general import is that brutality and illegal methods are not just wrong but also counter-productive. Two aspects of *The Detective* were to be echoed in later examples of the cop cycle. One was the theme of the dedicated, remorselessly honest, lone-wolf, street-level cop pitted against his bureaucratic superiors, who are more concerned with protecting their own promotion prospects by playing it safe than they are with law-enforcement. *The Detective* also foreshadows the rest of the cycle in its relentlessly brutal depiction of urban violence, seediness and decay.

Don Siegel's *Madigan* and Peter Yates' *Bullitt* together mark a transition from liberalism to presidential candidate Richard M. Nixon's hard law-and-order line. Both depict the tension between the pressure on policemen to clear up crime and the requirement that this is subject to 'due process of law'. Steve McQueen as Bullitt is an

*Top: Marcel Bozzuffi as a French gangster on the run in New York in* The French Connection; *in desperation he hijacks a train, but this move only briefly postpones his violent death at the hands of the police. Above: Steve McQueen as Bullitt with the dying witness (Pat Renella) he has tried to protect; the murdered man is actually a stand-in for the real witness, a gangster who intends to leave the country but is finally shot dead by Bullitt*

ambiguous character. He wastes cars, buildings and people with abandon yet he does not seem to relish the job. Violence is an unfortunate necessity. Perhaps the film's most memorable scene is the famous car chase on the precipitous streets of San Francisco, the most stomach-turning till *The French Connection*. *Madigan* does side with the tough, no-nonsense methods of Richard Widmark as Dan Madigan, a street-wise cop. But the liberal, rule-book-following commissioner, played by Henry Fonda, is viewed sympathetically, even if his values are untenable. Madigan's strong-arm tactics get his man – whom he had initially let escape when distracted by the suspect's nude mistress – but Madigan dies in the process. The final picture is of the city as a jungle, where toughness is the only viable response even if it ultimately solves nothing.

The city-as-jungle theme is most explicit in Siegel's *Coogan's Bluff*, showing the moral and physical confusion and decay of New York City through the eyes of an Arizona deputy sheriff (Clint Eastwood) who, complete with ten-gallon hat and cowboy boots, is tracking down a lost prisoner. Eastwood brings his cowboy persona to the role of Coogan, and the film clinches the connection between the traditional Western hero and the new police image (as does *McCloud*, the television series derived from it). The cop's displacement of the cowboy as folk-hero is best emphasized by the example of John Wayne; after turning down the part of Dirty Harry, he jumped on the paddy-wagon in *McQ* (1974) and *Brannigan* (1975).

The 'order before law' theme of *Madigan* and *Coogan's Bluff* was central in *Dirty Harry*, the next Eastwood-Siegel cop collaboration, a huge hit although condemned by liberals for its approval of police vigilantism. Eastwood's Harry Callahan justifies his disregard for civil rights by a victim-oriented perspective. In *Magnum Force*, the second Dirty Harry hit, Harry's targets are cops who organize a secret death squad to 'execute' a number of known and vicious gangsters whom the law cannot touch. Why Harry should oppose behaviour not unlike his own previous actions is never satisfactorily explained.

William Friedkin's *The French Connection* presents a message as bleak as – if more ambiguous than – *Dirty Harry*'s. Gene Hackman plays 'Popeye' Doyle

– based on real-life cop Eddie Egan, who appears in the film in a small part – as a brutal, boorish, boisterous bully, but one who usually gets results. He is a dedicated cop; but the pressures of the job have made him so cynical that his relentless pursuit of the heroin traffickers appears socially meaningless, an obsessive chase for its own sake. The ironic depiction of his ultimate failure could be interpreted either as a criticism of his rule-bending or as affirming the need for tougher laws and judges.

Following these hugely successful movies, a glut of derivatives flooded the screen. Jim Brown played a Poitier-like black sheriff in Ralph Nelson's *Tick . . . Tick . . . Tick* (1970). Poitier himself returned as Virgil Tibbs in Gordon Douglas' *They Call Me Mister Tibbs!* (1970) and Don Medford's *The Organization* (1971). Gene Hackman returned as 'Popeye' Doyle in John Frankenheimer's *French Connection II* (1975), while his real-life prototype, Eddie Egan, was the inspiration for Howard W.

## The adventures of real-life cops mixed blood and laughter in more than one winning combination

Koch's *Badge 373* (1973). Philip D'Antoni, producer of *The French Connection*, directed Hackman's erstwhile partner from that film, Roy Scheider, in *The Seven-Ups* (1973). Real-life Tennessee Sheriff Buford Pusser's exploits were narrated in Phil Karlson's *Walking Tall*, a low-budget, violence-filled sleeper that became a gigantic smash-hit and was followed by *Walking Tall II* (1975). Walter Matthau was a cop in *The Laughing Policeman* (1973) – which, despite its title and star, was a non-humorous, procedural account of the hunt for a mass-murderer – and in *The Taking of Pelham 123* (1974). Novelist Ed McBain's 87th Precinct heroes appeared in *Fuzz* (1972). Real-life prototypes of Starsky and Hutch, the New York cops Dave Greenberg and Bob Hantz, were portrayed in *The Super Cops* (1974); and a similar deadly duo were lampooned by James Caan and Alan Arkin in *Freebie and the Bean*.

Elliott Gould also sent up the police force in Peter Hyams' *Busting* (1974), with a performance reminiscent of *M\*A\*S\*H* (1970). George Peppard and Burt Reynolds played doomed cops in *Newman's Law* (1974) and *Hustle* (1975) respectively. Charles Bronson was a deadly, avenging cop in Michael Winner's *The Stone Killer* (1973), a dry run for his tremendous success as Mr Joe Average turned urban vigilante in the same director's *Death Wish* (1974). *Death Wish* was the most successful of a cycle of private vigilante movies that also included

*Top left: Detective Eddie Ryan (Robert Duvall) in* Badge 373 *conducts an interrogation to find out who killed his ex-partner and caused his own injured hand. Top: in* Hustle *a divorced cop (Burt Reynolds) falls in love with a call-girl (Catherine Deneuve) and plans to fly with her to Rome; but, on the way to the airport, he is killed in a liquor-store hold-up. Above: Charles Bronson plays a New York businessman who avenges his wife's death by shooting any muggers he can find in the streets*

and gun, Wintergreen dreams of becoming a stetsoned detective, like his idol Harve Pool (Mitchell Ryan). Temporarily assigned to assist the star investigator on a murder case, Wintergreen reveals his hero's impotence as both detective and lover. Back on motorcycle patrol, Wintergreen is gratuitously killed by hippies – an inversion of *Easy Rider*'s ending.

The films based on Joseph Wambaugh's novels are in a class of their own. Wambaugh was a 34-year-old Los Angeles police sergeant when he published the 1971 hit novel *The New Centurions*, which was filmed by Richard Fleischer in 1972 starring George C. Scott and Stacy Keach. Wambaugh's subsequent novels have also been filmed: *The Blue Knight* (1973, a television mini-series in the USA); *The Choirboys* (1977); *The Onion Field* (1979); and *The Black Marble* (1980). His work has also inspired two television series, *The Blue Knight* and *Police Story*. These movies are not law-

---

**The men in blue have to deal with everyday problems as well as shooting it out with the bad guys**

---

*Top: Serpico (Al Pacino) has made himself unpopular with his fellow-officers by publicizing police corruption; eventually they fail to back him up during a narcotics raid and he is seriously wounded. Top right: in Vanishing Point ex-racing driver Kowalski (Barry Newman) has taken a bet to drive from Denver to San Francisco in an impossibly short time; he nearly makes it, despite police pursuit, but deliberately drives the car into an unpassable road block. Above: The New Centurions of the Los Angeles police include a rookie cop (Stacy Keach) and a tough sergeant (George C. Scott) who teaches him some tricks of the trade*

*Gordon's War* (1973), *Framed* (1975), *Fighting Mad* (1976), *The Exterminator* (1980) – and, at a more serious artistic level, *Taxi Driver* (1976).

Whether reactionary, like *Walking Tall*, or liberal, like the Virgil Tibbs series, all these films eulogized their police heroes. But this love affair with the cops was only one side of Hollywood's treatment. In other genres, the police appeared less favourably. The counter-culture movies of the late Sixties, such as *Easy Rider* (1969) or *The Strawberry Statement* (1970), showed the cops as kill-joy pigs, an image echoed in the later contemporary-cowboy, driver and trucker movies, such as *J. W. Coop, Vanishing Point* (both 1971) and *Convoy* (1978).

A handful of films with cop heroes did not use the conventional crime-story framework. Sidney Lumet's *Serpico* (1973) told of the hero's hounding by colleagues and bosses as he tries to expose corruption within the force. He was based on the real-life cop whose revelations stimulated the Knapp Commission, reporting in 1972 on the wholesale corruption of the New York City Police Department. Al Pacino gave the central role a convincing quality of stubborn idealism.

*Electra Glide in Blue* (1973) was a probing exploration of the psychological roots of police machismo. Robert Blake played John Wintergreen, a short motorcycle cop who boasts of being the same height as Alan Ladd. Shown lovingly donning his boots

and-order homilies. The cop's struggle is to save his soul and preserve some minimum integrity and decency in an irredeemably savage and amoral world. The films show the routine phases of police work: rounding up prostitutes, spying on gays, rescuing would-be suicides or battered babies, acting as instant marriage-guidance counsellor to battling spouses, as well as shooting it out with liquor-store robbers. What Wambaugh's policeman must ultimately come to terms with is the futility of his efforts as the caretaker – 'centurion' – of a civilization that relentlessly breeds misery and degradation. So he has a tragic vision, a deep pessimism which precludes any hope of social change. The Wambaugh stories do share with the law-and-order cop movies the conflict between the real police work of the street cops and the bureaucratic bungling of their bosses. Wambaugh is a Hollywood maverick, who was so incensed by Robert Aldrich's treatment of *The Choirboys* that he took out an injunction against the use of his name in publicizing the movie. Dissatisfied with the handling of his earlier work, Wambaugh himself arranged the independent production of *The Onion Field*, undoubtedly his masterpiece as both book and film, and of *The Black Marble*, accepting only script credits. Despite glowing critical receptions, both of these excellent movies have not received the international acclaim that they deserve.

The late Seventies seem to have witnessed the demise of the cop cycle. Clint Eastwood's *The Gauntlet* (1977) continues the old theme of honest policeman versus corrupt hierarchy, but debunks his earlier lone-cop, machismo mystique. Eastwood plays a policeman proud of being selected for a mission to bring back an important witness, a prostitute played by Sondra Locke; but he has been chosen because his corrupt superiors regard him as the most incompetent cop on the force, and they want the witness killed before she can testify. The hero and heroine survive only because the erstwhile loner is repeatedly saved by the advice of the wisecracking girl he is meant to protect.

John Carpenter's *Assault on Precinct 13* (1976) is, like Carpenter's other films, a loving recreation of an old Hollywood staple in modern guise. It is a reprise of the Indian-fighting Western in an urban setting, with a stagecoach station or fort (paralleled

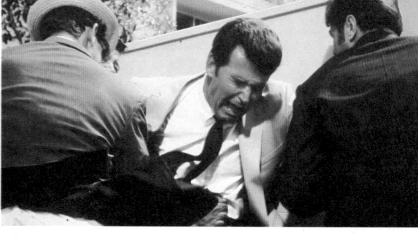

---

### The British bobby was replaced by the plain-clothes tough cop, with a gun instead of a truncheon

---

here by the police station about to be shut down) surrounded by savage redskins (the anonymous, weirdly-painted and oddly-attired youth gangs) and saved in the nick of time by the Seventh Cavalry (the Los Angeles police).

*The Private Files of J. Edgar Hoover* (1978) is a masterly, largely factual account of the history of the FBI, in the light of the critical reappraisal of the agency after the 1972 death of the man who had directed its fortunes for nearly half a century. Broderick Crawford seemed tailor-made for the title role.

Hollywood was not alone in exploring the law-and-order issue in the Seventies. In Britain, the traditional, cosy, *Dixon of Dock Green* image of the bobby had already received something of a blow in the early Sixties with the much more realistic *Z-Cars* television series and its successors, *Softly, Softly* and *Barlow*. In the Seventies the bobby mythology was replaced by a new cult of hard-drinking, swearing, womanizing and uncompromisingly tough cops, often with cockney accents, in such television series as *Target*, *The Professionals* and, above all, *The Sweeney*, which was successfully translated to the big screen with two features, *The Sweeney* (1976) and *Sweeney 2* (1978). A more sensitive exploration of the law-or-order dilemma was Sidney Lumet's *The Offence* (1972), with Sean Connery as a dedicated though authoritarian policeman who kills a suspected child molester during interrogation.

In Italy, Elio Petri's *Indagine su un Cittadino al di Sopra di Ogni Sospetto* (1970, *Investigation of a Citizen Above Suspicion*) probed the relations between police

and authorities in a satirical story of a police inspector who murders his mistress and then dares the department to expose him. The perennial political problem, first posed in Rome some two thousand years earlier, 'Who guards the guards?', has never been better explored on film.

Australia produced, in *Mad Max* (1979), a futuristic cop movie that outdirtied Harry and all his compatriots. Mel Gibson starred as the clean-cut cop of the title, seeking revenge against sadistic, marauding motorcycle gangs who blaze a trail of carnage through the outback. Essentially an exploitation picture which revels in graphic violence, *Mad Max* achieved a considerable cult following.

Although the characteristic law-enforcement hero of the late Sixties and Seventies was the cop, the more traditional Hollywood staples of the private eye and the gentleman sleuth were not neglected. There were numerous attempts to recapture the tone and atmosphere of the classic private-eye movies of the Forties. The two Raymond Chandler novels which had not yet been filmed at last reached the screen. Paul Bogart's *Marlowe* (1969) was based on Chandler's *The Little Sister* and had James Garner giving a very creditable performance in the title role. In *The Long Goodbye* (1973), Robert Altman brought Marlowe (played by Elliott Gould) up to date, placing him in contemporary Los Angeles. The film deviated pretty sharply from the original novel, but it succeeded in capturing Chandler's bleak vision of the great nowhere city. The two most successful of the Forties Marlowe films, *Murder, My Sweet* (1944) and *The Big Sleep* (1946), were remade as Dick Richards' *Farewell, My Lovely* (1975) and Michael Winner's *The Big Sleep* (1978), both starring the excellent Robert Mitchum.

Lew Archer, novelist Ross Macdonald's hero, was brought to the screen with a change of name by Jack Smight in 1966 with Paul Newman as *Harper*. Fast-moving and well-characterized, *Harper* was

*Top left:* The Choirboys *are ten cops on the night watch in Los Angeles, seen here in a publicity shot. Top:* Tony Rome *(Frank Sinatra) protects wealthy Rudolph Kosterman (Simon Oakland) from a murder attempt; Kosterman's wife Rita (Gena Rowlands) is being blackmailed into stealing her husband's diamonds. Above:* Marlowe *(James Garner) is roughed up by minions of the gangster Steelgrave, who wishes to prevent his affair with the film star Mavis Weld becoming public knowledge*

corruption through absolute power, and Faye Dunaway was a mysterious *femme fatale*.

Arthur Penn's *Night Moves* (1975) had Gene Hackman as a relentless pursuer of truth, hampered by domestic problems. Derived from an excellent script by Alan Sharp, *Night Moves*, with its bafflingly enigmatic plot, delivered the *coup de grâce* to the central thematic underpinning of the private-eye genre, that integrity and intuition for the moral worth of other people can succeed in resolving problems. Here the moral sensibilities and dedication of the hero lead to disaster for all the characters.

The Seventies also produced some excellent pastiches of the private-eye genre, possibly a sign of the dissolution of the moral assumptions of the straightforward variety. The delightful British *Gumshoe*, directed by Stephen Frears in 1971, starred Albert Finney as a small-time comedian who identifies with Bogart, getting involved in some Chandleresque action in Lancashire and London. In David Giler's *The Black Bird* (1975), George Segal played the son of Sam Spade, hero of *The Maltese Falcon*. Robert Benton's *The Late Show* (1977) had Art Carney as a private eye of pensionable vintage, complete with a hearing-aid which he has to remove before shooting, getting embroiled in a contemporary world of marijuana, murder and mayhem. Most satisfying of all was Richard

---

### The private eye made a come-back, but often as a comic character instead of a trench-coated hero

---

Dreyfuss' portrayal of a 'clapped-out Marxist gumshoe' (as another character calls him) in Jeremy Paul Kagan's *The Big Fix* (1978). A former college radical of the Sixties turned unsuccessful private eye, he pursues a complex web of political corruption, dragging in tow his Jewish momma and two small kids – his ex-wife dumps them on him as she follows the latest psychiatric fads.

The old-fashioned English detective mystery was also revived with great success in the mid-Seventies with Sidney Lumet's *Murder on the Orient Express* (1974). This version of Agatha Christie's classic whodunnit benefited from a stellar cast playing the train-load of suspects, and a remarkably convincing Albert Finney as the Belgian sleuth Hercule Poirot. *Death on the Nile* (1978), with Peter Ustinov as Poirot and an equally distinguished cast of suspects, was also a block-busting hit. Another Agatha Christie film, *The Mirror Crack'd* (1980), with Angela Lansbury as Miss Marple, marked the return of Elizabeth Taylor and Kim Novak to the screen after some years' absence.

Joseph L. Mankiewicz's *Sleuth* (1973), derived from Anthony Shaffer's brilliant play, questioned all the conventions of the whodunnit with a bamboozling and convoluted plot. Robert Moore's *Murder by Death* (1976), with a script by Neil Simon, was a hilarious send-up of the whole detective genre, with an all-star cast playing the best-known screen sleuths, in the traditional setting of a country-house weekend. The partnership of Neil Simon and Robert Moore attempted to repeat the success of this by lampooning the gumshoe genre in *The Cheap Detective* (1978), starring Peter Falk. Like the previously mentioned hits, these films show that the detective genre is very much alive, although largely in the form of pastiche or nostalgic tribute. The mantle of contemporary crime-fighter seems to have passed irrevocably to the cop.

ROBERT REINER

---

*Above: art-work from the publicity material for* The Late Show, *in which ageing ex-private eye Ira Wells (Art Carney) agrees to investigate the kidnapping of a cat belonging to Margo (Lily Tomlin), and finds that the trail leads by way of several murders to a final shoot-out which he wins only by faking an ulcer attack*

deservedly one of the most popular private-eye movies of the period. However, it was nearly matched by Gordon Douglas' *Tony Rome* (1967), with Frank Sinatra seemingly made for the Bogart-like role of a Miami-based private eye. *Lady in Cement* (1968) was a respectably workmanlike sequel from the Douglas-Sinatra team.

Gordon Parks' *Shaft* (1971) marked a departure for the private-eye movie in featuring a black detective hero. Richard Roundtree's portrayal of Shaft owed more to James Bond than to Philip Marlowe, with the emphasis being on the hero's prowess at sex and violence. Hugely successful, the film spawned two sequels, *Shaft's Big Score!* (1972) and *Shaft in Africa* (1973). Rather more in line with the traditions of the private-eye genre was Bill Cosby's black detective in *Hickey and Boggs* (1972), about a salt-and-pepper pair of down-and-out gumshoes, directed by Robert Culp, who also played Cosby's white partner.

In the Seventies, three films marked the culmination of the private-eye genre to date. Alan J. Pakula's adult thriller *Klute* starred Donald Sutherland in the role of a Tuscarora, Pennsylvania policeman who is hired by a wealthy acquaintance to leave the force and find a missing friend. The only clue is an obscene letter to a New York call-girl, Bree Daniels (Jane Fonda in an Oscar-winning performance). The tense, increasingly paranoiac atmosphere and acute characterization make for compulsive viewing, although the film finally reveals a soft centre as romance blossoms between Klute and the call-girl.

Roman Polanski's *Chinatown* (1974) successfully evoked both the physical and the moral landscape of the Forties *film noir*. Jack Nicholson was most effective as the private eye uncovering a tangled morass of political and private evil. John Huston, who as director had pioneered the genre with *The Maltese Falcon* (1941), played the personification of

Looking back over the Seventies, it is clear that the three most important movies in the commercial rise of the urban vigilante film were *Dirty Harry*, *Death Wish* (1974) and *The Exterminator* (1980). In the light of the two latter films it is now difficult to understand exactly why *Dirty Harry* caused all the stir and controversy it did when it first appeared. Its overt violence is minimal and what there is is hardly sadistic, at least not on the hero's part. Moreover, that hero is a policeman engaged in regular law-enforcement, rather than a private citizen carrying out a personal vendetta, and if his methods are rather unconventional and he chafes at the limitations imposed on him in his work by rules and regulations, at least the existence of these rules is acknowledged. In the end he throws away his police badge in a gesture of frustration but that can hardly be taken as an automatic sanction for everyone in the audience to go out after anyone who has somehow offended him.

All the same, in 1971 the film was freely accused of embodying a fascistic message and of endorsing Harry's most extreme digressions

1

2

3

5

6

from strict legality, thereby implying that the ends (the hunting down of an admitted psychopath) justified whatever means he might use. It is probable that Dirty Harry received such intense scrutiny because of its extreme efficacy as a piece of cinema entertainment: if Clint Eastwood is seen doing these things, supported by the film-making skills of Don Siegel, then the resulting effect on public morale might be expected to be that much more severe than if it was all happening in a lack-lustre programmer starring no-one in particular. And there was certainly no denying the overall class of the enterprise, any more than its logical place in the evolution of both Clint Eastwood's screen persona and the cinematic world of Don Siegel.

This was not the first film they had made together: it was preceded by Coogan's Bluff (1968), Two Mules for Sister Sara (1970) and The Beguiled (1971). Siegel also had a brief role in Eastwood's directorial debut Play Misty for Me (1971). After getting nowhere very much in Hollywood, Eastwood went to Europe and scored an enormous success in several 'spaghetti' Westerns direct-ed by Sergio Leone, starting with Per un Pugno di Dollari (1964, A Fistful of Dollars), in which he played a mysterious gunfighter with no apparent moral scruples and who used brutally ruthless tactics that were far from the cinema's time-honoured code of the West.

With Coogan's Bluff he made the vital transition from the West to the city: in it he plays a Western sheriff pursuing his man to New York and continuing to use the methods of the West, even though they mean exchanging horse for motor-bike and subsequently falling foul of his more bureaucratically-minded city colleagues.

Dirty Harry was a logical extension of this. Although Harry Callahan is San Francisco trained, he assumes an ignorance of city conventions which Coogan could naturally get away with, and evinces much of the ruthlessness that had made the Man With No Name of the Leone Westerns such a novelty; Harry flies in the face of police-thriller convention almost as much as his sinister predecessor does within the Western genre. There are a few attempts in the film to humanize and 'explain' him (by relaying how he lost his wife) but these seem to be mostly a matter of form and are not meant to be taken seriously. Essentially the character of Harry is given at the outset, derived more from the physical and emotional qualities of the star on screen than from any scriptwriter's dramaturgy.

On the whole, all explanation is kept to a minimum in Dirty Harry: the film's motivation is its action scenes. From the unsuccessful heist, stopped in its tracks almost single-handed by Harry early in the film, the tempo is created and kept up by the virtually wordless set-pieces that climax in Harry's running battle with the killer. This continuous momentum probably had more to do with the film's success than anything that might be construed as a 'message'. This, moviegoers felt, was the way they didn't make 'em any more: spare, hard-hitting muscular action such as is associated with the old-style macho-star vehicle.

It was no surprise that Eastwood went on to make two more films in which he played Harry Callahan: Magnum Force (1973) and The Enforcer (1976). It was also not too much of a surprise that in them he became more explicit about his mission, and that Siegel did not direct them. What had been fresh and spontaneous rapidly ran the risk of deteriorating into a formula, while as Eastwood became more established he tended to become more respectable. By 1976 a new star – also nurtured in Europe – emerged in Charles Bronson, and the genre had already moved on significantly with Death Wish. Nevertheless, Dirty Harry remains not only the first, but far and away the best of the bunch.

JOHN RUSSELL TAYLOR

**Directed by Don Siegel, 1971**
Prod co: Warner/Malpaso. **exec prod:** Robert Daley. **prod:** Don Siegel. **assoc prod:** Carl Pingatore. **sc:** Harry Julian Fink, Rita M. Fink, Dean Riesner. **photo** (Technicolor, Panavision): Bruce Surtees. **ed:** Carl Pingatore. **art dir:** Dale Hennessy. **set dec:** Robert DeVestel. **mus:** Lalo Schifrin. **sd:** William Randall. **ass dir:** Robert Rubin. **prod man:** Jim Henderling. **r/t:** 101 minutes.
Cast: Clint Eastwood (*Harry Callahan*), Harry Guardino (*Lt Bressler*), Reni Santoni (*Chico*), John Vernon (*the mayor*), Andy Robinson (*Scorpio*), John Larch (*Chief*), John Mitchum (*De Georgio*), Mae Mercer (*Mrs Russell*), Lyn Edgington (*Norma*), Ruth Kobart (*bus driver*), Woodrow Parfrey (*Mr Jaffe*), Josef Sommer (*Rothko*), William Patterson (*Bannerman*), James Nolan (*liquor proprietor*), Maurice S. Argent (*Sid Kleinman*), Jo de Winter (*Miss Willis*), Craig G. Kelly (*Sgt Reineke*).

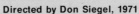

Inspector Harry Callahan of the San Francisco police force, known as Dirty Harry because of his ruthless methods (1) and tendency to accept unpleasant assignments, is given the job of capturing Scorpio, a rooftop sniper (2) who is attempting to hold the city to ransom. Scorpio kills twice to prove he means business, then kidnaps a girl.

Against his will, Harry finds himself with Chico, a new partner fresh from college (3). However, when Harry delivers the ransom money for the girl's release he is nearly killed and it is only Chico's intervention that saves him.

Chasing the wounded Scorpio to a football stadium, Harry manages to force him to reveal the girl's whereabouts before turning him in (4). The girl proves to be dead but Harry's use of strong-arm tactics while extracting the information enables the killer to be released on a legal technicality.

A disillusioned Chico leaves the force but Harry takes the law into his own hands and continues to pursue Scorpio, who retaliates by arranging for himself to be beaten up (5) in an attempt to frame Harry for assault. After this fails, Scorpio then kidnaps a bus-load of school-children.

Against orders, Harry rescues the children. Scorpio flees the bus (6), but Harry finally tracks him down (7) and 'executes' him (8). As he turns to walk away, Harry hurls his police badge into the river.

In the Sixties and Seventies Clint Eastwood seemed too good to be true. He transformed himself overnight from a smiling cowboy in a TV series into a deadly, inscrutable fantasy hero idolized by millions. Whatever he touched turned to gold, and so the biggest star in the world also became a highly successful director – but what does the future hold now for Clint?

# The Beguiler

There was an unexpected box-office lapse in the summer of 1980 – *Bronco Billy* didn't do very well. It should have been reliable business with Clint Eastwood's brushed leather face beneath a dashing white cowboy hat. He was surrounded by the people from previous hits. His deadpan reaction to mishap was funny, without destroying his authority. *Bronco Billy* had the air of a happy summer movie, as full of fights, laughs and male self-congratulation as *Every Which Way But Loose* (1978), the Eastwood Christmas film of two years before and a hit beyond anyone's wildest dreams. The latter was a departure: it was the first Eastwood film to try comedy action, as if to say, 'Look, this guy is 48, and he can't go around stomping on everyone for much longer'. It gave Clint an orang-utan to tuck under one arm, while the other retained its gentlemanly hold on Sondra Locke. The successful formula was repeated with *Any Which Way You Can* (1980), but *Bronco Billy* had been the first film to raise the possibility that Eastwood is not infallible.

## The Man With No Failures
For 16 years, he had enjoyed unrivalled success. Not every picture triumphed – one of the best, *The Beguiled* (1971), was too sardonic to please his following – but they all went about their business of entertaining large audiences. Eastwood didn't win much review space, and when he did it was because critics like Pauline Kael were alarmed by what they felt lay beneath the surface of violent cop movies like *Dirty Harry* (1971). Nevertheless, since 1964, about twenty Eastwood pictures had prospered. And if Eastwood was quiet, unstarry and inclined to stay at home at Carmel,

California, rather than play the talk shows, still he had gone from being actor to star to director and boss of his own company, Malpaso. That tight-knit operation made all his Seventies pictures – and took big profits from them.

No-one has ever begrudged him this glory. He handles himself gracefully, especially because he has acted on the notion that turning out pleasant movies is not that difficult. His pictures are not expensive and they never strive after the difficult or the pretentious. Twenty years earlier he was a good-looking Californian kid with hair like James Dean's and swimming-pool blue eyes. He would look better as he matured, but if it hadn't been for the shyness of someone who had reached six foot by the age of 13, he might have carried showbiz on the strength of beauty alone. Not since Gary Cooper had an American male in pictures had it in his power to stop the breath

*Above: death in the desert for adversaries of the Man With No Name – Eastwood in* For a Few Dollars More *(and right). Below left: Clint learns to ballroom dance at the Universal talent school around 1955. His partner was Italian actress Gia Scala*

of men and women in the audience alike. No matter how tough the roles, the skin, the eyes and the very soft voice have hinted at a Malibu Apollo.

## For a very few dollars . . .
He was born in San Francisco in 1930. The family was poor and Clint went from high school to manual labour, laying down the basis for that lean body. He was an army swimming instructor at Ford Ord, and then he started to study business at Los Angeles College. But physique and looks earned him offers from Universal – a starting contract at $75 a week. In 1955, he got a couple of walk-on parts in movies, including *Francis in the Navy*, starring Donald O'Connor and a talking mule.

Those were tough days. Clint looked too healthy and he spoke too clearly to fit the Brando style. He was in and out of work, taking acting classes by night and doing labouring jobs in the day. The body got harder, but he didn't put much faith in lessons or theory:

'The basic fundamental of learning acting is to know yourself, know what you can do. That's one big advantage of doing a series, if you can. You get to see yourself a lot, get to see what you can do wrong or right.'

His television series was *Rawhide*, and the role of Rowdy Yates was no more than an outline that a young actor could inhabit in front of the camera. Over two hundred episodes in seven seasons provided Eastwood with

that necessary view of himself. Now he is one of few screen stars with the instinctive assurance of knowing how a scene should be filmed. His face, his minimal reactions and his timing are a style such as Cooper and Bogart had possessed before him.

Even on *Rawhide* he was asking to direct some episodes. Eric Fleming, the lead star on the show, had no problems with Clint's ambitions. But CBS and the unions were very touchy and they restricted him to trailers. Still, it is a mark of Eastwood's love of movies that the urge to make them came early, apparently on a day when a stampede scene was being shot from a safe distance and Clint wondered why he couldn't carry a camera on horseback into the herd.

He could have been numbered with James Arness, Robert Horton or, indeed, Eric Fleming – stars in Western series who retired, got trapped in television, or in the case of Fleming, died in 1966 on the slide. Clint proved his initiative with what seemed an affront to Hollywood tradition. He went to Spain to make a Western for an Italian director. It was called *Per un Pugno di Dollari* (1964, *A Fistful of Dollars*) and he did it for $15,000: if the

*Above: a budding director has a look for himself during the filming of Don Siegel's* The Beguiled. *Right: Eastwood's directorial debut starred him as DJ Dave Garland who is plagued by the psychopathic woman (Jessica Walter) who asks him to* Play Misty for Me

'spaghetti' Western had proved cold and greasy the actor would have been thrown out in the garbage.

## Leone and the language of death

However, the film was a huge, international hit that changed Eastwood's life and, in the Man With No Name, created a role model that still works in TV advertising. The film was made by Sergio Leone, whose English was as limited as Clint's Italian. But they got on well and understood that the image of a laconic but lethal man musing on a cheroot until blazing guns appeared from beneath his serape, could be sensational.

The costume was bought by Eastwood in America. He conceived the character, and he rewrote or cut many of his lines. *A Fistful of Dollars* and its sequels – *Per Qualche Dollaro in Più* (1966, *For a Few Dollars More*) and *Il*

Buono, il Brutto, il Cattivo (1967, *The Good, the Bad and the Ugly*) – were full of pregnant pauses just because of the language problem on set, but that only stimulated Leone's visual imagination and allowed Clint to become an awesome assassin, above words, a face always gazing into the sun so that the eyes seemed to be glints of some rare and impervious metal. A ruthless, implacable honour grew around the silence and the eyes that would not look away. The movies were like mescal dreams, poised wonderfully between suspense and absurdity.

In later years, Clint was often willing to have his super-hero outsmarted – by women, an elderly Indian and that orang-utan. But that's not new. Leone's films were very violent, and they played the action straight – if that's the way you wanted to read it. Yet the exaggerated compositions, the mannered acting and the feeling of time oozing out as slowly as ketchup all suggested a satiric attitude on the part of the director and his star.

The *Dollars* trilogy kept Clint occupied in the mid-Sixties. When he returned to America, he set about making this new kind of Western at home: *Hang 'Em High* (1968), *Two Mules for Sister Sara* (1970), *Joe Kidd* (1972) and *High Plains Drifter* (1973) are all in the same vein. The lesson that he had learned was that the outsider hero suited him – not just a nameless figure, but a man without known allegiances. In 1968, for the first time, he teamed up with Don Siegel, a director of twenty years hard-earned experience and an expert story-teller with a predilection for toughness. Siegel had always found Hollywood stars squeamish when asked to be mean, but Clint was different:

'Eastwood has an absolute fixation as an anti-hero. It's his credo in life and in all the films that he's done so far . . . I've never worked with an actor who was less conscious of his good image.'

*Coogan's Bluff* – about an Arizona cop who comes on a manhunt to New York – isn't quite that heartless, but it did exploit the novelty of that handsome face snarling with hostility, of the Eastwood hero coolly laying any woman around. Siegel would be as important to Eastwood as Leone, but there were a few years of hesitation before the new partnership clicked. Eastwood was overshadowed by Richard Burton in Brian Hutton's *Where Eagles Dare* (1968) and by Lee Marvin in Joshua Logan's *Paint Your Wagon* (1969).

## Play dirty for Siegel

The year in which he emerged as a Hollywood giant was 1971. For Siegel he acted in *The Beguiled*, about a fugitive in the American Civil War taken in by a household of women who take sweet vengeance on his complacent stud attitudes by amputating his injured leg. Then he directed his first film, *Play Misty for Me*, a slick thriller about a disc jockey who is haunted and nearly killed by a woman who

*Above left: the calling of* Coogan's Bluff? *Eastwood in his first role as a vicious cop for Don Siegel. Above: as* Bronco Billy, *a Wild West show proprietor with problems. Below: Philo (Eastwood) and Clyde, trucking partners in* Every Which Way But Loose

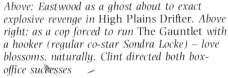

*Above: Eastwood as a ghost about to exact explosive revenge in* High Plains Drifter. *Above right: as a cop forced to run* The Gauntlet *with a hooker (regular co-star Sondra Locke) – love blossoms, naturally. Clint directed both box-office successes*

phones up with the request of the title. In both these pictures Clint was making himself the victim of women, and surely that owed itself to the good humour of a happily married man lusted after by so many strangers.

*Dirty Harry*, though, was the major event of 1971, and the most controversial film he has ever made. Siegel's direction guaranteed its impact, but the subject went beyond mere entertainment. Dirty Harry Callahan is a San Francisco cop with an old-fashioned belief in the law and the will that must enforce it. The film is in two parts: first Harry tracks down a loathsome killer, a nasty mixture of spoiled kid

psychopath and glib hippy; but then bureaucracy and the technicalities of the law let the killer go free whereupon Harry makes a private war on him, eliminating him with prejudice and then tossing away his police badge in disgust.

Some people felt that the picture encouraged vigilante fascism, that it was urging less liberal law-and-order programmes (Eastwood had backed Nixon in 1968). But the picture is more the manifestation of a very independent, romantic morality that shows in the star's aversion to publicity, extravagance and institutions:

'We, as Americans, went to Nuremberg and convicted people who committed certain crimes because they didn't adhere to a higher morality; we convicted them on that basis – and they shouldn't have listened to the law of the land or their leaders at that time. They should have listened to the true morality.'

## Softening the blows

It seems likely that he was affected by complaints about the violence in *Dirty Harry* and its successors, *Magnum Force* (1973), *The Enforcer* (1976) and *The Gauntlet* (1977). His anti-hero has mellowed to become a more relaxed, more amused and marginally less robust observer. That was the process of tolerance that worked so well in *The Outlaw Josey Wales* (1976), in which a righteous moral anger softens with time to become aware of foibles, frailty and humour. In many ways it is his most adventurous picture, a sign of the kindness he is often too shy or laid back to reveal.

Nor would anyone have expected *Breezy* (1973) from Eastwood. With William Holden and Kay Lenz, that was the story of a September-May romance, shamelessly sentimental but touching, solidly grounded and well acted. For Clint it was about a man who 'rediscovers life through the eyes of this young girl'. It was the first hint that he might be fearful of growing older, and it could have been a prelude to his own romantic interest in Sondra Locke. He resists confessions or the gossip press, but for some time he has worked with the younger, blonde actress who has not

really acted for anyone but Eastwood (though the failure of *Bronco Billy* apparently threatened their relationship).

He is over fifty now, with reason to wonder about his future. His face has begun to look strained; in the rather dull *Escape From Alcatraz* (1979) there was evidence of youth withering away. Gary Cooper made *High Noon* (1952) when he was 51, after several years of indecision. And at about the same age John Wayne yielded to paternal roles in *The Searchers* (1956) and *Rio Bravo* (1959). It may be that Eastwood's greatest test lies ahead. Can he find and prove himself in older parts? Is he inventive enough to discover a fresh character, or will his career wane? He might settle for directing and for running his own company, but if you have been as beautiful as Clint Eastwood, and as adored, it may be hard to give up being looked at.                DAVID THOMSON

**Filmography**
**1955** Revenge of the Creature; Lady Godiva (GB: Lady Godiva of Coventry); Francis in the Navy; Tarantula; Never Say Goodbye. '**56** Star in the Dust; The First Travelling Saleslady. '**57** Escapade in Japan. '**58** Lafayette Escadrille (GB: Hell Bent for Glory); Ambush at Cimarron Pass. '**64** Per un Pugno di Dollari (IT-GER-SP) (USA/GB: A Fistful of Dollars). '**66** Per Qualche Dollaro in Più (IT-GER-SP) (USA/GB: For a Few Dollars More). '**67** Il Buono, il Brutto, il Cattivo (IT-GER-SP) (USA/GB: The Good, the Bad and the Ugly); Le Streghe *ep* Una Sera Come le Altre (IT-FR) (USA: The Witches *ep* A Night Like Any Other). '**68** Hang 'Em High; Coogan's Bluff; Where Eagles Dare (GB). '**69** Paint Your Wagon. '**70** Gold Fever (doc. short) (appearance as himself); Two Mules for Sister Sara; Kelly's Heroes (USA-YUG). '**71** The Beguiled; Play Misty for Me (+dir); Dirty Harry. '**72** Joe Kidd. '**73** High Plains Drifter (+dir); Breezy (dir. only); Magnum Force. '**74** Thunderbolt and Lightfoot. '**75** The Eiger Sanction (+dir). '**76** The Outlaw Josey Wales (+dir); The Enforcer. '**77** The Gauntlet (+dir). '**78** Every Which Way But Loose. '**79** Escape From Alcatraz. '**80** Bronco Billy (+dir); Any Which Way You Can. '**82** Firefox (+dir); Honkytonk Man (+dir; +prod). '**83** Sudden Impact (+dir; +prod).

**Directed by Elio Petri, 1970**
**Prod co:** Vera Film. **prod:** Daniele Senatore. **sc:** Ugo Pirro, Elio Petri. **photo** (Technicolor): Luigi Kuveiller. **ed:** Ruggero Mastroianni. **art dir:** Carlo Egidi. **mus:** Ennio Morricone. **mus dir:** Bruno Nicholai. **sd:** Mario Bramonti. **prod man:** Romano Cardarelli. **ass dir:** Antonio Gabrielli. **r/t:** 115 minutes. Italian title: *Indagine su un Cittadino al di Sopra di Ogni Sospetto.*
**Cast:** Gian Maria Volonté (*police inspector*), Florinda Bolkan (*Augusta*), Salvo Randone (*plumber*), Gianni Santuccio (*police commissioner*), Arturo Dominici (*Mangani*), Orazio Orlando (*Biglia*), Sergio Tramonti (*Antonio Pace*), Massimo Foschi (*Augusta's husband*), Aldo Rendine (*homicide investigator*), Aleka Paizl, Vittorio Duse, Pino Patti.

Winner of a Special Jury prize at the 1970 Cannes Festival and a Hollywood Oscar the following year, Elio Petri's *Investigation of a Citizen Above Suspicion* belongs to a group of distinguished European films of the late Sixties and early Seventies in which their directors articulated leftist political views and attacked the social establishment. But unlike more serious treatments, Petri supplements his political allegory with a vein of sly humour, dark surrealism and eccentric characterization.

The film is dominated by a performance of operatic paranoia from Gian Maria Volonté as a police inspector who commits murder and

then, as a test of his own power, leaves tantalizing clues for his subordinates. Volonté's full-blooded fascist arias – 'Repression *is* civilization,' he declares at one stage – created something of a furore in Italy, not only because of the film's equation of authority with repression, but through its irreverence towards its policeman hero. He is a pathological and sensual inspector, thuggish and pathetic. His perpetual motion is that of a man unable to slow down for fear someone might get a glimpse of his hollowness and vulnerability.

The killing of his mistress had been provoked by taunts about his virility: murder becomes an almost

symbolic act. Augusta's criticism must be silenced because it is a revelation not only of the man's impotence but of the impotence of authority itself. The film has an Orwellian sense of totalitarianism as a denial of freedom not simply for the victims but also for the perpetrators, whose role as oppressor limits their own actions.

An inspector who describes police procedure as 'a drama staged to touch off one's deepest, most secret feelings' is essentially an actor, an overblown self-creation in love with the sound of his own voice, and a man with one foot in his own dream world. His distorted vision is echoed by the film's use of lurid colour and tinkling music, and by the bizarre decor of his mistress's flat, which allows him full indulgence of his fantasies. In his office, this psychological peculiarity is as far as possible suppressed by the glum constraints of normality. Here, appropriately enough, he seems more like a prisoner than many of the accused brought before him.

A certain tendency of the film to descend to melodrama has been criticized, but this style seems a

conscious attempt to convey the fevered vision of a disturbed personality – the camera seeking a rhetoric that matches the psychology of a man living on the edge of his nerves. Also, the director's adoption of the mode of suspense thriller is a skilfully calculated strategy: the detective story is an ideal vehicle for showing that social processes are, in reality, labyrinthine, often incredible and invariably cloaked in mystery.

Occasionally, the hero's idiosyncrasy threatens to reduce the film's general applicability as an antifascist polemic, but it also contributes to a certain originality. The corruptions practised by authority offer a ludicrous as well as disturbing spectacle, and the film's observation is tinged with an effective streak of black comedy. Having scattered clues about his crime, the inspector finds that his sycophantic staff ignore them all. 'The only guilty man in this room is me,' he remarks with ponderous irony, and this massively incriminating statement is met with deferential blankness. His attempts to reveal his guilt, as his self-loathing increases, are thwarted and culminate in an imaginative dream sequence where he is driven onto his knees to confess his innocence by superiors who convince him of the necessity of maintaining the *status quo* and the rule and respect of the law.

It is this tone of mischievous absurdity that justifies the reference to Franz Kafka's oppressive novel *The Trial* on the closing titles: 'Whatever impression he may give us, he is a servant of the Law, and therefore he belongs to the Law and is beyond human judgment.'

Petri shares Kafka's bleak view of the abuses and yet unimpeachability of the law, but also shares his satirical delight at human self-delusion. The effect is more exhilarating than depressing.

Elio Petri has made other notable films, particularly his debut work, *L'Assassino* (1961, *The Assassin*) and his futuristic thriller *La Decima Vittima* (1965, *The Tenth Victim*). But it is *Investigation of a Citizen Above Suspicion* which contains his most potent blend of spectacular style and mordant social commentary, his most vivid *mélange* of Marx and Freud. Petri and Volonté have a fine time energetically dissecting a citizen who is above suspicion but not quite beneath contempt. The actions and reactions of this demented protagonist embody a brave and forceful statement about the lunacy of power. NEIL SINYARD

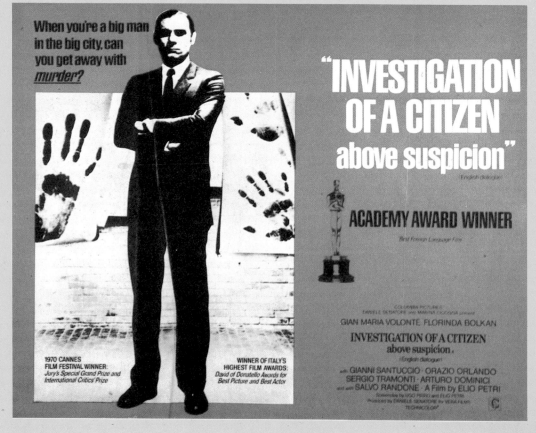

An influential police inspector, recently promoted to Head of Political Intelligence in Rome, murders his mistress Augusta (1). In flashback we learn of their strange sexual behaviour at her flat (2), where she had posed for photographs as a murder victim (3), teased him about his sexual prowess and revealed that she had another lover – an anarchist student, Antonio Pace.

The inspector leaves clues at the scene of the crime to test his inviolability before the law. He returns to examine the apartment (4), but none of his colleagues accept the evidence. Even when he openly confesses to a plumber and orders him to inform the police, the workman retracts his statement on realizing at the station who the inspector is (5).

While investigating a bomb explosion caused by young radicals (6), the inspector attempts to blame Pace for the murder (7). But Pace reports that he saw him leaving Augusta's flat. The truth becomes known and the inspector returns home to await arrest. There, he dreams that his superiors refuse to accept the confession he has submitted (8) and instead propose a toast to him before departing. On waking, he prepares for their arrival by drawing the blinds – leaving the viewer unsure whether or not he will be found guilty.

179

In 1972 Paramount decided to make *The Godfather* the centrepiece of their new production strategy. The aim was to find one film a year that would be a really big box-office success, a success large enough to carry all the other productions. The right film would have the benefit of both a large production and promotions budget, and it would be exhibited in such a way as to gain maximum impact – simultaneous, nationwide release backed by intense publicity. This impact would then be exploited by charging higher admission prices.

The choice of *The Godfather* proved inspired. The film was an extravagant commercial success. Within days of its release it had recovered all initial outlay, and within weeks had become an extremely profitable enterprise. In commercial terms *The Godfather* became a landmark, an indication of what could be achieved by Paramount's scheme. It was also a landmark in less tangible ways. The director, Francis Ford Coppola, was seen as a representative of the new generation of Hollywood film-makers, and the success of the film, not only guaranteed his artistic future but also improved the prospects of his contemporaries.

Although it was directed by a 'new' film-maker, *The Godfather* is essentially a traditional film: the subject-matter – the world of ethnic crime – is familiar and has provided the basis for many previous films; the main thrust is a narrative one, though ranging widely in time and space; the story is told vividly and clearly; the stars are a mixture of established faces, such as Marlon Brando and Sterling Hayden, and promising newcomers – Al Pacino, James Caan and Diane Keaton.

In many ways what separates *The Godfather* from previous gangster films is the amount of money spent on it. This is not as cynical a comment as it sounds, for the money is translated into artistic values on the screen. It allows the narrative to develop in a leisurely way, giving the actors the opportunity to develop characterizations and allowing settings and costumes to have strong dramatic presence. Overall, the money enables the film to be turned into a substantial spectacle.

Of course, the availability of money does not guarantee its effective use; it is up to the film-maker to take advantage of the resources money brings within reach. Coppola's contribution to *The Godfather* is undoubtedly a crucial one. As a director, his talents incline towards the creation of spectacle, and like a director of musicals, he is able to choreograph the movement of large numbers of people; the opening wedding reception is a superb example in this respect. He is always conscious of the expressive use of colour; the contrast between the light golden tones of the Sicilian sequences and the dark, sombre ones of the interiors inhabited by the gangsters is striking. Coppola also seems particularly sensitive to the emotional physical presence of actors and actresses.

1

4

7

PARAMOUNT PICTURES PRESENTS

# The Godfather

*The Godfather* is finely cast – Brando's considered authority, Al Pacino's controlled intensity, Robert Duvall's distanced influence, Diane Keaton's directness and vulnerability.

It has been said that *The Godfather* is a radical film. This is a difficult argument to sustain, for the point the film makes about the place of crime in American society (its intimate connections with the established representatives of law and politics, its control over legitimate enterprises, the analogies that can be made between the way crime and large corporations conduct their affairs) are all familiar ones, and hardly the marks of a radical view of American society. If anything, the film, with its admiration for a certain ideal of masculine purity based on honour, ruthlessness, the use of violence and the maintenance of the family, is reactionary in outlook.

The popular success of *the Godfather* is not easy to explain. The film's overall effect is rather cold and bleak and the ruthlessness of the central characters, their commitment to violence and repression of emotion make identification hard. A fictional world without moral basis, and characterized by bloody struggles, is not immediately attractive. However, some of the film's appeal can be explained. It has many of the pleasures of the nineteenth-century realist novel, providing an alternative social world that the reader or viewer can inhabit; it has a sense of the epic in its presentation of warring kingdoms whose rise and fall effect the lives of ordinary people, not just those of the chieftains.

But whatever *The Godfather*'s appeal, it certainly doesn't sustain the view of many film producers and critics that the popular audience is looking for easy identifications and comfortable reassurances. The popular response is far more complicated than that.

ALAN LOVELL

Don Vito Corleone (1) – head of an Italian-American criminal 'family' and 'Godfather' to the Italian immigrants in New York – holds a lavish reception for his daughter's wedding (2), periodically returning to his office to settle any 'business' that crops up during the day.

The Don's power is illustrated when Johnny Fontane, a singing star he has backed (3), seeks his help in getting a part in a Hollywood movie. The Don asks the producer, Jack Woltz, to give Fontane the part. When friendly persuasion fails, Woltz finds the severed head of his favourite horse in bed with him. Fontane is given the part.

Another family, the Tattaglias, propose that the Don join in their drug-running trade. When he refuses, the Tattaglias shoot him down in the street (4). The Don survives, but his younger son Michael (5) takes revenge by killing a Tattaglia associate (6). He flees to Sicily (7) where he settles down and marries a local girl.

After two years news of his brother Sonny's death reaches Michael. His wife is then killed by a car bomb meant for him (8) and he returns to America. When the Don dies of a heart attack Michael becomes the leader of the 'family'.

A series of ruthless measures finally reinstates the Corleone family's position. A new Godfather has emerged in his father's image (9).

**Directed by Francis Ford Coppola, 1972**
**Prod co:** Alfran Productions. **prod:** Albert S. Ruddy. **assoc prod:** Gray Frederickson. **sc:** Mario Puzo, Francis Ford Coppola, from the novel by Mario Puzo. **photo** (Technicolor): Gordon Willis. **sp eff:** A. D. Flowers, Joe Lombardi, Sass Bedig. **ed:** William Reynolds, Peter Zinner, Marc Laub, Murray Solomon. **art dir:** Warren Clymer, Philip Smith. **cost:** Anna Hill Johnstone. **mus:** Nino Rota. **mus dir:** Carlo Savina. **sd:** Christopher Newman, Les Lazarowitz, Bud Grenzbach, Richard Portman. **ass dir:** Fred Gallo, Tony Brandt. **prod des:** Dean Tavoularis. **prod man:** Fred Caruso, Valerio De Paolis. **r/t:** 175 minutes.
**Cast:** Marlon Brando (*Don Vito Corleone*) Al Pacino (*Michael Corleone*), James Caan (*Sonny Corleone*), Richard Castellano (*Clemenza*), Robert Duvall (*Tom Hagen*) Sterling Hayden (*McCluskey*), John Marley (*Jack Woltz*), Richard Conte (*Barzini*), Diane Keaton (*Kay Adams*), Al Lettieri (*Sollozzo*), Abe Vigoda (*Tessio*), Talia Shire (*Connie Rizzi*), Gianni Russo (*Carlo Rizzi*), John Cazale (*Fredo Corleone*), Rudy Bond (*Cuneo*), Al Martino (*Johnny Fontane*), Morgana King (*Mama Corleone*), Lenny Montana (*Luca Brasi*), John Martino (*Paulie Gatto*), Salvatore Corsitto (*Bonasera*), Richard Bright (*Neri*), Alex Rocco (*Moe Greene*), Tony Giorgio (*Bruno Tattaglia*), Vito Scotti (*Nazorine*), Tere Livrano (*Theresa Hagen*), Victor Rendina (*Phillip Tattaglia*), Jeannie Linero (*Lucy Mancini*), Julie Gregg (*Sandra Corleone*), Ardell Sheridan (*Mrs Clemenza*), Simonetta Stefanelli (*Apollonia*), Angelo Infanti (*Fabrizio*), Corrado Gaipa (*Don Tommasino*), Franco Citti (*Calo*), Saro Urzi (*Vitelli*).

# A River of Riches
## India's Parallel Cinema

**Nobody seems quite certain as to when India's 'alternative' cinema actually began. Was it with Satyajit Ray's historic *Pather Panchali* in 1955? Or did the setting up of the Indian government's Film Finance Corporation in 1960 provide the real spur for film-makers dedicated to socially-conscious art rather than easy audience appeal? Alongside the mainstream, there has always been a parallel tide of sorts, but it was the emergence of directors like Ray and Mrinal Sen that gave rise to the term**

There is no way that the Indian Parallel Cinema movement – whatever its starting date – can be considered coherent either in style or content. And its tragedy is that, despite the emergence of many fine talents, there are still very few cinemas in its home country prepared to foster their work. That undeniable fact has caused much argument in a perennially argumentative nation. A young director has infinitely more chance of making a film in India today than his equivalent in England, but to get it effectively released means that he has to face very similar problems. The complications in India are perhaps even greater because of language: at least a dozen official tongues make widespread dissemination almost impossible.

### In parallel streams

If Satyajit Ray and Mrinal Sen are the two most widely known Parallel directors, there is a third whose position has been pivotal over the last decade. He is Shyam Benegal, who comes from Bombay rather than Calcutta. Benegal, even more than the other two, has been determined to reach out to wider audiences as well as to make properly creative films. And if the followers – good and not so good – of Ray and Sen have been legion, it now looks as if Benegal has just as much influence as either. Ray's shadow is long and not easy to move away from; Sen is a maverick who can be copied only at some peril. Benegal, however, can more easily be followed into the marketplace – if he succeeds. Money breeds money in the Indian film industry, as in all others.

Born in the Hyderabad area in 1934, Bene-

gal moved early to Bombay and became a highly successful maker of commercials and documentaries. *Ankur* (1974, *Ankur – The Seedling*), his famous first feature, was financed by the advertising company for whom he worked, and was remarkably popular with middle-class audiences looking for more than the average Hindi spectacular could offer. The story is of a landlord's son sent to administer a rural estate and his love for a beautiful peasant girl, married to a deaf and dumb worker. The film shot the actress Shabana Azmi to stardom, and was generally admired for its sensitivity and social relevance. It also sent Benegal off on a career which has produced several features and moved him increasingly towards a wider audience.

*Nishant* (1975, *Night's End*), which came next, was again about the landlord class and the way gross injustice and feudal customs overwhelm even those determined to end them until the revolutionary process intervenes. Benegal then undertook a project unique in Indian film annals. This was *Manthan* (1976, The Churning) which was produced by 500,000 Gujarat farmers who each invested two rupees (about 10p) in its making. Naturally they all went to see the completed project, thus ensuring excellent returns.

The film is about a young vet who persuades farmers to start a co-operative and thereby to fight the landlords who had previously mulcted them of their profits. It is a stirring tale, with optimism in the final reel but no false hopes that this kind of organization could ever be easy in such a tradition-bound country.

*Bhumika* (1978, *The Role*) and *Kondura* (1978, The Boon) were less popular with the public and persuaded Benegal that to defeat a conservative industry meant being more thoroughly a part of it. *Bhumika* was a biography of a celebrated screen actress of the past that was designed to show how women – even if highly successful in their careers – still

*Left: the director Shyam Benegal in conference with his leading lady Smita Patil, who plays a village woman in* Manthan

had the odds stacked against them. But the censorship rating given to the film prevented men taking their wives to it, with the inevitable result that the very audience Benegal was seeking failed to see it in sufficient numbers.

*Junoon* (*Possessed*), which was made in 1979, caused no such restrictive practices. It was produced and acted in by Shashi Kapoor, the Bombay superstar, and its subject was the 1857 Sepoy Revolt. After seeing it, some felt that Benegal was selling out to the film establishment, while others thought that perhaps he was taking it over. What is certain is that Benegal is a technically assured filmmaker, able to secure subtle performances and to use significant themes in his attempt to move the Parallel Cinema out of its tiny arthouse ghetto.

## Flow of talent
At the other end of the spectrum are *auteurs* like Mani Kaul and Kumar Shahani who have a far greater concern about the films they make than the audiences that are attracted to them. Kaul has made five features, of which *Satah se Uthata Aadmi* (Rising From the Surface) – a film without formal plot, exploring reactions to Indian life – was shown at Cannes in 1981 and taken up by several French critics. He has been clearly more influenced by European rather than Indian film-making and remains a fascinating if difficult talent, who is unfortunately received in India with little understanding. Shahani, who has worked with Robert Bresson, is a similar case, ploughing a lonely furrow within an art cinema dedicated so often to countering big-budget fantasyland with small-budget neo-realism. But *Maya Darpan* (1972), his non-narrative first feature, is still a considerable achievement.

Another highly original, if less difficult, director is G. Aravindan, one of the leading figures of Malayalam (South India) culture. A cartoonist, painter, musician and devotee of the theatre. Aravindan has a wonderful eye for detail and a richness of imagination unequal-

led in the South Indian cinema. Two films, in particular, have been recognized in the West: *Thampu* (1979, The Circus Tent), about the effect of a travelling circus on the life of a faraway village, and *Kummatty* (1980, *Bogeyman*), a superb children's story with a much wider appeal than merely to the young.

One of the Parallel Cinema's greatest achievements – artistically if not commercially – was M. S. Sathyu's *Garm Hava* (1974, *Hot Winds*), the only major film set against the

*Above far left: Anant Nag as the landlord with Shabana Azmi as the maid he exploits in* Ankur – The Seedling. *Above left:* Kondura – *a moral tale about a magic root which brings tragedy to superstitious peasants. Above: when a helpless man loses his wife to powerful landowners, mass violence erupts in* Night's End. *Below: Ismat Chugtai, Jennifer Kendal, Nafeesa Ali and Shashi Kapoor in* Possessed; *set during the mutiny of 1857, it traces the love of a young Indian for a British girl*

controversial political canvas following the 1947 Partition with Pakistan. About a middle-aged muslim trader in Agra who refuses to leave for Pakistan despite the urgings of his friends, it was at first banned for instigating communal dissension, though finally given an all-India award for its contribution to national integration.

Two other film-makers of note sprang up in the Seventies: Girish Karnad and B. V. Karanth, who have made movies both together and separately – with Karnad also pursuing a highly productive acting career, and Karanth doing much work for the theatre. Karanth's best film is almost certainly *Chomana Dudi* (1975, Choma's Drum) which has a fine performance from Vasudeva Rao as a harijan (untouchable) who dreams of owning land but whose hopes disintegrate as caste and class put up insurmountable barriers. Karnad's breakthrough was *Kaadu* (1973, The Forest) in which two warring villages are watched through the eyes of a child growing up. He also made *Ondanondu Kaladalli* (1978, Once Upon a Time), an Indian samurai film with enough social concern to remind many of the Japanese director Akira Kurosawa, to whom it was dedicated.

## The newest waves

The latest wave of Indian directors – many obviously influenced by Benegal – is making strenuous attempts to reach wider audiences than in the past, often by appealing to specifically regional susceptibilities. And although only a few movies can be named here, it is important to understand that dozens are made each year which reject the usual commercial inanities, or at least use them with more intelligence.

Three are fully worthy of mention. The first is Saeed Mirza, whose polemical *Albert Pinto ko Gussa Kyon Aata Hai* (1981, What Makes Albert Pinto Angry?) provided a decisive change of gear from his somewhat elliptical first feature, *Arvind Desai ki Ajeeb Dastaan* (1978, The Strange Tale of Arvind Desai). Buddhadeb Dasgupta made *Dooratwa* (1979, Distance)

*Above: Vasudeva Rao (left) as an untouchable in* Chomana Dudi *by B. V. Karanth. Below: Albert Pinto is a flashy young garage mechanic finding his way in an unfriendly society. Below right: Amina (Gita) and Shamshad (Jalal Agha) in M. S. Sathyu's* Hot Winds

about the emotional sterility of the Indian middle-class, and followed this with *Neem Annapurna* (1980, Bitter Morsel), describing the fatal lure of the big city for the hopeful petit bourgeois. And Govind Nihalani – whose impressive *Aakrosh* (1981, Cry of the Wounded) shared the main award at the 1981 Delhi Festival – showed how much he has developed as a film-maker after years as Benegal's cameraman. It is directors such as these who look set to alter the face of the Indian cinema, and they have made it impossible to ignore the fact that something special now exists.

DEREK MALCOLM

184

# ORIENTAL SPLENDOUR

**India, China and Hongkong have encompassed a variety of traditions in film-making, a rich panorama too little-known in the West**

India is the biggest film-producing country in the world – in 1980 about seven hundred and twenty films were released. Though outnumbered by films in the Tamil and Telugu languages of the South, many of these were still the traditional Bombay films – romantic musical melodramas made in the Hindi language (the traditionally dominant all-India language), and often described by serious critics as insipid, hidebound, hybrid, outlandish and escapist.

India has a long heritage of cinema. The first movies were shown in Bombay, the principal city of the West Coast, on July 7, 1896. Film production started in 1913, and early films often imitated Hollywood models. At the end of the silent era, the film pioneer Ardeshir Irani – inspired by Universal's *Show Boat* (1929) – produced and directed the first full-length talkie in Hindi, *Alam Ara* (1931, Beauty of the World). Audiences welcomed the changeover to sound, and new studios were set up in various parts of the country.

The growth of the studio system in India was similar to that in Hollywood. In 1929, V. Shantaram, S. Fatehlal, V. G. Damle, K. R. Dhauber and S. B. Kulkarni – five young film-makers of ambition and total dedication – formed Prabhat Film Company in Kolhapur, south of Bombay in the state of Maharashtra. In 1933 they were able to buy a sprawling estate on the outskirts of Poona, south-east of Bombay, and launch a regular studio with four stages and a number of outdoor locales, at which they made films mostly in the Marathi language. The high quality of the studio's resources was responsible for the visual richness and realistic sound in their films. The use of spoken dialogue, which sound made possible, enabled the Prabhat film-makers to examine the psychological and social sides of their themes. It also helped them to bring out the contemporary relevance of traditional literature about saints – Damle and Fatehlal's *Sant Tukaram* (1937, Saint Tukaram) is one of the highest achievements of the sound period, and won a prize at the Venice Film Festival.

Shantaram's first sound film *Ayodhyecha Raja* (1932, The King of Ayodhya) starred Durga Khote, a high-caste girl, making her debut. In the early silent period, no decent women appeared in films and most females were played by boys. In 1936 Shantaram made *Amar Jyoti* (Eternal Light) in Hindi – also shown at the Venice Film Festival. His other notable films were *Duniya Na Mane* (1937, The Unexpected), about the problem of a May-December marriage and the customs restricting the life of a widow, and *Admi* (1939, The Man), which challenged traditional attitudes about the prostitute's place in society.

Another prominent studio at the time was Bombay Talkies, founded by the husband-wife team of Himansu Rai and Devika Rani, who had learned about film production in England and Germany. One of their most respected social pictures was *Acchut Kanya* (1936, Untouchable Girl), about a girl from the lowest Hindu social group who falls in love

with a Brahmin upper-caste youth. Most of the Bombay Talkies films were concerned with social reform.

In Calcutta, West Bengal (in the eastern part of the country), the producer B. N. Sircar recruited Dhiren Ganguly and Debaki Bose in 1930 to direct films for his newly-founded New Theatres company. Bose showed his talents in *Chandidas* (1932), the story of a poet-saint of the sixteenth century. It included songs based on the work of Chandidas, and also used specially-written background music for the first time in Indian cinema. Next he made *Puran Bhagat* (1933, The Devotee) in Hindi, which brought New Theatres into a wider market than their previous Bengali features. In 1937 Bose's *Vidyapathi*, another film about a poet-saint, was released in both Bengali and Hindi versions. Also for New Theatres, P. C. Barua made *Devdas* (1935), attacking the arranged-marriage system in India; its quietly-performed songs, its realistic dialogue and its tragic ending were all new to Indian films.

From the late Thirties, as the war produced a boom economy, there was an influx of new independent producers who attracted the star actors as well as the top directors and technicians from the established studios by offering bigger money. The

*Above: in Mrinal Sen's* Akaler Sandhane *(1981,* In Search of Famine*), a contemporary film crew comes to a Bengali village to make a film about the wartime famine, a man-made disaster that was also the subject of Satyajit Ray's* Ashani Sanket *(1973,* Distant Thunder*). The villagers help them to re-create this tragedy from the past*

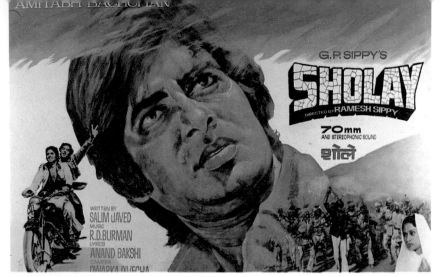

*Above:* Sholay *was a great commercial success in India. Its tale of two brave men defending a village against bandits clearly drew on the themes of popular Westerns. Right: a film from Sri Lanka, Lester James Peries'* Dese Nise *(1976, The Eyes) tells the story of an ugly man who marries a beautiful blind girl. Her sight is restored by a hermit healer, who attempts to seduce her; but she prefers her husband, though she laughs aloud when she first sees him*

stars soon realized their crowd-pulling capacity and recognized the value of independence from the strict discipline of the studio system. Prithviraj Kapoor (the father of Raj Kapoor and Shashi Kapoor and the grandfather of today's star Rishi Kapoor) had already shown the way by making a great success of freelancing. Following the example of their stars, some of the leading directors broke away. V. Shantaram left Prabhat in 1941 to start his own company, Rajkamal Kalamandir. Mehboob Khan left Sagar Movietone to work under his own banner.

In 1947 India was freed from British colonial rule. The British administration left behind a clumsy system of rationing raw film stock, severe censorship of films in order to control the nationalistic sentiments of patriotic Indians during the struggle for independence, and heavy taxes of up to sixty per cent on film-makers. Much of this heritage survived the departure of the British, as did the system of illicit payments to avoid taxation.

By now there was a fixed formula for the success of any film – one or two stars, six songs, three dance sequences, a bit of crying, a bit of laughter, extremes of emotion – but in 1948 S. S. Vasan's *Chandralekha*, made in the Tamil and Hindi languages and the biggest extravaganza of its time,

## Singing and dancing are essential ingredients in the entertainment mixture of popular Indian films

started a successful new trend with its chorus-dance sequences. In the same year Uday Shankar, brother of the musician Ravi Shankar, made a film on the classical dances, *Kalpana* (*Imagination*); but the film was not generally well-liked, perhaps because of the growing popularity of light music and westernized themes.

Mehboob Khan made many multi-star films such as *Aan* (1952, *Savage Princess*) and *Bharat Mata* (1957, *Mother India*), which were unprecedentedly successful at the box-office, combining sensitivity and commercial ingredients, and always including some reference to the oppressed classes of society. On the other hand, Raj Kapoor was involved in making entertainment films, such as *Awara* (1952, *The Vagabond*), that were basically musicals and showed the sublimity of love. Bimal Roy was meanwhile making offbeat films such as *Do Bigha Zamin* (1953, *Two Acres of Land*) and *Sujata* (1960) about subjects like poverty, money-lending and untouchability. K. A. Abbas scored international critical success with *Munna* (1954, *The Lost Child*), the story of an orphan.

In the South, where Madras was the main production centre, films were similar in theme and treatment to those of Bombay. Madras films were usually musicals, melodramas and stories about the problems of the joint family system. Though Tamil was the language of the region, many films in Telugu were also produced in Madras.

Films for the Sri Lanka (formerly Ceylon) market were shot in the studios of the South. Only the dialogue was written by the Sri Lankans in the Sinhalese language; the rest of the production was done entirely by the South Indians. Most of these films were carbon copies of typical Tamil and Hindi films. Then Lester James Peries made *Rekava* (1957, *The Line of Destiny*) on location, using a neo-realist style; this was recognized as the first truly national film to appear from Sri Lanka. His third film *Gamperaliya* (1963, The Changing Village) won the Grand Prix at the third International Film Festival of India, the first Sinhalese film to gain an international award.

In the East, Calcutta showed promise when Satyajit Ray made *Pather Panchali* (1955, *Song of the Little Road*) with meagre resources. Ray was the first Indian director to win world-wide fame and esteem. *Pather Panchali* took the critics completely by

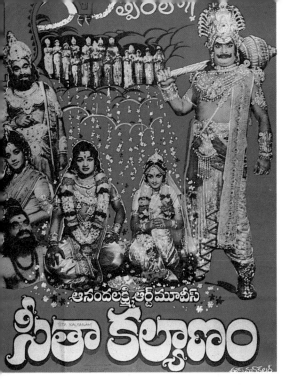

surprise and led them to much fresh thinking by its truthful portrayal of village life. The film refused to fall into any familiar pattern or set category – Ray had rebelled against the prevailing styles of Indian cinema.

The S. K. Patil Committee, which inquired into the working of the film industry in the early Fifties, suggested many reforms, including the setting up of a government-sponsored institution for financing films. The Committee clearly saw that many of the worst ills of Indian cinema arose from the lack of institutional finance on reasonable terms. The Film Finance Corporation (FFC), which came into operation in 1960, was supposed to make money available to the film industry as a whole, not solely to art cinema or popular movies. In its early years it pursued a cautious policy, supporting experienced directors such as Shantaram and Ray, but still managed to lose money. It then changed its policy to encourage low-budget productions. In 1969 the FFC announced the completion of six films made by aspiring directors, including Mrinal Sen's *Bhuvan Shome*. These were regarded as representing a 'New Wave' in Indian cinema. Subsequently several first features were supported. Though the FFC was able to balance its annual budgets in the Seventies, its

contribution was arguably marginal to the mainstream of Indian cinema.

For all that, the Seventies have seen the creation of some remarkable films, and the emergence of directors who have won formidable reputations the world over. Shyam Benegal, beginning with *Ankur* (1974, *Ankur – The Seedling*), was the first Indian since Ray to gain international recognition. After the Bombay-based 'New Wave', the major breakthrough was in the South with Pattabhi Rama Reddy's *Samskara* (1970, Funeral Rites), which was followed by *Vamsha Vriksha* (1971, The Family Tree), co-directed by Girish Karnad and B. V. Karanth, and then Karnad's *Kaadu* (1973, The Forest) and Karanth's *Chomana Dudi* (1975, Choma's Drum). In Bombay too, the 'New Wave' continued as Saeed Mirza developed into one of India's most promising directors.

The commercial cinema had its own ups and downs. The producer G. P. Sippy's *Sholay* (1976, Embers) has been the biggest blockbuster in the history of Indian cinema. An action-packed film, a mixture of the thrills of the Western with Indian music and emotions, the film started a new trend, the making of colossally-budgeted films. But the success of *Sholay* could not be repeated. In Bombay the film industry was caught in a vicious financial circle from which it was unable to extricate itself on its own, while the government swallowed as much as forty to fifty per cent of box-office income. The only hope for a better cinema lay in the increased sponsoring of production by the various states of India in their own regional languages.

RAKESH MATHUR

*Left: a South Indian film made in the Telugu language,* Sita Kalyanam *(1976, Sita's Wedding) was based on the* Ramayana, *a classical epic of Indian mythology. Praised for its authenticity, the film depicts the marriage of Rama, incarnation of the god Vishnu, and Sita, adopted daughter of King Janaka. Above: a production shot from Girish Karnad's* Ondanondu Kaladalli *(1978, Once Upon a Time), which concerns two warring brothers in medieval India, each of whom hires a mercenary general; but the mercenaries eventually join forces against their squabbling masters, turning the fight into a struggle between classes. Bottom left: Li Shizhen was a real-life 16th-century Chinese pharmacologist whose ambition in life was to revise the standard text on herbal medicine, a task he accomplished despite great difficulties; but his great work in 52 volumes was not published until three years after his death*

Although film was introduced into China in 1896 and indigenous production started six years later, it was not until the Mingxing Company was founded in 1922 that Chinese cinema began to establish a firm base and an identity. Mingxing's greatest success was the martial-arts series *Huoshao honglian si* (1928–31, The Burning of the Red Lotus Monastery). Several episodes were banned by a government fearful of social unrest. Most companies had fallen into bankruptcy and China had become one of the world's biggest markets for American films. To counter the industry's escapism, the Communist Party established a base within Mingxing in 1932. The writer Xia Yen joined the studio, bringing with him a group of young radical talents from the theatre. The studio then produced more popular films: comedies and dramas modelled on Hollywood formulas but subverted by sharp social realism. The audience responded to seeing itself on screen in a realistic context for the first time. The financial success of these films encouraged other studios to experiment and this first flowering of a Chinese cinema established stars and directors who

remained central to its development.

These advances ended abruptly with the Japanese bombing of Shanghai in 1937; the left-wingers dispersed to the countryside and the studios fell to the Japanese. The film-makers re-converged on Shanghai in 1946 and formed the Kunlun Film Company. For three years, as civil war raged, this studio produced the most outspoken films China had ever seen. After *Yijiang chunshui xiang dong liu* (1947, *The Spring River Flows East*) enjoyed massive critical and box-office success for its attack on opportunism and decadent luxury, censorship became even tighter and Kunlun had to toe the line. In 1948 it started to shoot *Wuya yu maque* (1949, *Crows and Sparrows*), a scathing picture of Shanghai slum life; but the film was so critical of the ruling Kuomintang, the Chinese nationalist party, that production was halted by force, and the film was completed only after the Communist victory. All film-making was soon brought under government control. The veterans of the Thirties were put in charge and film was encouraged by the government. The purpose of film now was to educate the masses in the need for and structure of the new society, and the cinema became subject to the vagaries of political policy. A brief freedom was enjoyed in 1956–57 during Mao's 100 Flowers Campaign and films like *Li Shizhen* (1956) treated unusual subjects – in this case, the life of a pharmacologist – with delicacy and grace. Despite the ensuing anti-rightist purge, the film industry recovered and by 1964 was producing works of real sophistication. Then the Cultural Revolution swept China in 1966 and all film production was halted for over four years.

The Cultural Revolution produced 'model' operas and ballets, full of static revolutionary tableaux, and a few features that tried, within strict limitations, to raise political debates. But almost all of the talents who had created a once-huge industry were imprisoned or sent to hard labour in the country. Only after the overthrow of the Gang of Four in the late Seventies could the film industry begin to re-establish itself.

The task is immense: the survivors of the Thirties are too old to re-create a truly Chinese cinema and the young have been for so long denied access to their own film history that everything must be learned anew. Recent films betray a level of naivety. However, there is no doubt that, in time, China will produce works as interesting and as accomplished as the films of its rich past.          SCOTT MEEK

It was the flood of martial-arts films into western markets in 1972–73 that brought the Hongkong film industry to the notice of the West in a way that sporadic screenings of films from Hongkong at festivals had been unable to.

In general, the history of film-making in Hongkong has been intimately bound up with that of China. Genres structured around classical literary sources, stories from myth and folklore or from cycles of tales of knight-errantry, low-life comedies, melodramas, subjects drawn from opera, drama and history are common to both from silent days. The key events in China's history – the marathon struggle that began in the late Twenties between the nationalist ruling party, the Kuomintang, and the Communist Party, the long and bitter war with Japan, the Communist victory in 1949 and the subsequent changes in political line – were equally decisive in that of the colony island. For one thing, the disruption of China's film industry and cultural production resulted, from the Twenties onwards, in an influx of intellectuals, performers and writers from both film and theatre into the colony in successive waves.

The first Hongkong production company was established in 1921. Ten years later, some five major companies were in operation, surrounded by a host of smaller ones. But Hongkong as a producer remained under the shadow of Shanghai – the Hollywood of the East – until that city was occupied

*Top, left to right: in* Shiwu guan *(1956, Fifteen Strings of Cash)* and Wutai jiemei *(1964, Two Stage Sisters), Chinese film-makers enjoyed unusual but quite brief freedom of artistic style;* The Secret *starred Chang Ai-chia*

by the Japanese in 1937.

The situation is complicated by the existence of two Hongkong cinemas. The arrival of sound in the late Thirties led to the development of a (northern Chinese) Mandarin-language cinema alongside the local Cantonese-dialect one. Mandarin cinema found its market – until 1954 – on the mainland and then increasingly in South-east Asia, eclipsing Cantonese cinema in the mid-Sixties. But it was within Cantonese cinema that Hongkong's first important and popular series of martial-arts films was produced.

During the Sino-Japanese War, Tianyi, one of Shanghai's major studios, moved to Hongkong. Its studio manager was one of the Shaw brothers, Runde Shaw. The company began turning out popular Cantonese genre films before switching to Mandarin around 1950 to enable it to service the chain of Shaw theatres in South-east Asia. Its main rival during the late Fifties and early Sixties was an offshoot of the Singapore-based Cathay Organization, Motion Picture & General Investment (MP & GI). By 1965, Shaws had comfortably overtaken MP & GI, after emerging as Shaw Brothers, a new

---

## The slap of fist and foot, the clang of steel resounded through Hongkong's martial-arts movies and made the world take notice as they became a popular cult

---

company headed by Run Run Shaw, in 1957. They moved from their small Kowloon studio to Clearwater Bay, completing their legendary Movietown studio in 1961. Their aim seems to have been to maintain a large output, initially 50 films a year (dropping to something like half that in the Seventies) while establishing superior Shanghai-style production values.

Shaws made their push at exactly the right moment. By the early Sixties, Hongkong had recovered from the wartime occupation and the cinema was a boom industry. By the mid-Sixties, production on the mainland virtually ceased. Shaw Brothers turned out the romances and musicals that MP & GI had made a success of, and also began to make something of a speciality of the historical drama, a genre that Mandarin cinema, with its larger market and therefore larger budgets, could mount with some authenticity. Films were made in colour and then on widescreen. A number of important directors worked for Shaws during this period including Hu Chin-ch'üan (King Hu) and Chang Cheh, both of whose martial-arts films have been screened in the West.

It was the sensuous sophistication of the films of Li Han-hsiang that provided Shaws with the money-spinners that helped seal their reputation. A graduate of the Peking Art Institute, Li was attracted to Hongkong in 1948, aware of the possibilities in Hongkong's fumbling attempts to rival mainland production, and signed on as a contract director at Shaws in 1955. He turned gradually from small-scale socially-orientated themes to more classic subjects, which he lent increasingly epic and lavish dimensions. His major box-office success was Liang Shan-po yü Chu Ying-t'ai (1963, The Love Eterne), an opera adapted for the screen and co-directed with King Hu, who three years later was to revivify the martial-arts film with his Ta tsui hsia (1966, Come Drink With Me), also for Shaws.

The apogee of the historical drama was reached during Li's work for his own company in Taiwan after leaving Shaws in 1963. Taiwan's situation as a

film production centre has been very much a direct function of its political situation, with a very stringent code of production in operation, and equally stringent censorship. Production has been dominated by the output of the government-owned Central Film Studio. Escapist contemporary melodrama has been the most notable genre. But Taiwan has also operated as something of an offshoot of Hongkong, as in Li's case. Li returned to Shaws in 1971, but not before such films as Hsi Shih (1967, Hsi Shih: Beauty of Beauties) and the remarkable Ti Ying (1970, The Girl Who Saved Her Father), with their quite extraordinarily expressive use of landscape and performers, had revealed the limitations inherent in the studio system as it operated in Hongkong.

Although the martial-arts film dominated production from about 1966 for the next ten years, no list of key films of the Seventies could escape including half a dozen by Li Han-hsiang. Undeniably the most ambitious films of the decade were those comprising his two-part epic, Ch'ing-kuo ch'ing-ch'eng (1975, The Empress Dowager) and Ying-t'ai ch'i hsüeh (1976, The Last Tempest). The two films examine the declining years of the Ch'ing dynasty and the rise of the Reform Movement; quite hypnotically powerful and enormously resonant, they draw beautifully modulated performances from a number of Shaws' key actors. Other central works, if in a more modest vein, are the two-part satire on power and corruption consisting of Ta chün-fa (1972, The Warlord) and Ch'ou-wen (1974, Scandal), and a number of compendia of erotic fables such as Ch'in p'ing shuang yen (1974, Golden Lotus), a seductive and entertaining version of the Chinese erotic novel, and Feng hua hsüeh yüeh (1977, Moods of Love).

Distinctive balletic interpretations of the martial-arts film appeared in the work of King Hu, including Hsia nü (1969, A Touch of Zen), Ying-ch'un-ko-chih feng-po (1973, The Fate of Lee Khan) and Chung-lieh t'u (1974, The Valiant Ones), or the superlative philosophical swordplay thrillers directed by Ch'u Yüan at Shaws.

The martial-arts films that are best known internationally star the charismatic Bruce Lee, who died in 1973. However, it was a series of three comedies that pointed to the development of a new and distinctive cinema for Hongkong. Hsü Kuan-wen (Michael Hui), a television personality and an ex-Shaw Brothers actor-turned-director, gave a fresh twist to the low-life Cantonese comedy in Kuei ma shuang hsing (1974, Games Gamblers Play), T'ien-ts'ai yü Pai-ch'ih (1976, The Last Message) and Pan-chin pa-liang (1977, The Private Eyes), which centred humorously on the problems of survival in contemporary Hongkong.

Hui, with his studio experience, forms a bridge between the Hongkong cinema's veterans with their mainland backgrounds and a group of new film-makers, many of whom have both international film-school and television experience. These younger film-makers found that the stringent economic climate during the mid-Seventies and the concomitant unadventurousness on the part of the major studios blocked any hope of entry into the industry. Directors such as Allen Fong, with Yüan-chou-tsai-chih ko (1977, Song of Yuen Chau-chai), and Hsü An-hua (Ann Hui), with Feng chieh (1979, The Secret), attempted films that spoke with some urgency to the situation of life in Hongkong while acknowledging both that island's legacy of Chinese culture and the lively grassroots industry where drug and embezzlement scandals become instant thrillers. As China opens up during the Eighties, the situation will again undoubtedly change.

VERINA GLAESSNER

*(Sylvia Chang) as a girl trying to solve a murder case. Above:* The Private Eyes *is a comic view of a Hongkong private-detective agency. Below:* The Fate of Lee Khan *tells of the Chinese struggle against Mongol invaders*

# Fighting for their lives

# Martial-arts movies

**In the cinema of Hongkong and Taiwan the martial-arts film has been both a crown and a millstone. It has catapulted this corner of the Far East to worldwide attention – though the very success of the genre with foreign audiences has prevented wider appreciation of what these countries have to offer. However, there is no denying the contribution this uniquely Chinese film form has made – and continues to make – to international cinema**

The West was late to catch on to the martial-arts film (in Chinese *wu-hsia p'ien* – literally 'martial chivalry film'), but when it did, it did so with a vengeance. After trying to attract western distributors since the mid-Sixties, Shao Yi-fu (Run-run Shaw) of the Shaw Brothers distribution company finally succeeded in selling the director Cheng Ch'ang-ho's period action drama *T'ien-hsia ti-yi ch'üan* (1972, *King Boxer*) to Warner Brothers. It had a sudden and amazing box-office impact, and Golden Harvest, Shaw Brothers' main rival, soon responded with *Ching-wu men* (1972, *Fist of Fury*), directed by Lo Wei and starring Bruce Lee, who was immediately established as the first Oriental superstar. The term 'Kung Fu', literally meaning 'skill' or 'technique', began to enter the filmgoer's vocabulary, and the floodgates opened. The boom reached its climax in 1974 with the release of the rest of the Lee films, but declined in 1976 in a wave of reissues and double-bills. Yet the memory lingers on – the days of Lee-fever may be over but Hongkong is no longer a blank space on the film-going map.

## Kicking off
In Hongkong it has been a different story. The martial-arts genre made its first impression back in mainland China in the late Twenties

and early Thirties with the *Huoshao honglian si* (The Burning of the Red Lotus Monastery), a series of stylized, stage-influenced works which finally fell victim to their own lack of imagination. It was the prolific *Huang Fei-hung* series, begun in Hongkong in 1949, which finally set the genre rolling – these black-and-white Cantonese quickies, about a famous martial-artist-cum-doctor at the turn of the century, celebrated communal Cantonese values within a more realistic staging of martial-arts skills. The character has since appeared in some eighty films and thirteen television episodes, and has effectively set the pattern for the future – with clearly defined moral opposites, a wealth of authentic detail in martial-arts styles and highly characterized protagonists.

When the Cantonese industry petered out in the early Sixties, there was a lull in martial-arts productions as Mandarin film-making asserted itself as the cinematic *lingua franca*. The success of *Hao-hsia chien ch'ou* (1964, *Tiger Boy*), directed by Chang Ch'eh, helped to pave the way for the genre's wholesale revival, confirmed a couple of years later by the runaway success of *Ta tsui hsia* (1966, *Come Drink with Me*) and *Lung-men k'o-chan* (1967, *Dragon Gate Inn*), both directed by Hu Chin-ch'üan (King Hu), and Chang Ch'eh's *Tu-pi tao*

(1967, *The One-Armed Swordsman*). These were 'new style' martial-arts films, celebrating general Chinese rather than specific Cantonese values and traditions.

## Farewell to arms
In 1970 the genre went through the first of its many subsequent transformations. *Lung-hu tou* (The Chinese Boxer), directed by Wang Yü, star of *Tiger Boy*, featured unarmed fighting techniques with an almost obsessive interest in their perfection and innate superiority. The arrival of Bruce Lee in *T'ang-shan ta hsiung* (1971, *The Big Boss*) set the pattern for what came to be known as Kung Fu films, and as worldwide attention focused on Hongkong and Taiwan a flood of imitations followed, urged on from mid-1973 by the industries' desperate search for a superstar to replace Lee after his death. Often less elaborately staged, and set in Republican times rather than the

remote past, the Kung Fu films were cheaper to produce and avoided the more decorative fantastic style pioneered by Hu and Chang.

Flamboyance returned to the genre in the mid-Seventies when Shaw Brothers embarked on a series of adaptations of the popular swordplay novels of Taiwanese writer Ku Lung. Shaws director Ch'u Yüan brought Ku's novels to the screen in an increasingly baroque series of adaptations consisting of some twenty films, beginning with *Liu-hsing, hu-tieh, chien* (1976, *Killer Clans*).

By this time the genre was rapidly diversifying, to keep pace with both local television and the capricious tastes of the audience. At the same time as the works of Ku Lung and Hongkong writer Chin Yung were being plundered for material, another Shaw Brothers director, ex-martial arts choreographer Liu

Chia-liang, was already steering things in a different direction. With *Shen ta* (1975, *The Spiritual Boxer*) and *Hung Hsi-kuan* (1977, *Executioners from Shaolin*), Liu blended traditional elements of Mandarin martial-arts cinema – both swordplay and unarmed combat – with a Cantonese taste for the irreverent and opportunistic. The definitive move in the demystification of the Mandarin martial-arts films came with director Yüan Ho-p'ing's *She-hsing tiao shou* (1978, *Snake in the Eagle's Shadow*) and *Tsui ch'üan* (1978, *Drunk Monkey in the Tiger's Eyes*), both films which capitalized on the cheeky skills of Ch'eng Lung (Jackie Chan). At last, after five years, Hongkong cinema had produced in Chan another superstar worthy of the mantle of Bruce Lee, and it was again Golden Harvest that was to promote him internationally, first in *Shih-ti ch'u-ma* (1980, *The Young Master*) and then in *The Big Brawl* (1980).

## Slow, slow, kick, kick, slow

In the rampantly plagiaristic world of Hongkong and Taiwan cinema, originality is the preserve of very few, but two directors of martial-arts films who can truly be called original are King Hu and Chang Ch'eh, both of whom are known internationally – the former on the festival circuit, the latter for more than half-a-dozen dubbed productions released abroad during the boom in martial-arts films. Hu is rare in Chinese cinema in that he is a painstakingly slow director for whom the finest details of decoration and authenticity are paramount. His works attempt to tap the mystical currents in Chinese culture, and the flurries of action which punctuate his films merely give overt expression to these hidden realms. Perhaps his finest and most fluid work is *Ying-ch'un-ko-chih feng-po* (1973, *The Fate of Lee Khan*), a life-and-death game played out

with chess-like ritual in a remote Shenhsi inn. With the later *Shan-chung ch'uan-ch'i* (1979, *Legend of the Mountain*), a film on an epic three-hour scale, Hu delved again into the mystic qualities of Taoist poetic literature, further refining the same qualities found in his earlier film *Hsia nü* (1969, *A Touch of Zen*).

## Death or glory boys
Chang Ch'eh, renowned for promoting some of the greatest personalities of martial arts films, inhabits a different world. His works of the mid-to-late Sixties are set in a ruthless universe in which revenge and self-annihilation offer the only reason for existence. In *Chin yen-tzu* (1968, *The Girl with the Thunderbolt Kick*) self-centred superheroes vie for glory, climaxing in the dying cry of mutilated Silver Roc (Wang Yu): 'As always, I'm the master swordsman'.

*Above: in* Executioners from Shaolin, *Hung (Ch'en Kuan-t'ai) battles his way up the temple steps in an attempt to take revenge on the evil hermit who had killed the chief priest. Below: Jackie Chan in* The Big Brawl

From the early Seventies onwards, Chang started to explore the ethics of unarmed-combat techniques in such films as *Shao-lin tzu-ti* (1974, *The Dragon's Teeth*), one of many to feature the mythic hero Fang Shih-yü. Most of his films rely almost completely on an obsessive interest in training and technique, the simple revenge plots becoming merely a peg on which rival fighting styles are hung and analysed.

If all these varying sub-genres have anything in common, it is a respect for the pyramidal structure of the traditional martial-arts film in which the heroes overcome the limitations of the body to meet their final apotheosis face to face with their equal. Even the Cantonese martial-arts films of the late Seventies respect this code beneath their more relaxed, opportunistic philosophy. It is a structure found also in the Hollywood Western and particularly the Italian 'spaghetti' Western. The ramifications, however, are, even at their most 'pulp' level, recognizably Chinese.

## Big brawlers
Yet, in the final instance, the Chinese martial-arts film is a cinema of personalities. It is the actor's presence, his screen persona, by which the genre is illuminated. To experience the coiled-spring, animalistic intensity of Bruce Lee's performances is to glimpse the vehemence of his personal anguish over East-West relations – Lee was canonized by Chinese audiences as much for his naked nationalism as for his manifestly genuine skills. The Taiwan-trained Mao Ying (Angela Mao) exhibits an almost Lee-like spunkiness and austerity in director Huang Feng's classic *Ho-ch'i tao* (1972, *Hap-Ki Do*). In *T'ieh wa* (1973, *The Kung Fu Girl*) and *Hu pien tzu* (1974, *Whiplash!*) actress-dancer Cheng P'ei-p'ei exhibits an elegance and supple grace of almost icy sensuality. In Ti Lung there is a Clint Eastwood-like charisma, and in Wang Yü, hacking his way through *The Girl with the Thunderbolt Kick* or *Chan-shen t'an* (1973, *Beach of the War Gods*), a violently obsessive masochism. It is such performances that linger in the mind long after the sound of the final swordthrust has faded from the soundtrack.          DEREK ELLEY

**Bruce Lee was master of the martial-arts movies. He was fiery and yet cool – controlled but uncontrollable. Already a star in his homeland, his death before the release of many of his films in the West helped to make him into a legendary figure**

There is a massive double irony in the short but spectacular career of Bruce Lee. For overseas Chinese he was a strident symbol of their often compromised identity – but one who never conquered Hollywood on his own terms. For westerners, Lee's films provided something quite new – a simple, unabashed, chauvinistic heroism and an electric physical presence. Yet a few months after he stormed western markets he died in Hongkong, of acute cerebral oedema, on July 20, 1973, at the age of 32.

Bruce Lee was born in San Francisco, in the Year of the Dragon, on November 27, 1940, the fourth child of touring Cantonese opera star Li Hai-chüan and his Eurasian wife Grace. His original name, and the one which appears on his gravestone, was Li Chen-fan (Lei Tsen-fan in Cantonese). His parents returned to Hong-kong in 1944 and soon afterwards Lee began a career as a child actor in the busy Cantonese industry, appearing in numerous films under the name Li Hsiao-lung (Lei Siu-lung in Can-tonese – 'little Dragon Lee'). Despite being raised in a comfortable neighbourhood, Lee had always shown a liking for the tougher side of Hongkong life: his childhood involved a long succession of different schools and street-gang brawls. Later, he was to confess, 'If I hadn't become a star, I would probably have ended up a gangster.'

At the age of 18 Lee returned to San Francisco, and shortly afterwards moved to Seattle, studying by day and working as a

*Left: Bruce Lee in* Enter the Dragon. *Below: as Chen Chen in* Fist of Fury, *Lee devastates members of a rival Japanese karate school*

waiter by night. In his spare time he continued to practise his beloved martial arts and after he enrolled at Washington University as a philo-sophy student, he began teaching friends and enthusiasts. In 1964 he married and moved to California, where he opened his second martial-arts school. Appearances at public tournaments led to his being cast as the oriental sidekick Kato in the television series *The Green Hornet* (1966–67), which, ironically, proved enormously successful in the Far East. So much so that Lee went on a promotional tour and, while in Hongkong, was approached by producer Raymond Chow.

Lee, convinced that Hollywood stardom was just around the corner, turned Chow down. Back in America, bit-parts in television fol-lowed, then a brief but dynamic role in *Mar-lowe* (1969) opposite James Garner, and then a supporting role in the pilot for a television series entitled *Longstreet* (1971–72). Despite Lee's many friends in the film business – most of them pupils at his school – success remained elusive. Finally, Raymond Chow contacted him again, and within a couple of days Lee decided to return to Hongkong to star in *T'ang-shan ta-hsiung* (1971, *The Big Boss*).

Directed by Lo Wei, *The Big Boss* unexpec-tedly broke numerous box-office records in the Far East. Lee had returned to Hollywood for more *Longstreet* episodes and only reluctantly agreed to return to Hongkong to make a follow-up – *Ching-wu men* (1972, *Fist of Fury*). Also directed by Lo Wei, this was an even greater success, and by the spring of 1972 Lee was Hongkong cinema's undisputed super-star. Chow and Lee co-produced their next

blockbuster, *Meng lung kuo chiang* (1972, *The Way of the Dragon*), and by this time the martial-arts boom had begun – Hollywood came to Lee.

Lee and Chow had already started shooting *Szu-wan yu-hsi* (1978, *Bruce Lee's Game of Death*), but suspended production at the pros-pect of a Hollywood deal, the result of which was the English-language *Enter the Dragon* (1973). On its release in late 1973, Lee was already ensconced in modern-day Chinese myth; yet the West's thirst for him and his art was only just beginning . . .     DEREK ELLEY

**Filmography**
**1941** Chin-men nü/Golden Gate Girl/Tears San Francisco (extra). **'46** Fu-kuei fu-yün/The Beginning of a Boy/The Birth of Mankind/The Transience of Riches. **'48** My Son A-Chan. **'50** Hsi-lu Hsiang/The Kid/Kid Cheung. **'51** Jen-chih ch'u/Infancy. **'53** Tz'u-mu lei/A Mother's Tears; Fu-chih kuo/Blame It on Father; Ch'ien-wan jen-chia/Countless Families; Wei-luo ch'un-hsiao/In the Face of Demolition. **'55** Ku-hsing hsüeh-lei/An Orphan's Tragedy; Erh-nü chai/We Owe It to Our Children; Ku-erh hsing/Orphan's Song. **'56** Cha-tien na-fu/The Wise Guys Who Fool Around; Tsao chih tang ch'u wo wu chia/Too Late for Divorce. **'57** Lei-yü/Thunderstorm/Thunder and Rain. **'58** The Orphan Ah-Sam. **'61** Jen-hai ku-hung/A Goose Alone in the World. **'69** Marlowe (USA). **'71** T'ang-shan ta-hsiung/The Big Boss (also GB title) (USA: Fists of Fury). **'72** Ching-wu men/Fist of Fury (also GB title) (USA: The Chinese Connec-tion); Meng lung kuo chiang/Way of the Dragon (also GB title) ( +dir; +sc; +martial arts dir) (USA: Return of the Dragon). **'73** Ch'i-lin chang/The Unicorn Fist (guest); Lung-cheng-hu tou/Enter the Dragon (USA-HK). **'75** Le Retour du Dragon (French compilation of *eps* from USA TV series; The Green Hornet, 1966–67). **'78** Szu-wan yu-hsi/Game of Death (GB: Bruce Lee's Game of Death); Circle of Iron (co-sc. only) (USA) (GB: The Silent Flute).
*No reliable listings exist for Lee's films as child actor.*

SHASHI

Far left: the glamorous dancer and star Hema Malini in Mrig Trishna (1975, Mirage), directed by R. N. Shukla. Left: Prayag Raaj's Pap aur Punya (1974, Sin and Virtue), which featured Shashi Kapoor in a story about brothers on different sides of the law. Above: I. F. Pran and top male star Amitabh Bacchan in the smuggling intrigue of Don (1978)

## Mythical roots

In the early days of the Indian silent cinema, audiences went to see their favourite gods and goddesses on the screen, for movies were adaptations of the mythological stories from the epic texts of the *Mahabharata* and the *Ramayana*. As a result, Indian film did not develop the codes and conventions that are peculiar to cinema, but was closely allied to the conventions of literature, and also to theatre, music and dance. Since the texts were very familiar, the plots contained no surprises. Audiences were only interested in how each story was going to be depicted, so film-makers concentrated on creating spectacular extravaganzas with lavish costume and scenery. This was a significant shift from classical Indian drama, which used no scenery and depended exclusively on descriptive poetry to inform the spectator about the action, as well as incorporating music and dancing into the narrative structure to create atmosphere. Owing to the lack of emphasis on dramatic construction and the absence of a linear narrative, the film characters did not have to develop psychological complexities. From the outset these characters were firmly fixed with their respective moral attributes, representing the forces of either 'good' or 'evil' – the eternal preoccupation of the gods. This was how the Indian cinema arrived at its character stereotypes, which are conveyed through well-established codifications of dress, gesture, colour and so on, and which recur in every story.

Film narrative is usually propelled by strict dramatic 'rules'. In India it proceeds by emphatic shifts of tone – each scene or sequence having a specific mood or atmosphere. This system has evolved from the honoured traditions of Sanskrit – the classical language and literature of the Hindu inhabitants of India – where representational practices are strictly coded in terms of the nine *rasas*, or moods (love, anger, villainy, sacrifice, devotion and so on). Each *rasa* is conveyed through specific expressive gestures described by Philippe Parrain, in his book *Regards sur le Cinéma Indien* (Editions du Cerf, 1969), as various:

'. . . facial expressions (themselves broken into distinct positions and movements of the head, the eyes, the eyebrows, the eyelids, the nose, mouth) . . . gestures, rhythms, costume, colour, tutelary divinity and so on. The totality constituting a complete vocabulary that can be articulated in subtle and ingenious ways. . . . Films are built on a series of catalogued feelings which are established as such without any ambiguity. Scenes can be easily be broken down into a series of expressions which are meant to represent the emotions successfully experienced by the protagonist . . . which is difficult to square with an overall continuity of the action.'

Audiences unaware of these codes cannot distinguish ineptitude from consummate artistry and tend to interpret them through western notions of ham acting and histrionics.

As the plots of the films made in India today come directly from Hollywood rather than from Sanskrit drama, they have a peculiar mix of two distinct conventions, which inflect each other and produce something entirely original. This can be clearly seen in films like Ravi Chopra's *The Burning Train* (1980), a combination of the American films *Silver Streak* (1976) and *The Cassandra Crossing* (1977), or Ramesh Sippy's blockbusting success *Sholay* (1976, Embers), which draws on *The Magnificent Seven* (1960), *C'Era una Volta il West* (1968, *Once Upon a Time in the West*) and *Butch Cassidy and the Sundance Kid* (1969). The pacing of *Sholay* is completely baffling to anyone not used to Indian cinematic conventions. The tense and exciting sequence in which the two heroes outwit their opponent is followed by a song routine involving them in some horseplay with the heroine – a scene totally unrelated to the rest of the action. Yet the combination of tightly-knit drama (modelled on the Western) and unmotivated 'spectacle' which breaks up the narrative and makes the film seem so endless for a western viewer, is one of the reasons why *Sholay* has been incredibly successful, running in one cinema in Bombay since 1975.

## Indian love songs

The fusion of songs, instrumental music and dancing has existed in Indian drama since the time of the poet Kalidasa in the fourth century, and this unity is preserved in the cinema today. In fact, the cinema popularizes all national music and draws upon Indian classical and folk, as well as western pop music, to create a special type of 'film music'. Music directors are as important as film directors, and the films are sold on the popularity of the songs, which sometimes supersedes the appeal of the stars, as was the case with *Qurbani* (1980, A

Sacrifice).

Within the fragmented structure of the Indian film, certain elements take precedence – song picturization, for instance. The content of many of India's ancient miniature paintings shows an attempt to pictorialize and reflect classical music; the music itself is organized around *ragas*, which refer to 'states of mind' and are appropriate to certain times of day. This tradition has continued into the popular music of films and has progressed and evolved from clichéd images – for example, a man and a woman gazing into each other's eyes by moonlit pools filled with lotus leaves, denoting love. Most Indian lyrics have taken on new pictorial meanings, as evidenced by Raj Kapoor's epic *Sangam* (1964, Meeting) which backs its music with scenes of Rome, London and Paris. The 'transition' from song to story in the rest of the film is very smoothly achieved, as the lyrics often reflect aspects of the narrative. This is also true of *Bharat Mata* (1957, *Mother India*), where the peasants singing in the fields elaborate on the action.

## A cut above Hollywood

The sophistication of editing in Indian film, which has developed through the cutting of lyrics and dance movements in unison, is far more advanced than in American musicals such as *Saturday Night Fever* (1977) and *Grease* (1978), simply because the technique is in constant use. Vijay Anand's films, including *Guide* (1965) and *Ram Balram* (1980), are fine demonstrations of this.

Dancing was introduced into Indian film at the same time as sound, without the slightest regard to the purity of styles, although drawing upon the four major types of classical dancing: Bharat Natyam, Kathak, Kathakali and Manipuri. Because most of these 'pure' dance styles are exclusive to their dramatic conventions and cannot be used to illustrate other forms of recital, each screen actor and actress was left to create his or her own style, basing it on the school he or she knew best. As a result a new school of dance emerged, an arbitary mixture of all the other styles – which initially horrified the purists. In fact, when the top female star Hema Malini first came to Bombay from the Madras studio, she was bombarded with angry fan letters for attempting to adapt the traditional Bharat Natyam gestures to suit the Bombay film medium. However, Faubion Bowers, a great admirer of

Indian dance, has observed that the cinema variety will eventually become India's fifth major school of dancing.

Four main genres can be distinguished in Indian cinema, although they often merge into each other. The first three are the spectacle epic, usually continuing the tradition of the mythological stories; the family melodrama; and the crime thriller modelled on the American Western. These latter two are often combined with a popular plot involving two brothers, one good (generally a policeman) and the other living on the margins of the law; having been parted at birth, due to some freak of fate, the brothers are eventually reunited in the presence of the mother who instinctively recognizes her lost sons. The various combinations of this plot have produced outstanding successes such as *Amar Akbar Anthony* (1977), where three brothers unaware of their kinship are involved in donating blood to a patient, who of course turns out to be their mother. The fourth genre is the reformative social-problem drama, which has become very reactionary with its hollow rhetoric and glorification of the hero. An example of this is Yash Chopra's box-office flop *Kaala Patthar* (1979, Black Stone), supposedly based on the Chasmeena mine disaster.

## All-in entertainment

The demographic changes in India – especially the continuous influx from the rural areas to the cities – creates more than just social and economic problems. The new city-dwellers find themselves cut off from the traditional cultural life of the village, which provides folk drama, dance, fairground entertainers and storytellers. Thus a visit to the cinema has to give them what film critic and director K. A. Abbas calls 'omnibus entertainment', which would normally have gone on through the night in the village: the average two-and-a-half to three-hour length of the Indian movie is comparatively modest.

An unusual factor of the Indian film industry is that exhibition rather than production is the most powerful element. The lack of cinemas in rural areas, the over-production of

*Right:* Awara (1952, The Vagabond) *was directed by and starred Raj Kapoor. Below right: poster for Vijay Anand's* Ram Balram. *Below left: the film actor Saeed Jaffrey in the BBC TV series* Gangsters (1976)

films, and the abundance of independent financiers and producers who speculate on potential profits enable exhibitors to put immense pressure on the producers, who have to adhere to proven box-office formulas. The main ingredient for success is the current favourite superstar, inevitably a man since the action is totally organized around the male actors, with the actresses providing embellishment and erotic spectacle. The saleable male star charges anything between £60,000 to £120,000 and the top male star Amitabh Bacchan can demand up to £133,000. The female star charges between £18,000 to £50,000, with the leading actress Hema Malini getting a maximum of £60,600. The escalating costs of film production are attributed to the high prices charged by the stars, who consider they deserve a substantial amount of the takings because the whole basis of a picture is constructed around selling their personas.

Bacchan was a new phenomenon as a superstar because his lanky body and dark complexion did not conform to the tradition of good looks set by North Indian standards – the fair skin, light eyes and slightly plump physique of the inimitable Kapoor family, the all-

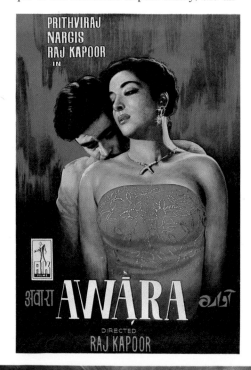

time favourite Dilip Kumar and Rajesh Khanna. It suggests perhaps that India, in a post-colonial age, is looking for less western models of beauty.

The inaccessibility of Indian genres and aesthetic conventions to western audiences is a luxury the Indian film enjoys because the native industry has always managed to retain a degree of autonomy from the USA. Also, as India never entered into any vigorous capitalist trading with Japan or the western world, the rapid process of modernization, which is a result of such competition, did not occur. There is a degree of imitation, if not outright plagiarising of Hollywood, yet an uncompromising difference exists between Indian and American film. India's home market is also so large that the industry does not have to cater to foreign markets, though Indian exports are high (in 1977 Indian films were exported to 77 countries). Since the rural areas lack cinemas, there is also massive room for expansion.

BEHROZE GANDHY

*This article is based upon material from the BFI dossier* Indian Cinema, *edited by Paul Willemen and Behroze Gandhy*

*Right: Dharmendra, one of India's 'virile' male leads, with Sharmila Tagore in* Chupke Chupke *(1975, Quietly Quietly). The actress was first cast by Satyajit Ray as the beautiful and tragic heroine of* Apur Sansar *(1959, The World of Apu). Below: one of the big entertainment films of 1980*

BR FILMS

B.R.CHOPRA'S

THE BURNING TRAIN

STORY & DIRECTED BY
RAVI CHOPRA

SCREENPLAY & DIALOGUE
KAMLESHWAR

LYRICS
SAHIR

MUSIC
R.D.BURMAN

in 70mm
Stereophonic Sound

# Oshima's Empires

Nagisa Oshima – a one-man 'New Wave' at the start of his career – is now regarded as the father of a revolutionary young generation of Japanese film-makers. But in the West he is best known for the erotic *Ai No Corrida (Empire of the Senses)*

Nagisa Oshima has been called the least in-scrutable of Japanese directors. But as leader and chief theoretician of the 'New Wave' movement, which started in Japan at the same time as it did in France, he has also been thought both difficult and inaccessible. He is, however, a remarkable film-maker, known widely in the West mainly through *Ai No Corrida* (1976, *Empire of the Senses*), a treatise on physical sex, made for a French producer, that rivalled Bernardo Bertolucci's *Ultimo Tango a Parigi* (1972, *Last Tango in Paris*) for notoriety. To some, it was a strange movie for so radical and socially conscious a director, but to him, Sada and her lover are not crazed libertines; they are drop-outs from society at a time (in the Thirties) when Japanese imperia-lism was imposing a puritanical ethos upon the nation. 'Make love, not war' was at least a subsidiary text in the film.

## Cruel story of youth

Oshima was born on March 31, 1932 in Kyoto. His father, the descendant of a samurai, was an accomplished amateur painter and poet who died when the boy was six, leaving a library which included a large number of Marxist and socialist texts. These Oshima read in the soli-tude of a lonely childhood, and by the time he left high-school he was ready to become a fully-fledged student activist as well as embryo writer and dramatist. Studying law at Kyoto University, he led a student group that got into trouble with the authorities: when the Em-peror visited the campus, the group held aloft placards imploring him not to allow himself to be deified because so many had died during the war in the name of his divinity.

When he graduated, he joined the Shochiku Film Company in 1954 as an assistant director,

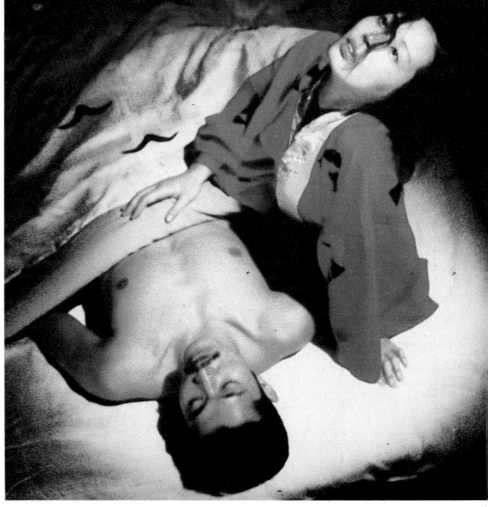

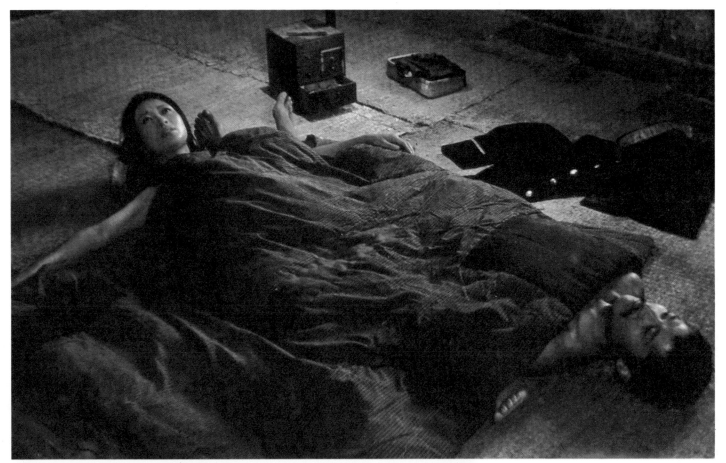

*Left*: Ai No Corrida, *the candidly erotic tale of the self-destructive passions of Kichi (Tatsuya Fuji) and his lover Sada (Eiko Matsuda).*
*Above*: *revealing the sex problems of a young man,* Diary of a Shinjuku Thief *has a deliberately documentary quality*

*Above: in* Ai No Borei, *a discharged soldier embarks on a torrid affair with a peasant woman. After killing her husband, they live together in constant fear, tormented by the ghost of the dead man*

despite his reputation as a 'red student' and the fact that there were over 2,000 applicants for only five jobs. Five rather desultory years later, he was entrusted with his first films as director: *Ai To Kibo No Machi* (1959, *A Town of Love and Hope*) and *Seishun Zankoku Monogatari* (1960, *Naked Youth*), two of the teenage *yakuza* (gangster) genre then popular. In 1960 he also made *Taiyo No Hakaba* (*The Sun's Burial*), a violent story about slum life in which a community of tramps, junkies and the unemployed sell their blood for food and clothing.

Each of these films contained obvious social comment as well as the kind of excitements required of a commercial director, but his fourth film, also made that year, lost him his job. *Nihon No Yoru To Kiri* (1960, *Night and Fog in Japan*) was an attack on both the traditional Left and the muddled activists of the student movement, calling for real action from a new radicalism. When a socialist leader was assassinated a few days after the film's release, it was hastily withdrawn from circulation.

Oshima reacted by setting up his own production company and making *Shiiku* (1961, *The Catch*), in which a black American airman is imprisoned and eventually killed by villagers who are unaware that World War II has finally ended. It was an angry rejection of traditional moral values, suggesting that Japan's fierce nationalism and hatred of foreigners were responsible for the war. Only the village children are seen as a hopeful portent – in the last sequence a young boy moves away from the communal fire and quietly builds one of his own.

## The man who left Japan on film

His next features were all highly critical of Japanese society, and made in an easily-assimilated naturalist tradition that he finally began to eschew in 1967 with *Nihon Shunka-ko* (*A Treatise on Japanese Bawdy Songs*). In this extraordinary film, a band of students visiting Tokyo react to the alienation they feel by singing the songs and end up, in a fantasy scene, strangling a rich girl who has been the object of their erotic dreams.

In *Muri Shinju: Nihon No Natsu* (1967, *Japanese Summer: Double Suicide*) he again left realism behind with a story about a man who wants someone to kill him and a woman who wants a lover. The two meet, get involved, are mixed up in gang warfare and ultimately kill each other before the police can get them. Oshima's pessimism at this time seemed to know no bounds.

His first film to be shown extensively in the West was *Koshikei* (1968, *Death by Hanging*), based on the true story of a young Korean in Japan who raped and killed two girls and was hanged years later after he had confessed and reformed. In the film, the hanging fails and the hypocritical and mindless authorities force the Korean to go through a re-enactment of the crime before killing him. By now Oshima's films had become frankly revolutionary in

both form and content, and were influenced as much by Jean-Luc Godard as those of many other radical directors of the day all over the world. And again the West was to be startled by *Shinjuku Dorobo Nikki* (1969, *Diary of a Shinjuku Thief*), a fractured story full of life and vitality about the sex problems of a young student who steals books in Tokyo's version of Soho.

*Tokyo Senso Sengo Hiwa* (1970, *The Man Who Left His Will on Film*) developed from this anarchic superstructure, its protagonist being a young man who photographs student demonstrations in Tokyo, and tries to find within all his footage how a friend has disappeared. What he discovers, in fact, is that he himself has almost disappeared in the general worthlessness of his own life.

## Empire of disillusion

But between these two films came a remarkable change of course, as if Oshima was trying to find some way of appealing to a wider audience. *Shonen* (1969, *Boy*) was a much more direct narrative, a moving story, again based on actual events, about a couple who wander across Japan, having trained their small son to run in front of passing cars and pretend to be injured so that they can claim compensation. Eventually they are cornered, but the boy – loyal to the last – cannot be made to confess. Using the child as a pathetic yet amazingly dignified emotional shuttlecock within a family of parasites, Oshima constructs an almost classical film which does not so much accuse the parents as blame a society that has produced such a perversion of the norm.

*Gishiki* (*The Ceremony*), made in 1971, was less obviously universal in appeal but perhaps Oshima's finest demonstration of the film-making art. The chronicle of a wealthy provincial family from the end of World War II to the present, it is punctuated by the marriages and funerals at which the family is drawn together. Dominated by an authoritarian grandfather, the older members show themselves to be both militaristic and feudal in their outlook, much

*Right: the family saga* The Ceremony *is a complex allegory of political degeneracy and a seeming attack on reactionary Japanese society, seen through the eyes of one son, suffering under an authoritarian grandfather*

to the disillusion of the younger elements. The film, formal in structure and stunning to look at, yields riches even to western eyes trying to decipher its many layers of meaning. By contrast *Natsu No Imoto* (1972, *Dear Summer Sister*) is virtually impenetrable without knowing that Okinawa – where it is set – was once part of the Japanese empire and also Japan's Ulster. Even then, this story of a Tokyo girl looking round the island for her long-lost brother and finding he is the tourist guide with whom she has had an affair, seems an allegory without a centre.

It scarcely prepared the world for *Ai No Corrida*, based on an incident during the Thirties when a Tokyo woman was found wandering the streets with her lover's severed penis in her hand. He had literally died of love, allowing himself to be strangled and mutilated in a final ecstasy of pleasure. It is all superbly filmed – an illustration of French writer Georges Bataille's thesis that equates the orgasm with *la petite mort*. But if the West was amazed and sometimes scandalized, in Japan the film was regarded as a blow for sexual equality, since, in their sexual encounters, the maidservant and the owner of the geisha house are shown as having become absolute equals, giving and taking what each wants. The woman on whom the film was based, incidentally, has long been a heroine of the women's movement in Japan, and Oshima underlined why.

## After passion

In 1978, Oshima made another film in France for the same producer, and the fact that it was called *Ai No Borei* (*Empire of Passion*) suggested to some that he was trying to repeat that box-office triumph. In fact, the film was a ghostly thriller in which an adulterer is hounded by the police after plotting with a woman to kill

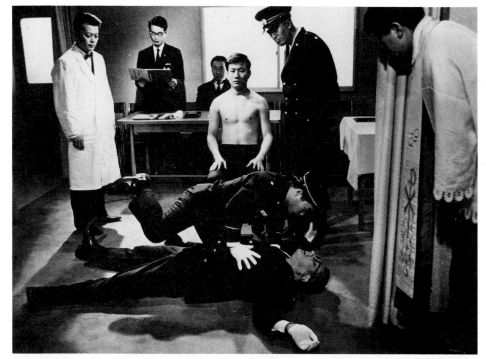

her husband. There were social but hardly political implications, suggesting that Oshima, the 'activist samurai', might be beginning to lose his way. Yet, over all, he is undoubtedly as significant and skilful a director as most of the great Japanese film-makers of the generation before him. If he only occasionally evinces the universality of a Kurosawa or Ichikawa, his concerns are different and less reliant on commercial appeal.

Oshima clearly sees Japan developing blindly, its old values corrupted and its new ones worthless. Once a politicized director, he now says: 'No matter what political system we live under, people at the bottom stay there.' It is those people with whom he is most concerned, who await a revolution that never seems to come. In particular, the plight of the Japanese woman interests him greatly – for some time in the mid-Seventies he hosted a programme especially for them on Japanese television, with huge success.

Perhaps it was the impossibility of making his sort of films without compromise that drove him to France for two of his features and has led him to think of an international future. Whatever the reason, it is a major risk for one so concerned about his own homeland and so accurate about it. Yet, wherever he is, he is bound to make good films. His concern is, after all, for the world not for one people. And there is no reason to suppose that a wider focus will be any less clear.                    DEREK MALCOLM

**Filmography**
1959 Tsukimiso (sc. only); Donto Ikooze (co-sc. only); Ai To Kibo No Machi (+sc) (USA/GB: A Town of Love and Hope). '60 Seishun Zankoku Monogatari (+sc) (USA: Naked Youth); Taiyo No Hakaba (+co-sc) (USA/GB: The Sun's Burial); Nihon No Yoru To Kiri (+co-sc) (USA/GB: Night and Fog in Japan). '61 Shiiku (USA/GB: The Catch). '62 Amakusa Shiro To-kisada (+co-sc) (USA/GB: The Revolt). '64 Chiisana Boken Ryoko (+co-sc) (USA/GB: A Child's First Adventure); Watashi Wa Bellett (+sc) (USA/GB: I Am Bellett). '65 Etsuraku (+sc) (USA: The Pleasures of the Flesh); Yunbogi No Nikki (doc. short) (+prod; +sc; +comm) (GB: Yunbogi's Diary). '66 Hakachu No Torima (USA/GB: Violence at Noon); Ninja Bugeicho (+co-prod; +co-sc) (USA/GB: Band of Ninja). '67 Nihon Shunka-ko (+co-sc) (USA/GB: A Treatise on Japanese Bawdy Songs/Sing a Song of Sex); Muri Shinju: Nihon No Natsu (+co-sc) (USA/GB: Japanese Summer: Double Suicide). '68 Koshikei (+co-prod; +co-sc; +narr) (USA/GB: Death by Hanging); Kaette Kita Yop-parai (+co-sc) (USA/GB: Three Resurrected Drunkards). '69 Yoiyami Semareba (short) (sc. only) (USA/GB: When the Evening Comes); Shinjuku Dorobo Nikki (+co-sc; +ed) (USA: Diary of a Shinjuku Burglar; GB: Diary of a Shinjuku Thief); Shonen (USA/GB: Boy). '70 Tokyo Senso Sengo Hiwa (+co-sc) (USA/GB: The Man Who Left His Will on Film). '71 Gishiki (+co-sc) (USA/GB: The Ceremony). '72 Natsu No Imoto (+co-sc) (USA/GB: Dear Summer Sister). '76 L'Empire des Sens/Ai No Corrida (+sc) (FR-JAP) (USA/GB: In the Realm of the Senses/Empire of the Senses). '78 L'Empire de la Passion/Ai No Borei (+sc) (FR-JAP) (GB: Empire of Passion). '83 Merry Christmas, Mr Lawrence (+co-sc) (JAP-GB).

# THE BRITISH EMPIRE STRIKES BACK

In the films of the Seventies the brilliant technicians toiling away in Britain's special-effects industry seized control of the seas, the skies and the galaxies beyond and filled them with all manner of superbly designed spacecraft and monsters that appeared to live and breathe. But can the British continue to win the special-effects war as American computer technology becomes more and more sophisticated?

'We thought at the time that *2001* would start a big trend. It really didn't. The main effect was that people said no-one's ever going to do this again. No-one's ever going to have the patience, the money or the talent to pull it together.'

These are the words of Douglas Trumbull, special-effects supervisor on *2001: A Space Odyssey* (1968). The special-effects business was in the doldrums after this film. John Brosnan's definitive book on the subject, *Movie Magic: The Story of Special Effects in the Cinema* (published in 1974), is filled with effects men lamenting the lack of work and contracting opportunities.

## Star Jaws

Arguably, *The Exorcist* (1973) and the disaster-movie cycle of the mid-Seventies made producers aware of the value of effects. Certainly the success of *Jaws* (1975), with Bruce-the-$250,000-mechanical-shark, made producers

realize the possibilities. But it was *Star Wars* (1977) that gave effects not just the artistic respectability of *2001* but solid financial standing too. It brought in around $200 million on first release, having cost only $9 million – about $2.5 million of that for effects. It was relatively cheap because it was shot in Britain. Director Steven Spielberg claimed that if he had shot *Close Encounters of the Third Kind* (1977) in Britain his $19 million film would have cost only $12 million; since then, most of the big effects movies have come to Britain: *Superman, The Movie* (1978), *Alien* (1979), *Superman II, Flash Gordon, The Empire Strikes Back* (all 1980), *Outland* and *Dragonslayer* (both 1981). The list goes on. Britain has established a justified reputation for quality and cost-effectiveness. But it is a success under threat.

One of Britain's highest-paid effects supervisors, when pressed, admits:

'The side of *Star Wars* that really made the film – the optical effects – the Americans did

*Above left: the mechanical dragon designed by Brian Johnson at Pinewood comes to grief in* Dragonslayer. *Above: Roger McQuarrie's pre-production artwork for* Star Wars *shows the Empire's climactic attack on the Death Star; Grant McCune supervised the model-making and John Dykstra the special effects*

that. John Dykstra, with the backing of American studio money, perfected a new system. A lot of money was spent. You see, America still has studios with special-effects departments and we don't any more. We're all freelance here.'

It is a generalization, but British effects men do tend to be all-rounders working on a totally freelance basis. American technicians tend to specialize either within the traditional studio system or within facility companies contracted to the major studios or large corporations. In the Seventies, when pure talent was of paramount importance, the British benefited. They

*Above: Britain's cottage industry in operation – Martin Bower (of Bowerhouse Models Associates) at work in his garage, airbrushing the model of the space-shuttle used in* Outland. *Top: the shuttle in action with jet streams of liquid nitrogen blasting from gas jets fitted by another effects team*

had been trained on low-budget movies or in television: many of today's top effects men worked on Hammer horrors or Gerry Anderson productions – such as *Stingray*, *Fireball XL-5* and *Thunderbirds* – in the Sixties. They had to think of the cheapest rather than the easiest or the most obvious way to create a good effect. The late Les Bowie, who is more responsible than anyone for today's British effects talent, once created the world in six days for £1200 – on Hammer's *One Million Years BC* (1966) – using porridge for lava and tap-water to create a deluge.

## Optical disillusion

In the more technological Eighties, specialized effects equipment threatens to destroy British pre-eminence in effects work. Low production costs and the pool of creative talent still attract producers to Britain, but the vital 'optical' effects work on *Star Wars*, *The Empire Strikes Back*, *Flash Gordon* and other major movies

went to America, while the physical effects (created live in the studio or on location) were shot in Britain. The danger was already there in the Seventies and the threat has increased in the Eighties.

The key is research and development: both take time; both cost money. Large corporations, studios and facilities houses can afford the investment but isolated, individual technicians cannot. Disney developed two new camera systems for *The Black Hole* (1979); the company invested $100,000 in the sophisticated Matte Scan system and an undisclosed amount on the more complex computer-controlled ACES (Automated Camera Effects System). The Star Wars Corporation built a complete new special-effects 'factory' for *The Empire Strikes Back*. Both these huge investments took place in California, because that is where the new technology, the finance and the trained computer-biased film technicians are based.

Brian Johnson, the British effects man who supervised *Alien*, *The Empire Strikes Back* and *Dragonslayer*, warns:

'We don't have the equipment to do an *Empire Strikes Back* movie in its entirety in Britain. We can cope with the live-action and incidental effects. But, with regard to 'optical' content, there's no way we could have done it all here. We just don't have the equipment. We've got to get some soon or we'll go under because of the motion-control systems that are coming up in the States.'

To understand the nature and the magnitude of the threat to British supremacy in

Left: the four-legged Imperial Walkers that attack in the snow in The Empire Strikes Back were animated by Phil Tippett and John Berg for Brian Johnson using the 'stop-motion' technique in which movements are shot frame by frame. Above: massive model work and a nest of snakes for Raiders of the Lost Ark (1981). Right: Roger Dicken holds his models of the 'face-hugger' and the 'baby', which bursts out of the hero's chest in Alien

special effects, it is necessary to understand some basic effects techniques. One vital component of much effects work is the matte. Matte technique involves the 'jigsawing' together of separate elements. When a frame measuring 35mm across is projected onto a cinema screen perhaps 35 feet across, miniscule imperfections are magnified. If the join between the different elements in the picture is not exact – if the camera has moved the merest fraction of an inch – the dividing-line becomes visible; thus the black lines round parts of the picture in less expensive effects movies. For decades, this difficulty has meant that cameras involved in matte shots have had to remain static. On 2001, British effects supervisor Wally Veevers designed a very basic mechanical motion-control system ('the sausage machine'), which meant he could repeat camera movements accurately. Modern American systems are computer-linked.

Computer-linking means the exact position of the camera can be determined at any point in a pre-set movement. Thus the camera can be moved as well as, or instead of, the objects filmed, and individually-shot elements will still jigsaw together perfectly in a final composite shot. In the Star Wars 'dog-fights', the cameras panned and tilted with the fast-moving spacecraft (most of which were actually static), giving a sense of excitement which could not have been achieved from a series of static camera viewpoints.

### Very close encounters

Computer technology gives a precision that could not be achieved manually or mechanically. Douglas Trumbull claimed that his Motion Tracking System on Close Encounters of the Third Kind could repeat a camera movement as often as required to an accuracy of one ten-thousandth of an inch. On complex shots, this accuracy is vital. One sequence in The Empire Strikes Back involves a spacecraft flying through an asteroid belt pursued by enemy craft. The sequence as seen in the movie is made up of over forty shots; some of these 'individual' shots contain around twenty-eight separately-shot elements and, to create the final 'single' shot, these twenty-eight elements had to be doctored so that, in all, about a hundred pieces of film passed through an 'optical printer' and were jigsawed together. Optical work on the British-based The Empire Strikes Back was supervised by Richard Edlund at the Star Wars facility in California.

British effects supervisor Derek Meddings managed to shoot the slightly less complex space scenes for Moonraker (1979) without a motion-control camera after the producers decided the system was too expensive. With extraordinarily precise pre-planning, Meddings' team simply wound the film back inside the camera and shot the different elements in different parts of the frame, helped by the blackness of space. For the snow scenes in The Empire Strikes Back, Brian Johnson and Richard Edlund had to develop a white matte system.

British effects talent in the model, optical and physical fields was employed on Outland, though American-invented and American-financed Introvision equipment was used on a few sequences. The system involves matting out sections of the picture and replacing them with identical sections behind which or into which live-action figures can disappear. This means actors can enter a photograph or painting of a doorway in the two-dimensional picture of an expensive-looking model set which does not have to be built full-scale. Introvision also involves front-projection, a technique popularized by 2001.

In front-projection, actors and foreground objects are shot in front of a highly-reflective screen. Between the actors and the camera is a two-way mirror with the mirrored side facing the actors at an angle of 45°. A projector is aimed at the mirrored side and positioned at right-angles to the actors and camera. While the camera shoots through the clear glass, a projected background is bounced off the mirrored side at the exact point through which the camera is shooting. As a result, the projected background hits the reflective screen behind the actors from the exact viewpoint of the camera and 98 per cent of the light is reflected back in a straight line through the two-way mirror and into the camera lens. The result is a brightly lit live-action foreground and an equally bright background fitting together exactly.

On 2001, Wally Veevers used front-projection in many scenes, including the opening Dawn of Man sequence, which was shot entirely at Borehamwood–Elstree using front-projected plates of African landscapes. The effect is almost impossible to detect except in one shot of a leopard whose eyes shine brightly because they, like the background scene, are reflecting projected light directly back into the camera lens.

### So you believed a man could fly?

A much-publicized development of front-projection was the Zoptic (Zoom Optic) system which, it was claimed, made Superman 'fly'. In

*Top: production shots from* Excalibur *(1981) showing the scene with Merlin on the clifftop as it was filmed (left) and as it was seen on the screen (right) with the castle (a painting) and clouds (filmed elsewhere) matted in. Above right: Princess Aura's spaceship from* Flash Gordon – *designed in the comic-strip style of the Thirties*

fact, many different techniques were used and, on *Superman II*, the new system's limitations of movement proved almost as great as its advantages. But Zoptic is still an important advance. It was developed in Britain by Zoran Perisic, a former *2001* rostrum cameraman, and involves synchronized zoom lenses on camera and projector. In *Superman, The Movie*, the actor was static while the camera and projected background 'moved' using zooms. The result was that Superman appeared to move within the frame and in realistic relation to the background.

Flying is obviously a special effect, but Superman is a prime example of the audience not being aware of effects. For one of his many effects on *Superman, The Movie*, Derek Meddings designed a huge miniature of the Golden Gate Bridge, which straddled the giant water tank at Pinewood. His effects team crashed model cars on the model roadway of the bridge, but most viewers assume they are watching full-scale crashes. For *Superman II*, Meddings designed a superbly detailed model of the Eiffel Tower for the opening sequence and a vast miniature of 42nd Street on which, again, he crashed model cars and caused miniature mayhem. Here audiences believe they are watching events on a full-size street because Meddings moved model pedestrians

*Above: a waterfall panorama created by Les Bowie for Hammer's* When Dinosaurs Ruled the Earth *(1970). The background is a painting on glass. The moon is a spotlight shining through part of the glass where the paint has been scratched off. The sparkle of the sea is created by a semi-mirrored surface reflecting twinkling lights. The waterfall is not water but*

*running salt. The water leading to the sea is tap water which runs under the background painting. The cliffs are polystyrene. The figures are live actors but they are not in front of the camera. The background has a mirror inset that reflects the actors – who are standing in another part of the studio. Nothing, therefore, is real*

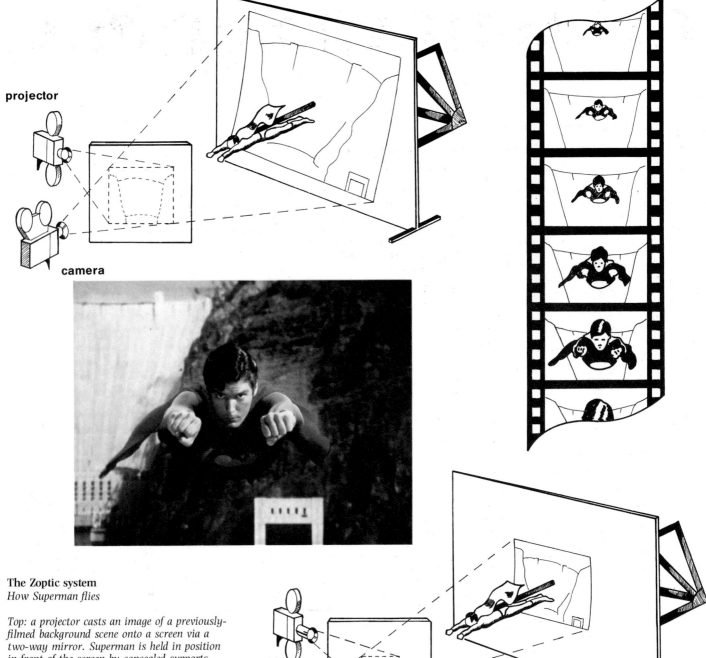

## The Zoptic system
*How Superman flies*

*Top: a projector casts an image of a previously-filmed background scene onto a screen via a two-way mirror. Superman is held in position in front of the screen by concealed supports. The camera shoots through the two-way mirror and films both the projected background and the 'live' Superman.*

*Right: the projector and the camera are both fitted with zoom lenses which are synchronized. The process by which Superman is made to fly occurs in two separate, but simultaneous stages: the projector lens zooms in, causing the background to diminish in size. At the same time, the linked camera lens zooms in to compensate, so that the diminishing background (which would otherwise appear to get smaller) remains the same size as seen by the camera. Because Superman is 'live' he, of course, remains the same size but appears to get bigger as the camera zooms in (film strip, above right). The overall effect is of Superman 'flying' towards the audience. The effect is paradoxical, for what appears to move (Superman) is actually static, and what appears to be static (the background on film) has actually moved. Variations of this technique can make Superman 'fly' away or from side to side. Zoptic was invented by Zoran Perisic.*

along the sidewalks in the background. For the scenes at the villain's headquarters in *The Spy Who Loved Me* (1977), he used moving model guards and miniature helicopters to confuse the viewers' sense of scale.

Meddings' miniature work on scenes involving explosions and water is remarkable because neither fire nor water can be realistically scaled-down. To overcome this on *The Spy Who Loved Me*, he designed a 63-foot-long, 12-ton 'miniature' oil-tanker, fitted with water disturbers on the hull, which he filmed and sank at sea off the Bahamas.

## Adverse effects
When economic conditions in the Seventies dictated that high-budget American movies should be shot in Britain, British technicians were able to provide high-quality results cost-effectively. That was a bonus for Hollywood producers, but it was not the reason they initially came to Britain. The profits from movies like *Star Wars* returned to America, where they helped develop the home effects industry. When, in the future, the exchange rate and other factors dictate that big-budget American productions are based abroad, it is unlikely that the effects work for those films will come to Britain if the British, whatever their native talent, do not have the technology to provide an all-round service. Without capital investment, Britain's big success story of the Seventies could fade away in the Eighties.
MARTYN SADLER

# GALACTICA, DEMONICA

Chaos is come again in Seventies fantasies, whether in the gleaming
metallic future or in a disaster-prone, blood-smeared present

A major feature of Seventies cinema was the extraordinary popularity and creativity of its science-fiction and horror films. During the decade, these previously minor genres gained a new vigour and a firm standing at the box-office. *Jaws* (1975) and then *Star Wars* (1977) became the biggest commercial successes the industry had known, according to *Variety*'s 1979 listing.

The major screen manifestation of science fiction in the Sixties had been such impressive television shows as *Dr Who* (1963 onwards), *The Outer Limits* (1963–65) and *Star Trek* (1966–69), to which *Star Trek – The Motion Picture* (1979) was a late follow-up. In the cinema, the genre was not as prolific, although this decade saw the rise of the big-budget treatment of science fiction which was one of the characteristics of the Seventies strain. *The Time Machine* (1960), *Robinson Crusoe on Mars* (1964) and *Fantastic Voyage* (1966) all boasted impressive visuals, although the real precursor of the Seventies high-technology sheen was Stanley Kubrick's *2001: A Space Odyssey* (1968).

The superproduction aesthetic really arrived with George Lucas' *Star Wars* and *The Empire Strikes Back* (1980, produced by Lucas but directed by Irvin Kershner) and Steven Spielberg's *Close Encounters of the Third Kind* (1977) – ravishing audio-visual experiences which demonstrate the spectacle, power and excitement of high technology. Indeed, this auditory and visual clamour works against the faculty of analysis, in contrast to *2001* which uses its technology and effects to disorientate and alienate. Countering the ability to think clearly is perhaps a necessary strategy, since *Star Wars* and

*The Empire Strikes Back* ask the audience to accept the contradiction of a group of 'rebels' who wish to restore the old patriarchal order, and *Close Encounters of the Third Kind* forwards the proposition that lack of communication between the common man and the authorities can be resolved only by some sort of alien, quasi-divine intervention. It very much seems that, in the absence of actual communication with an alien culture, these films stand in as objects of awe and reverence.

*Star Wars* itself spawned a series of derivatives, which sometimes even included cute pet robots. The most obvious is *Battlestar Galactica* (1978), based upon the pilot episode of the television series about the survivors of a doomed planet in search of a new home; but this totally lacks the imagination of its model. *L'Umanoide* (1979, *The Humanoid*), a 'spaghetti' science-fiction film, also flatters by imitation but fails to impress. The only real contender is the underrated Disney production *The Black Hole* (1979). This is almost a remake of *20,000 Leagues Under the Sea* (1954) set in space, with Maximilian Schell playing the mad scientist intent on pushing his knowledge to the very limits.

*Star Wars* and *Close Encounters of the Third Kind* express a naive faith in space, almost as a new and exciting West to be opened up and explored, which is not necessarily shared by all science-fiction productions. *Alien* (1979) has similar production values, with stunning photography by Derek Vanlint and genuinely other-worldly designs by H. R. Giger, but it fascinatingly tries to combine the cool, abstract manner of Kubrick with the Fifties monster movie – having much the same story as *It! The*

*Star Wars creates imaginary
worlds populated by all manner of
creatures, the product of a fruitful
union between the fertile
imagination of George Lucas and a
popular tradition of fantastic
stories in comic-books, paperbacks
and movie serials*

*Above: when the* Poseidon, *a luxury liner on its last voyage, capsizes in the Mediterranean, the passengers' New Year's Eve celebrations are greatly disrupted;* The Poseidon Adventure *was based on a popular novel by Paul Gallico. Top: the hero (Christopher Reeve) of* Superman, The Movie *flies effortlessly over the streets of New York, thanks to British special-effects artists. Top right: the world's tallest building goes up in flames, with the aid of two studios, 20th Century-Fox and Warners, and Irwin Allen, who also produced* The Poseidon Adventure

*Terror From Beyond Space* (1958). *Alien* is a menacing, brooding film, with fear and paranoia rife as a virtually indestructible life-form stalks the corridors of a spaceship eating its way through the crew one by one. The heroine stands up to this image of male sexual aggression, just as she withstands an attack from a male member of the crew, and comes through as the only survivor in a genre where men usually reign supreme.

Male fantasies are also the subject of two more super-productions, *Superman, The Movie* (1978) and *Flash Gordon* (1980). Both filter the original comic-strip images, and also those drawn from earlier films, through a knowing Seventies sensibility to achieve a finely balanced ironic distance from the material. *Superman, The Movie* is particularly successful because of its range of feelings, from the outrageously comic to a spectacular love scene in the skies over New York City. *Flash Gordon* celebrates the artifice of the original Buster Crabbe series, and along the way exposes the fallacy that only women, and never men, are supposed to be ornamental in films.

Loosely connected to the social-catastrophe element of science fiction (the havoc wrought by falling meteors, marauding monsters, dangerous chemical contamination or atomic blasts), and growing to fill the vacuum left by the passing of the spectacular epic, the disaster movie has claimed its share of the box-office in the Seventies. Very much in the manner of an epic for modern times, the disaster movie imagines the breakdown of social order and then dusts off old movie stars for their iconographic significance as heroic saviour figures. Generally the disasters take the form of attacks by one or several of the elements, as if to caution the audience that catastrophes are natural and not avoidable by political means.

At the conclusion of these films, all the marital and romantic problems that have been set out are resolved and old values are restored. The disaster movie may well be an older generation's way of rejecting life as it has developed in the allegedly 'cynical' Seventies and finding solace in the male screen heroism of Richard Harris in *Juggernaut*, Charlton Heston in *Airport 1975* and *Earthquake* (all three 1974), George C. Scott in *The Hindenburg* and Lorne Greene in *Tidal Wave* (both 1975), Rock Hudson in *Avalanche* (1978) and Sean Connery in *Meteor* (1979). But the genre cannot be too easily dismissed. *The Poseidon Adventure* (1972) depicts a world of order so dizzily inverted that the whole film takes place within a liner turned upside down. *The Towering Inferno* (1974), deservedly the most popular film of this type, holds together its various centres of interest with great skill and manages to make the consuming flames profoundly disturbing as they destroy an enormous new skyscraper.

For the variety of themes it tackles and the directorial talent it has attracted, the horror film is certainly one of the most interesting areas of Seventies cinema. As the critic Robin Wood has pointed out:

'It is a commonplace that the (ostensibly) celebratory family film disappeared from the American cinema in the Fifties. What happened was that its implicit content became displaced into the horror film. What is enacted symbolically in *Meet Me in St Louis* (1944) is "realized" in *Night of the Living Dead* (1968).'

In Vincente Minnelli's 1944 film, the child Tootie symbolically destroys her family through attacking a group of snowmen; in George Romero's later film, a daughter kills and then tries to eat her mother. One more late-Sixties film to suggest that the horror derives from within the family was Roman Polanski's *Rosemary's Baby* (1968), in which Rosemary (Mia Farrow) actually gives birth to the Antichrist.

With this trend proceeding into the Seventies, there developed some deeply disturbing visions of values in transition, of growing doubts about the sanctity of the nuclear family and its role in society. Children themselves, traditionally symbols of innocence, and young people are seen as monstrous progeny in *Dead of Night* (1972), *The Exorcist* (1973) and *Exorcist II: The Heretic* (1977), *It's Alive* (1974) and *It Lives Again* (1978), *The Omen* (1976) and *Damien – Omen II* (1978), *Carrie* (1976), *Martin* (1977), *The Fury* (1978) and *The Brood* (1979). The family itself is the collective monster in such films as *Frightmare* (1974) and *The Hills Have Eyes* (1977); and the home becomes the deadliest of traps in *Burnt Offerings* (1976) and *Full Circle* (1977). The overwhelming impression given by the best of these films is of a dark fantasy on the theme of Ken Loach's hard-hitting social drama *Family Life* (1971), in which her family and collusive authorities pressurize an independent-minded young woman into a mental home.

The new film-student generation of film-makers seems to have been particularly attracted to fantasy forms. The result has been innovation and exploration, but also a notable amount of homage to the cinematic past. Understandably, Hitchcock is the key influence, both in his identification mechanisms and in the various suspense techniques. The most stylistically self-conscious of the new directors are Brian De Palma, Steven Spielberg and John Carpenter. De Palma especially seems constantly to be remaking old Hitchcock films, heightening the Hitchcockian elements of style into delirious parody. The best of his films is probably *Sisters* (1972), derived from *Psycho* (1960), but his most ambitious project was the spectacular but misogynistic *Carrie*, in which a young girl's coming to

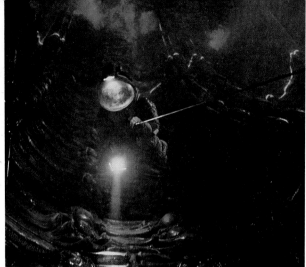

womanhood coincides with her development of destructive powers.

Spielberg began his career in features with small-scale but scary television movies: *Something Evil* (1971) is an assured Gothic horror tale with Sandy Dennis; and *Duel* (1971), with an excellent Richard Matheson screenplay, involves a motorist who finds himself menaced by an unseen but murderous truck-driver in a monstrous juggernaut. This is a simple, though terrifying, articulation of his favourite theme, the ordinary man in extraordinary circumstances. *Jaws* is on an altogether bigger scale, poised with great commercial acumen between straight thriller, monster movie and the disaster genre in its tale of a marauding shark. It

## Children, sharks, ghosts, even truck-drivers could be a source of supernatural fear and menace in movies that touched on raw nerves

utilizes Hitchcockian detail, suspense and shock tactics with outstanding assurance; it is regrettable that the film's sexual undercurrents are so firmly directed against women.

John Carpenter is basically a frustrated old-time studio contract director. As if to stress the B-feature origins of cinematic science fiction, he dismantles the whole elaborate machinery of such space operas as *2001* in the glorious genre romp *Dark Star* (1974). In his hands, the genre has the intimacy and imagination of a good George Pal production, such as *The Time Machine*. Carpenter's two horror thrillers, *Assault on Precinct 13* (1976) and *Halloween* (1978), invoking respectively the worlds of Howard Hawks and Alfred Hitchcock, are among the most sheerly terrifying films ever made, turning the human attackers in each film into deeply disturbing monsters. *The Fog* (1980) is a straight horror picture, showing the return of a ghostly shipwrecked crew to wreak vengeance upon the descendants of their murderers. Embodiments of deep guilt, the ghouls stagger out of the luminous fog in a movie that itself summons up the ghost of the delicate, brooding intensity of Val Lewton's RKO horror productions in the Forties.

Carpenter is one of several newer directors whose movies have been made at a fraction of the cost of the average Seventies Hollywood product. His films still look quite polished, though, compared to the tacky, small-budget productions of such directors as David Cronenberg, Larry Cohen and George Romero. The least interesting of these three directors is Canadian David Cronenberg, whose *The Parasite Murders* (1975, released in Britain as

*Shivers*), *Rabid* (1977) and *The Brood* reveal beneath their squalid nastiness an immature attitude towards sexuality and a misogynistic tendency as pronounced as Brian De Palma's.

Larry Cohen and George Romero, on the other hand, make horror films which suggest progressive political attitudes. Cohen's *It's Alive* and *It Lives Again* manipulate images of the home with a creepy accuracy as they relate the stories of mutant babies on the rampage. *Demon* (1976) has been criticized as muddled on the level of sexual politics because of its treatment of the dual-sexed villain; but it ingeniously combines detective movie, science fiction and horror to attack the repressiveness of organized religion.

Romero's brand of political horror is demonstrated by such films as *The Crazies* (1973), about a small rural community fighting back in reaction to being accidentally contaminated with a germ-warfare bug, and *Dawn of the Dead* (1979, released in Britain as *Zombies*), a grim parody of consumerism involving a small group trapped within a huge hypermarket by hordes of flesh-eating zombies. The black sense of humour running through these films surfaces most distinctly in *Martin*, a vampire film that merely *refers* to the genre conventions as it concentrates upon the theme of sexual repression. Its use of a depressing contemporary suburban location to create atmosphere and its poetic conciseness in exploring Martin's pathological disturbance make it one of the finest films of the Seventies in any genre.

In science fiction of the Seventies, the director is by no means the only effective creator of such films

*Top left: the dead captain (Joe Saunders) of a spacecraft is kept on ice for his brain's advice. Top: a space patrol explores the entrails of a strange planet and picks up from it a deadly* Alien. *Centre:* Star Trek – The Motion Picture *deploys more elaborate technology than did the TV series. Above: publicity material for* Battlestar Galactica, *a TV spin-off starring Lorne Greene as Adama*

heads, in a futuristic world that denies love or personal identity, reveal a really inventive use of cinema and the genre. Crichton, originally a medical doctor and a novelist, has singlemindedly pursued the theme of dehumanization by technology. He wrote the novels upon which are based the excellent *The Andromeda Strain* (1971) and *The Terminal Man* (1974), and he scripted and directed both *Westworld* (1973) and *Coma* (1978). *Westworld* remains his masterpiece, a highly inventive vision of an eerie adult Disney World which strips away male power fantasies through allowing his protagonists to indulge in re-enacting the myths of the West with robot figures.

Outside the USA and Canada, fantasy has been well represented, although on a smaller scale. From Italy, for example, Dario Argento came out with *Suspiria* (1977), a stylish horror film about demonism in a music college which plays on genre conventions and suspense mechanisms in a fasci-

## Maybe filmgoers needed cinematic shocks to help them cope with real life in a disaster-prone decade

nating way. Roman Polanski's French movie *Le Locataire* (1976, *The Tenant*) is a horrific tale of loneliness and the bizarre illusions that can lurk beneath deadpan urban existence. Australian director Peter Weir's *The Cars That Ate Paris* (1974) is a consumer fantasy about a community that survives by crashing strangers' cars and then cannibalizing the wreckage.

The Russian Andrei Tarkovsky's coolly abstract and metaphysical *Solaris* (1972) portrays an alien planet's ability to manifest visitors' unconscious desires. There is an electric atmosphere generated by some images, but as the critic David Thomson has commented: 'An episode of *Star Trek* explored this theme with more wit and ingenuity, less sentimentality and a third the length.'

It was an error for Tarkovsky to have attempted to follow *2001*, a cinematic cul-de-sac, especially with a less dramatic use of decor and technology. Kubrick's film may have given fantasy a new respectability; but the way ahead paradoxically proved to be in the backward glance, sometimes with great self-consciousness, at the styles and iconography of an earlier Hollywood – yesterday's dreams and nightmares reassessed in the light of the troubled Seventies.                    MARTIN SUTTON

*Above: two brothers fight a mental duel to the death as they struggle for control of each other's brain, with the fate of the world at stake, in David Cronenberg's* Scanners *(1981). Top:* The Fog *comes to a Californian town, bringing with it the vengeful ghosts of sailors whose ship had been deliberately wrecked a century before. Top right: the robots of* Westworld *strike back when their control system goes wrong and they cease to be mere victims of holidaymakers pretending to be Western gunslingers*

as *Battlestar Galactica, Star Wars, Close Encounters of the Third Kind, Star Trek* and *Alien*. With new techniques in miniature photography, computer-linked cameras and automatic systems of mattes, special-effects teams led by such talented people as John Dykstra, Douglas Trumbull and Carlo Rambaldi provided the highly believable physical embodiment of the writers' visions. These manufactured dreams are heady indeed, and their formidable nature seems very much to be the implicit subject of *Star Wars, The Empire Strikes Back* and the last forty-five minutes of *Close Encounters of the Third Kind*. The former pair reduce the rich philosophical possibilities of science fiction to a galactic pinball game; and *Close Encounters of the Third Kind*, despite throwing up ideas on the urban nightmare, is ultimately dependent upon its thunderous conclusion, where the dumbstruck extras stand in for the audience's quasi-mystical experience in watching the film.

Two directors whose names have been especially linked with science fiction in the Seventies are George Lucas and Michael Crichton. Lucas, despite his later epics, will perhaps be most kindly remembered for his first feature *THX 1138* (1970). Its abstract images of white chambers and shaved

# DONALD PLEASENCE
# Slightly Sinister

**Donald Pleasence lurks surreptitiously in the corners of his scenes. Sometimes it is hard to remember his face – but then the memory clears and his deadpan expression comes stealthily to the fore. Particularly in his work with the director John Carpenter it is noticeable just how much he conjures up a strangeness, an eeriness that is hard to forget**

There can be little doubt that the most crucial event in the career of Donald Pleasence was his appearance in the original 1960 stage-production in London of *The Caretaker*, written by Harold Pinter. Pleasence had just turned 40, and perhaps that is what was most significant: with his baldness and lack of a conventionally impressive physique, there has always been something inherently middle-aged about him – but, conversely, he seems not really to have aged to a marked extent over the following 20 years.

More particularly, however, it was an exact matching of performer and role. Pinter's play, about a tramp invited by two brothers to share their attic room, was an immediate cult success though very far from being a popular hit, and Pleasence made the part of the tramp Davies fit him like a glove. Davies is by turns wheedling, ingratiating, bullying, but always ambiguous. He is evasive even about his origins, answering a query as to whether he is Welsh with, 'Well, I've been around'. Pleasence brought a marvellously suggestive vocal range as well as an indefinable air of menace to his mundane, yet sinisterly poetic,

*Above: Donald Pleasence as a member of an evil family of marauding villains who torment the lives of innocent settlers in* Will Penny. *Below: as the tramp, Davies, in the screen version of* The Caretaker

flights of fancy, the most frequently quoted of which concerns his need to go to Sidcup to retrieve his papers. His playing of this role is, happily, preserved on film in the faithful movie version directed in 1963 by Clive Donner, although something of the theatrical power of the original work was lost in the transition.

Donald Pleasence was born in England in the Midlands in 1919 and was educated in Ecclesfield near Sheffield. By the age of 20 he was working as a stage manager on the Isle of Jersey but his career was interrupted by World War II, the latter part of which he spent in a German POW camp. After the war he played Mavriky in Peter Brook's 1946 production of *The Brothers Karamazov* and then spent the next five years appearing with numerous repertory companies. It was a role in Jean-Paul Sartre's *Vicious Circle* that led to him being invited to join Laurence Olivier's touring company, which resulted in appearances on Broadway in both *Caesar and Cleopatra* and *Antony and Cleopatra*. By the mid-Fifties he began to concentrate more on live television drama and became popular in England as a result of these appearances. It was also around this time that Pleasence started to combine his busy theatrical and television career with a number of supporting roles in British films. Of these, probably the most worthwhile were as the repressed, puritanical Welsh second-in-command to Trevor Howard's tramp-steamer captain in *Manuela* (1957) and as the petty and prejudiced market inspector in the expanded screen version of *Look Back in Anger* (1959).

However, it was in the Sixties that Pleasence became a really recognizable presence in the cinema, and it was predominantly with varieties of menace that he was associated. Although he was effectively cast in the title

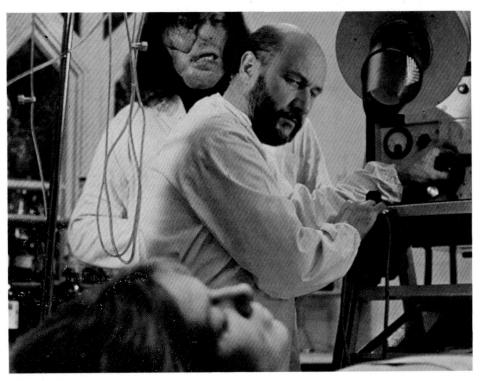

role in the generally nondescript *Dr Crippen* (1963), the majority of his roles were not usually representative of the sidelong domestic menace associated with Pinter, and his most Pinteresque screen appearance – outside *The Caretaker* – was probably in Roman Polanski's black comedy *Cul-de-Sac* (1966). But in this film – as the male half of a strange couple living in isolation on Holy Island and playing involuntary hosts to a pair of escaping gunmen – he was on the whole more menaced than menacing.

By this time, crucially, he had been adopted by Hollywood, and was being introduced to a wider audience – primarily in the guise of a deep-eyed villain. In fact, he was satanic in the fullest sense in director George Steven's biblical blockbuster *The Greatest Story Ever Told* (1965),

where his 'Dark Hermit', it is implied is, an incarnation of the Devil himself. Despite an excursion into barnstorming comedy to play the leader of a band of vehemently anti-temperance miners in the rather forcedly

*Above left: Pleasence as* Dr Crippen *and Coral Browne as the bombastic wife he eventually murders in order to run away with his mistress. Above right: in one of his many British horror movies* The Mutations, *this time as a bio-chemist searching to combine plant and animal life and using circus freaks as the subjects of his experiments. Below: Pleasence and Françoise Dorléac as a bizarre couple in* Cul-de-Sac, *with Lionel Stander as one of the escaping gangsters who intrudes on their secluded island life*

humorous Western *The Hallelujah Trail* (1965), Pleasence's most notable performances in the next few years were as conspicuously unlikeable types.

In the science-fiction thriller *Fantastic Voyage* (1966), a bizarre yarn about a team of scientists and their submarine who are temporarily 'miniaturized' to infinitesimal proportions in order to journey inside the body of an injured scientist and perform an ultra-delicate brain operation, Pleasence plays a character who – after histrionic displays of cowardice – is ultimately revealed as a would-be saboteur. Not only do his plans come to nought but his tiny being is finally reduced to smithereens in the deadly embrace of a shoal of antibodies in the patient's bloodstream.

Shortly afterwards, in *Will Penny* (1967), an off-beat, 'realistic' Western that was a cherished project of its star Charlton Heston, Pleasance essayed a more flamboyantly malignant figure, that of the maniacally vengeful frontier badman 'Preacher' Quint. If his villainy in this film had a scenery-chewing edge of relish to it, this is perhaps due to the fact that he had just had bestowed upon him the accolade for cinematic villainy, that of being cast as chief heavy in a James Bond opus. The film was *You Only Live Twice* (1967), and Pleasence made Blofeld, head of the dreaded 'Spectre', into a scar-faced projection of comic-book fear, superciliously fondling a pet cat whilst not attending to pressing affairs of international disruption.

The ensuing decade saw no slackening in the frequency of Pleasence's screen appearances, as he commuted between American, British and European productions, but on the whole the quality of his roles showed a decline. On home ground, he figured forgettably in such off-the-peg horror items as *Tales That Witness Madness* (1973), *The Mutations* (1974) and *From Beyond the Grave* (1974), and impersonated historical personages in cameo roles as diverse as Thomas Cromwell in *Henry VIII and His Six Wives* (1972) and Heinrich Himmler in *The Eagle Has Landed* (1976).

In America he was a stock heavy in *Soldier Blue* (1970) but otherwise tended to be found in more whimsical, if not always very rewarding, circumstances. Thus, he was an eccentric publisher in the attractive comedy *Hearts of the West* (1975), and – continuing the literary association – he played the novelist Boxley in director Elia Kazan's flawed screen version of *The Last Tycoon* (1976) – scripted by none other than Harold Pinter.

More recently, he has appeared in the guise of the avaracious recording boss in the peculiar musical *Sgt. Pepper's Lonely Heart's Club Band* (1978) and as Seward, keeper of the asylum, in the director John Badham's lavish new version of *Dracula* (1979), in the latter a perhaps unexpectedly low-key presence amid the prevailing theatricality. But he brings a degree of theatrical credibility to John Carpenter's *Escape From New York* (1981), as the kidnapped President of the United States, who has to be rescued from a New York that has been turned into a prison for three million convicts.

But of Pleasence's later screen roles, easily the most striking – and one of the few instances in his movie career of his receiving top billing – has been in John Carpenter's stylishly-made and phenomenally profitable spine-chiller *Halloween* (1978). Here he is cast as a psychiatrist on the trail of an escaped pathological killer, but one whose prognostications of his patient's likely intentions, to quote critic Richard Combs, 'owe nothing to Freud and everything to Jeremiah'.

The rather self-effacing, even hangdog, characterisation that Pleasence affects chimes in neatly with the semi-abstract quality of the movie as a whole. The character may – somewhat irrelevantly – be named Sam Loomis after one of the characters in Hitchcock's *Psycho* (1960), but it is easy to make a different association: somehow Loomis' preoccupied air gives the impression of being ascribable to a need to retrieve his papers from Sidcup.
TIM PULLEINE

*Above: Pleasence as the Russian villain in the intriguing spy story* Telefon *(1977). Below: on the trail of a killer in the director John Carpenter's spinechiller* Halloween

### Filmography
**1954** The Beachcomber. **'56** 1984. **'57** The Man in the Sky; Manuela/Stowaway Girl. **'58** A Tale of Two Cities; The Heart of a Child; The Man Inside. **'59** Look Back in Anger; The Battle of the Sexes. **'60** The Shakedown; Flesh and the Fiends; Hell Is a City; Circus of Horror; Sons and Lovers; The Big Day; Suspect (USA: The Risk). **'61** No Love for Johnnie; Les Mains d'Orlac/The Hands of Orlac (FR-GB); Spare the Rod; The Horsemasters. **'62** The Inspector (USA: Lisa); A Story of David. **'63** Dr Crippen; Maniac; The Great Escape (USA); The Caretaker (USA: The Guest). **'65** The Greatest Story Ever Told (USA); The Hallelujah Trail (USA). **'66** Cul-de-Sac; Fantastic Voyage (USA). **'67** The Night of the Generals/La Nuit des Généraux (GB-FR); You Only Live Twice; Eye of the Devil; Matchless (IT); Will Penny (USA). **'68** Mister Freedom (FR); The Madwoman of Chaillot. **'70** Soldier Blue (USA); **'71** THX 1138 (USA); Outback (AUS); Kidnapped/David and Catriona. **'72** The Jerusalem File (USA-IS); The Pied Piper (GB-GER); Henry VIII and His Six Wives; Innocent Bystanders. **'73** Death Line (USA: Raw Meat); Dr Jekyll and Mr Hyde (orig. TV) (USA); The Rainbow Boys (CAN); Wedding in White (CAN); Tales That Witness Madness. **'74** From Beyond the Grave; The Black Windmill; The Apprenticeship of Duddy Kravitz (CAN); The Mutations; Arthur, Arthur (orig. TV) (USA); Barry McKenzie Holds His Own (AUS). **'75** Escape to Witch Mountain (USA); . . . Altrimenti ci Arrabbiamo (IT-SP) (GB: Watch Out, We're Mad); Hearts of the West (USA) (GB: Hollywood Cowboy). **'76** I Don't Want to be Born (USA: The Devil Within Her); Trial by Combat (USA: Dirty Knight's Work); Journey Into Fear (USA); The Count of Monte Cristo (USA); The Devil's Men (USA: Land of the Minotaur); The Last Tycoon (USA); The Eagle Has Landed. **'77** Goldenrod (CAN); The Uncanny (GB-CAN); Oh, God! (USA); The Passover Plot (USA-IS); Telefon (USA); Les Liens de Sang/Blood Relatives (FR-CAN). **'78** Tomorrow Never Comes (GB-CAN); Sgt. Pepper's Lonely Hearts Club Band (USA-GER); L'Ordre et la Sécurité du Monde (FR); Out of Darkness; Power Play (CAN-GB); The Defection of Simas Kudirka (USA). **'79** L'Homme en Colère/The Angry Man/Jigsaw (FR-CAN); Good Luck Miss Wyckoff (USA). **'79** Dracula (USA); Jaguar Lives (USA). **'80** All Quiet on the Western Front (USA). **'81** The Monster Club; Escape From New York (USA); Race to the Yankee Zephyr (NZ-USA); Halloween II (USA). **'82** Alone in the Dark (USA).

You'll believe a man can fly.

ALEXANDER SALKIND PRESENTS MARLON BRANDO · GENE HACKMAN IN A RICHARD DONNER FILM
SUPERMAN
STARRING
CHRISTOPHER REEVE · NED BEATTY · JACKIE COOPER · GLENN FORD · TREVOR HOWARD
MARGOT KIDDER · VALERIE PERRINE · MARIA SCHELL · TERENCE STAMP · PHYLLIS THAXTER · SUSANNAH YORK
STORY BY MARIO PUZO · SCREENPLAY BY MARIO PUZO, DAVID NEWMAN, LESLIE NEWMAN AND ROBERT BENTON
CREATIVE CONSULTANT TOM MANKIEWICZ · DIRECTOR OF PHOTOGRAPHY GEOFFREY UNSWORTH B.S.C.
PRODUCTION DESIGNER JOHN BARRY · MUSIC BY JOHN WILLIAMS · EXECUTIVE PRODUCER ILYA SALKIND · PRODUCED BY PIERRE SPENGLER
DIRECTED BY RICHARD DONNER · PANAVISION® TECHNICOLOR® AN ALEXANDER AND ILYA SALKIND PRODUCTION

After the commercial success of *The Three Musketeers: the Queen's Diamonds* (1973) and *The Four Musketeers: the Revenge of Milady* (1975), which were shot as one film and then released as two (to the consternation of many of the actors paid for only one), the producers Ilya and Alexander Salkind and Pierre Spengler lit another controversial fuse with the announcement of their intention to resurrect the ultimate all-American comic-book hero – Superman. The five years of planning that followed saw an excessive and, of course, expensive period of hype, beginning with full-page ads in *Variety*, laser shows and hot-air balloons before a shooting-script had even been agreed.

Coupled with this paid advertising was the enormous press and media coverage garnered by this momentous production, highlights of which include Marlon Brando's $3.7 million fee, the search for a director and for a woman to play Lois Lane, and – the most saleable novelty – the search for Superman himself. Almost every leading actor in Hollywood was rumoured to have been offered the part, but the final decision was delayed until almost a month before production when predictably an unknown, Christopher Reeve, was cast.

After problems with the fee demanded by Steven Spielberg and the reluctance of expatriate English director Guy Hamilton to return to Pinewood Studios, the producers decided on Richard Donner as director of *Superman, The Movie*. Riding high on the success of *The Omen* (1976), Donner eschewed all temptations to make a camp version. Wisely, he hoped that a modern audience would accept the limitations inherent in such fantasy entertainment and enjoy rather than mock the adventures of a being unencumbered with human frailties. As the director said:

'The main aim of our own interpretation is to uphold and enhance the American myth. It is real within its own framework.'

Fortunately for the production team of *Superman, The Movie*, the previous celluloid representations were, despite their popularity, very wooden translations of the DC Comics hero. They ignored the science-fiction element and relied too heavily on the truth and justice aspect. Kirk Allen, star of the Columbia serial, and television star George Reeves were tied mainly by low-budget handicaps, and became flying G-Men in search of a good script. The only real inspiration for the new film-makers were the magnificent animation effects created in Max Fleischer's Superman cartoons of the Forties. They were, and still are, wonderfully concise films, clearly displaying Superman's alien abilities in true DC style. Colourful and adventurous, they come closest to the current notions of 'man of steel'.

Aided and abetted by the most convincing actor who ever pulled on a pair of bright blue tights, Donner was also fortunate to have a 'no expenses spared' special-effects department. Being veterans of *Star Wars* (1977), their patient work (it took years to create the illusion of flight) was certainly worth the wait, and the sequence when Superman saves Lois and catches a helicopter in mid-air is quite breathtaking.

What makes *Superman, The Movie* the best screen version to date is not the amazing effects, but the excellent acting from the benevolent aliens. Marlon Brando as Jor-El sets the mood perfectly, his awesome presence pervading the rest of the film after his early disappearance. His fatherly wisdom and fairness leave no-one in any doubt at all that Superman must be perfect. Through sheer hard work, Christopher Reeve conveys the essence of Jerry Siegel and Joe Shuster's' original character. His Clark Kent – a bumbling innocent, shy and nervous – contrasts superbly with his macho alter-ego, though this romantic, old-fashioned gallant is not quite believable as a match for Margot Kidder's Lois, whose persona is probably a victim of too many scriptwriters.

The other small disappointment in *Superman, The Movie* is that it is never really possible to believe that a man can fly. For all the faultless effects, the suspension of disbelief is often shattered by the stiff-limbed posture of Reeve, necessary for the complicated harness worn in the flying scenes. Regardless of the drawbacks (many of them self-inflicted by the anxious producers, who continued to face litigation from unhappy actors long after the film's release), *Superman, The Movie* is a masterpiece of Seventies science fiction, which relies heavily on the fantastic effects but boasts at least one great acting performance . . . from Christopher Reeve.   STEPHEN WOOLLEY

Just before the destruction of the planet Krypton, Jor-El, a member of the ruling council, and his wife Lara (1) launch their son in an earth-bound projectile (2). Minutes later their planet is spectacularly engulfed by a nearby sun. Due to molecular changes in the earth's atmosphere, the infant is invested with superhuman powers (3). He is absorbed into society, but when his foster parent, Pa Kent, dies, he decides to head for the Arctic wastes where – in a giant glacier – he is reunited with the spirit of Jor-El.

After twelve years, he returns to civilization in the guise of mild-mannered Clark Kent, reporter for the Daily Planet – a busy newspaper in Metropolis. Although ignored by colleague Lois Lane (4) in his alias as a newsman, he is adored by her and millions of others whilst fighting crime and injustice as the flying hero Superman (5).

Diabolical villain Lex Luthor (6, right), aware of Superman's superior powers, plans to disable him with Kryptonite, a fragment of his planet, and then destroy parts of California. His evil plan is disrupted by Eve Teschmayer (6, left), one of his own assistants, who sympathetically releases Superman, but too late to prevent one of Luthor's deadly missiles from exploding. Superman miraculously repairs the country (7) and pulls Lois' car out of a rock-fall (8), only to find her dead. Distraught, yet undaunted, he circles the globe at unimaginable speed, reversing time itself, and with Lois once again breathing, he returns Luthor and his villainous accomplice Otis to the authorities. His mission complete, he is reunited with Lois, but still keeps his true identity from her.

**Directed by Richard Donner, 1978**
**Prod co:** Dovemead, for International Film Production. **exec prod:** Ilya Salkind. **prod:** Pierre Spengler. **assoc prod:** Charles F. Greenlaw. **sc:** Mario Puzo, David Newman, Leslie Newman, Robert Benton, based on characters by Jerry Siegel, Joe Shuster. **creative consultant:** Tom Mankiewicz. **photo** (Panavision, Technicolor): Geoffrey Unsworth. **model photo:** Paul Wilson. **creative sup/sp eff:** Colin Chilvers. **creative sup optical visual eff:** Roy Field. **creative sup mattes and composites:** Les Bowie. **creative dir process photo:** Denys Coop. **dir and creator model eff:** Derek Meddings. **sp visual eff des/main titles des:** Denis Rich. **creative sup sp visuals:** Stuart Freeborn. **Zoptic sp eff:** Zoran Perisic. **sup ed:** Stuart Baird. **ed:** Michael Ellis. **prod des:** John Barry. **sup art dir:** Bill Brodie, Maurice Fowler. **mus:** John Williams, The London Symphony Orchestra. **cost:** Yvonne Blake. **sup sd ed:** Chris Greenham. **flying co-ordinator:** Dominic Fulford. **stunt co-ordinators:** Alf Joint, Vic Armstrong, Alex Stevens. **r/t:** 143 minutes.
**Cast:** Christopher Reeve (*Clark Kent/Superman*), Marlon Brando (*Jor-El*), Susannah York (*Lara*), Margot Kidder (*Lois Lane*), Gene Hackman (*Lex Luthor*), Ned Beatty (*Otis*), Valerie Perrine (*Eve Teschmayer*), Jackie Cooper (*Perry White*), Marc McLure (*Jimmy Olsen*), Trevor Howard, Harry Andrews, Vass Anderson, John Hollis (*elders*), Jack O'Halloran (*Non*), Maria Schell (*Vond-Ah*), Terence Stamp (*General Zod*), Sarah Douglas (*Ursa*), Glenn Ford (*Pa Kent*), Phyllis Thaxter (*Ma Kent*), Jeff East (*young Clark Kent*), Diane Sherry (*Lana Lang*), Jeff Atcheson (*coach*), Billy J. Mitchell, Robert Henderson (*editors*), Larry Lamb (*first reporter*), Larry Hagman (*missile-convoy major*), Rex Reed (*himself*).

**Directed by Steven Spielberg, 1977**
**Prod co:** Phillips/Columbia/EMI. **prod:** Julia Phillips, Michael Phillips.
**assoc prod:** Clark Paylow. **sc:** Steven Spielberg. **photo** (Metrocolor,
Panavision)**:** Vilmos Zsigmond, William A. Fraker, Douglas Slocombe. **col:**
Robert M. McMillian. **add photo:** John Alonzo, Laszlo Kovacs, Steve Poster.
**sp photo eff:** Richard Yuricich, Dave Stewart, Robert Hall, Don Jarel, Dennis
Muren. **anim sup:** Robert Swarthe. **anim:** Harry Moreau, Carol Boardman,
Eleanor Dahlen, Cy Didjurgis, Tom Koester, Bill Millar, Connie Morgan.
**visual eff sup:** Steven Spielberg. **sp photo eff sup:** Douglas Trumbull. **sp
photo eff co-ord:** Larry Robinson. **project co-ord:** Mona Thal Benefiel. **eff
unit project man:** Robert Shepherd. **video tech:** 'Fast' Eddie Mahler. **ed:**
Michael Kahn. **art dir:** Dan Lomino. **design:** Joe Alves, Phil Abramson,
Matthew Yuricich, George Jensen, Carlo Rambaldi. **sp mech eff:** Roy
Arbogast, George Polkinghorne. **mech design:** Dom Trumbull, John
Russell, Fries Engineering. **electronics design:** Jerry L. Jeffress, Alvah J.
Miller, Peter Regla, Dan Slater. **models:** Gregory Jein, J. Richard Dow, Jor
Van Kline, Michael McMillen, Kenneth Swenson, Robert Worthington.
**mus/mus dir:** John Williams. **songs:** 'Chances Are' by Al Stillman, Robert
Allen, sung by Johnny Mathis; 'When You Wish Upon a Star' by Leigh
Harline, Ned Washington; 'The Square Song' by Joseph Raposo; 'Love
Song of the Waterfall' by Bob Nolan, Bernard Barnes, Carl Winge, sung by
Slim Whitman. **cost:** Jim Linn. **makeup:** Bob Westmoreland. **titles:** Dan
Perri. **sd:** Gene Cantmessa, Buzz Knudson, Don MacDougall, Robert
Glass. **Dolby sd sup:** Steve Katz. **sd eff:** Frank Warner, Richard Oswald,
David Horton, Sam Gemette, Gary S. Gerlich, Chet Slomka, Neil Burrow.
**tech adv:** Dr. J. Allen Hynek. **sp consultants:** Peter Anderson, Larry
Albright, Richard Bennett, Ken Ebert, Paul Huston, David M. Jones, Kevin
Kelly, Jim Lutes, George Randle, Jeff Shapiro, Rourke Engineering. **tech
dialogue:** Colin Cantwell. **stunt co-ordinator:** Buddy Joe Hooker. **ass dir:**
Chuck Myers, Jim Bloom. **r/t:** 135 minutes.
**Cast:** Richard Dreyfuss (*Roy Neary*), François Truffaut (*Claude Lacombe*),
Teri Garr (*Ronnie Neary*), Melinda Dillon (*Jillian Guiler*), Bob Balaban
(*David Laughlin*), J. Patrick McNamara (*project leader*), Warren Kemmer-
ling (*Wild Bill*), Roberts Blossom (*farmer*), Philip Dodds (*Jean Claude*), Cary
Guffey (*Barry Guiler*), Shawn Bishop (*Brad Neary*), Adrienne Campbell
(*Silvia Neary*), Justin Dreyfuss (*Toby Neary*), Lance Henriksen (*Robert*),
Merrill Connally (*team leader*), George DiCenzo (*Major Benchley*), Amy
Douglass, Alexander Lockwood (*implantees*), Gene Dynarski (*Ike*), Mary
Gafrey (*Mrs Harris*), Norman Bartold (*Ohio Tolls*), Josef Sommer (*Larry
Butler*), Rev Michael J. Dyer (*himself*), Roger Ernest (*highway patrolman*),
Carl Weathers (*military policeman*), F. J. O'Neil (*ARP project member*), Phil
Dodds (*ARP musician*), Randy Hermann, Hal Barwood, Matthew Robbins
(*returnees from Flight 19*), David Anderson, Richard L. Hawkins, Craig
Shreeve, Bill Thurman (*air traffic controllers*), Roy E. Richards (*Air East
pilot*), Gene Rader (*hawker*), Eumenio Blanco, Daniel Nunez, Chuy Franco,
Luis Contreras (*federales*), James Keane, Dennis McMullen, Cy Young,
Tom Howard (*radio telescope team*), Richard Stuart (*truck dispatcher*), Bob
Westmoreland (*load dispatcher*), Matt Emery (*support leader*), Galen
Thompson, John Dennis Johnston (*special forces*), John Ewing, Keith
Atkinson, Robert Broyles, Kirk Raymond (*dirty tricks*).

Riding high on the success of *Jaws*
(1975), Steven Spielberg began his
ambitious project – initially entitled
'Watch the Skies' – with full studio
backing. He constructed an enormous set in an airplane hangar in
Mobile, Alabama, while shooting
certain outdoor scenes in a section
of Indiana desert land reminiscent
of Jack Arnold's locations in *It
Came From Outer Space* (1953) and
*Tarantula* (1955). Over a year was
spent shooting and re-shooting
scenes on various other international locations with the help of
some top cinematographers. These
sequences jigsawed together for
two versions, the first demanded by
an impatient Columbia, released in
1977, and the second – Spielberg's
authorized version – released three
years later.

Although the *Special Edition*
(1980) contains additional scenes,
the overall effect of the two films is
the same. Both are wonderful, brilliantly constructed science-fiction
drama featuring complex special
effects which are enhanced by
Spielberg's single-minded, all-
American, all-Hollywood vision. It
is a mammoth spectacle, as gripping as Hitchcock, as magical as
Disney's early animated features,
and as humanely optimistic as the
best of the Sixties television series
*The Outer Limits* (1963–65).

The story is presented from three
simultaneous viewpoints: that of
the innocent child and his distraught mother, of an intrigued
electrical engineer, and of a group
of scientists led by François Truffaut playing in his first American
movie. Everything revolves around
five or six breathtaking set-pieces;
the narrative intercuts between
these 'close encounters', excitingly
revealing the clues which lead to
the moving climax when the extra-
terrestrials come to rest on Devil's
Tower. Superbly edited throughout,

the film moves at an extraordinary
pace, teasing the audience with
constant references to the other
beings as Lacombe and his UFO
investigators discover the secret of
the five musical tones – a signal
continuously broadcast from outer
space.

In the first sighting is encapsulated all the success of *Close Encounters of the Third Kind*: around
the curve of the road come three
multicoloured, gyrating shapes at
incredible speed but slow enough
to be in full view of witnesses and
the audience. By shooting the special effects in 70mm and the rest in
35mm, which is then blown up to
70mm, the quality of the print is
consistent so that the spacecraft
look completely real. It is the im-
maculate special effects, integrated so perfectly with the heart-
stopping narrative, which are the
true stars of *Close Encounters*. The
final sequence – the arrival of the
mothership on Devil's Tower – is as
startling as Cecil B. DeMille's part-
ing of the waves in *The Ten Commandments* (1956). Anyone would
find it difficult not to believe that this
great citadel in the sky, twice as
high as the mountain, really exists.

Unlike the swashbuckling
heroics of that other high-budget,
cosmic adventure movie *Star Wars*
(1977, dir. George Lucas), the effectiveness of *Close Encounters*
lies in our ability to believe that
beyond the stars superior powers
are benevolent and caring. In those
closing moments the audience is
allowed the kind of emotional participation not felt in cinemas since
Judy Garland walked over the rainbow and Dumbo flew: perfect escapism for our troubled times.

STEPHEN WOOLLEY

**Lost on the road while trying to
establish the cause of a massive
power-cut, Roy Neary sees a set
of bright lights approaching.
Instead of passing straight by, the
intense rays rise above his truck
(1), and immediately there is a
loss of all gravitational force in
his cab.**

**In another part of the same
black-out a young boy awakes to
find the entire house in bizarre
confusion; all the electrical
appliances have switched
themselves on. Amused and
amazed, he runs into the night
pursued by his fearful mother,
and mysteriously appears at the
edge of a hill-top road where Roy,
Jillian and the boy witness three
of the alien spacecraft.**

**Spurred on by newspaper and
television reports, interested
people turn up for these sightings
(2). Meanwhile, a group of
scientists led by Claude Lacombe
has found evidence in other
continents that a certain musical
pattern can be linked with the
aliens' efforts to communicate.**

**Jillian's son is invisibly
kidnapped by the extra-
terrestrials (3), and Roy alienates
his own family by building a clay
model of the visions he has seen
of a flat mountain (4). As soon as
he realizes, along with Jillian,**

CLOSE ENCOUNTER
OF THE FIRST KIND
Sighting of a UFO

CLOSE ENCOUNTER
OF THE SECOND KIND
Physical Evidence

CLOSE ENCOUNTER
OF THE THIRD KIND
Contact

WE ARE NOT ALONE

CLOSE ENCOUNTERS
OF THE THIRD KIND

A COLUMBIA-EMI Presentation

1

2

3

4

5

6

that the model in his living room is the Devil's Tower in Wyoming and that the aliens want them to be there, he and Jillian race across country.

On arrival they find everything cordoned off by Lacombe (5) and the military who have simulated a nerve-gas scare. All the unwelcome humans drawn there are rounded-up for interrogation (6), but Roy and Jillian escape.

An exciting chase culminates in the discovery of a colossal runway, a giant electronic board covered with coloured strips, and a powerful musical keyboard. All their former paranoia is calmed by this sight, and their weird obsessions and premonitions now seem crystal clear.

A fleet of dancing, whooshing, neon-lit spaceships precede the landing of the huge mothership. Communication between the scientists and the craft is initiated by the playing of the five mystical notes, and culminates in an extra-terrestrial duet. Roy eventually enters the mothership surrounded by the aliens (7) – their embryonic features clear and their intentions obviously harmless. With sadness Lacombe and his team watch the friendly visitors leave (8). From a vantage point, Jillian and her son see the craft move off (9).

7

8

9

# INDEX

220